Afghanistan Crisis

Decoding Engagement of Major and Regional Powers

Vinod Khobragade

ATLANTIC

PUBLISHERS & DISTRIBUTORS (P) LTD

Published by

ATLANTIC

PUBLISHERS & DISTRIBUTORS (P) LTD

7/22, Ansari Road, Darya Ganj, New Delhi-110002
Phones : +91-11-40775252, 40775214, 23273880, 23275880
Fax : +91-11-23285873
Web : www.atlanticbooks.com
E-mail : orders@atlanticbooks.com

Printed & bound in India by Atlantic Print Services

Preface

Afghanistan has always been the realm of global power politics since long time. The rivalry between the regional as well as the external major powers has kept Afghanistan boiling for various reasons such as political and economic domination in the region. Amongst these rivalries, the great game between the Britain and the USSR was prominent. In fact, Soviet Russia has always influenced the domestic politics of Afghanistan which was full of internal chaos and crisis between/amongst the ruling and political elites. During the cold war politics between the US-led Western Block and the USSR-led Eastern Block, the Soviet Russia grabbed opportunity to intervene Afghanistan in support of Afghan's Communist government and stayed there from December 1979 to February 1989. At the same time, the regional (Pakistan and others) as well as major powers such as the US, China, and others in tandem hatched conspiracies against the Soviet Union's occupation of Afghanistan. This further led to bringing of Afghanistan and the region under the shadow of cold war politics.

Furthermore, the entry of the Taliban in the political picture of Afghanistan imposed huge turmoil in and beyond Afghanistan. The Taliban Regime (1996-2001) further pushed Afghanistan in the category of failed states. Pakistan played shrewdly adroit politics in the region further increasing the mess in Afghanistan and always wanted and supported Taliban rule. The nexus between Taliban and Pakistan is notorious. The United States intervened Afghanistan in 2001 to throw out the Taliban regime after the 9/11 incidence and remained there till 2021. During the US's long war against terrorism, other regional actors such as Russia, China, Iran, and Pakistan played dysfunctional role against the US and its presence in Afghanistan. In fact, all these countries played functional/dysfunctional and direct/indirect role against the US and the democratic government of Afghanistan. However, largely, these states formed their nexus with the Taliban, the boiling factor of the Afghanistan's crisis. They indulged in supporting and strengthening Taliban against the US. Consequently, the anti-US collective forces failed the US in Afghanistan. Therefore, gradually, after realising the role of the Taliban, the US also entered in agreement with the Taliban before withdrawing its forces from Afghanistan. Eventually, the US vacated space for return of the Taliban in power in August 2021.

So far as India's role is concerned, New Delhi has always supported the democratic government in Afghanistan and contributed for the infrastructure development and the nation building there aiming at the well-being of the people. For this, the US presence there was more crucial in view of India's constructive involvement. As a result, India became most favourable country for the Afghan people. In fact, India's role in Afghanistan largely premised on soft power. However, India, being a democratic and peace loving country, always opposed and abstained from establishing contact with the violent Taliban. Therefore, Taliban's regaining of power recently, created dilemma for India given its huge investment in Afghanistan. Amongst the states involved in Afghanistan's crisis, India adopted the policy of non-engagement with the Taliban, and always supported the Afghan-led peace process. In fact, India failed to realise the Taliban as the most crucial factor for Afghan's peace process.

Significantly, despite the immense efforts by the various emperors and major state-actors towards occupying the region or Afghanistan, no one could conquer Afghanistan, and all they met with great economic and human loss. Especially, the Great Britain, the USSR, and the US (2001-2021) failed in their political or military objectives there. As has been observed, Afghanistan is a very tough and difficult country to occupy and govern. The empires after the empires and the nations after the nations have badly failed to win or normalize Afghanistan. As a result, Afghanistan is known as the "Graveyard of Empires".

Therefore, given the involvement of various regional and major actors, this book is an attempt to map their engagements in Afghanistan.

Vinod Khobragade

Contents

1

Afghanistan: The Graveyard of Empires

Introduction

Afghanistan has a long and great history. It has seen many emperors tried to conquer and establish their empires in Afghanistan. As a result, the Afghan land became the battlefield of many wars amongst the aspiring rulers or dynasties and foreigners to rule over. Significantly, these rulers also contributed by building major historical monuments and structures making Afghanistan beautiful that further attracted the world, however, these monuments are lost now. For example, the Bamiyan Buddha Statue of 6th century, the largest in the world, was destroyed by the Taliban in 2001. However, the present-day life in Afghanistan became so worst to give any happy news to the world. The killings and deaths, and wars and conflicts have been the routine occurrences there. The people are desperately struggling for peace and stability. The adversity, poverty, and deprivation of the Afghan citizens and also the mutual misunderstanding among its leaders and lust for domination offered the major countries like the UK, the USSR, and later the US and others to make Afghanistan as pawn in their hands for their personal interests. In fact, the collective leadership of the country plays major role in nation building and keeping the other countries away from contravening its right of sovereign state. But Afghanistan has always been remained unfortunate to move and initiate the process of its nation building, and consequently, the divided people are being used by the others for their self-interests, personal gains and making the land a battlefield for their mutual wars. Many actions within the state began struggle in the name of 'holy war' but shifting it into the gorge of 'civil war'. Because of the incessant civil wars and foreign invasions, situation in Afghanistan became mostly worst and pathetic. Given its geo-politically strategic significance, Alam Payind stated, "just in the past 100 years, Afghanistan was invaded either partially or completely six times by outsiders,"[1] and later by the United States of America in 2001. In a recent UN report, it has reported that in a war-torn country, three million Afghan peoples are suffering from the shortage of food and they need it urgently. Therefore, saving of humanity became the more significant objective of the UN and the global community. In fact, Afghan's people believe that "...in the absence of a legitimate and effective central authority, their country will continue to serve as a battlefield where the contradictory interests of various Afghan ethnic and linguistic groups and of Afghanistan's neighbors converge," and "...these conflicts and wars have forced changes in traditional relations among various Afghan ethnic and linguistic communities."[2]

Afghanistan is a landlocked country situated in heart of the South-Central Asia. It links Central Asia with South Asia. Before the colonial era, Afghanistan had been significant for the ancient Silk Road, and indeed, its gateway to the north, south, east, and west for commercial and civilizational interactions. Afghanistan was a "crossroad of ancient trade routes and human migrations. The main east-west trade routes passed through its northern and southern plains, and through its mountain passes before the ascendency of waterborne trade between Europe and the Far East."[3] Afghanistan has about 6,52,864 sq. kilometers geographical area and has common borders to the east and south Pakistan (Durand Line, 1510 miles), to the west is Iran (582 miles), and to the north, it is surrounded by the Central Asian countries; Turkmenistan (462 miles), Uzbekistan (89 miles) and Tajikistan (810 miles) and to its extreme northeast, Wakhan Corridor, which shares short border (47 miles) with the Xingjian province of China. Significantly, Afghanistan is rich in natural resources such as natural gas, petroleum, chromate, coal, copper, talc, barites, sulfur, lead, zinc, iron ore and salt, and precious and semi-precious stones like emeralds, rubies, lapis lazuli, etc. However, unfortunately, Afghanistan is very poor in terms of water resources. Afghanistan has also some agricultural resources such as grazing land and fertile land in some provinces such as Helmand in south and Kondoz in north. Moreover, the major rivers in Afghanistan are: the Amu Darya (800 kms), the Harirud (850 kms), the Helmand (1000 kms), and the Kabul (460 kms).[4] The population of Afghanistan is reported about 36.5 million in 2018. Afghanistan is a multi-ethnic country; about 99 percent Muslims dominated by the Sunnis and its population is divided into various ethno-linguistic groups or officially there are 14 ethnic groups:[5] Pashtun (42%), Tajik or Farsi of Iranian origin (27%), Hazara (10%), Uzbek (9%), Aymāq (4%), Turkmen (3%), Baloch (2%), and others (5%) such as Pashai, Nuristani, Gujjar, Arab, Brahui, Pamiri, etc. The Afghan Constitution has mentioned a total of 14 ethnic groups.[6] It is a multi-lingual state and many languages are spoken, however, Dari and Pashto are the official languages. As estimated, there are about seven major and about 40 minor languages in Afghanistan.[7] About 29 percent population is urban and rest is rural. Most of the Afghans, except Afghan Turks, and West Pakistani people have cultural and ethnic commonalities. Pashtun is the largest ethnic group that lives both in Afghanistan and Pakistan. It has believed that Afghanistan has about 45 percent population of Pashtun and Pakistan has three times more Pashtun than that of Afghanistan. Besides, Afghanistan and Iran share many important historical, cultural, religious, ethnic, linguistic, and economic ties. For Afghanistan, Iran is a very significant source of various essential products such as fuel, electricity, food, pharmaceuticals and medicines, chemicals, and important site of pilgrimage for the Shiite Muslims.[8]

Afghanistan, because of its vast ethnic diversity, is one of the extremely fragile and conflict-affected countries in the world which has been suffering from the range of turmoil from state security to human security that including the problem of security of people, absence of united community cohesion and resilience, shambling health situation, failed economy, ethnic crisis, and the major problems of violence and instability. With the international intervention led by the US in 2001 overthrowing the Taliban regime (1996-2001) to establish an elected government, Afghani people developed optimistic expectations towards the reconstruction of New Afghanistan to enjoy peaceful and better life. However, since 2014, with the partial withdrawal of international forces led by the US,[9] the turmoil in Afghanistan re-surfaced. The internal security and economic development sprouted as the major challenges. The terrorist violence causing deaths of many became routine in Afghanistan. Since 2014, the Taliban's attacks mushroomed in various parts of Afghanistan pushing the Afghani population again into the suffocating quagmire of agony and deadly violence. It has reported that the Taliban's 2016 'Spring Offensive'—a series of attacks, the group used to launch each year after the end of winter, included a major bombing in Kabul in April, which killed and injured more than 400 people. In June, security guards at the Canadian embassy in Kabul were attacked; in July, the Taliban drove a truckload of explosives into a foreign military facility; in August, militants stormed the campus of the American University of Afghanistan in Kabul.[10] Moreover, there are more attacks continuing even today by the other militant groups. "The role-call of deaths has been increasing—according to the UN, 11418 people were killed in Afghanistan in 2015 and 2016, of which at least 24 percent are children, and 2017 has seen 1700 deaths so far".[11] In August 2017, the NATO forces were attacked. Moreover, both the Taliban and the Islamic States indulged in creating inhuman and deadly chaos in Afghanistan. And Pakistan's support to Taliban further increased Afghani's pain. The various factors forced Afghanistan falling into the category of fragile and failed states. In fact, even during the democratic government in Afghanistan, the Taliban continued to grab more Afghan's territory under its control and influence.

In fact, the failed state is the country in which the government is unable to use its authority adequately in controlling the bad situation and also fails in providing the necessary political goods to its citizens. "The category of fragile and failed states in international relations is a post-Cold War phenomenon that developed to address new threats to regional and international security originating from conflict-prone, politically fractured, socially divided and economically collapsing states in Asia, Africa...."[12] According to Robert I. Rotberg, "failed states are tense, deeply conflicted, dangerous, and contested bitterly by warring factions. In most failed states, government troops battle armed revolts led by one or more rivals. Occasionally, the official authorities in a failed state face two or more insurgencies, varieties of civil unrests, different degrees of communal discontent, and a plethora of dissent directed at the state and at groups within the state...failed states cannot control their borders....They loose authority over sections of territory".[13] The other features of the failed states are: enduring violence and growth of criminal violence, destroyed infrastructures, limited supply of political goods, flawed institutions, unparallel economic opportunities (only for privileged few), declining GDP and loss of government's legitimacy.[14] Moreover, the three key variables operational around the world to identify states' failures, as mentioned by Nurruzman, are: first, a country's low level of material well-being (measured in terms of infant mortality), second, its degree of trades openness (in terms of imports and exports in percentage of GDP), and finally, the presence of major civil conflicts between two or more bordering states. Further, it has argued that the policy of military intervention by the great powers or the superpowers have done more damages than good to the failed states. The Soviet Russian military intervention in 1979 in Afghanistan is said to be responsible for opening the conflicts such as ideological conflicts between communism and Islam, ethnic conflicts between Pashtuns and non-Pashtuns and other sectarian conflicts. However, Afghanistan, though was economically poor and weak, but was stable. Besides, the American military intervention in 2001 in the name of war against terror further deteriorated the situation at the cost of human life and material loss without achieving peace and stability in Afghanistan.[15] In fact, gradually, Afghanistan transformed into a failed state.

Historical Background

Throughout history, Afghanistan has often played a pivotal role between the superpowers of any particular era. In the ancient world, the Greeks of Alexander the Great's Macedonian hegemony: Persians; Mongols under Genghis Khan and his successors; and a host of other groups have vied for control, often leaving ethnic traces within a complex tribal and ethnic makeup in modern Afghanistan. In the nineteenth century it was part of the "Great Game" between Great Britain and Russia; in the twentieth and twenty-first centuries, there have been both Soviet and NATO incursions; and now, Afghanistan retains a pivotal role between India and Pakistan, China, Iran and former Soviet Republics. NATO is engaged in a task of "declared nation building", and also to ostensibly make the streets of Western cities safe. But is this not just a "great game" but a "grand illusion"? Afghanistan has often been internally divided, but has never welcomed foreign domination, an experience which tends to bring Afghans together against the invader. Foreign troops, however well intentioned, propping up an unpopular central government, usually leads to resentment and the opposite of what was intended.[16]

The urban civilization, as believed, began in the modern Afghanistan between 3000-2000 BC. This region was controlled for the first time by Iranian Achaemenian Dynasty from 550 BC to 331 BC. Between 330 and 327 BC, Alexander the Great emerged in scene to defeat the Achaemenian Emperor Darius III and also subdued the local resistance in the territory that known as Afghanistan. It was believed that Darius fled the battlefield in a war with the Alexander giving him victory. Darius requested a peace treaty with the Alexander by writing letter to him, but, the Alexander told Darius to surrender unconditionally. The historians reported that during the winter of 330-329 BC, Alexander furthered into Afghanistan.[17] From here, he also tried to capture India (as was considered as "far end of the world"), but could not succeed and returned back.[18] After Alexander's death in 323 BC, his successor Seleucids captured the northern region of Afghanistan establishing the Seleucids dynasty by Seleucus and he was engaged in continuing the infusion of the region with the Greek cultural influence. After the death of the Alexander, the beginning of the Hellenistic[19] period in Afghanistan was reported.[20] Emperor Seleucus had expanded its empire close to the Indus River in India, and in 305 BC, Seleucus and the Mauryan King Chandragupta Maurya engaged in wars, however, ultimately, after facing severe defeat, Seleucus reached to an agreement with the king of Mauryan Dynasty.[21] In fact, after Alexander, Afghanistan was divided into two Empires, one by Seleucides in the north and other by the Maurya dynasty in the Southern Afghanistan. Subsequently, the Mauryan Empire Asoka, the passionate emperor of charity, compassion, and humanity, introduced Buddhism there and across the entire Mauryan Empire. The Southern Afghanistan remained under the control of the Maurya from 305 BC-185 BC.[22] However, after the death of Asoka, the Maurya dynasty began declining because of its weaker kings. In 185 BC, during the Sunga coup, the Sunga leader Pushyamitra Sunga killed the last Maurya king Brihadratha and established the Sunga Empire.[23] Further around 150 BC, nomadic Kushans could successfully establish empire there making it the cultural and commercial centre. It has believed that this dynasty long lasted till 224 AD. And later, from the third century AD (the end of the Kushans) to the seventh century, the region was observed fragmented and was controlled by the Iranian Sassanian Empire.[24] It was also believed that along with the Sassanian period, the influence of Hinduism was also renewed in Afghanistan.[25] In fact, "the region of Afghanistan has for much of history been part of the Persian empire. From time to time it has been linked with the northern plains of India, as under the Kushan dynasty of the 2nd century AD. Very occasionally, as in the time of Mahmud of Ghazni, it has existed as a kingdom approximating more closely to the modern borders of Afghanistan."[26] It has believed that "during the pre-Islamic period in Afghanistan, the cultural religious beliefs functioned mainly under the threefold influence of Hellenistic, Buddhist and Hindu cultures. China and Rome also had influence on the region as indicated in the artesian artifacts found in Afghanistan."[27]

The Islamic and Mongolian Period: The year 642 AD has been believed as the beginning of the Arab conquest of the Middle East, and in this year, in the battle of Nahavand, the Arab Islamic rulers overpowered the Sassanian dynasty. And in 652, the Arabs had invaded and conquered Afghanistan and began introducing the Islamic faith in Afghanistan.[28] They further continued conquering the Afghan tribes for very long time and they also rapidly spread Islam throughout Afghanistan, and, gradually, Afghanistan became the centre of the many dominant Islamic rulers. By the tenth century, the rule of the Arab Abbasid Dynasty and his successor in Central Asia, the Samanid Dynasty, were collapsed. The Ghaznavid Dynasty (offshoot of Samanids) became the first great Islamic Dynasty to rule Afghanistan from 962 to 1151 and this empire was considered as the most significant as "it was the first considerable Islamic empire that spread across the Asia," and it was also believed that they have spread Islam into India.[29] Besides, "the centre of the Ghazni Empire was the pinnacle of prestige, enjoying artisans, poets, musicians, and philosophers amidst the backdrop of opulent palaces, gold-encrusted mosques, and abundant gardens that spread to India."[30] Later the Ghori Empire was established in 1151 in Afghanistan by Muhammad Ghori by defeating Sultan Bahram Shah, the last king of the Ghanzi Empire. The Ghori Empire reined Afghanistan from 1151 to 1219. In 1220, the Mongol forces of Genghis Khan occupied the entire Central Asia. And until 1380s, Afghanistan remained fragmented and Timur (famously known as Tamerlane) had ruled and expanded the Mongol Empire. The Mongol Empire remained and continued by Timur's descendants in Afghanistan till the early sixteenth century.[31] It is believed that "in AD 1219, the empire and the land of Afghanistan would be ransacked and overthrown by a ferocious Mongol warriors likes of which the world had never seen."[32]

The Pashtun Rulers: In 1504, the Mughals of North India entered the region and continued contesting for the Afghan territory with Iranian Safavi Dynasty for the next two centuries. Further with the death of the most prominent Safavi leader, Nadir Shah in 1747, the indigenous Pashtun (also known as Durrani), began ruling Afghanistan that lasted till 1978. "The beginning of modern Afghanistan can be dated to 1747, when the Afghans in Nadir Shah's army return home after his death. Their leader, Ahmad Khan Abdali, enters Kandahar and was elected king of the Afghans in a tribal assembly. He takes the title Durr-i-Durran ('pearl among pearls') and changes the name of his tribe to the Durrani."[33] He had formed "Tribal Confederacy".[34] The historians reported that the first Durrani leader Ahmad Shah also known as "the father of Afghan Nation", united the Pashtun tribes and by 1760 built an empire that expanded and spanned till Delhi and Arabian Sea, and even from the Amu River to the Indus River. It is believed that he had established the name 'Afghanistan' and made Kabul its capital. Kabul was built as a beautiful city. On Kabul's beauty, Ahmad Shah Durrani wrote, "Whatever countries I conquer in the world, I would never forget your beautiful gardens. When I remember the summits of your beautiful mountains I forget the greatness of the Delhi throne."[35] Depicting the beauty of Kabul and comparing it with paradise, Alexander Burnes described Kabul as: "There were peaches, plums, apricots, pears, apples, quinces, cherries, walnuts, mulberries, pomegranates, and vines, all growing in one garden. There were also nightingales, blackbirds, thrushes, and doves... and chattering magpies on almost every tree," and today, as Rajiv Dogra stated, "that paradise-like city is unrecognizable; so complete has been its destruction over the years. The desolate patchwork that greets the visitor now bears hardly any fruit and hosts almost no bird. But even back then, the glory did not last long."[36] However, the region could not stay united and fragmented after the death of Ahmad Shah in 1772. It has stated that "after the death of Ahmad Shah, Afghanistan became an 'orgy of intrigue, treachery, murder...and betrayal'."[37] In 1826, Dost Mohammad, the leader of the Pashtun Muhammadzai tribe restored the power in Afghanistan.[38] In 1880, Abdur Rehman, a Durrani ruler occupied power there and reigned till 1901.[39] It has observed that most of the significant changes in Afghanistan under the Pashtun rule since 1747 took place in his reign.[40] However, it has also believed that the Afghan rulers since Abdur Rahman had believed the policy of keeping Afghanistan "inaccessible as the best method of keeping the powerful neighbours at arms length," and though this policy could maintain Afghanistan's independence, but "it also kept the Afghan society out of reach for the benefits of modern educational technological and social developments."[41] Therefore, because of the past irrational policies, the Afghan society has been facing major socio-economic and political problems today.

The Great Game of the Great Empires: The geo-political or strategic position of Afghanistan in the Central Asian region significantly had major influence in and out of the region and has been "the victim of external intervention throughout modern history." And therefore, because of its significance, by the nineteenth century, it was caught between two rival great powers and the Central Asian region and Afghanistan became the battlefield of the Great Game[42] between the Britain from the south and east, and Czarist Russia from the north, however, they were failed in their objective to dominate and control Afghanistan.[43] In other words, Afghanistan had become the buffer state between the British Empire and the Russian Empire, and both the empires had, so-called, permanent rivalry, which, however, benefited neither country of them. In fact, according to the British, continuous instability in Afghanistan led to the small wars becoming hot wars: 1839-42, 1878-80 and 1919, in which the British failed and frustrated.[44] "Between 1839 and 1919, Britain fought three brutal wars in Afghanistan to counter Russian influence in the region."[45] In the first Anglo-Afghan War 1839-42, Britain overthrew the Dost Mohammad rule, however, they abandoned their stronghold in Afghanistan in 1842. After this, Soviet Russian forces reached to the northern border of Afghanistan. Furthermore, in 1878 in the second Anglo-Afghan war, Britain invaded and occupied most of Afghanistan. In fact, it was stated that "for twenty-five years at the end of the nineteenth century everybody was certain that one day Britain would fight Russia in Asia,"[46] and their fight came in reality as the great game for Afghanistan. In 1880, Abdur Rehman started a 21 years reign focused on maintaining of Soviet Russia and British interests, consolidation of Afghan tribes, and reorganization of civil administration to create a modern state of Afghanistan. During this time in 1893, the Durand Line was established by the agreement between the British India and Amir Abdur Rehman Khan of Afghanistan. Further from 1901 to 1919, Habibullah, son of Abdur Rahman, ruled Afghanistan and continued the administrative reforms and maintained Afghan neutrality in WWI.[47] Moreover, along with carrying his father's legacy, he also introduced "a small degree of modernization, to education, to infrastructure and to the army."[48] In fact, "the British tried a number of strategies against Pashtun tribes during the Anglo-Afghan wars. One was 'butcher and bolt,' the practice of slaughtering unruly tribesmen and then moving quickly to pacify new areas. But they were unable to conquer country," as the tribesmen were "brave and warlike race."[49] Moreover, the Afghans are also believed as "a brave, hardy and independent race...with their indomitable hatred of rule, and their love of individual independence."[50] The Durand Line was marked by the British which passes through the present-day Pakistani provinces of Khyber Pakhtunkhwa, Federally Administered Tribal Areas (FATA) and Baluchistan, and ten provinces in Afghanistan.[51] The Pashtun tribes that habitat in both the sides of line see the province of both sides as Pashtunistan.

Afghanistan got independence on 19 August 1919 from the British Rule by signing a treaty of Rawalpindi that ending the Third Anglo-Afghan war. Even for that matter, during the two world wars period, Afghanistan maintained balance between the two world powers. Further, from 1919-29, Habibullah's son Amanullah ruled Afghanistan further maintaining the balance between the great power rivalry between the Soviet Russia and Britain. During his regime, Amanullah introduced Afghanistan's first constitution in 1923. After him, in 1933, his nephew, Mohammad Zahir Shah became the king of Afghanistan and ruled over 40 years till 1973 when he was overthrown by his cousin Mohammed Daud Khan with the help of Soviets. In 1978, Daud Khan abolished Monarchy and became President declaring Afghanistan as a Republic state. In fact, even during the cold war politics between the US-bloc and the Soviet-bloc after the Second World War, Afghanistan remained non-aligned, but despite that Afghanistan had strong relationship with the Soviet Russia.[52] It has observed that since the Soviet invasion of

Afghanistan in December 1979, Afghanistan has consistently been victim of the conflicts and wars, and incessantly struggling for peace and stability. Peace became a nightmare or mirage to Afghan people. After the Soviet occupation, Afghanistan became the victim of cold war politics between the US and Soviet Russia until the Soviets withdrawn from Afghan soil in 1989. The US had supported and funded the Mujahedeen militants group against the communist government supported by the Soviet forces in Afghanistan. And thereafter, Afghanistan was encompassed with the civil war between the Mujahedeen and the communist group. However, in this conflict, the Mujahedeen eventually occupied power in Kabul on 15 April 1992.

Civil War in Afghanistan

The decade of 1970s brought multiple changes in the overall scenario of Afghanistan. With the emergence of Mohammed Daud Khan in power in 1973, the opposition forces that including communists and fundamentalists became active and started severe struggle against the Daud government. The Daud government had taken some harsh reforms and adopted the policy of suppression despite making the democratic promises, and besides, could not introduce development and other required programmes that resulting to the beginning of opposition to the government of the day by the masses. Even for that matter, he also had planned suppression of all the opposition parties and leaders. The power of the Afghan President Mohammed Daud Khan came to a violent end through a coup led by the insurgent troops or PDPA[53] (this coup was called as Saur Revolution) on 27 April 1978. Subsequently, this coup further deteriorated the situation and the People's Democratic Party of Afghanistan (PDPA) emerged in power only, later, to form government in Afghanistan with the support of the Soviet communists on the promise by the PDPA that the socialism would be established in Afghanistan, and subsequently, Nur Muhammed Taraki of the PDPA became the head of government of the Democratic Republic of Afghanistan. However, it has observed that since then with the involvement of Soviets, Afghanistan became the battleground of cold war politics. However, this rivalry between the USSR and the USA was not limited to that epoch, but even today both the US and Russia still are involved functionally or dysfunctionally in Afghanistan. It has stated that by enjoying the Soviet communists support, the PDPA leadership started imposing "its will upon the people and to take a line of action towards establishing an authoritarian regime in Afghanistan based on fear and coercion."[54] Besides, it has stated that the PDPA government prosecuted and murdered the Afghan elites, religious establishments and intellectuals, as a result, because of the unjust role of the government, the civilian revolt began in the eastern Afghanistan in 1978, and subsequently, the previous Prime Minister and Minister of Defense, Hafizullah Amin, seized power in the late 1979. However, new regime was also somewhat unstable and the country saw "The new ruler attempted to remove his PDPA opponents, hurting party morale and promoting dissatisfaction in and outside the government."[55] In this context, it was reported that

> The new government in Afghanistan after assuming power began to introduce radical transformations in the country and implement an impractical maximalist course. In a feudal society with deep rooted remnants of a gentile tribal order and the domination of Islam in all spheres of life they proclaim their intentions to establish socialism in the shortest possible period, for which there was neither a social or an economic basis, nor mass support. Concentrating their main efforts in three basic directions; the agriculture sector, the national question and religion, they ruined the system of village management, shaped over the centuries, exacerbated ethnic tensions, and provoked a harsh negative reaction from the clergy.[56]

This government, in fact, was failed in addressing people's problems and grievances of social life. Therefore, by and large, the PDPA government's unacceptable transformations for the rapid achievements by means of radical reforms and the use of force, invited antagonism and resistance from the opposite forces that created the atmosphere for the inception of civil war in the country. In fact, the government and its leadership of the day resulted to be weak and unsuccessful and the party began facing an internal strife and crisis of leadership. Furthermore, in a juncture of socio-political vulnerabilities, the superpower rivalry further added fuel in only to worsen the situation. However, all these developments in the politically disordered Afghanistan offered an opportunity for the opposition forces to be more proactive only to form the coalition with the help and support from the countries of the Islamic world and the USA. And besides, the internal tribes started fighting, because of which thousands of refugees fled to Pakistan and Iran.[57] Moreover, Pakistan provided asylum to the Afghan rebels to establish their military camps. The military camps in Pakistan became the centre for the Afghan counter revolution and it has also stated that, through Pakistan, the Afghan rebels received the financial assistance from the US, arms from China and all other support from the Western and the Islamic countries.[58] In fact, it has argued that "Afghanistan is difficult both to defeat and to control, but it has seldom shown a serious inclination to control itself. Peace and order in the country have often suffered because of internecine conflicts and wars," and besides, "Afghans are ardent nationalists, but their actions weaken national unity and integration. They are known for their spirit of fierce independence, but this independence may have been jeopardized by the intermeshing of internal conflicts and external intervention.[59]

The Soviet Intervention: The Afghan leadership of the day could not control the worsening situation in and around Afghanistan, as a result, they (Prime Minister Hafizullah Amin and President Nur Mohammad Taraki) invited military assistance from the communist Soviets to deploy their forces in Afghanistan to suppress the anti-government forces and their activities. It has stated that in March 1979, Taraki had made such request from the Soviet government when the Herat uprising had taken place, however, Taraki's request was turned down, and the Soviets had sent the shipments of military equipments. It has reported that after prolonged deliberations and discussions and repeated request (about 20 requests) from the PDPA government, on 12 December 1979, the Soviet Union decided to support the Afghan government by sending troops to Afghanistan, however, on the perception of security threats.[60] In fact, it has also stated that the refusal of the political advice of the Soviet by the Amin government forced the Soviet troops to enter Afghanistan in December, and after that Amin was killed by the Soviet forces, and appointed Babrak Karmal as a Prime Minister.[61] But he also failed to rule efficiently and that offered an opportunity to Mujahedeen to rise against the Kabul government. But it has stated that the Soviet's troops deployment further intensified the internal Afghan conflicts as this could not repair the worsening military and political situation in Afghanistan. By 1981, the Soviet forces were deployed across the country and had started direct combating with the Mujahedeen who had launched a national resistance against the PDPA government. The Mujahedeen were consisted of the several factions/groups organized on the personalities and the ethnic lines, and they had expanded the attacks on the Soviet back-forces.[62] In 1985, seven guerrilla organizations came together against the Soviet forces and strengthened Mujahedeen's power. However, again due to inefficiency to rule, Karmal was replaced by Muhammad Najibullah, but even he also sailed the same boat with Karmal. It has stated that between 1983 and 1986, Afghanistan experienced the large number of fatalities and violence because of the Soviet forces increased their large-scale attacks. During this time, Soviet forces had changed their combating strategy from "a tactic of driving the Mujahedeen from the countryside, to forcing the population out of contested areas, with widespread use of aerial bombardment".[63] Even for that matter, the Soviet forces, as reported, were indulged in targeting the civilians regularly and also had deployed land mines across the country even in the urban localities. Furthermore, the level of violence was also escalated as the Mujahedeen had intensified their warfare activities with new weaponry that was provided by the United States.[64]

The US's Pro-Mujahedeen Policy: The Soviet's troops deployment further invited the international reaction especially by the US, the NATO countries, Islamic World, and even China. They perceived that Soviet's military deployment in Afghanistan had abruptly disturbed the prevailing balance of power in the regional and global level. This development made the US uncomfortable, and therefore, the US started providing large amount of arms and other supplies to the Mujahedeen and also "reinforced the western military presence in strategically important zones in the region" in view of rebalancing the power equations in the region.[65] In fact, the developments in Afghanistan destabilized the US influence in the region, and moreover, the US was also unable to interfere directly in Afghanistan to support the forces in opposition. Therefore, pondering as an alternate, the US administration planned to use Pakistan and other Islamic states like Saudi Arabia in this direction and by taking quick decision, decided to send arms and technical supplies and a sum of 100 million dollars to Pakistan. As a result, as Liakhovsky stated, "Pakistan, which on the eve of Afghan war had been facing the threat of economic and political bankruptcy, was transformed into a front line state and started to receive an extensive military and economic aid from the US and Saudi Arabia."[66] Furthermore, after becoming the US partner for the Afghan strategy, Pakistan also expressed its reaction against the Soviet's military intervention in Afghanistan on the plea of the Soviet's presence close to its borders. Besides, the states like Egypt, Saudi Arabia, Kuwait, Sudan, Tunisia, and the UAE had expressed displeasure and negative reaction against the Soviet's troops deployment in Afghanistan, while others such as pro-Soviet Islamic countries welcomed it. Moreover, China also condemned the Soviet action in Afghanistan and expressed its support to the US initiative against the Soviet Union because of its rivalry and competition with the latter and hence joining the anti-Soviet forces such as Pakistan and the US, provided small weapons to the anti-Soviet resistance/Mujahedeen.[67] China had held the Afghan-Soviet agreement as "Soviet Hegemonism".[68] Reacting to the Soviet invasion, on 31 December 1979, China's Ministry of Affairs expressed, "Afghanistan is China's neighbour...and therefore the Soviet armed invasion of that country poses a threat to China's security. This cannot but arouse the grave concern of the Chinese people", and Chinese people "will never tolerate the Soviet hegemonist invasion of our neighbour."[69] By and large, however, China had perceived the Soviet invasion in Afghanistan as a threat to China's security and also a threat to peace and security in Asia and the entire world. Such anti-Soviet reactions definitely forced the group of countries to openly move a confrontation with the Soviets and all these countries declared their support to the opposite forces or groups in Afghanistan. Explicitly, Afghanistan felt isolated at the international level having support only of the Soviet Union. During those days, "The United States launched a propaganda campaign aimed at demonstrating to the leaders and the people of the Islamic States that the USSR, and not the US, was the mortal enemy of Islam."[70] On CIA's strategy against the Soviet intervention in Afghanistan, Steve Galster stated:

> The CIA was especially resistant to calls for providing the mujahidin with US-made weaponry. Traditionally, the Agency purchased foreign, usually Soviet-styled, weaponry in order to "plausibly deny" US involvement if the need arose. Throughout the Afghan war, the CIA purchased Soviet-designed weapons from Egypt, China and elsewhere and transported them to Pakistan. Cables reveal that Chinese and Egyptian AK-47 rifles and SA-7 anti-aircraft missiles arrived in Pakistan as early as 1980. This covert purchasing process not only covered US tracks, but ensured the availability of weapons that were compatible with the kind captured by the rebels from their Soviet-supplied enemies.[71]

Furthermore;

> Despite signs of corruption in both the military and humanitarian aid programs as early as 1982, Congress ultimately provided nearly $3 billion in covert aid for the mujahidin.... By 1987, the United States was providing the rebels with nearly $700 million in military assistance a year. In 1984, Congressman Charles Wilson used his powerful position on the House Intelligence Committee to tack on an additional $50 million for Afghan covert aid and convinced the CIA to purchase high-quality, Swiss-designed Oerlikon anti-aircraft missiles, which could pierce the heavy armor of the USSR's most formidable counterinsurgency machine, the Hind Mi-24 helicopter. The CIA went even further in 1985, purchasing the sophisticated British-made Blowpipe anti-aircraft missiles. And in 1986,...the CIA provided the

> mujahidin with US-made Stinger missiles, the most effective shoulder-held anti-aircraft weapon in the world.[72]

Subsequently, after having suffered substantial losses and incurred excessive costs in the country, the USSR decided to withdraw from Afghanistan. During the period of Soviet forces deployment in Afghanistan, 14,500 Soviet soldiers and one million Afghanis died.[73] The USSR realized that military was not the solution to the Afghan problem. Therefore, because of frustration, the USSR, in 1988, signed a Geneva Accord with the Afghan government and decided the time period for the complete withdrawal, and in 1989, the Soviets were withdrawn completely from the Afghan soil. It has believed that "the Afghan War contributed to the collapse of the Soviet empire."[74] In context of the USSR intervention, it was observed that

> The war in Afghanistan had a major impact on domestic politics in the Soviet Union. It was one of the key factors in the delegitimization of Communist Party rule. Civil society reacted to the intervention by marginalizing the Afghan veterans. The army was demoralized as a result of being perceived as an invader.... The image of the Soviet Army fighting against Islam in Afghanistan also contributed to a rapid rise of Islamic fundamentalism in the Central Asian republics and possibly to the strengthening of the independence movement in Chechnya, both of which continue to pose major security threats to Russia....[75]

In the words of Gregory Feiffer,

> The Soviet War in Afghanistan again confirmed that no power ever successfully conquered that land, which, for all its remoteness, lies at a strategically important crossroad of empires. The Persian ruler Cyrus the Great invaded it in the sixth century BC. Alexander the Great followed three hundred years later, as did the British in the nineteenth century. They vied for control over Afghanistan with the Russian Czarist empire for decades in what came to be called the Great Game. But while foreign forces have often moved into Afghanistan with relative ease, they've never been able to maintain control. The country's long history

> of invasion helped spawn a culture of warfare among disparate local tribes and ethnic groups, which fought relentlessly among themselves until united by the common goal repelling outside encroachers.[76]

Afghanistan After the Soviet Withdrawal: The fact has been that the ten long years period of the Soviet occupation and the struggle against it, there could not be a single story of success in Afghanistan and even the masses of this land could not form a collective sense of nation or nationhood rather they remained divided on the line of ethnic and sect-based factors. The presence of the Soviet forces in Afghanistan could not dilute the civil war in Afghanistan. Even after the withdrawal of the Soviet troops, the situation in Afghanistan had not changed as expected but worsened further as the fighting among the Afghans themselves increased. As a result, it was clearly appeared that the presence of the Soviet forces was not the only reason for the civil war in Afghanistan, but the other factors also. Later, on 30 April 1992, after a prolonged military and economic assistance from the USSR, the Najibullah government was overthrown from the Afghan's seat of power and Mujahedeen government was formed and Sibghatullah Mojadeddi was made acting president of Afghanistan from April to June 1992, and on 30 August 1992 Burhanuddin Rabbani became the new President of Afghanistan.[77] It has believed that the Mujahedeen's coming into power was welcomed by most of the Afghan people with the high expectation that they would transform the war-ravaged country into peaceful and ordered situation. But their expectation soon went down and even Mujahedeen indulged in continuing civil war. Between February and September 1993, fighting began between Hekmatyar and other Mujahedeen factions including Mohaqiq's Hazara dominated 'Hizb-e-Wahdat', the 'Jamiat-e-Islami' and Dostum's newly formed 'Jumbish-e-Milli'. Further, between January 1994 and May 1995, Dostum and Hekmatyar joined hands to oust Rabani and Mohaqiq and the Taliban emerged as the important player on the Afghan's political platform.[78] The Taliban had destroyed almost all the other groups in Afghanistan and some fled out of it. However, since then Afghanistan had two main opposition groups—the Taliban and the United Front (UF) or the National Alliance (United Islamic Front for the Salvation of Afghanistan), which was said to be emerged as an anti-Taliban faction in 1996. It was said that "The UF was a tactical alliance, or confederation, between warlords (or commanders) of different militias across Afghanistan who had differences among themselves...."[79] On Afghanistan, Chandra quoted what Commander Abdul Haq stated that:

> For us Afghanistan is destroyed. It is turning to poison, and not only for us but for all others in the world. If you are a terrorist, you can have shelter here, no matter who you are. May be one day they (the Americans) will have to send hundreds of thousands of troops to deal with that, and if they step in, they will be stuck. We have a British grave in Afghanistan. We have a Soviet grave. And then we will have American grave."[80]

The Emergence of Taliban

The Taliban Movement of Islamic Students was set up in 1994 in the southern province of Kandahar amidst the Afghan civil war by Mullah Mohammed Omar, a Pashtun Muslim cleric and a junior Mujahedeen commander during the anti-Soviet war, who took up arms,[81] and later, the Taliban captured Kandahar in November 1994 to "pacify the crime-ridden southern city", Herat in 1995, and on 25 September 1996, seized power in Kabul and emerged as a major political and military force. By doing this, the Taliban transformed the state structure into the "Islamic Emirate of Afghanistan" in 1996, and adopted two-track governance system in Kandahar and Kabul.[82] The word 'Taliban' is a word used for student. The Taliban are believed to be a group of private rural-based Islamic religious schools (madrasa) in Afghanistan and the bordering areas of Pakistan. The Mujahedeen's who were fought against the Soviet forces were recruited from these schools. The Taliban leaders are the religious leaders from the Kandahar province trained in madrasa which were affiliated to the Deobandi Movement in both Afghanistan and Pakistan.[83] It has believed that "the movement attracted popular support in the initial post-Soviet era by promising to impose stability and rule of law after four years of conflict (1992-96) among rival mujahedeen groups."[84] As a result, the Taliban regime had territorial control over about 90 percent of the country before it was toppled in 2001 by the US. The emergence of the Taliban has two main domestic or internal and external factors. Internally, it was a product of the civil war during the anarchic environment that prevailed in Afghanistan, and externally it was the product of the region politics especially Pakistan's regional ambitions.[85] Due to the failure and inability of the Mujahedeen government in Afghanistan, the Taliban sought the support of Pakistan and Saudi Arabia. These states provided military and financial support to the Taliban to emerge as an effective military force, and it has also stated that the Taliban forces comprised of the large number of the non-Afghans such as nationals from Saudi Arabia and other Gulf countries.[86] In fact, the Talibans were successful in gaining local legitimacy quickly as they portrayed themselves as saviours of the Afghan society, and as a result, with its increasing popularity, many people started joining it.[87] It has stated that:

> The predominantly Pashtun Taliban emerged...as a messianic movement made up of Taliban (literally students) from Islamic Madrassa (seminaries) who were living as refugees in Pakistan. They vowed to bring peace to Afghanistan, establish law and order, disarm the population, and impose Shariah Islamic law. Welcomed by the war-weary Pashtun population, the Taliban were at first remarkably successful and popular until they captured Kabul...and expressed no desire to rule the country. But ever since they then—abetted by their Pakistani and Saudi backers and inspired by ideological mentor such as Bin Laden—The Taliban have committed themselves to conquering the entire country and more.[88]

Within two days of assuming power, the Taliban shot Najibullah in his head and hung his 'beaten and bloated' body to crane in Central Kabul.[89] In fact, the Taliban were puzzled and incapable to understand how to rule or run the government or controlling of economy that led to the situation bad to worst in Afghanistan and even they opposed the modernization process and continued focusing much on traditional practices.[90] As of coming in power, they started rejecting and neglecting the state's core functions that including even the discarding of social services and welfare of the masses imposing more stringent rules based on religious faith or laws and because of some anti-human practices and violations of basic human rights, they were internationally isolated.[91] The women were the worst victims of the Taliban rule. However, during this time the main countries that supported and recognized the Taliban as Afghanistan's legitimate government were Pakistan, Saudi Arabia and United Arab Emirates (UAE), however, the latter two had maintained limited diplomatic presence in Afghanistan. It has reported that "in 1998 alone, Pakistan provided $6 million to the Taliban."[92] In context of Pakistan's support to the Afghan regime, it was said that "Islamabad supported the Taliban as a force that could unify and stabilize Afghanistan while staving off Indian, Iranian, and Russian influence."[93] Further, in February 1997, the US had received Taliban delegation. In fact, Pakistan and Saudi Arabia had links with the Taliban in December 1994 and the US had tacitly supported the student's movement, which later came to be known as the Taliban.[94] It has also stated that "The Taliban is a creature of Pakistan, and now Pakistan is in danger of becoming a creature of the Taliban."[95] The Taliban had centered in the border region of Afghanistan and Pakistan, and "the Taliban were supported by Pakistan both diplomatically and materially and harboured Osama bin Laden...."[96] Pakistan by providing major support including arms and funds, "could manipulate Taliban clerics, and...ensure a stable and acquiescent Afghanistan, as well as secure routes to open trade to the newly independent Central Asian states."[97] Significantly, the safe heaven provided to the Taliban by Pakistan has been considered as the major strength of the Taliban to rise up. In this context, Human Rights Watch reported

> Of all the foreign powers involved in efforts to sustain and manipulating the ongoing fighting, Pakistan is distinguished both by the sweep of its objectives and the scales of its efforts, which include soliciting funding for the Taliban, bankrolling Taliban operations, providing diplomatic support as the Taliban's virtual emissaries abroad, arranging training for Taliban fighters, recruiting

> skilled and unskilled manpower to serve in Taliban armies, planning and directing offensives, providing and facilitating shipments of ammunitions and fuel, and on several occasions apparently directly providing combat support.[98]

Furthermore, Liakhovsky narrated the actions of the Taliban as "The Taliban had stepped forward with the slogan to clean the country of violence, murders, and lawlessness, but instead of the promised relief, they threw millions of Afghans into conditions of great severity the likes of which had never been seen in the past."[99] During the Taliban regime, Mullah Omar extended sanctuary to Al-Qaeda on the condition not to act against the US, but, Osama bin Laden, by breaking promise made to Omar, launch a terrorist attack on the US embassies in Nairobi and Dar es Salaam in East Africa in 1998, and later in 2001, terrorist attack on the US which is known as 9/11 attack. It has believed that "the Taliban was fundamentally parochial while al-Qaeda had its sights set on global jihad."[100] In fact, Afghanistan had become the main land of international terrorism. Osama bin Laden launched war against the US by "accusing the Americans occupying Arabia, plundering its riches, humiliating its leaders, attacking Iraq, and (claiming that) the United States had declared war on Islam and its people."[101] As a result, Laden declared a jihad against the US. In fact, throughout the Taliban regime, Afghanistan was complete in bloods as the Taliban and other groups like the United Front were continuously fighting against each other. It has reported that "the Taliban forced civilians from their homes and then set fire to houses and crops, and destroyed irrigation canals and wells, ostensibly to rout opposition synthesizers but effectively preventing the residents' return.[102] In March 2001, the Taliban destroyed the Bamiyan Buddha statue.

Eventually, as a revenge of the 9/11 terrorist attack, the US (Operation Enduring Freedom by the Bush Administration) in 2001 launched military attack on the Taliban-led Afghanistan for harbouring al-Qaeda, and toppled their government, but the US failed to defeat them. In fact, the United Nations had sanctioned military action against the terrorism. The Taliban force consisted of about sixty thousand fighters and has been the most vigorous insurgent group in Afghanistan and holds strong influence over the civilians near its strongholds in Afghanistan's south and east regions. Moreover, "it has also metastasized in neighboring Pakistan, where thousands of fighters in the country's western tribal areas wage war against the government", and since their ousting from power, the Taliban had been threatening of the destabilization of the region and harbouring terrorist groups with global ambitions, and also hampered the process of economic development and consistently sabotaging the human rights and violence and killings of the people in the areas where it dominantly prevailed.[103] After the US attack, the Taliban fled from Afghanistan and regrouped across the border in Pakistan from where they started insurgency against the US-supported government in Afghanistan.[104] In the civil war in Afghanistan, both the Taliban and the United Front committed severe crimes of killings and violations of human rights. However, the Taliban has been held as more deadly organization against the human rights violations of Afghan nationals. As has observed that the Taliban's functional approach has been a mixture of rural-urban insurgency that depending on which regional command of the country was analyzed. "Overall, the insurgency is rural, protracted, and funded through rents acquired from illicit economies. Its approach or fighting strategy, has alternatively been described as asymmetric, Fourth Generation, Maoist, and that of the war of the flea."[105]

Post-Taliban Afghanistan (Since 2001)

In the post-Taliban period, the people of Afghanistan experienced multiple and diverse changes and developments as compared to the oppressive rule of the Taliban, however, that varied from region to region or depending on the geographical location of the people. Importantly, many people felt the sigh of relief from the repressive Taliban regime. Furthermore, socio-economic and educational reforms also began taking place. But even many were uncertain about the future of Afghanistan, and, in some provinces new sources of insurgency, instability and fear were also identified. Further, with the changing circumstances, unfortunately, fear, and problems of the Afghan people continued increasing. The Taliban, even being out of the power, continuously kept affecting the Afghan people to suffer the worst life. However, with the retreat of the Taliban from Afghanistan in 2001, Afghanistan began its new positively hopeful journey led by Hamid Karzai under the umbrella cover or protection of the international forces led by the US. In fact, "ensuring security, stabilizing democratic polity and promoting steady development processes" were the major challenges for Karzai.[106] Therefore, in the direction to decide on the better future of the post-Taliban Afghanistan, with the efforts of United Nations, a conference was held in Bonn (Germany) from 27 November to 5 December 2001 (also known as Bonn Agreement). The nation building and the reconstruction of Afghanistan, which was ruined by the Taliban, was the most important and challenging objective for the interim government and the foreign actors. And Bonn Agreement was one such effort. The participants in this conference were the representatives of the four Afghan opposition groups, observer representatives from neighbouring countries and other important states that including the US. This agreement created the interim government of Karzai "to serve as the repository of the Afghan sovereignty and outlined a political process for producing a new constitution and choosing a new Afghan government."[107] Further, according to the provisions of the Bonn Agreement, "A large meeting of Loya-Jirga (Afghan Parliament), was held in June 2002, at which Hamid Karzai was elected head of the new Afghan Transitional Authority. A New Constitution was adopted in January 2004, presidential elections, in which Karzai was elected, were held in October 2004, and National Assembly elections were held in September 2005."[108] In fact, after the end of Taliban regime, since 2001, Afghanistan faced multiple problems such as the weak government, corruption, patronage and alliances, growing insurgency and even "Iraq also emerged as a fatal distraction in the affairs of Afghanistan" and even for that matter, the leadership of Karzai was also seen weak lacking in adequate decision and strategy making.[109] Even after the success in elections, Afghanistan further, in the summer of 2006, saw increase in violence, and the Afghan and international forces failed to provide security adequately as the security situation required more troops.

Since 2001, in fact, Afghanistan was never been peaceful and without violence. The US also made various new strategies to control and stabilize the situation in Afghanistan. However, during such critical time, observing the pathetic situation in Afghanistan, international community started generous donations, financial assistance and optimum cooperation for the better future of Afghanistan. With the help from international community, Afghanistan achieved many gains in various sectors such as "the revival of the education sector, economic development, and rule of law, democracy, civil liberties, human rights, women's rights and health."[110] More importantly, the education of the girls and women restarted which was banned during the Taliban regime. As reported by Syed Zabiullah Langari,

> Afghan women and girls who were either veiled or in burqas during the Taliban regime and denied any form of education, were once again allowed to go to school and university—they were able to contribute to the development of their country. With the passage of time, school doors once again reopened and millions of Afghan children were enrolled in educational institutions. Alongside state-run schools, hundreds of private schools and higher educational institutions were also established in the country. The revival of the education sector is often noted as one of the biggest achievements of the new political system in Afghanistan.[111]

However, the Taliban continued increasing its strength, power and engaged in actions against Afghan government. "From 2002 to 2005, the Taliban rebuilt its cadres with drug money, charity from donors in the Gulf states, and help from Al-Qaeda. Their sanctuaries in Pakistan enabled them to rearm, refit, and retrain."[112] Further, from 2005, the Quetta Shura Taliban led by Mullah Omar, the Hiz-i-Islami Gulbuddin led by Hekmatyar, and the Haqqani Network led by Jalaluddin Haqqani and his son Sirajuddin came together to subvert the Karzai government and in this year, "the Taliban began a nationwide offensive to spread its influence."[113] The Taliban's offensive since then continued incessantly. In many provinces of Afghanistan, the Taliban had 'shadow governments' and even the many provinces where it had none or less influence, the Taliban remained the significant factor there. With the change and need of circumstances, the Taliban has achieved sophistication in almost all the areas of warfare such as intelligence information, weaponry and other logistics, and strongly fighting against the Afghan Security forces and the international security forces. Further, since the 2014 international forces drawdown, the Taliban insurgency expanded its presence across the countryside. And because of the increasing presence of the insurgents, the Afghan forces appeared to be weak in tackling with them.[114]

Post-2014 Afghanistan

From very long time as discussed in the beginning of this chapter, Afghanistan had been an important land for the international politics. And therefore, it became a battlefield of great powers and even after that the role of external forces in Afghanistan remained continuously vital. Since after the end of the Taliban regime, many actors in and out of the region remained engaged and involved in Afghan affairs by supporting or opposing the Afghan parties or groups against each other. The roles and involvement of Russia, China, Pakistan, India, Iran, the US and the Central Asian countries are significant and are dealt in separate chapters of this book. The year 2014 has been remarkably seen in context of Afghanistan, because, President Barak Obama had declared the complete withdrawal of the US and NATO forces from Afghanistan in 2014. In fact, it has believed that during 2013, the gradual withdrawal of the international security forces led by the US began and by the end of 2013, 90 percent of 800 military bases of international security forces were closed.[115] However, the complete withdrawal could not occur and the anti-government forces and even some of the states involved in Afghanistan got frustrated because of the re-deployment and further continuation of the existing international forces there. And since then, further, Afghanistan has been facing severe consequences of the prolonged civil war. The Afghan Security Forces and the international forces jointly fought against the Taliban and other militant groups. The Taliban had further intensified its fighting against the government establishments and the forces. The Taliban's severe attacks on various cities in the urban Afghanistan had stunned everyone including the Afghan government and the US. They incessantly remained engaged in bombings on the government establishments and confusing the security plans of both the Afghan and the American forces regarding securing the population centers in Afghanistan. They have killed thousands of the soldiers and the innocent people. In fact, the strong international force along with the Afghan forces was seen failing to destroy the Taliban and their strategy. Therefore, the Taliban appeared stronger moving towards winning and the US as failing side in the Afghan war. However, out of frustration and learning the military solution as a futile exercise, the US began focusing on the political or diplomatic solution to the conflicts in Afghanistan. In fact, the Taliban expected that all the parties or the countries engaged with the Afghan government in view of stabilizing the country and also to seek their stakes in Afghanistan should accept its conditions. Moreover, the Taliban seen interested in peace talks with the US and not with the Afghan government, and also not ready to stop violence against humanity. They learnt that the countries in and around the region held the role of Taliban as vital for any expected development, peace or stability in Afghanistan, and its role could not be ruled out. Therefore, taking it as an opportunity, they put forward their conditions for the objectives in Afghanistan. The Taliban had asked the US to release the Taliban members from its custody to boost the peace talks further.

On 24 April 2015, the Taliban began its spring offensive in the northern province of Kunduz in the districts of Imam Sahib, Aliabad, and Qala-i-Zal as well as other areas, and after the Taliban offensive was launched, the head of the provincial council estimated that more than 65 per cent of the province was under Taliban control. The offensive was targeting and aiming the "foreign occupiers especially their permanent military bases, their intelligence and diplomatic centers, officials of the stooge regime (read Afghan Government), their military constellations, especially their intelligence, interior ministry and defense ministry officials and other pernicious individuals," and as the fighting techniques, they focused on

> Martyrdom seeking attacks for the devastation of infidels (read suicide attacks), infiltration attacks among the enemy

> ranks (read insider attacks where Afghan security forces personnel target their own or Coalition forces), attacking the huge and relatively fortified centers of the enemy with heavy and long-range missiles, confrontational attacks against the already demoralized mercenary forces of the enemy and guerrilla attacks in all major cities.[116]

According to Sediq Sediqi, the then spokesperson of the Interior Ministry of Afghanistan, "the terrorists are coming from Pakistan and that they include foreign fighters as well—Chechens, Uzbeks and also from other regional countries."[117] In 2014, 5400 Afghan Police and Army personnel were killed in the struggle against the Taliban. But already in the first 15 weeks of 2015, some 4950 personnel were killed or wounded.[118] Furthermore, since 2017, Afghanistan had been facing an intensification of the fighting between its forces and the Taliban forces that led to the large number of civilian casualties, killings of soldiers and security personnel and also the destruction of institutional and other establishments, and the human rights violations. Besides this problem, Afghan security forces were fighting against the militants of Islamic State of Khorasan Province (ISKP), the Afghan branch of the Islamic State in the Nangarhar province in Afghanistan. It has reported that the Islamic State emerged in Afghanistan in 2014, and in 2015, it created the ISKP as its branch in the Khorasan province of Afghanistan. Between January to November 2016, the 6785 Afghan forces were killed and another 11777 forces were wounded, and in 2016, the 3498 civilians were killed and 7920 were wounded.[119] Further on 21 April 2017, the Taliban's gunmen and suicide bombers attacked the Afghan military base in the Northern Balk province killing more than 100 military and other personnel and injuring many more.[120] The deadly suicide attacks in the urban areas that killed and wounded many people across the country. Besides, between January and September 2017, about 8,000 civilian casualties were recorded. According to a special report on terrorists targeting places of worship, religious leaders, and worshipers, the United Nations Assistance Mission to Afghanistan (UNAMA) documented 850 civilian casualties that resulted from 51 attacks, most of which were planned outside of Afghanistan.[121] Further, it has reported that in the first nine months of 2018, about 2700 civilians were killed, the highest number of killings of civilian since 2014.[122] Moreover, the Taliban attacks had made the Afghan's members of Shia Hazara minority community its target in large number and they have been continuously facing harassment and increased attacks. Even during their oppressive regime from 1996-2001, the Taliban had committed human rights violations against the Hazara group. According to the reports, in its advances in the Ghazni province (especially Jaghori and Malistan districts) which is dominated by the Hazara ethnic group, the Taliban fighters had been attacking them. The continuation of the battle reported in the Central province of Uruzgan between the Taliban and the Hazara militia group created panic of violence in the community, and, as a result, they fled to the neighbouring Ghazni province. Even for that matter, as has reported, the Hazara people could not escape from the attacks of the Islamic state too. The Afghan forces were deployed there for the protection of the Hazara community. However, the Taliban had denied that they had been targeting "any specific race, ethnicity or sect" and stated that their attacks were against the Afghan's regime and the US hireling positions in the region.[123] The Taliban were indulged in attacks on civilians and their homes, plundering of residential properties and kidnapping of the locals also. Besides, they "had also blocked supply routes, making it impossible to provide food and medicines to the locals. It also disrupted communication towers effectively cutting the civilians off from the rest of the country."[124] As a result, the Hazara community lived traumatized severely. Moreover, because of the US's military operations, civilian casualties were reported to be increased. The Human Rights Watch reported that the civilian casualties had taken place more due to US's operations and less by the Afghan forces. As a result, the US presence in Afghanistan had become the target to criticize by the masses and the Taliban. It has also reported that "both the Taliban and ANSF used schools for military purposes, which, together with countrywide insecurity, deprived many children, especially girls, of access to education."[125] However, despite many peace announcements by the Afghan government, the terrorist's assaults on the civilians and the security forces could not stop. According to Human Rights Watch Report 2018:

> The United Nations Assistance Mission to Afghanistan (UNAMA) documented 2,640 war-related civilian deaths and 5,379 injuries in the first nine months of 2017, a slight decrease over the same period in 2016.... The number of internally displaced persons (IDPs) who fled from their homes due to the conflict surged as fighting intensified. More than 250,000 were displaced in the first 10 months of 2017, bringing the nationwide total to at least 1.7 million people. Among the displaced were hundreds of thousands of refugees coerced out of Pakistan with the support of the United Nations High Commissioner for Refugees (UNHCR) in 2016. Attacks on civilians contributed to depression and other mental disabilities....[126]

The Amnesty International also reported that "The Gender-based violence against women and girls persisted by state and non-state actors. An increase in public punishments of women by armed groups applying Shari'a law was reported. Human rights defenders received threats from both state and non-state actors; journalists faced violence and censorship. Death sentences continued to be imposed..."[127] In fact, the US lavishly spent over $70 billion on Afghan's security services since the beginning of the war. However, despite that about 30-40 Afghan soldiers and policemen were killed every day, and in 2016, this number was 22, and in 2017, 10,000 soldiers were killed.[128] The year 2018 has been reported as the deadliest year of the war in Afghanistan since 9/11. According to the UN data, seven Afghan adults and two children on an average were killed every day in the first six months of this year, and 19 civilians injured every day, and more than 90 percent of these attacks are believed to be conducted by the Taliban.[129] During October 2018 Parliamentary elections, which were organized for the first time and run by Afghan's themselves, the Taliban and the other terrorists groups stayed engaged in violence and deadly attacks on the voters, and even the candidates fighting the elections could not be escaped. About ten candidates were killed and hundreds of people dead in electoral violence. In some places like Paktia in South-eastern province bordering Pakistan, the election officials were beaten up and the ballot boxes were snatched and taken away and even people in some major cities of some provinces could not vote.[130] However, despite the threats of the Taliban attacks and violence, the people's turnout for vote was reported as high. The leaders in Afghanistan stated that the voter's turnout in large numbers showed the rejection of the Taliban ideology. Afghanistan's Chief Executive Abdullah Abdullah stated, "The Taliban wanted to build a stream of blood, but the Taliban was defeated and the Taliban's thoughts and ideas were rejected."[131] In fact, this election was delayed by three years because of the security and political problems. Earlier it was originally scheduled in 2015. There had been many flaws in the management of elections as reported. Just before the elections, Afghan Army's General Abdul Raziq was killed. He was considered as one of the most powerful security and political personalities, and also a staunch rival to the Taliban in its southern province of domination. It has believed that for America, General Raziq was "bulwark against the Taliban" and for the Human Rights Watch, he was Afghanistan's "torturer-in-chief".[132] Raziq was also held towering personality who built his relationships with both former presidents Hamid Karzai and Ashraf Ghani. General Raziq's death created vacuum and thereafter consequences had created severe concerns before the Afghan government. By and large, Afghanistan regularly experienced new developments such as the emergence of the Islamic State in Afghanistan, new approaches of the Afghan government and new Great Game and the tense relations amongst the US, Russia, Iran, China, Pakistan and even India. As, with the declaration of New Afghan Policy by the then US President Donald Trump, Afghanistan had to envisage uncertain developments in the country and the region around it. President Trump declared the US policy in Afghanistan to "win the war". Furthermore, "Afghanistan's neighbours," especially Pakistan, as observed was "more aggressively promoting what they perceive to be their own national security interests,"[133] as Pakistan's relations with Afghan government were very strained at that time and it had always been unwilling to facilitate talks between the Taliban and the Afghan government and had continuously kept extending its support to the Taliban. Pakistan was also indulged in allowing the insurgents to recruit, fundraising, planning and conducting operations from safe havens inside its territory. However, Pakistan, contrarily, remained grudging and accusing "the Afghan government of at best turning a blind eye, if not actively supporting, Pakistani tribal militants conducting cross-border attacks from Afghan territory against Pakistan."[134] And therefore, observing Pakistan's dysfunctional attitude, Maley rightly stated, "the greatest threat to order in Afghanistan arises from the sanctuaries in Pakistan that the Taliban employ."[135] Further, as Haidari reported:

> The Taliban, which operate from safe sanctuaries and enjoy institutional support in Pakistan, provide an enabling operational environment for all other terrorist groups in Afghanistan. Without this overarching umbrella and operational platform, foreign militants could have hardly gained a foothold to destabilize Afghanistan, the region, and the world at large. These intertwined networks of terror, violence, and death-maintained by state-sponsorship of terrorism-drive drug production in Afghanistan. The Taliban alone make some $200 million off the illicit drug business. This sum finances their terrorist activities across Afghanistan.[136]

In fact, despite knowing Pakistan's dysfunctional role in destabilizing Afghanistan, the US continued its economic and military support to Pakistan rather taking stringent action against it. However, President Donald Trump dared an action against Pakistan by limiting or curbing economic assistance, but the officials in his administration still tried in vain efforts to prevail upon Pakistan. Pakistan also rather falling under the US pressure joined the anti-US states such as Russia and China. The major players like the US, Russia and China have strategic interests in maintaining their engagement with Pakistan. Haidari stated in 2017,

> The Afghan army and police forces have continued to fight what is a regional and global war against terrorism and organized crime. It has long been clear that the conflict in Afghanistan is an imposed one. It is not a civil war among Afghans but a war over Afghanistan where more than a dozen regional and transnational terrorist groups have converged to undo the country's gains of the past

> (17) years, to weaken and topple the Afghan state, and to exploit the Afghan soil for launching attacks against targets in the region and beyond.[137]

Even during the continuation of peace talks between the US and the Taliban, the latter continued its attack against the people, soldiers and the Afghan government's establishments. Director of the US National Intelligence, Dean Coats stated that though Afghan forces had secured cities and other government strongholds, but the Taliban had increasingly continued large scale attacks, and "the Afghan security suffers from a large number of forces being tied down in defensive missions, mobility shortfalls, and lack of reliable forces to hold recaptured territory..." besides, he said, "...neither the Afghan government nor the Taliban will be able to gain a strategic military advantage in the Afghan war in the coming year if coalition support remains at current levels."[138] According to SIGAR as reported by the International Crisis Group, by 1 February 2017, the Afghan government had control over only 57.2 percent of total districts in Afghanistan and the rest under the control of Taliban.[139] However, further, Taliban, as reported, despite its heavy violent activities and attacks especially in the urban areas, with the changing power game politics in Afghanistan had also adopted additionally new approach and started people-orientated welfare activities in the areas controlled by them to lure and put positive impact on the Afghan people and managed to construct legitimacy in the areas of its domination as they started providing services such as "conflict resolution—which some people considered to faster and fairer than the state's practices," and in some cases, the Taliban had responded the local demands positively better than the government.[140] In other words, as observed by the researchers, "Over time, Taliban policies in areas of control shifted from repressive violence to cooperation and public relations. By 2011, Taliban leaders had signed agreements with 28 aid organizations, including permission to conduct polio vaccination drives. As NATO forces withdrew, Taliban professionalism grew."[141] In some provinces as reported, "Instead of destroying the schools, clinics and courts," the Taliban started "running them by co-opting or replacing local officials who remain on the government's payroll." They also tried to "demonstrate the governance skills" in the country.[142] According to a study "Life under the Taliban Shadow Government" by Ashley Jackson, as reported by Pamela Constable, the Taliban ran "sophisticated system of parallel governance," "with commissions for each area of service such as health, justice and finance, operating in numerous districts fully or partly controlled by the insurgents."[143]

Afghanistan's Neighbourhood Dilemma

Afghanistan and Pakistan have commonness in various aspects because of which they seem to be cousin-nations in nature, and, so, their bilateral tension is termed as "Cousin Rivalry".[144] Both have common frontier with common historical, cultural, and religious traditions. Despite common geographical frontier, both have been indulged in prolonged hostility. The main cause of prolonged hostility had been considered as the Afghanistan government's demand of Pashtunistan, immediately after the independence of Pakistan in 1947. The Pashtuns of Afghanistan and the Pashtuns living in Pakistan have commonality in all the aspects of socio-cultural life. The Afghanistan government had a proposal of integrating these people of both the countries to make an autonomous state. This had become the major factor of irritation that invited Pakistan's resentment. According to the United States Institute of Peace (USIP) report coauthored by Rubin and Abubakar Siddique,

> The long history of each state offering sanctuary to the other's opponents has built bitterness and mistrust between the two neighbors. Afghanistan sheltered Baloch nationalists in the 1970s while Pakistan extended refuge and training to the Mujahedeen in the 1980s and then later supported the Afghani Taliban. Following the Soviet invasion of Afghanistan in 1979, Pakistan's then military ruler Zia ul-Haq promoted the jihad in Afghanistan, funded thousands of Islamic madrasas, armed domestic Islamist organizations, and in the process militarized and radicalized the border region.[145]

Both the states are divided by 'The Durand Line' which is considered to be the main nub of contentions between Afghanistan and Pakistan. This line divides the ethnic Pashtuns and Baloch people living in both the sides. However, Afghanistan has never accepted and recognized this line demarcated by the British. And Pakistan has always been found making efforts to create zone of influence in Afghanistan by extending various support to Taliban. In fact, the Taliban regime in Afghanistan has always benefited Pakistan and, as a result, Pakistan always wished an unstable Afghanistan to accomplish its interests in the region. Pakistan is said to be a state-sponsorer of terrorism against Afghanistan since a very long time. Afghanistan has been blaming Pakistan for its dire and burning situation. In this direction, without directly mentioning Pakistan, Afghanistan in August 2017 expressed that it wanted the international community to take action against countries using 'non-state actors' to forward their foreign policy goals. In this context, Afghanistan's Ambassador to the US Hamdullah Mohib stated that "The ideal solution be the end to using non-state actors and terrorists to bring havoc upon a people who deserve peace and security, who have suffered far too long. If there isn't an end to the support, we would like the international community to take some actions in order to discourage and to prevent such states from continued usage of non-state actors."[146]

In fact, during democratic non-Taliban governments, Afghanistan has witnessed some of the worst terrorist attacks killing a number of people for which Kabul blamed Pakistan-based terror groups for these attacks. Because of this, in June 2018, Afghanistan had cut all ties with Pakistan after a deadly bomb attack which the country's intelligence agency blamed on militants backed by Islamabad. Afghanistan accused Pakistan for allowing the Taliban and Haqqani terror network to operate from its soil for planning attacks in Afghanistan. As a result, because of Pakistan's support to terrorist groups, Afghanistan's then President Ashraf Ghani accused Pakistan for launching an "undeclared war" on Afghanistan by covertly supporting several terror networks, including the Taliban.[147] On Afghan-Pakistan tensions, one of the Afghan Security Officials stated, "This is war and we are at war, with Pakistan, a war for the very existence of our nation...neither the US, nor NATO, nor Iran, nor anyone else are agreed how to turn off the toe of terror which is located in Pakistan."[148] It has stated that "Different terrorist groups are using ISIS as a cover. ISIS has become a brand in Afghanistan. The groups are Haqqani, Tahreek-e-Taliban Pakistan (TTP) and Taliban. Terror has become a weapon in the hands of some countries."[149]

Further, the government of Afghanistan had faced threats not only from Pakistan in its east, but from west, Iran also. Iran supported Taliban, and by extending this support, Iran had further added fuel in already boiling Afghanistan. In fact, it has stated that Iran's support to the Taliban was not against Afghanistan, but against the US. The role of Iran in Afghanistan is dealt in details in a separate chapter. It has said that Iranian campaign had accelerated to step into a vacuum left by departing the US forces. This was held as Iran's biggest push into Afghanistan in decades. In Afghanistan, Iran aimed to make sure that foreign forces should leave eventually and that "any government that prevails will at least not threaten its interests and at best be friendly or aligned with them. One way to do that...is for Iran to aid its one-time enemies, the Taliban, to ensure a loyal proxy and also to keep the country destabilized, without tipping it over. Iran does not want stability in Afghanistan,"[150] as it was criticized by the Afghans. Iran's intensification of covert intervention in Afghanistan came out recently. It has revealed that Iran was providing local Taliban insurgents with weapons, money, and training and also has offered Taliban commanders sanctuary and fuel for their trucks. However, with the expansion of the NATO mission in Afghanistan, it has argued that, "the Iranians quietly began supporting the Taliban to bleed the Americans and their allies by raising the cost of the intervention so that they would leave. Iran has come to see the Taliban not only as the lesser of its enemies but also as a useful proxy force," and in fact, by and large, Iran's involvement was to fail the US's longest Afghan mission which costing about half trillion dollar which it spent for the stability in Afghanistan.[151] Besides, it was also alleged that both Iran and Russia had held meetings with Taliban, and, Iran had facilitated meeting between Taliban leader and Russian officials for securing funds and weapons from Russia for the insurgents. In fact, it has argued that America created vacuum that encouraged the other countries to get involved in Afghanistan.[152] This way, the Afghan government faced multiple challenges from both the neighbours, Pakistan and Iran, having cordial relations with the Taliban. As both Iran and Pakistan failed in talking with the Afghan government, they rendered more importance to the Taliban.[153]

The Afghan government always proposed that the peace process should be entirely Afghan government led/owned and always expressed its unwillingness for the inclusion of the Taliban in the peace process unless they relinquished the violence and inhuman attacks on the civilians, and, because of which the earlier attempts at the peace talks could not be yielded the decisive outcome, contrarily, that led to further escalation of violence. The Taliban, having its sanctuaries in Pakistan, had successfully mounted pressure on the Afghan government by escalating terror attacks despite the strong security establishment. As a result, Afghanistan mourned the civilian casualties of more than 10,000 in 2017. Therefore, because of the prolonged escalation of violence and rising civilian casualties that had been inhumanly perpetrated by the Taliban insurgency, which even the US forces failed to control and stop, the then Afghan President seemed to be, out of frustration and fear, haplessly changing his political strategy to share reasonable power with the Taliban. So, subsequently, the Afghan government had also offered peace negotiation with the Taliban. President Ghani wanted to reduce the prevailing bloodshed in Afghanistan by adopting any workable means. The former Afghan President Karzai had also expressed that negotiation with the Taliban might have been the only solution to peace, and had discarded the US's initiative of military solutions. The Taliban also are Afghans and there was need to seat with them to talk on peace. Therefore, the US's stand would have further caused war in Afghanistan further instigating suffering to Afghans.[154] Similarly, in this direction, during the Kabul Process, an international security conference on 28 February 2018, the Afghan President Ashraf Ghani proposed a comprehensive offer to the Taliban. The proposal offered the Taliban a chance to end the war at the negotiating table.

In exchange for a ceasefire, the government stated that those Taliban members willing to renounce violence could have been enjoyed a peaceful and respectful life. Moreover, the government had also offered to recognize the Taliban as a political party and allowed them to contest the election, prisoner release, passports to Taliban members and visas to their families, as well as office space in Kabul had they been agreed to ceasefire and worked with the constitution of the land. In fact, it has reported that President Ghani's offer came forward immediately after the Taliban sent an open letter to the American people calling for the direct talks with the US to find a peaceful resolution to the prolonged war.[155] On Taliban's letter that circulated in the US, C. Raja Mohan said, "the Taliban was playing on the sentiments of those Americans who think that the US war in Afghanistan, now in its 17th year, is not winnable," and the letter stated that even "if the policy of using force is continued for another one hundred years, the outcome will be the same...America must end her occupation and must accept all our legitimate rights including the right to form a government consistent with the beliefs of our people."[156] However, some analysts saw Ghani's peace offer as highly risky, while others felt it a better initiative. The renowned scholar Steve Coll held it as "a positive development" and stated that "adding some talks to the fighting is essential to reducing the violence. The reasons to talk are many, including to making sure that humanitarian assistance reaches people in need."[157] Interestingly, the pro-Taliban government of Pakistan had also welcomed Ghani's peace offer to the Taliban promising the extension of wholehearted support to the peace process. But, Pakistan's credibility in this direction was dubious. Pakistan has always been interested in controlling the political situation in Afghanistan. In fact, the world players like Russia, China, and Pakistan were also indulged in cooperation with the Taliban to establish peace and to end violence in Afghanistan. The then US Defense Secretary Jim Mattis, in context of peace deal with the Taliban, also positively expressed that victory or political settlement in Afghanistan was possible by facilitating reconciliation between the Afghan government and the Taliban and not possible on the battlefield or through military solution.[158]

Return of Taliban Regime 2.0

With the final withdrawal of the US forces came nearer, the power and influence of the Taliban also increased substantially. And eventually, after the withdrawal of the foreign forces as a deal between the US and the Taliban, on 15 August 2021, the Taliban captured Kabul second time after 20 years of war. The entire world was highly shocked and surprised on the dramatic coming back of Taliban in power. However, though Taliban returned back in power, they have been facing many major challenges especially from governance to social and economic issues. The Taliban's untrained soldiers are unable to tackle the inside situation related to law and order and especially unaware of how to deal with the people including women. They are trained for wars only. However, the Taliban government has pledged and assured the international community specially the Western countries that it would not allow the terrorists to use Afghan land to strike against the Western countries. Moreover, the Taliban also changed its political attitude and domestic policies framing them little liberal as compared to its earlier regime, 1996-2001. However, the Taliban has been struggling for the international legitimacy. They are facing economic, social, and political and governance problems and the security threats as well. The men in the Taliban government need special training of governance. By and large, Afghanistan will be dependent on international assistance as long as it does not get economic stability, and the future of Afghanistan also seems uncertain given the increasing activities of extremist organizations.

Notes and References

1. Alam Payind, Afghanistan's Relations with Its Neighbors, *Critique: Critical Middle Eastern Studies*, Vol. 5, No. 8, Spring 1996 (online 2007), p. 61.
2. *Ibid.*
3. Marc Haber et al., Afghanistan's Ethnic Groups Share a Y-Chromosomal Heritage Structured by Historical Events, PLoS ONE 7 (3), e34288, Penn Libraries, University of Pennsylvania, 2012, https://repository.upenn.edu/anthro_papers/38/?utm_source=repository.upenn.edu%2Fanthro_papers%2F38&utm_

medium=PDF&utm_campaign=PDFCoverPages, accessed on 7 September 2018.

4. Country Profile: Afghanistan, The US Library of Congress-Federal Research Division, August 2008.
5. Afghanistan: Country Profile, Ministry of Foreign Affairs, Islamic Republic of Afghanistan, http://www.mfa.gov.af/about-afghanistan/country-profile.html, accessed on 8 September 2018.
6. Ethnic Groups of Afghanistan, World Atlas https://www.worldatlas.com/articles/ethnic-groups-of-afghanistan.html, accessed on 7 September 2018.
7. What Languages are Spoken in Afghanistan?, World Atlas, https://www.worldatlas.com/articles/what-languages-are-spoken-in-afghanistan.html, accessed on 8 September 2018.
8. Amin Saikal, *The Arab World and Iran*, Palgrave Macmillan, New York 2016, p. 146.
9. The US troops poured in Afghanistan are as; in April 2002, 7425 troops; April 2006, 23300; May 2011, 100,000; December 2009, 69000; in 2010, President Obama announced surge of 30000 troops; February 2014, 34000 and at present there are 8400 troops that are deployed in Afghanistan, and in 2017, the President Trump has approved sending up to 4000 more to train and advise the Afghan Army. For details see, Varghese K. George, Trump links India's Afghan role to trade surplus, *The Hindu*, 23 August 2017, p. 12, also see, Vinod Khobragade, Reconstructing the Failed States: China's Role in Afghanistan, *South Asian Journal of Socio-Political Studies* (*SAJOSPS*), Vol. XVIII, No. 1, July-December 2017, pp. 5-12.
10. Angela Stanzel, China's Interests in Afghanistan, China Policy Institute: Analysis, 5 September 2016, https://cpianalysis.org/2016/09/05/chinas-interests-in-afghanistan/, accessed on 31 July 2017.
11. Jyoti Malhotra, In terror-struck Afghanistan, waiting for Trump to see the light, *The Indian Express*, 8 August 2017, p. 7.
12. Mohammed Nuruzzman, Revisiting the Category of Fragile and Failed States in International Relations, *International Studies*, 46(3), 2009, pp. 271-94.
13. Robert I. Rotberg, *State Failure and State Weakness in a Time of Terror*, Brookings Institution Press, Cambridge, 2003, p. 5.
14. *Ibid.*

15. M. Nurruzman, 2009.
16. Peter Gilbert, Afghanistan—the "great game" without end?, *International Journal of Leadership in Public Services*, Vol. 8 Issue: 1, 2012, pp. 59-72, https://doi.org/10.1108/17479881211230673, accessed on 16 January 2019.
17. Stephen Tanner, *Afghanistan: A Military History of the Alexander Great to the Fall of the Taliban*, Da Capo Press, 2003.
18. Meredith L. Runion, *The History of Afghanistan*, Greenwood Press, Westport, 2007, p. 31, also see Stephen Stanner 2003.
19. Spread of Greek influence over non-Greek cultures.
20. Runion 2007, p. 39.
21. *Ibid.*, p. 41.
22. *Ibid.*, p. 42.
23. *Ibid.*
24. Country Profile: Afghanistan, The US Library of Congress-Federal Research Division, August 2008.
25. Runion, 2007, p. 48.
26. History of Afghanistan, History World, http://www.historyworld.net/wrldhis/PlainTextHistories.asp?historyid=ad09#ixzz5QJEEf4Ga, accessed on 6 September 2018.
27. Runion, 2007, p. 48.
28. *Ibid.*
29. *Ibid.*, p. 49.
30. *Ibid.*
31. Library of Congress, August 2008.
32. Runion, 2007, p. 50.
33. History of Afghanistan, History World.
34. Ijaz Khan, *Afghanistan: A Geopolitical Study, Central Asian Survey*, Vol. 17, No. 2, 1998 (online 2007), p. 489.
35. Rajiv Dogra, *Durand's Curse: A Line Across the Pathan Heart*, Rupa Publications India, New Delhi, 2017, p. 9.
36. *Ibid.*
37. *Ibid.*, pp. 9-10.
38. Library of Congress, August 2008.

39. He was known as Iron Amir, Father of the Nation and Amir ul-Momineen or leader of the faithful; who was also held as strong leader; punishing his enemies, putting down rebellions and ruling through terror and also he was notorious for his cruelty. For details, see Christopher Wyatt, Afghanistan in the Great War, *Asian Affairs*, Vol. 46, No. 3, 2015, p. 387.
40. Ijaz Khan, 1998, p. 489.
41. *Ibid.*, p. 490.
42. The phrase 'Great Game' was first used by Captain Conolly in 1840 in context of Zcarist Russia and Central Asia, and in the contemporary international politics, the phrase is used to analyse the US-Russia rivalry. For details see, Seymour Becker, "The 'Great Game': The History of an Evocative Phrase", *Asian Affairs*, Vol. 43, No. 1, 2012, pp. 61-80.
43. J.K. Baral, The Afghan Game: Interests and Moves, *Strategic Analysis*, Vol. 37, No. 6, 2013, p. 701.
44. For details see, Kaushik Roy, *War and Society in Afghanistan: From the Mughals to the Americans, 1500-2013*, Oxford University Press, New Delhi, 2015.
45. Seth G. Jones, *In the Graveyard of Empires: America's War in Afghanistan*, W.W. Norton & Company, London, 2009.
46. Edward Ingram, A preview of the great game in Asia-II: The proposal of an alliance with Afghanistan, 1798-1800, *Middle Eastern Studies*, Vol. 9, No. 2, 1973, p. 157.
47. The US Library of Congress, August 2008.
48. Wyatt, 2015, p. 388.
49. Jones, 2009.
50. Quoted in Ian Cummins, Afghanistan: 'The Great Game' or Domino Theory?, *Australian Outlook*, Vol. 34, No. 2, 1980, p. 141.
51. Dogra, 2017, p. 121.
52. Afghanistan History, Afghanistan's Website, http://www.afghanistans.com/Information/History/Default.htm, accessed on 7 September 2018.
53. PDPA was founded on 1 January 1965 by Nur Muhammed Taraki.
54. General Major A. Liakhovsky, The Civil War in Afghanistan, *National Security and the Future*, 1(1), 2000, p. 187.

55. Jenna Lempesis, The Civil War in Afghanistan: AN Overview, https://www.mtholyoke.edu/acad/intrel/afp/afghanoverview.htm, accessed on 15 September 2018.
56. Liakhovsky, 2000, p. 187.
57. *Ibid.*, p. 188.
58. *Ibid.*
59. J.K. Baral, 2013, p. 700.
60. Liakhovsky, 2000, p. 189, also see, Svetlana Savranskaya, The Soviet Experience in Afghanistan: Russian Documents and Memoirs, Volume II: Afghanistan: Lessons from the Last War, The National Security Archives, 9 October 2001, https://nsarchive2.gwu.edu//NSAEBB/NSAEBB57/soviet.html, accessed on 14 September 2018.
61. Jenna Lempesis, 2018.
62. Bennett, Andrew, *Condemned to Repetition? The Rise, Fall and Reprise of Soviet-Russian Military Interventionism 1973–1996*, Belfer Center for Science and International Affairs, Cambridge, 1999, p. 283.
63. William Maley, *The Afghanistan Wars*, second edition, Palgrave Macmillan, New York, 2009, pp. 40-41.
64. World Peace Foundation, Afghanistan: Soviet Invasion and Civil War, 7 August 2015, https://sites.tufts.edu/atrocityendings/2015/08/07/afghanistan-soviet-invasion-civil-war/#_edn4, accessed on 14 September 2018.
65. Liakhovsky, 2000, p. 194.
66. *Ibid.*
67. S. Bose and A. Panda, 2016, Indian and Chinese Foreign Policy Imperatives and Strategies vis-à-vis Afghanistan, *India Review*, Vol. 15, No. 4, 2016, pp. 391-92.
68. A.Z. Hilali, China's Response to the Soviet Invasion of Afghanistan, *Central Asian Survey*, 20:3, 2001, p. 326.
69. *Ibid.*, p. 327.
70. Liakhovsky, 2000, p. 195.
71. Steve Galster, Volume II: Afghanistan: Lessons From the Last War, Afghanistan: The Making of US Policy, 1973-1990, The National Security Archives Electronic Briefing Book No. 57, 9 October, 2001, https://nsarchive2.gwu.edu//NSAEBB/NSAEBB57/essay.html, accessed on 14 September 2018.

72. *Ibid.*
73. Jenna Lempesis, 2018.
74. Adam Roberts, Afghanistan and International Security, in Michael N. Schmitt (ed) The War in Afghanistan: A Legal Analysis, *International Law Studies*, vol. 85, p. 6.
75. Svetlana Savranskaya, October 9, 2001.
76. Gregory Feiffer, *The Great Gamble: The Soviet War in Afghanistan*, HarperCollins ebook, p. 5.
77. Avinash Paliwal, *My Enemy's Enemy: India in Afghanstan from the Soviet Invasion to the US Withdrawal*, HarperCollins Publishers India, Noida, 2017, p. 87.
78. *Ibid.*, p. 101.
79. *Ibid.*, p. 118.
80. Vishal Chandra, 2015, p. 7.
81. Timeline: Taliban in Afghanistan, Al Jazeera, 4 July 2009, https://www.aljazeera.com/news/asia/2009/03/2009389217640837.html, accessed on 19 September 2018.
82. For details see S. Yaqub Ibrahimi, The Taliban's Islamic Emirate of Afghanistan (1996-2001): 'War-Making and State-Making' as an Insurgency Strategy, *Small Wars and Insurgencies*, Vol. 28, No. 6, 2017, pp. 947-72.
83. Human Rights Watch, Afghanistan—Crisis of Impunity: The Role of Pakistan, Russia and Iran in Fueling the Civil War, Human Rights Watch Report, NEW York, Vol. 13, No. 3, July 2001, p. 11.
84. Zachary Laub, The Taliban in Afghanistan, Council on Foreign Relations, 4 July 2014, https://www.cfr.org/backgrounder/taliban-afghanistan, accessed on 20 September 2018.
85. S. Yaqub Ibrahimi, 2017.
86. Human Rights Watch, 2001, p. 1.
87. Florian Weigand, 2017.
88. Ahmad Rashid, The Taliban Exporting Extremism, *Foreign Affairs*, Vol. 78, No. 6, Nov-December 1999.
89. Avinash Paliwal, 2017, p. 98.
90. Joseph J. Collins, *Understanding War in Afghanistan*, National Defense University Press, Washington D.C., 2011.
91. Zachary Laub, 2014.

92. Joseph Collins, 2011.
93. Zachary Laub, 2014.
94. Avinash Paliwal, pp. 103-05.
95. Quoted in Avinash Paliwal, 2017, p. 149, also see, The Taliban, Council on Foreign Relations, https://www.cfr.org/interactives/taliban?cid=marketing_use-taliban_infoguide-012115#!/taliban?cid=marketing_use-taliban_infoguide-012115, accessed on 19 September 2018.
96. Nasreen Akhtar, Pakistan, Afghanistan and Taliban, *International Journal on World Peace*, Vol. 25, No. 4, December 2008, pp. 49-73.
97. The Taliban, Council on Foreign Relations.
98. Human Rights Watch, Afghanistan—Crisis of Impunity, New York, 2001, p. 23.
99. Liakhovsky, 2000, pp. 203-04.
100. Zachary Laub, 2014.
101. Joseph Collins, 2011.
102. Human Rights Watch, 2001 p. 17.
103. The Taliban, Council on Foreign Relations.
104. Zachary Laub, 4 July 2014.
105. Colin P. Clarke, An Assessment of the Taliban Insurgency in Afghanistan, Analysis, No. 258, ISPI, June 2014, p. 1.
106. Rajen Hershe, Situating Afghanistan in a Globalising World in Rajen Harshe and Dhananjay Tripathi edited Afghanistan Post-2014, Rutledge, New Delhi, 2016, p. 25.
107. Catherine Dale, War in Afghanistan: Strategy, Operations, and Issues for Congress, Congressional Research Service, 7-5700, R40156, 9 March 2011, p. 5, www.crs.gov
108. *Ibid.*
109. William Maley, Afghanistan: An Historical and Geographical Appraisal, *International Review of the Red Cross*, Vol. 92, No. 880, December 2010, pp. 859-76.
110. Syed Zabiullah Langari, A Look at Education in Post-Taliban Afghanistan, TOLO News, 9 January 2017, https://www.tolonews.com/opinion/look-education-post-taliban-afghanistan, accessed on 24 October 2018.
111. *Ibid.*

112. Joseph Collins, 2011.
113. *Ibid.*
114. International Crisis Group, Afghanistan: Growing Challenges, 30 April 2017, https://www.crisisgroup.org/asia/south-asia/afghanistan/afghanistan-growing-challenges
115. Vanda Felbab-Brown, Security and Political Developments in Afghanistan in 2014 and After: Endgame or New Game, in Wolfgang Taucher, Mathias Vogi, Peter Webinger (eds.) Afghanistan: 2014 and Beyond, Outlook on Security, p. 6.
116. V. Mahalingam, Implications of the Taliban's 2015 Spring Offensive, Institute for Defence Studies and Analyses, 6 May 2015, https://idsa.in/idsacomments/ImplicationsoftheTalibans2015SpringOffensive_vmahalingam_060515
117. Originally by Bill Roggio, "Taliban launch offensive in northern Afghan province," *Long War Journal*, April 27, 2015, accessed on 8 November 2018, also see V. Mahalingam 6 May 2015.
118. David J. Lynch, "Afghan Forces Suffer Heavy Toll in First Taliban Battles," *Bloomberg*, May 3, 2015, http://www.bloomberg.com/news/articles/2015-05-03/afghan-forces-suffer-h..., accessed on 8 November 2018.
119. International Crisis Group, 2017, also see SIGAR.
120. *Ibid.*
121. M. Ashraf Haidari, Afghanistan in 2017: Achievements and Challenges, *The Diplomat*, December 28, 2017, https://thediplomat.com/2017/12/afghanistan-in-2017-achievements-and-challenges/, accessed on 13 November 2018.
122. Security in Afghanistan: Ballots Amid Bullets, *The Indian Express*, 29 October 2018, p. 11.
123. Agence France-Presse, Hazaras fear Violence as Taliban Advances, *The Hindu*, 9 November 2018, p. 12.
124. Ruchi Kumar, Hazara Shias of Ghazni Come under Siege, *The Hindu*, 25 November 2018, p. 6.
125. For details see Afghanistan Events of 2017, Human Rights Watch, https://www.hrw.org/world-report/2018/country-chapters/afghanistan, accessed on 23 October 2018.
126. *Ibid.*
127. Amnesty International, Afghanistan 2017/2018, https://www.amnesty.org/en/countries/asia-and-the-pacific/afghanistan/report-afghanistan/, accessed on 24 October 2018.

128. Security in Afghanistan: Ballots Amid Bullets, 2018.
129. Shubhajit Roy, In Polls Under Taliban Shadow, Test for Two Countries and an old Bond, *The Indian Express*, 6 November 2018, p. 8.
130. Security in Afghanistan: Bullets Amid Ballots, 2018.
131. Afghan Leaders Say Election Turnout Shows Voters are Rejecting The Taliban, RadioFreeEurope RadioLiberty, 22 October 2018, https://www.rferl.org/a/afghan-leaders-say-election-turnout-shows-voters-are-rejecting-the-taliban/29557289.html, accessed on 24 October 2018.
132. Security in Afghanistan: Ballots Amid Bullets, 2018, p. 11.
133. International Crisis Group, 2017.
134. *Ibid.*
135. William Maley, 2010, p. 876.
136. M. Ashraf Haidari, 2017.
137. *Ibid.*
138. Lalit K. Jha, Pak-backed Groups will Continue Attacks in India, Afghanistan, says US Intel Chief, *The Indian Express*, 31 January 2019, p. 10.
139. International Crisis Group, 30 April 2017.
140. Florian Weigand, Afghanistan's Taliban—Legitimate Jihadist or Coercive Extremists?, *Journal of Intervention and State Building*, Vol. 11, No. 3, 2017, p. 359.
141. Pamela Constable, The Taliban has successfully built a parallel state in many parts of Afghanistan, *The Washington Post*, 21 June 2018, https://www.washingtonpost.com/news/worldviews/wp/2018/06/21/the-taliban-has-successfully-built-a-parallel-state-in-many-parts-of-afghanistan-report-says/?noredirect=on&utm_term=.441773d35ce5, accessed on 15 October 2018.
142. Rakesh Sood, Seeking a Managed Exit, *The Hindu*, 22 September 2018, p. 8.
143. Pamela Constable, 2018.
144. Michael Semple, Torbor: Pakistan and Afghanistan's Cousin Rivalry in Chris Ogden edited, New South Asian Security, Orient BlackSwan, New Delhi, 2016, p. 45.
145. Jayshree Bajoria, The Troubled Afghan-Pakistan Border, Council on Foreign Relations, 20 March 2009, https://www.cfr.org/

backgrounder/troubled-afghan-pakistani-border, accessed on 14 July 2017.

146. Lalit Jha, Afghanistan Calls for Action against Countries that Use non-state actors, *The Indian Express*, 4 August 2017, p. 12.
147. *Ibid.*
148. Jyoti Malhotra, 8 August 2017.
149. *Ibid.*
150. Carlotta Gall, As American Presence wanes, Iran Gains Ground in Afghan, *The Indian Express*, 7 August 2017, p. 12.
151. *Ibid.*
152. *Ibid.*
153. Some part of this chapter has been taken from my earlier published paper. For details see, Vinod Khobragade, Reconstructing the Failed States: China's Role in Afghanistan, *South Asian Journal of Socio-Political Studies*, Vol. XVIII, No. 1, July-December 2017, pp. 5-12.
154. Vidya Ram, India should not Fall for US Designs, *The Hindu*, 5 October 2017, p. 12.
155. Ruchi Kumar, An Offer for Peace with Taliban, *The Hindu*, 4 March 2018, p. 5.
156. C. Raja Mohan, Kabul's Risky Overture, *The Indian Express*, 6 March 2018, p. 9.
157. Steve Coll in an interview given to Jyoti Malhotra, China's India anxiety is inseparable from its deep Pakistan, *The Indian Express*, 8 March 2018, p. 9.
158. Robert Burns, US: Victory in Afghanistan possible by facilitating Taliban reconciliation, *The Indian Express*, 14 March 2018, p. 12.

2

USA: The Failure of the Longest War

Introduction

The dire situation in Afghanistan did not offer any opportunity for the success of the US strategy despite engaging in a long-standing war of more than seventeen years. The American involvement in the state resulted into a serious loss. However, in fact, it has observed that because of its hegemonic recognition, the US was not interested to lose its global status and wanted not to offer vacuum in Afghanistan for its rival powers of the cold war and post-cold war period. The US realized its strategic failure in Afghanistan, but, was not ready to leave. The Afghan platform had become the matter of prestige for all Presidents of America. Not a single US President ostensibly thought of surrendering its Afghan mission or to yield to the Taliban's fierce opposition, as the world community or other great powers would have seen the US as a losing or declining great power, and the world terrorists groups would have been more vociferous against the US. In its Afghan mission, the US gained little and lost more in terms of soldiers, money, and reputation. In context of the US intervention, it has believed that "military interventions have traditionally been a source of controversy in the United States. But America's appetite for the dispatch of armed forces has been diminished greatly by factors that have primarily emerged in the twenty-first century," and these included, "most painfully, the protracted campaigns in Afghanistan and Iraq that have made

US political and military leaders more cautious about waging wars to end tyranny or internal disorder in foreign land."[1] In fact, prior to 9/11, according to Goodson and Johnson,

> American policy toward Afghanistan had been largely to ignore what was a Central Asian backwater, outside of American alliance structures and essentially a remote and deeply underdeveloped extension of the Soviet Central Asian republics. Indeed, virtually for all of Afghan history with the exception of the Soviet occupation period (1979-1989), US policy toward the country and its surrounding region was to treat it as a minor and peripheral interest.[2]

The US involvement in Afghanistan for first time has been considered in 1934, when the US had officially extended recognition to Afghanistan's independence and had established its embassy in Kabul. During 1930s, the ruler of Afghanistan, King Amanullah Khan had appealed the world powers to support financial assistance for the reconstruction and development of backward and underdeveloped Afghanistan. So, perceiving the geo-political significance of Afghanistan, the US had responded Afghanistan. The United States had provided $20 million loan to Afghanistan for construction of the Kandahar-Herat highway in 1945 and later this was extended to $51.75 million in 1954. In 1946, the US Morrison-Knudsen Company had further agreed to provide $20 million loan to Afghan government for the construction of irrigation systems and others.[3] However, further, the US's interests of investment in Afghan's oil field could not materialize, though the Soviet Union posed no threat to the US till 1979. But, further, the major challenge was posed by the increasing proximity between the Soviet Union and Afghanistan especially with the Soviet intervention in 1979 that led to forming the pro-Soviet government in Afghanistan. In this context, Goodson and Johnson stated that "the year 1979 proved to be a watershed in US relations with Afghanistan and the South Asian region.... The Soviet invasion of Afghanistan...presented the United States with an opportunity to bleed the Soviet Union, which had become a persistent and unremitting rival during the Cold War."[4] With these developments, the US further strongly started peeping into Afghanistan by supporting the anti-Afghan government forces.

During this time, as a cold war rivalry, the US had supported the Mujahedeen against the Soviet Russian intervention and during the civil war in Afghanistan. And therefore, the period from 1979 to 1988 had made the US more uncomfortable because of the Soviet Union's a decade long staying in Afghanistan. The influence of the US in the region had started fumbling, and the Afghan issue suddenly became the issue of concerns for the US. Because of the increasing Soviet and Afghanistan relations, the US held the "Soviet policy towards Afghanistan as the gravest threat to world peace since World War II." And the then US Security Adviser Zbigniew Brzezinski had held that the pro-Soviet developments in Afghanistan could pose grave threats to the US interests in Afghanistan and the region.[5] Further keeping the cold war politics in mind, Brzezinski postulated that "the Soviets' intention was to use Afghanistan in order to exert its power and influence over the neighboring countries of Pakistan and Iran, and eventually over the entire region of South Asia. Every measure, it was decided, must be taken to counter the possibility of Afghanistan turning communist."[6] Therefore, the US started strategies to counter the Soviet influence and the Afghan government by contacting with the rebellion groups in Afghanistan. In this task, Pakistan was the main ally of the US. In fact, it has reported that the US's full involvement in Afghanistan had been designed before the six to eight months earlier to the Soviet's intervention. And the reason that was put forward behind providing secret or covert aids to the Afghan rebels (Mujahedeen or fighters for the faith and their jihad; a war for the faith) by the US was that the US wanted to "draw the Russians into the Afghan trap."[7] The US, in fact, had specific national security interests/objectives behind the support to the rebellions in Afghanistan that to increase the cost of war of the USSR that ultimately compelling the withdrawal of Soviet military from Afghanistan.

Later after the departure of the Soviet forces, Afghanistan saw many transformations in its domestic politics, and the Taliban started consolidating its power. After the withdrawal of the Soviet troops from Afghanistan, the US's interests in Afghanistan declined and had stopped providing economic, military and other assistance to Afghanistan and also designed no plan for the further reconstruction, development, and rebuilding of Afghanistan. However, the US handed over this task in Afghanistan to its allies such as Pakistan and Saudi Arabia to resolve the problems and provided them free hand in the country. But, as stated, the US's this sort of stand was held as betrayal with the Afghan people. It was stated that "the absence of the US had the effect of leaving a major power vacuum, creating a situation which lent itself to more chaos, destruction, and in-fighting amongst Afghanistan's many warlords, who, all out to consolidate their own individual power, proved unable to unite."[8] This situation prevailed till 1994, and further taking the advantage of the situation, in 1996, the Taliban took over the power and declared the legitimate government in Afghanistan. With this, Pakistan had provided full support to the Taliban and also provided military training to the members of the Taliban. It has stated that the training grounds which were established by the US during the Afghan civil war were made camps and refuge for the terrorists including Osama bin Laden. The US supported the Taliban government during 1994-96 to get the Taliban support for its interest in the oil fields.[9]

US Military Intervention

The US was aware of the terrorist activities of the Al-Qaeda in and from Afghanistan, but had not indented of eliminating them or had not assumed that the Al-Qaeda terrorist would pose any probable threat to the US's interest in the homeland and outside the country, and as a result, the US remained dormant. In this context, the 9/11 report had stated four kinds of failure from the US side; imagination, policy, capabilities, and management. According to the report, "after the end of the cold war, there was a general sense of satisfaction and it was hard to perceive an attack from an organization based in one of the poorest, most remote and least industrialized countries of the world," and further, "to US, Afghanistan seemed very far away. To members of Al-Qaeda, America seemed very close. In a sense, they were more globalized than we were…and it was a failure of imagination."[10] Later, Al-Qaeda compelled the US to change its policy towards Afghanistan when they perpetrated a terrorist attack on the US, 9/11 incidence, that forcing America to devise a strategy to destroy Al-Qaeda and its establishments and networks, and even not to allow or making impossible the anti-American terrorists to operate from in and around Afghanistan.

By hijacking four commercial planes, the Al-Qaeda had crashed them in the World Trade Centre in New York and the Pentagon in Washington D.C. on 11 September 2001 that leading to the killings of about 3000 people. It has reported that although Afghanistan was the base of the Al-Qaeda, but none of the highjakers was Afghan national. The Al-Qaeda's attack had completely shocked the world order which the US was trying to rebuild, as a sole superpower, after the end of the cold war, and even for that matter, Al-Qaeda challenged the US, a leader of the unipolar world, and also had threatened the peace-loving people of the world community.[11] With this major attack, which never happened in the history of the US, the then US President George W. Bush declared to begin war against terrorism, and for this, he also received worldwide unconditional support. George Bush and his administration accused that the Taliban government in Afghanistan had provided asylum to the Al-Qaeda and its leader Osama bin Laden, who had masterminded the 9/11 terrorist attacks. Initially, the US had asked the Afghan (Taliban) government to hand over Osama bin Laden, but the Taliban government refused it. It has stated that the Taliban government had offered to hand over Osama bin Laden for trial, but only to a third country, rather than directly to the United States. But by refusing the Taliban offer, the Bush administration on 7 October 2001, with the British support, invaded Afghanistan (Operation Enduring Freedom) by launching air and ground attacks, which was joined shortly thereafter by the US allies (NATO forces). Consequently, the Taliban leadership quickly lost the control of the country and ran to hide in Pakistan, and later by 2002, the other Taliban and Al-Qaeda foot soldiers and unit commanders relocated in the south-eastern Afghanistan and also migrated across the border to Pakistan.[12] However, subsequently, they consolidated their base there and from there, they began insurgency against the Western-backed government in Afghanistan, the Afghan National Security Forces and the US led international troops (NATO forces). After 2006, the US faced very staunch resistance from the Taliban, and here, without doubt, Pakistan's support to the Taliban cannot be discarded. After Bush, in 2009, Barak Obama became the President of America and initiated very crucial decisions both in economic and foreign policy affairs, and brought new shifts in the US's foreign policy. "President Obama made it clear that the role of the US in world politics should not be defined by the global war on terror", and initiated policy to withdraw the US troops from Iraq to "focus on Afghanistan."[13] Moreover, it has observed that President Obama had focused two major points in the US's Afghanistan policy: "First, the recognition of the fact that the Pakistan-Afghanistan border was the central hideout of the Taliban and Al-Qaeda forces. Second, to increase the number of ground troops in Afghanistan to concentrate on counter-terror activities."[14] Moreover, the coalition between the Taliban and Al-Qaeda had become reportedly stronger. As a result, with the stiff Taliban resistance, further, on 17 February 2009, President Barak Obama declared a plan to send 17,000 more troops in December of the same year. He further had committed an additional 30,000 troops. By this way, the US's troop's deployment in Afghanistan had reached to 100,000 in August 2010 during the Obama administration. However, further to deal with Afghan's domestic problems, on 2 May 2012, the US and Afghanistan signed the Enduring Strategic Partnership Agreement and both the parties committed to strengthen long-term strategic cooperation in areas of mutual interest that included advancement of peace, security, and stability; strengthening state institutions; supporting Afghanistan's long-term economic and social development; and encouraging regional cooperation. Moreover, the agreement emphasized on their strong commitment to the sovereignty, independence, territorial integrity, and national unity of Afghanistan. However, President Obama declared, on 27 May 2014, the withdrawal of the International Forces beginning from December 2014 and the complete withdrawal by the end of 2016 from Afghanistan, but it could not take place, and contrarily, his successor, President Donald Trump decided not to withdraw its forces completely rather adding more in. In fact, when, Trump was not president, he had opposed and criticized the deployment of the US forces in Afghanistan. But subsequently, during his Presidentship, there were around 14,000 US soldiers in the country, along with smaller detachments of NATO troops. But despite the large number of forces in Afghan territory, the US could not kill Laden there in Afghanistan, but in the soil of its earlier ally Pakistan during the Obama administration. In fact, killing of Laden could be seen just as a moral victory to the US rather than substantive gains as the US struggled hard, in vain, to destroy the roots of terrorism in the Af-Pak region or elsewhere around the world. It was highly formidable to destroy the Taliban completely in Afghanistan as had determined by Trump.

US Interests in Afghanistan

War in Afghanistan has been the longest and most difficult among the US's various interventions around the world. There had been, however, various US's vital interests too in Afghanistan that included the protection and preservation of its myriad political, economic, and security and strategic gains since its intervention in 2001. Moreover, the internal instability in Afghanistan had a larger regional ramification as Pakistan, India, Iran, and Russia and others indulged in competition to influence Afghanistan. Therefore, looking at all these, the US also became a stakeholder in Afghanistan.[15] The US has been seeking its interest in terms of "Pakistan's stability and security of its nuclear weapons..., the transnational drug trade and Iranian regional influence, which are both likely to grow if western forces withdraw in unfavourable circumstances, and humanitarian considerations, as the bloodbath in a collapsing Afghanistan would likely dwarf the recent civil wars in Libya and Cyria."[16] According to Leonid Gusev, in 2008, the US Senator Richard Lugar had stated that "it was in the US interest to establish a multilateral and effective system in the Caspian and Central Asian regions for supplying oil and gas to Europe and other markets in order to reduce the dependence of European and Central Asian countries on the Russian energy monopoly."[17] And therefore, keeping all this in view there has been certain interests/objectives of the US in Afghanistan.

Geo-economic and Political Interests: Engaging in Afghanistan and the Central Asian region was of more significance for the

US in terms of 'Geo-economics'. It was aimed at redirecting Oil in the Central Asian countries from China towards a market controlled by the stock exchanges in New York, London, Tokyo and Singapore and also looking for the ways to transport Caspian Sea resources without going through Iranian territory. Moreover, the United States was unhappy with the construction of the gas pipeline from Turkmenistan to China via Uzbekistan and Kazakhstan that started operating in the fall of 2009. Besides, the US had also been making major efforts in resolving the geopolitical problems in Central Asia in order to neutralize or to counter-balance the Russian traditional presence and its dominance in the region. The US has also been intending to counter the growing influence of China in the region. The US sees both Russia and China as its main strategic rivals. Therefore, the US military presence in Central Asia especially in Afghanistan allowed them to monitor the activities of its main rivals in the region and to maintain a military base there. As a result, the US kept trying "to recover their bases in Uzbekistan and increase their usage of Kazakhstan's airfield network to support military operations by coalition forces in Afghanistan."[18] However, it has stated that from President George Bush to President Donald Trump, the US military engagement with Afghanistan was never focused on the rich minerals in Afghanistan. But, as has expressed, the "American interests in the region have been keeping the region's countries engaged in American regional and global strategies by means of economic, military, political, ideological, cultural and humanitarian influences."[19] In other words, the US strategy has always been based on the idea that the other anti-US countries in the region not to be allowed to grow stronger. Furthermore, the increasing US military-political presence in Central Asia aimed to possibly intervene in Iran's affairs, containing China militarily, and putting pressure on Russia. In fact, it was also held that "the US's presence in the region was also to have monitoring on India in the future, and also to ensuring India's capability for reacting quickly to actions by international terrorists and Islamic radicals in Afghanistan, Pakistan and other South Asian countries."[20] By and large, the US and its Western allied countries have been seen keenly exhibiting their interests in consolidating their overall political, economic, and cultural influence in and around Afghanistan, especially including the Central Asian countries. Besides, they have been trying to be "a major force in the distribution and consumption of energy and other natural resources in the region."[21] In context of Economic Interests, "the US had seen of gaining access to the energy resources of Central Asia and surrounding areas; controlling supply routes to world markets; creating conditions for organizing a raw materials embargo of China and India, as required; and ensuring control over strategic reserves of uranium ore."[22]

Counterterrorism and Elimination of Terrorists Sanctuaries: With the major human loss that occurred because of the 9/11 terrorist attacks, the US government since then had always focused the policy of war against terrorism and the elimination of sanctuaries provided to the terrorists. The US President George W. Bush started the US's counter-terrorism policy, which all his successors have been seriously following so that the American nationals should not be the terrorist's targets again. In his speech on 20 September 2001, President Bush stated:

> The terrorist practice a fringe form of Islamic extremism... the terrorist are traitors to their own faith...these terrorist kill not merely to end lives but to disrupt and end a way of life...they are the heirs of all the murderous ideology of the 20th century...either you are with us, or you are with the terrorists...this is civilization's fight...the civilized world is rallying to America's side...freedom and fear, justice and cruelty, have always been at war, and we know that God is not neutral between them.[23]

Further, in context of the continuation of the US's war on terror, on 17 August 2009, in his speech, President Barak Obama said:

> We must never forget: this is not a war of choice. This is a war of necessity. Those who attacked America on 9/11 are plotting to do so again. If left unchecked, the Taliban insurgency will mean an even larger safe haven from which Al-Qaeda would plot to kill more Americans. So this is not only a war worth fighting. This is fundamental to the defense of our people.[24]

In fact, the counterterrorism policy was aimed at the elimination of extremism and its leadership especially the Al-Qaeda and the Taliban. And in this objective, with the new tactics and resources added by the Obama administration in conjunction with the traditional tactics of counterterrorism, the US, as believed, could gain demonstrable progress against the Taliban insurgencey.[25] However, the clear observations showed that in case of Al-Qaeda, the US could not achieve substantial success as expected, except the killing of old and abundant leader Osama bin Laden during the Obama administration. The US strategy that was evolved by 2010, as stated by Tellis and Eggers, was "to focus on transitioning the conflict's resolution to be an Afghan responsibility, with Washington underwriting its financial costs", and, further, taking the cognizance of the Afghan situation especially its poor infrastructure, fumbling and weak state capacity, and the sever problem of the insurgency, the Obama administration aimed at the stabilization of Afghanistan by means of "robust economic development and transformed governance," however, "by the end of Obama's presidency, both the open-ended conflict with the Taliban and Washington's prolonged financial commitment to Kabul became suspect."[26] In context of the complete elimination of the terrorism from Afghanistan during the Obama regime, Rajiv Dogra narrated the message of the leaders in Central Asian states that "if America targets terrorist in Afghanistan, it will only be trimming the branches. If it wants to strike out terror once and for all, it must destroy the roots of terror in Pakistan."[27] But contrarily, America made Pakistan its strong partner to fight against terrorism that further motivated Pakistan indirectly to indulge in supporting terrorist acts in Afghanistan. In this direction, Dogra further stated that "If the reality on the ground is the test of Pakistani sincerity to American concerns, then the harsh fact is that even as Obama was making that address, Pakistan was giving shelter to Mullah Omar and his Quetta Shura, besides hiding Osama bin Laden."[28] In this regards, Goodson and Johnson pointed that President Obama had adopted the unconventional strategy of counterterrorism, in which, the US administration used unconventional forces, clandestine intelligence gathering and new technology that had proven to be effective in the unique and more complex situation.

Obama believed and used the method of striking the Pakistani-based militants with missiles fired from drones, the technique that Bush administration had adopted in 2004 and lasted till 2008. The Obama administration introduced a surge of US troops in Afghanistan that began in 2009, however, "a tactic of choice was the cross-border drone strike into Pakistani territory, with President Obama himself reportedly personally approving the targets of the strikes."[29] However, by and large, despite, its mega-policy on terrorism, the US failed in destroying the roots of terrorism by means of hard power or military in Afghanistan, and, as a result, the US learnt the necessity of political diplomacy or dialogues and soft policy with the Taliban. In this direction, the US-Taliban engagement has taken place and moved towards the peace deal which reached to the drafting of the framework of peace deal in January 2019 in their negotiations in Doha, Qatar, where the Taliban holds a political office.

Counter-narcotics or Anti-Drugs Policy: The controlling of drug trafficking was also on the US agenda in the region. Initially, as has reported, the US was not interested in drugs- or opium-related matters of Afghanistan on the pattern of Colombia, in which the US with the help of the Colombian government had flushed off the narcotics industry. But after learning from the various survey that the Taliban had been raising their funds from the opium production, the Bush administration had adopted the anti-drugs policy in its war strategy in Afghanistan. But it was stated that the US had to face the perils of the opium trade if left unaddressed. However, after taking the cognizance of the Taliban and the opium production, the Bush administration decided about "the exploding of poppy problem in Afghanistan" and to make efforts for its eradication. Therefore, in this direction, President Bush had appointed a new ambassador on drugs and corruption in Afghanistan and started new counternarcotics and poppy eradication efforts. For this purpose, the US Congress had sanctioned more than $1 billion to overt counternarcotics policy in Afghanistan for the two years between October 2006 and October 2008.[30] Further, Steve Coll stated, "Bush's adaptation of Plan Colombia for Afghanistan constituted the most significant change in US policy in the war since 2002.... The most dramatic aspect of Plan Colombia was the aerial spraying of coca crops with herbicide. In late 2006 and early 2007, for Afghanistan, Bush advocated strongly for spraying poppy crops from airplanes in the heart of Taliban country".[31] On the drug eradication, the US delegation had strongly told the Afghan President Karzai, "Future US aid to Afghanistan could be erode if poppy cultivation was not brought under control", and replying to this, Karzai had promised to "eradicate as much poppy as it could."[32] However, the US could not succeed in eradication of the problem of opium or drugs in Afghanistan and its anti-drug policy failed. Because, during 2007, even Karzai also had aborted the efforts against the poppy production in Afghanistan and also opposed the US military role in fighting drug production. In fact, it has stated that war in Afghanistan promoted the poppy production as of the destruction of the irrigation system and non-poppy farming. "The prolonged stalemate over Plan Afghanistan (similar to Plan Colombia) during 2007, wasted American money and effort."[33] Despite the deadlock on the resolution over the poppy and the Taliban connection, during 2008 and 2009, the US administration had taken the decision to send thousands of US Marines to Helmand, the heartland of the poppy economy.[34] The policy of drug in Afghanistan was aborted during the Barak Obama administration. It has reported that since the beginning of the US war in Afghanistan, the US administration spent $7.55 billion in the efforts of counter-narcotics till 30 September 2014.[35]

However, it has alleged that the US troops presence in Afghanistan had covert interests and strategy. As has believed, "The war on Afghanistan is a profit driven Resource War (and), US military bases in Afghanistan are also intent upon protecting the multibillion narcotics trade."[36] It has stated that

> America's covert war, namely its support to the Mujahedeen 'Freedom fighters' (aka Al-Qaeda) was also geared towards the development of the Golden Crescent trade in opiates, which was used by US intelligence to fund the insurgency directed against the Soviets...the drug trade developed over the years into a highly lucrative multibillion undertaking. It was the cornerstone of America's covert war in the 1980s. Today, under US-NATO military occupation, the

> drug trade generates cash earnings in Western markets in excess of $200 billion dollars a year.[37]

At present, as reported, the Taliban alone is involved in about $200 million illicit drug business, which they financed their terrorist activities across Afghanistan. And "a deepening symbiotic relationship between terrorism and drug production is responsible for the 87 percent increase in opium production in Afghanistan" in 2017.[38] By and large, the American Afghan policy exhibited as what, in 2014, the US President Barak Obama stated, "After 2014, we will support a unified Afghanistan as it takes responsibility for its own future..., a small force of Americans could remain in Afghanistan with NATO allies to carry out two narrow missions: training and assisting Afghan forces and counterterrorism operations to pursue any remnants of Al-Qaeda."[39] As Douglas C. Lovelace Jr. stated, the US objectives behind adopting the strategy of complete finishing of the Al-Qaeda, rebuilding Afghanistan and regionalize strategy had been especially "...to contain the threats of terrorist attacks in its homeland and threats to its national security interest, to prevent the proliferation of the weapons of mass destruction from the region and significantly to establish ambience to ensure regional stability and to contain the domination and influence of the other competitive powers in the region."[40]

The US Role in Reconstruction and Development

Nation-building or reconstruction of the failed state is based on three important efforts that any government or state needs to make: security, governance, and the economic development. In case of Afghanistan, the situation in all these three areas has been dismal from very long time, and to balance or manage these fields is a very difficult task especially when the state has been going through civil wars or has a despotic/theocratic regime. In other words, Afghanistan's reconstruction or nation-building hinges on the adequate security mechanism, good or functioning governance system and, vitally, the level of economic development to bring all the multi-faceted changes in social, political, and economic life of the Afghan people. And in this direction, the US administration has always been forerunner and its efforts attracted high appreciation, despite flaws in its policy efforts. And therefore, reconstruction had become the important component of the US mission in Afghanistan. The reconstruction program aimed "to help the Afghans recover from the unbelievable brutality of the Taliban and will have a society that's capable of meeting needs of its people."[41] In context of the US efforts for the well-being of the Afghan people, the US Department of State stated:

> We (the US) focus our development assistance on promoting economic growth, building the capacity of civilian institutions, improving the performance of the justice system, and helping the government maintain, and improve upon, the gains made over the last decade in health, education, and women's rights. The United States also provides support for Afghan civil society, promotes increased respect for human rights, helps to fight the illegal trade in narcotics, and continues to provide significant humanitarian support.[42]

The US has contributed significant blood and treasure, spending over a trillion dollars and losing lives of its thousands soldiers in pursuing the longest war (17 years) in its history. Out of the total amount spent so far, about $120 billion has been spent on reconstruction and development, more than the inflation-adjusted expenditure under the Marshall Plan for rebuilding Western Europe after World War II. And the rest amount has been contributed by the international community.[43] In fact, the US contribution for the reconstruction of Afghanistan has always been appreciated by the Afghan community and the others also. Perhaps, no other country could contribute for the well-being of the Afghan people as what has been contributed by the US. In April 2002, during his speech in Virginia Military Institute, President George W. Bush had called for the reconstruction of Afghanistan and stated that "by helping to build an Afghanistan that is free from this evil and is a better place in which to live, we are working in the best traditions of George Marshall," in fact, evoking the post-World War II Marshall Plan. The US Congress had appropriated over $38 billion in humanitarian and reconstruction assistance to Afghanistan from 2001 to 2009.[44] In

2010 alone, $105 billion went to Afghanistan, and in 2011 the figure was $117 billion.[45] In 2012, of the bulky amount of the $12.9 billion in aid to Afghanistan, $9.95 billion went towards spending on military and security assistance to arm and train Afghan military and police forces. However, according to an article published by the *Journal of World Affairs* in 2013, "The Money Pit: The Monstrous Failure of US Aid to Afghanistan," the aid has been exactly that, a failure. Since 2002, about $110 billion has been appropriated for aid to Afghanistan, and "all of that has not brought the United States or Afghanistan a single sustainable institution or program."[46] According to USAID, in 2014, Afghanistan received $7.3 billion in foreign assistance from the US, of which more than half went toward conflict prevention and security. The planned amount of American aid for Afghanistan in 2017 was reported to be $4.7 billion.[47] As on 30 September 2014, the US had appropriated $104.1billion for the relief and reconstruction in Afghanistan. This fund was allocated for the variety of fields such as security, governance and development, counternarcotics, humanitarian, and civil operations.[48] According to the SIGAR report of Sopko, more than $120 billion spent by the US administration on Afghan's reconstruction. According to the US Department of State, in October 2016, in the Brussels Conference on Afghanistan, the United States along with other international donors committed to provide Afghanistan $15.2 billion in civilian assistance through 2020 and, in its turn, Afghanistan also committed to strengthen the domestic conditions such as "governance, rule of law, fiscal sustainability, and human rights." All these commitments are said to be codified in the "Self-Reliance through Mutual Accountability Framework" (SMAF) and, furthermore, the United States used the "bilateral incentive programs and the SMAF to hold the Afghan Government accountable to mutually agreed reform commitments."[49] However, the Stockholm International Peace Research Institute (SIPRI) report stated that

> Afghan businesses have failed to capitalize on the loads of greenbacks that have rained down on the country.... The Afghan private sector has thus far failed to fulfill its potential as an engine of economic growth or an instrument

> of social inclusion. While there is a prospect of tapping this potential, the country's economy is currently mostly deadlocked.... The report found that only around 10 percent of the Afghan economy is legitimate. The rest is black market commerce that discourages entrepreneurs from investing and hiring.[50]

The United States and its allies, as it was reported, together contributed more than $5 billion annually in civilian assistance to Kabul.[51] The SIPRI report further stated that the "popular dissatisfaction with unequal access to economic resources, flawed public services and goods, the adverse security situation, and predatory government activity undermine an effective and sustainable private sector." It has also criticized that the foreign countries and other donor or aid groups provided too much money to Afghan government, which the Afghan government could not spend it appropriately and wisely. Even though aimed at improving government and to grow businesses, "the aid became a crutch that sustained kleptocrats and stifled entrepreneurship."[52] However, it has stated that the nation-building efforts of the US in Afghanistan were suffered and restricted because of the lack of commitment, inadequate institutional capacity, and absence of functional infrastructure, which was ravaged due to its prolong destructive war.[53] The US provided huge amount of economic aids to Afghanistan for over the years since its war on terrorism, but, the US economic assistance to Afghanistan, as reported, decreased from 2010 to 2017, however, it saw little increase in 2018.[54]

Security Assistance

The adequate security situation of any country is most vital factor for overall and comprehensive development of the country and its people in terms of economic, political, social, standard of education and industrial/technological development. The world has experienced that the countries that have been internally insecure and unable to provide adequate security to its citizens are facing myriad of challenges in human life and economic and infrastructure development. Afghanistan is also case of such poor and failed countries. In Afghanistan, the incessant Taliban insurgency remained the most debilitating challenge that

Afghanistan faced despite the security arrangements controlled by the international forces and the US trained Afghan national forces, besides, the multiple other immense efforts of the US. The US policy in Afghanistan especially during the Obama period was to weaken Taliban insurgency in the field which had been continued even during Trump's period till the peace talks did not begin between the US and the Taliban. The Obama administration provided security training and military assistance to the Afghan forces and people to defend themselves and helped the Afghan government in providing basic services to the people, and also tried to deprive the insurgency of the popular support and to create the conditions for the sustainable security. In fact, this strategy was devised looking at the post-2014 withdrawal of the US and NATO forces.

Initially after the US attack in Afghanistan (during the Taliban regime), the formation of the Afghan National Defense and Security Forces (ANDSF) in 2002 was the most crucial contribution of the US government under President Bush to assist the international forces in setting security structure in Afghanistan. The ANDSF was raised, trained, and equipped by the US to provide security to Afghanistan from the internal and external threats emanating from terrorists and also to prevent the re-establishments of safe havens to the terrorists. In this direction, the US spent $70 billion. Besides, in the sphere of security of Afghanistan, the US also helped in developing the Afghan National Army (ANA).[55] It was stated that initially the US policy in Afghanistan was aimed at the military operations against the terrorism and was not aimed at the construction and strengthening of the Afghan Army, or police or any other security institution. The US's counter-terrorism policy was aimed to undermine the creation and role of the Afghan army and police forces.[56] In the direction of security in Afghanistan, Building on the Enduring Strategic Partnership Agreement between the Islamic Republic of Afghanistan and the United States of America, was signed on 2 May 2012, and the two countries signed the Bilateral Security Agreement (BSA) on 30 September 2014. The BSA reaffirmed that Afghanistan and the United States were committed to strengthen long-term strategic cooperation in areas of mutual interest, including: advancing peace, security, and stability, strengthening state institutions, supporting Afghanistan's long-term economic and social development, and encouraging regional cooperation.[57] Under Defense and Security Mechanism for Afghanistan, both the states made agreement to: develop appropriate measures of effectiveness for the analysis and strengthening of Afghanistan's use of available defence and security resources; cooperation in developing and sustaining Afghanistan's defence capabilities; development of the process for accurate and effective cooperative assessments of internal and external threats to Afghanistan and enhancement of information and intelligence sharing and evaluation.[58] Moreover, according to the BSA, about 10,000 US troops were decided to be stayed in Afghanistan even after the international forces were to be withdrawn in 31 December 2014. The BSA came in force on 1 January 2015 and was also decided to be remained in force "until the end of 2024 and beyond" unless it was terminated by either side with two years' notice.[59] According to the US Department of State,

> In 2003, NATO assumed leadership of the United Nations-mandated International Security Assistance Force Mission (ISAF). At its height, ISAF included more than 130,000 troops from 51 NATO and partner nations. ISAF forces fought alongside the Afghan National Defense and Security Forces (ANDSF) as the international community worked to improve ANDSF capabilities. The US force levels peaked at roughly 100,000 in 2011, and began to decrease through 2014, as the ANDSF gained strength. The ISAF officially ended on December 31, 2014, with the ANDSF taking over full responsibility for security in Afghanistan on January 1, 2015, when the United States and NATO formally ended their combat role in Afghanistan and transitioned to a new mission. On January 1, 2015, NATO launched the Resolute Support Mission (RSM), a non-combat mission focused on providing training, advice, and assist support to the ANDSF. The BSA and a NATO Status of Forces agreement signed in September 2014 provide the legal basis for US and NATO forces to remain in Afghanistan.

> The United States had approximately 9,800 troops in Afghanistan in 2015 and 2016, drawing down to 8,400 in January 2017.[60]

Furthermore, the US was the part of a coalition of more than 100 countries and organizations around the world that provided both security and civilian assistance to Afghanistan, and, the US and more than 30 other nations provided financial support to the ANDSF. The international community collected and made available about $5 billion for the ANDSF in 2016, in which the US had largest share. Besides, the countries pledged in the NATO Warsaw Summit in July 2016 to keep extending their financial support for the ANDSF through 2020.[61] Between 2001 and 2016, as stated, there had 2,247 US military deaths in Afghanistan and more than 20,000 US service members were wounded in action there.[62] Moreover, the US's Afghan war and reconstruction efforts have cost the US more than $841 billion or perhaps the trillions of dollars that may be estimated by some others. However, despite initially supporting the US withdrawal from Afghanistan, President Trump appeared supporting more US troops to be added, however, without specifying the detailed figures, he stated that "America's enemies must never know our plans, or believe they can wait us out. I will not say when we are going to attack, but attack we will."[63] However, despite the US administration, from Bush to recent past, spent billions of dollars in raising, training and equipping the Afghan security forces, but, the Afghan forces could not become capable of securing their own land and people. In this direction, the report of the Special Inspector General for Afghanistan Reconstruction (SIGAR) pointed out major flaws in making its Afghan mission successful and viable with respect to extending the adequate security mechanism in Afghanistan:

> Providing advanced Western weapons and management systems to a largely illiterate and uneducated force without appropriate training and institutional infrastructure created long-term dependencies, required increased US fiscal support, and extended sustainability timelines. The lag in Afghan ministerial and security sector governing capacity hindered planning, oversight and the long-term

> sustainability of the ANDSF. Police development was treated as secondary mission for the US government, despite the critical role the ANP played in implementing rule of law and providing local-level security nationwide. ANDSF monitoring and evaluation tools relied heavily on tangible outputs, such as staffing, equipping, and training levels, as well as subjective evaluation of leaderships. This focus masked intangible factors such as corruption and will to fight, which deeply affected security outcomes and failed to adequately factor in classified US intelligence assessments.... The ANDSF was ill-prepared to deal with deteriorating security after the drawdown of the US combat forces.[64]

It has reported that the US security assistance to Afghanistan fall between 2013 and 2016, however, since 2017 it has observed its rising up further.[65]

US's New Afghan Pollcy: The Trump Administration

Barack Obama as the President of the US declared the withdrawal of the US forces from Afghanistan starting in December 2014, however, that could not happen, instead the troops flow further increased by his successor President Donald Trump. After assuming office of the US President, Trump outlined the American strategy toward Afghanistan in which he called for the increasing of thousands of military troops to assist and train Afghan forces in view of accomplishing the desired objectives. However, very surprisingly, President Trump discarded the US's vital role in 'reconstruction and nation building' of Afghanistan. And also decided to put pressure on Pakistan to curb its support to the Taliban and the other terrorist outfits active against Afghanistan and also urged India to be a partner to assist the economic and development projects in Afghanistan.[66] President Trump held that US's war in Afghanistan, a prolonged war, as a costly war. Before assuming the powers as the US President, he had urged to pull out its forces criticizing the policy of Obama administration for Afghanistan. In this context, it has stated that the US's security establishment that including the then National Security Adviser, General H.R. McMaster and the Secretary of

Defence General James Mattis "persuaded Trump to give the US another shot at turning the tide."[67] Moreover, the international analysts described the war as "a stalemate with the Taliban continuing to grow stronger while rampant corruption continues to plague the Afghan government, hampering US military initiatives."[68] As has reported, between the years 2001 and 2017, the US administration spent about $830 billion in fighting the war in Afghanistan.[69] Further, Haidari analyzed the significance of the US New Strategy for Afghanistan that the new strategy's full implementation would have helped addressing the challenge of narco-terrorism in three aspects: First, the strategy's regional component was aimed at the shutting down of terrorist safe havens in Pakistan and this was also aimed at targeting not only its symptoms, but the root of the narco-terrorism threat. Second, an increase in the number of US and NATO forces had already started making major difference in favor of the Afghan forces in the Afghan's battlefield. And third was that the new strategy had "given increased authorities and resources to the Resolute Support Commander in prosecuting a results-driven war against the Taliban."[70] Moreover, it has also reported that since when the Trump Administration announced its New South Asia strategy in August 2017, the US Government had "increased the amount of troops and equipment for war in Afghanistan, increased offensive strikes against the Taliban, expanded training and assistance for Afghan forces, and sought to pressure Pakistan to eliminate terrorist safe havens." In fact, by and large, the strategy sought to push and persuade the Taliban to engage into negotiations for a political settlement with the Afghan's government.[71]

No to Nation-Building, Only to Win the War: Since the beginning, the war in Afghanistan comprised of three components: A counter-terrorism mission to prevent Al-Qaeda and later ISIS from gaining a safe haven, a counter-insurgency strategy aimed at the Taliban, and a nation-building component to form something resembling a liberal democratic society in Afghanistan. But by bringing change in the US foreign policy towards Afghanistan, President Trump sidelined the policy of nation-building of Afghanistan. His war in Afghanistan was completely focused on the component of counter-terrorism and with a nod to counterinsurgency only as a means aiming to confirm the success in disallowing the safe havens to global terrorist and likeminded radicals. The former President Obama had declared the pulling back of the US soldiers from Afghanistan, but Trump declared to fight for the victory in Afghanistan. President Trump said, "Our troops will fight to win. We will fight to win." In this context, he said, "From now on, victory will have a clear definition, attacking our enemies, obliterating ISIS, crushing Al-Qaeda, preventing the Taliban from taking over Afghanistan and stopping mass terror attacks against America before they emerge." However, on the end of the US role in Afghan's nation-building, Trump stated:

> We want them to succeed, but we will no longer use American military might to construct democracies in far-away lands or try to rebuild other countries in our own image...America will continue its support for the Afghan government and the Afghan military as they confront the Taliban in the field. Ultimately, it is up to the people of Afghanistan to take ownership of their future, to govern their society and to achieve an everlasting peace. We are a partner and a friend, but we will not dictate to the Afghan people how to live or how to govern their own complex society. Those days are over. We are not nation-building again. We are killing terrorists.[72]

In fact, Trump realized the economic overburden of the American people, as what Eikenberry had rightly stated on the economic factor of the US interventions in Afghanistan and Iraq that

> Americans view the serious domestic fiscal and political problems that the US has experienced...as related in part to its involvement in the wars in Afghanistan and Iraq. The difficult experience of trying to rebuild an economy devasted by unprecedented deficit spending in support of lengthy foreign wars left the American people with a deeply diminished appetite for armed intervention. While defence outlays were far smaller than social-welfare and interest payments, the military, diplomatic, economic and human costs of two increasingly unpopular wars were politically more visible.[73]

Further, beyond the counter terrorism, the US policy was defined to maintain regional stability. The internal situation of instability in Afghanistan had optimum potentials to affect the situation in Pakistan that was to lead to destabilize the surrounding of these countries including the Central and the South Asian region as a whole. And therefore, the US needed cooperation of Pakistan in dealing with the terrorists so that to stabilize and balance the situation. However, on 22 August 2017, President Donald Trump announced a 'New Afghan Strategy', a strategy for the war in Afghanistan and, further extended and deepened the US involvement in the mission to support the government of Afghanistan in its fight against terrorism especially the Taliban and other terrorist groups. Trump's new Afghan policy involved the sending of additional troops to Afghanistan, and reorienting the definition of success away from time tables toward a conditions-based approach. In June 2017, the NATO promised and urged to increase the troops under then ongoing Resolute Support Mission to continue to train, advise, and assist the Afghan National Defense and Security Forces (ANDSF), besides, replacing of South Asian partner in war against terrorism. It has observed that in the year 2017, the US military moves were observed increased against the so-called Islamic State—Khorasan Province (ISIS-KP); the IS's local affiliate that having presence in the eastern provinces of Afghanistan. And therefore to destroy their holds, in April 2017, "the US dropped the most powerful conventional weapon in the military's arsenal, the GBU-43/B Massive Ordnance Air Blast (the Mother of All Bombs), on a network of caves controlled by the Islamic State in Nangarhar Province, along the border with Pakistan." But, the terrorist attacks continued further and in May 2017, the IS militants attacked the military hospital in Kabul that killing and wounding many people.[74]

President Trump's new strategy vitally was focused on the defence and military autonomy in Afghanistan, and also demonstrated the integration of the military, diplomatic, and economic mechanisms of the US power in the direction of a successful victory in the Afghan war. Trump extended powers of the US defense authority to increase the troop levels in Afghanistan by several thousand, however, he did not declare specific numbers of the US military saying that, "We will not talk about numbers of troops or our plans for further military activities.... Conditions on the ground, not arbitrary timetables, will guide our strategy from now on. America's enemies must never know our plans or believe they can wait us out." Moreover, the major military shift that Trump, in his new strategy, had declared about the strengthening of the US military authorities to attack the Taliban and the other terrorists in Afghanistan. In this direction, Trump said, "Micromanagement from Washington, DC, does not win battles.... These killers need to know they have nowhere to hide, that no place is beyond the reach of American might and American arms.... Retribution will be fast and powerful." Further, Trump said that "the US would give military commanders the authority to act in real time and expand the authorities for the US armed forces to target terrorists and criminal networks in Afghanistan." However, earlier, it has reported that Obama had put major restrictions on the US offensive operations in Afghanistan.[75]

More significantly, Trump also emphasized on the political solution to the Afghan War, which indicated that Trump did not discard, and believed in the negotiation with the Taliban, but, was skeptic whether the Taliban would join the negotiation table and also thought that he would not invite the Taliban for the purpose. However, this was also pondered by the earlier President Obama, but, Trump expressed that his plan was different, and discarded the time-bound approach and emphasized that there was "no timelines on the withdrawal of US troops." In this context, Trump said, "I've said it many times how counterproductive it is for the United States to announce the dates we intend to begin or end military operations.... Someday after an effective military effort, perhaps it will be possible to have a political settlement that includes elements of the Taliban in Afghanistan, but nobody knows if or when that will ever happen."[76] Moreover, Trump promised and committed to work with the Afghan government and asked them to take on its share of the military, political, and economic burden and need to exhibit their determination and progress to continue taking the US support, and he said that the US support "is not a blank check."[77] Trump also believed that "The stronger the Afghan security forces become, the less we will have to do."[78]

No to Pakistan, Yes to India: President Trump found determined to bring about a change in American policy. In a new policy, while authorizing a limited increase in US troops presence in Afghanistan, Trump was found critical of Pakistan. By learning the fruitless role of Pakistan in its mission against terrorism, Trump maneuvered New Afghan Policy sidelining Pakistan. He vehemently declared the change of approach against Pakistan in reference to safe havens given by Pakistan to Taliban terrorists as well as a connection between the US funding and Pakistan's change in behavior. More vitally, Trump emphasized on the furtherance of 'Strategic Partnership' with India for the US's South Asian concerns and earnestly urged assistance from India in Afghanistan. The US learnt that India holds better relationship with Afghanistan, and Afghanistan appreciates India for its democratic tradition and its clean-hands in dealing with the Afghan's domestic affairs. Therefore, in his New Strategy for Afghanistan, Trump advocated India's significance in the region. Trump urged India to help the US by playing proactive role in establishing peace and stability in Afghanistan by means of economic and developmental aids, and he also proposed India to play bigger role in the war-torn country to its trade surplus with the United States. He said, "We appreciate India's important contributions to stability in Afghanistan, but India makes billions of dollars in trade with the United States, and we want them to help us more with Afghanistan, especially in the area of economic assistance and development". In fact, by inviting India to be its partner in Afghanistan, the US over ruled Pakistan position.[79] Earlier the US held Pakistan as partner and India as a friend, however, according to Trump's new policy, the US made India its partner-cum-friend by criticizing Pakistan as an 'enemy'. By learning Pakistan's negative role, the US President declared Pakistan as 'a dysfunctional force'. Trump used harsh language for Pakistan in his new policy for the region and rightly highlighted the problem by mentioning Pakistan's patronage and support to the Taliban that had put a strategic impediment in the US's longest war against terrorism. And "an effective policy in order to win the Afghan war demands addressing the sanctuaries that Pakistan has continued to provide in pursuit of its objectives in the region."[80] Trump stated that the US would no longer keep silence over Pakistan's 'safe havens' for terrorist organizations. And consequently, at that time, the US-Pakistan relationship in terms of Afghanistan and South Asia became the issue of day-to-day mutual allegations and critical debates. Furthermore, Trump said:

> We have been paying Pakistan billions and billions of dollars; at the same time they are housing the very terrorists that we are fighting. But that will have to change, and that will change immediately.... Today, 20 US-designated foreign terrorist organizations are active in Afghanistan and Pakistan—the highest concentration in any region anywhere in the world. For its part, Pakistan often gives safe haven to agents of chaos, violence and terror.[81]

President Trump acknowledging Pakistan's sacrifices, however, further added that "no partnership can survive a country's harbouring of militants and terrorists who target US service members and officials".[82] After the declaration of New Strategy, the Trump administration put pause in disbursing of $255 million military financial assistance to Pakistan from the $1.1 billion promised in 2015, until Pakistan proves its credentials on terrorism front. Discarding the US major financial support, however, Pakistan held the US financial assistance as 'peanuts'. Despite its 'stronger than steel' relationship with China, it has stated that Pakistan cannot cut itself off from the alliances with the Western countries. In fact, despite critical stand against Pakistan, the US still held Pakistan as significant factor in the peace-building process in Afghanistan. In this context, the US Secretary of States Rex Tillerson stated, "Pakistan has suffered greatly from terrorism and can be an important partner in our shared goals of peace and stability in the region. We look to Pakistan to take decisive action against militant groups based in Pakistan that are a threat to the region. It is vital to US interests that Afghanistan and Pakistan prevent terrorist sanctuaries."[83]

The US's New Policy increased distance between the US and Pakistan as they had been very strong allies since very long time.

This development further created diplomatic impasse between them. Since then both rescheduled their high-level bilateral meetings for indefinite period. Pakistan's National Assembly also passed a unanimous resolution rejecting the US's accusations, and Pakistan condemned the wider space provided for India's role in Afghanistan by the Trump administration claiming the move as highly detrimental and dysfunctional to the regional stability. Pakistan's then Prime Minister Shahid Khaqan Abbasi, while declaring 'zero role' for India in Afghanistan said that they didn't foresee any political or military role for India in Afghanistan. He further said, "I think it will just complicate the situation and it will not resolve anything. So if they want to do economic assistance, that's their prerogative, but…we don't accept or see any role politically or militarily for India in Afghanistan."[84] Moreover, along with this issue, without failing to follow the traditional political practice of Pakistan, he spoke on Kashmir as a core issue for improvement in bilateral relations with India, and, he said that the conflicts in Afghanistan and Kashmir are linked. Further, condemning criticism over Pakistan for the asylum to terrorists, he said that the movement of cross-border terrorism in the region was from Afghanistan to Pakistan and not reversed. Pakistan side accused that "US will go to every extent to scapegoat Pakistan for its Afghanistan failure. With someone as unpredictable as Trump, the government believes that there is no hope for thaw in relations soon."[85] Further, Pakistan accused the US of ignoring the threats to Pakistan emanating from India. Pakistan's Defence Minister Khurram Dastgir Khan said, "The US knows all, but ignores the threats faced by us because of its strategic interest". He further claimed that a nexus existed between the US, India and Afghanistan that was threatening Pakistan.[86] Besides, Pakistan's Foreign Minister Khwaja Asif stated that Trump has not been focusing on Afghan's internal multiple serious dimensions that could bring stability in Afghanistan, but just focusing on Pakistan's alleged support to the Taliban, and such thinking of the US has been setting itself up for defeat. By strongly opposing Trump's stand on Pakistan, Asif stated that Pakistan could not be used as a "whipping boy" for the US's failure in the region, and therefore, Pakistan would not tolerate the language of threat and intimidation to Pakistan. Moreover, on the US's accusations on Madrasas in Pakistan, Asif said, "these madrasas were nurseries for American jihad in Afghanistan."[87]

However, despite all this, Pakistan's significance in the US's mission in Afghanistan was further held up by the US Defence Secretary James Mattis stating that "we intend to work with Pakistan in order to take the terrorists down, I think that's what a responsible nation does."[88] And Pakistan also has been looking forward for the resumption of the diplomatic dialogues. Trump's New Afghan Policy is summarized by Jim Molan as:

> While short on specifics…as comprehensive, aggressive, resolute, more lethal and waged across a wider area with less restrictions on field commanders than before. It can fairly be considered to be new because, in the 16 years of this conflict, a sustained, open-ended military presence and real pressure on the neighbours—especially Pakistan, and non-specified support from India—has not been tried.[89]

On January 1, 2018, Trump opined that the US foolishly gave Pakistan more than "33 billion dollars in aid over the last 15 years," and they have given nothing to the US, but "lies & deceit, thinking of our leaders as fools." "They give safe haven to the terrorists we hunt in Afghanistan, with little help. No more!" Subsequently, the suspension of all military assistance to Pakistan took place, as a result, the waves of resentment further flown in Pakistan. However, the doubt was raised that whether this move would bring about a change in its army's behavior.[90] Besides, the US Defense Secretary Jim Mattis stated that "There have been changes in Pakistan's behavior (since the South Asia strategy announced) with respect to fight against terrorism…. Pakistan military's operations are helping the US efforts against terrorism."[91] Trump's, as it was apparently appeared, determination against Pakistan seemed more vehement and irreversible. In February 2018, the Financial Actions Taken Force (FATF—an inter-governmental anti-money laundering watchdog) pulled Pakistan in its 'gray list' of the countries. The motion, in this regards, was jointly moved by the US, the UK, France and Germany. On Pakistan's inclusion in the gray list, Joshua White, senior adviser on South Asia to the Pentagon and the White House during Barack Obama's presidency, stated, "The FATF decision would have an impact on Pakistan's financial position, making it more difficult to raise capital on international markets, and making outsiders even more wary of foreign direct investment.... And it would, as a result, put continued pressure on Pakistan's foreign reserves...."[92]

Though this did not affect the China Pakistan Economic Corridor (CPEC), but, this had obviously put a pressure on Pakistan and affected Pakistan's standing in the international financial market. Furthermore, it was believed that the full implementation of the US's strategy would have helped in achieving positive results in war against the Taliban.[93]

India's Reaction on New US Policy: The India-US relationship appeared as a paradigm shift in the international politics with the leadership change in both the sides: Narendra Modi and Donald Trump. Both the leaders seemed to be like-minded having extremely high ambitions in the world politics, and, accordingly, they appeared playing very proactive role especially in Asia, which has emerged as the centre of the world politics or the great power game. However, it has stated that "the India-US relationship has a strong logic of its own; relationship between the world's largest and the world's oldest democracies. It is a relationship based on convergence of fundamental values, freedom of individual liberties."[94] In the struggling and unstable Afghanistan, both the US and India engaged by means of their own strategies in the direction of establishing peace and stability. The Trump's New Policy was held as positive and was welcomed in India by expressing that "India shares the US's concerns over Pakistan which provides safe havens to terrorists." In this context, India's ambassador to the US Navtej Sarna said:

> On terrorism, India and the US have a strategic convergence in a host of areas, including in its fight against terrorism.... We welcome the new Afghan policy because we share the concerns and the objectives that the safe havens that have been given to terrorists in Pakistan. The cross-border operations that are carried out from there concern us as much they are for the people of Afghanistan. Therefore, we

> share the policies announced by the Trump Administration which we welcome.[95]

Besides, India's MEA stated, "We welcome President Trump's determination to enhance efforts to overcome the challenges facing Afghanistan and confronting issues of safe havens and other forms of cross-border support enjoyed by terrorists. India shares these concerns and objectives." Further the Ministry while expressing India's commitment in establishing peace, stability in Afghanistan stated, "We are committed to supporting the government and the people of Afghanistan in their efforts to bring peace, security, stability and prosperity in their country. We have been steadfast in extending reconstruction and development assistance to Afghanistan in keeping with our traditional friendship with its people. We will continue these efforts, including in partnership with other countries."[96]

In fact, Trump expected India to help the US in "working with Afghanistan's domestic factions widening and buttressing the political legitimacy of the current government and also to improve its governance."[97] C. Raja Mohan opined, "Trump's new Afghan strategy could be a potential game-changer for South Asia or a brief exception to the familiar pattern of US-Pak relations. While recognizing the potential shadow between Trump's words and deeds, Delhi must bet on its own activism that can influence future outcomes in Afghanistan."[98] For India's proactive role in Afghanistan by viewing the new US's policy by President Trump in Afghanistan, it has expressed that

> ...India's highest priority is to prevent Afghanistan from becoming a sanctuary for radical militants, which could adversely affect Indian security, leading it to reject inclusion of the Taliban in any final political solution. While India has contributed to the reconstruction of the Afghan state, despite repeated pleas, its military assistance has been limited due to fear of legitimizing Pakistani security concerns. However, the stakes are too high for continued hesitancy. To defeat the Taliban and thus ensure its own security, India must overcome its self-imposed restraint on military aid to Afghanistan, both qualitatively and quantitatively, short of directly fighting the Taliban.

> Moreover, a closer assessment of the conflict situation suggests that reconciliation with the Taliban is unlikely, and that India would be better off helping the United States in its fight rather than a political settlement.[99]

Trump's New Policy, however, even 'without Pakistan' or 'with India' could not be successful. The US's so-called breakup with Pakistan further has not offered any other solution to the prevailing problems. Earlier Pakistan's engagement with the US in war against terrorism was hypocritical, while India has its own limitations. Though Trump did not push any military role for India to share with the US troops to play in Afghanistan, but it seemed that Trump was seeking to put moral responsibility on India in sharing the burden of its mission in Afghanistan. During the US Defence Secretary James Mattis's visit to India, 26-27 September 2017, India's then Defence Minister Nirmala Sitharaman had clearly declared that India would not send its troops to Afghanistan; however, the other assistance to the war-torn Afghanistan would be continued. Mattis said, "We applaud India's invaluable contributions to Afghanistan and welcome further efforts to promote Afghanistan's democracy, stability and security." The US held that "India has as many legitimate security interests in Afghanistan as Pakistan."[100] In fact, India perceived that the US was not reliable over the Af-Pak region as India was engaged in Afghanistan not because of the US's support but because of its own interests, and was engaged in myriad capacities. However, it was also true that India could dare engagement with Afghanistan because of the US's security built up there.

The US's so-called new role in the Afghan cauldron was also held skeptic. The world observed Trump as a man of unpredictability. Therefore, Trump's unreliability and uncertainties created dilemma for India over the alliance with the US in Afghanistan. The more significant factor that clearly enunciated in the policy was that unlike his predecessor Obama, President Trump clearly indicated that the US mission for stability in Afghanistan would not be time-bound and the US troops would stay there as long as necessary or till the objective was not accomplished. In fact, the security situation in and around Afghanistan needed the US troops to be present there. In terms of India's point of view also, without doubt, the US's continuous presence in Afghanistan certainly helped India to accomplish its interests in and around Afghanistan, but, unfortunately, it has observed that as long as the US troops extended its presence, the Taliban extremism and violence also prevailed, which killed the possibilities of the peace and stability in Afghanistan. However, C. Raja Mohan argued that India must be prepared for the possibility of the US slipping back to its old ways on Pakistan, and therefore, India's current emphasis must be on taking advantage of the Trump's discontinuity in the American policy towards the Indian Subcontinent and, in this context, that of India's approach would involve three elements—economic, security, and diplomatic.[101] In context of Trump's new policy, C. Raja Mohan outlined a set of parameters while engaging with Afghanistan, that; "...India must ramp up its economic diplomacy in Afghanistan to bring immediate benefits to Kabul amidst the deteriorating conditions in the country...Delhi must step up security cooperation with Afghanistan, especially in the training of its police and armed forces and intelligence sharing..." and, diplomatically, "...India must counter the emerging argument that Trump's new approach will intensify the 'Indo-Pak rivalry' in Afghanistan and the old one that Kashmir holds the key to peace in Afghanistan."[102]

It was also expressed that "The US needs to ensure better security situation for the Indian development work to have the expected impact and the US should also bring in Japan, the European Union and others into the developmental framework of Afghanistan."[103] Besides, it was also opined that India was "being recognized as a clear force for the good, a sponsor of democratic values and stability".... It wasn't "a tacit endorsement, but a loud one that has huge implications for India in South Asia where it jostles for influence with a mercantile China.... India must play its cards well."[104] Ahmad and Gopalswamy stated that although the scope of possibilities for India's support to Kabul was vast, India's assistance could have proved indispensable in two critical areas: The first was strengthening Afghanistan's intelligence, surveillance and reconnaissance (ISR) capabilities, and second, India could support Afghanistan in air space surveillance.[105] Furthermore, it was also suggested that India should extend its support to

Afghanistan in terms of military hardware that including the artillery, armored vehicles and tactical communication equipment, training of Afghan intelligence personnel in signals and imagery intelligence and deploying advisory teams to train the technical and maintenance staff of the Afghan air force.[106] However, despite the US's new policy offered all-well situation in favour of India's strategic interest in Afghanistan, the former Afghan President Hamid Karzai alerted India by expressing that India should abstain from falling into the US's new approach towards Afghanistan rather India should follow its own independent approach while engaging with Afghanistan. On India-US new arrangement in the region especially towards Afghanistan, Karzai further expressed that India has been a friend and an ally and a traditional civilizational friend of his country but he wanted India to continue its traditional wise man's approach to the region. It was too deep a civilization to be taken away by an American design...and too big a nation to be in any temporary arrangement with this or that country.[107]

Aptly to argue that by upholding India's significant role in pulling Afghanistan out from its unfortunate quagmire, the Trump administration tried to enhance India's confidence further to play proactive role for the good sake of Afghanistan. Therefore, in this direction, India further dared Pakistan's negativity in the Af-Pak region and continued its commitment in training Afghan police officers in India under the UNDP programme. The training to the Afghan police officers was aimed as helpful in protecting various irrigation, housing, school and other projects from the Taliban and other extremist groups in Afghanistan. In fact, India exhibited its gesture that India would not be deterred from assisting Afghanistan for its security. This was a very clear message to Pakistan and the other countries of the region which were dealing with the Taliban and were playing monstrous role against the interest of Afghanistan. Moreover, India also decided to send the engineers to Afghanistan to repair and refurbish the non-functional planes and helicopters given to Afghanistan. From this it was crystal clear that India adopted its own method to rebuild Afghanistan rather following the US's way of action.[108] Further, C. Raja Mohan argued that "Delhi has good reasons to see Trump's current policy as a consequential moment in India-US relations as well the geopolitics of the subcontinent. Any sustentative India-US strategic coordination in Afghanistan and Pakistan's inevitable reaction to it could presage a major change in the regional politics of South Asia."[109]

Reaction of the Afghan Government: Afghan President Ashraf Ghani also welcomed the Trump's New Policy extending the use of hard words against Pakistan for its sponsorship to terrorism. He termed the new US approach as a "game changer", and he stated that the new policy would provide "a clear pathway for regional countries to end support for non-state actors."[110] However, despite dysfunctional role of Pakistan against the interests of Afghanistan, President Ghani, while addressing the UN General Assembly on 19 September 2017, appealed Pakistan to work together to curb extremism. Welcoming the new developments, Ghani stated,

> We welcome this strategy, which has now set us on a pathway to certainty. The Afghan people have looked to the US for this type of resolve for years...we now also have an opportunity for a dialogue with our neighbours on how we can work together earnestly to eliminate terrorism and contain extremism...I call upon Pakistan to engage with us on a comprehensive state to state dialogue on peace, security and regional cooperation leading to prosperity.[111]

President Ghani further stated that the strategy had sent a signal to Taliban guerillas that they could not win on the field and must negotiate the peace as Trump has further influx more troops in Afghanistan to fight against the extremists. By condemning Pakistan Prime Minister's 'Zero role' of India in Afghanistan comment, the Afghan's Ambassador to India Shaida Mohammad Abdali said, "No country has right to dictate or manipulate Afghanistan's foreign policy," and also called Pakistan Prime Minister having old cold-war era mindset.[112] After the New Policy, he expressed that the 'Trilateral India-Afghanistan-US partnership' would have optimum opportunity to work together to enhance cooperation in the field of economic and development in Afghanistan, and to achieve success in the broadly set objectives against the terrorism and other inhuman activities. However,

Karzai raised the doubt and concerns towards the US's New Policy that it would not bring peace and stability in Afghanistan but further heightening of pain and suffering of the Afghan people. In this context, he stated, "Everyday Afghan told the US of the sanctuaries outside our borders. The US knew they were there but couldn't do much because Pakistan was an ally."[113] In fact, the US was not there only aiming at the ending of extremism, but, has strategic interest and playing the strategic game in the region given the Chinese influence in and beyond the region. However, while meeting with the US Defense Secretary Jim Mattis in March 2018 in Kabul, Ghani had expressed his appreciation for the US's military's sacrifices over the years and offered the praise for the US's new war strategy in Afghanistan.[114]

Challenges to the US's Afghan Policy

War in Afghanistan that had been prevailing from very long time resulted in the pervasive destruction of Afghan's state institutions, armed and police forces, national economy and overall development that left the people into dismal and painful situation. The US involvement in the Afghan conflict was the longest war by more than seventeen years. Despite all the burdens, the US and its international allies made considerable progress in settling the life of the Afghan people. The US made great efforts in the reconstitution and reconstruction of the Afghan state, Afghan security forces making them a responsible national institution, and more importantly, boosting the economy in proper order to bring improvements in the human development, though the pace was slow. In fact, it will not be exaggeration to state that only the US could dare to do this for the sake of humanity, though it has multiple interests there. The US efforts in Afghanistan can be apprehended as "a work of real hegemon." In other words, no other superpower other than the US could dare to wage a war against the enemies of humanity; the terrorism. In 2018, the US faced 4260 casualties in Afghanistan.[115] Dan Feldman, Special Representative for Afghanistan and Pakistan, United States Institute of Peace, Washington D.C., listed the US's momentous achievements in Afghanistan such as "access to education, improving the role of women and girls, health and longevity, independent media, infrastructure, and GDP growth.

Afghanistan is simply not the country it was when the Taliban ruled."[116] It was also stated that the offensive operations that had launched by the US helped in reducing the Afghan forces casualties by 20 percent in few months of 2017, while the "sustained pressure on the enemy had driven their casualties high." However, the terrorists had increasingly changed their tactics such as "carrying out frequent suicide attacks in Kabul and provincial centers." In 2017, the Afghan forces with the help of the US forces could gain through their counter-narcotics efforts that "destroyed more than 2 tons of heroin, 64 tons of morphine, 400 tons of opium, 25 tons of hashish, and a large amount of precursor chemicals. The street value of these seized drugs in Afghanistan is estimated at $352 million."[117] In fact, Chinese scholar Sun Tzu had rightly opined that "There has never been a protracted war from which a country has benefited."[118] And this happened with the US. However, despite the positive efforts, the US faced many challenges in offering Afghanistan peace, security, and stability. Among many, the main challenges were: security, weakness in national government and politics, political and military corruption, expansion of militarism; the Taliban and the IS, great powers rivalry and break-up with Pakistan as a long-standing partner in war against terrorism and many more.

Political Weakness and Expansion of Militancy: With the political turmoil that weaken the national government, the Taliban insurgency was mushroomed further and the Islamic State was also consolidating its footsteps in Afghanistan. It was observed that along with the Taliban, the IS also began the terrorist attacks in Afghanistan killing many people. Even for that matter, the Taliban also rejected the peace offer of the Ghani government. This development posed dual terrorist challenge to the US policy in Afghanistan. In fact, since the 2014 drawdown of the US troops, the Taliban insurgency was expanded rapidly around the country covering around 40 percent of its territory. It has observed that the Afghan's national government was facing internal instability, mutual disagreements amongst the members and also the government's dysfunctions that were undermining the fighting capacity of the Afghan National Defence and Security Forces (ANDSF) to counter the Taliban insurgency. Moreover, the government's capacity in confronting the significant governance, economic, humanitarian and other challenges also were weak. The civilian and military casualties, the numbers of conflict-displaced and those in need of urgent humanitarian assistance were continued growing.[119] Despite a long standing of more than 17 years in Afghanistan, the ANDSF continued facing of significant challenges in holding territory and defending population centers, while the Taliban continued contesting districts and continued carrying out suicide attacks in major cities. More than 2,500 ANDSF service members were killed and over 4,200 were wounded in the first four months and, in the first six months of 2017, record-high number of civilian casualties were documented by the UN; 1,662 civilian deaths and 3,581 civilian injuries.[120] There were more than a dozen regional and transnational terrorist groups strongly active in diminishing the improved situation and to convert it into more unstable and pathetic situation which was prevailing despite the US presence in Afghanistan, to weaken the Afghan state and to use the Afghan soil to launch terror attacks in the region and beyond especially against the antagonist ideologies. According to the International Crisis Group,

> Preventing the loss of more territory to insurgents, particularly during the anticipated spring offensive, is an urgent priority, notably in order to limit the scope of ungoverned spaces that could be exploited by regional extremists and transnational terror groups.... Tackling the security situation also will require addressing widening internal disagreements and political partisanship that permeate all levels of the security apparatus and have undermined ANDSF command and control structures. Intra-governmental divisions likewise have impeded implementation of reforms necessary to mitigate the effects of corruption, nepotism and factionalism in the Afghan National Army (ANA) and particularly the Afghan National Police (ANP).[121]

Moreover, it has stated that the US was not getting adequate help from the international community in Afghan turmoil. The "allies had less than 3,000 troops on the ground in Afghanistan.

In 2011, the United States and its partners had some 130,000 troops in Afghanistan."[122]

Corruption in Afghanistan: Establishment of peace, stability, and economic development hinges on the institutionalization of good governance and the rule of law. But, corruption in Afghanistan remained the major obstacle in looking for the peaceful settlement of the country's multiple problems. This problem was widely rooted in both the Afghan's National Government and its armed forces, and had also put impediments in the US humanitarian and military efforts. It has reported that in March 2017, more than 1,000 Afghan army service members were fired following corruption charges.[123] It was argued that "Corruption weakens Afghanistan's nascent state and empowers its enemy. It is the mother of all threats to Afghanistan's stabilization and sustainable development."[124] In fact, according to the analysts of international relations, the war created a stalemate because of the Taliban's continuously growing stronger and making rampant attacks. Besides, the level of rampant corruption was high that plaguing the Afghan government, and also hampering US military activities. It has also argued that President Trump's plans for Afghanistan remained much like those of President Obama: to strengthen the Afghan government forces on the battlefield in hopes a bloodied Taliban would come to "the negotiating table to negotiate a political solution."[125] However, it has stated that breaking of the prevailing stalemate against the Taliban would be possible if more additional troops were to be influxed in Afghanistan aiming to serve in two roles: counterterrorism missions and training the Afghan forces. But, it was also believed that only increasing the number of US or international troops in Afghanistan would not work positively. The US had already experimented the larger number of troops in Afghanistan that could not resolve the problem. Julie Vitkovskaya pointed out few specific factors that kept the US war in Afghanistan continue; first, despite the deaths, more soldiers were continued to be deployed in the region. About 8,500 US troops were present in Afghanistan since when Obama officially ended the combat mission there (and Trump further increased more US troops). Moreover, there were NATO troops also that worked with the US forces to train, advise and assist Afghan security forces. Besides, there were US Special Operations forces on a separate counterterrorism mission were engaged in targeting Al-Qaeda and the Islamic State. Second, the US has spent billions of dollars fighting this prolonged war in Afghanistan. More than $700 billion has been spent for the reconstruction programmes and the war efforts in Afghanistan, and further the troops increase would have added billions of dollars more as a cost of the conflict. The military strategists predicted that the US spending could have increased up to $840 billion. And third, the Islamic State and the Taliban inclined to continue the launching of major terrorist attacks. The Taliban remained responsible for many deadliest attacks in Afghanistan that killed hundreds of Afghan soldiers and the civilians. The incessant attacks were the major blows to the US war efforts aiming to help the Afghan army become self-sustaining especially against the Taliban.[126]

However, in context of the US failure in its Afghan Mission, Daniel L. Davis in *The National Interest* expressed that America's Afghan mission no longer serving its purpose, and also stated three reasons for the US not being successful in Afghanistan.

First, the objective itself is impossible to attain. Afghanistan is a vast, untamed and mountainous country.... Even with the highest concentration of US, NATO and Afghan security forces, major sections of the nation were beyond the troops' ability to control. Even then, the Taliban had freedom of maneuver in large portions of eastern, central and southern Afghanistan. Today, the government controls less than 60 percent of its territory. It is impossible, therefore, to set as a policy intent to "prevent" terrorists from using Afghanistan as a launching pad for planning attacks against the United States. *Second,* even if theoretically it were possible to drive all the terrorists out of the country, the successful accomplishment of that goal would be meaningless...terrorists in the modern age do not need specific pieces of terrain to conceive and practice attack plans. They use the internet, telephones, text messages and other electronic means to coordinate and plan. In those cases when physical meetings are required, terrorists will convene in locations where the security environment is the most permissive. *Lastly,* whatever aspiration

Washington may seek, there is effectively no strategy governing the conduct of operations on the ground in Afghanistan... currently it is difficult to discern an overall, coherent strategy for Afghanistan.[127]

Dealing with the situation in Afghanistan was appeared to be very complicated and formidable which needed very comprehensive strategy. Since a long time, the US was logistically dependent on Pakistan to carry out its operations in Afghanistan, Pakistan's negative approach in this context had put many problems in the US mission, and therefore, big challenge was how to deal with Pakistan. Trump's hard gesture against Pakistan could not offer possible solution to the problem. Though it has suggested that to deal with Pakistan, a multi-pronged approach and coercive pressure on Pakistan, for providing its support to insurgents and to stop using terror as an instrument of foreign policy, should have been adopted and applied. However, Pakistan did not fall under any US pressure given China-Pakistan proximity. The US had to prevail upon China for the sake of humanity; however, it was very tough and formidable task as both are the opposite players of the great power game or New Cold War. The US Ambassador to Afghanistan, John R. Bass called Pakistan as a source of "significant challenges" in Afghanistan that "enabling the Taliban to rest and refit, plan coordinated attacks." However, further, he expressed that "US will not succeed if we do not have the support and cooperation of Pakistan, its neighbours and the wider circumference of significant countries in the wider region."[128] However, according to the Transparency International's Corruption Perception Index-2019, "Afghanistan, from its low base, has made a gain of eight points."[129]

Great Game Rivalry: The US v/s China-Pak-Russia

By exhibiting rivalry gesture against the US, both the superpowers China and Russia also criticized and opposed Trump's New Afghan Policy which vehemently blamed Pakistan for its inaction. In fact, in the post-2014 period, China's engagement in Afghanistan multiplied in terms of economic and military assistance in view of accomplishing its objectives of Belt and Road Initiatives and to curb extremism in Xinjiang province. Therefore, Afghanistan particularly and the region generally experienced the possibility of the complex problems if the interests of both the US and China had clashed across. It was stated that, "Beijing is willing to provide a cushion to Pakistan against America physically upping the ante. Washington would have to be very careful in ratcheting up conflict in the region because it would involve Chinese interests pertaining to the one-belt-one-road project."[130] Besides, it has also argued that "If the US is angry, Pakistan has got a new master and financier—China."[131] Therefore, it was observed that "the global power equations and the position in South Asia were far more complex...for Washington to carry out another attack...on a Pakistani military check-post"..., because, there was "China in the equation, with greater power and capacity to play a role."[132] China strongly supported and held Pakistan's role as crucial in Afghanistan which Trump's strategy had marginalized. However, such developments if had taken, there would have been obviously a fire-test for India how to adjust its interest adroitly in changing power equations in Afghanistan and the region. In this direction, Pakistan's commentator Khaled Ahmed has aptly stated:

> Pakistan is counting on China to balance India-US bonhomie. Afghanistan will likely to be the theatre of engagement. US President Donald Trump's challenge to a double dealing Pakistan has provoked commentators in the country to invoke the threat of a cold war-like confrontation between America and China—with Pakistan safely operating on the Chinese side while India draws closer to the US.[133]

Furthermore, Russia also termed Trump's New Policy as a 'Dead End.' Both Russia and China assured Pakistan for every possible support after Trump's anti-Pakistan posture. They had diplomatically stated that they would use veto power against any 'US move' in the United Nations to impose any sanctions against Pakistan. Against Trump's New Policy, Pakistan also started approaching the key international and regional powers and diplomatic offensive to garner support for Pakistan.[134] In fact, Russia, China, Iran, and Turkey and other few more anti-US states were supporting Pakistan against US's new strategy in Afghanistan and that created perplexing situation for India. Apparently, Russia-Pakistan proximity developed at a time when the relations between the US and its cold war ally were unraveling over the war against terrorism in Afghanistan. During the presence of the Soviet Forces in Afghanistan (1979-88), Pakistan helped the US to flow weapons and the US activities across the border to support and aid to the Afghan fighters against the Soviet forces. Nevertheless, both the Pakistan and Russia developed military, economic, and diplomatic relationship which was completely dormant for several decades. Interestingly, both also cultivated links with the Taliban militants against the US troops. By and large, the vacuum that created in Pakistan by the US through de-aligning with, Russia occupied it. Besides, the presence of the Islamic States (IS) in the region also brought both together as the IS started its attacks in Pakistan, and Russia grappled with panic that if the IS reaches to the Russian border through Central Asia. It was criticized that Russia was openly legitimizing the Taliban. And even Iran was also extending its support to the insurgents in Afghanistan to weaken and undermine the US presence there. In fact, the United States, on one hand, and the Iran and Russia together on other, had tensions over the conflict in Syria, which had created concerns that it would put repercussion to hurt the possibilities of peace and stability in Afghanistan. Both Iran and Russia were pushing for the US withdrawal from Afghanistan from very long years. It has reported that "Now, as the Taliban gains ground and the White House appears to lack a clear Afghan policy, Iran and Russia have boosted support for insurgents and sidelined the United States from regional diplomacy on the war."[135]

The US's new policy clearly defined that the US's forces in Afghanistan were not for the reconstruction of Afghanistan but to kill or defeat and finish the extremist groups in and around Afghanistan. In fact, Pakistan emerged as 'a global bad boy (state)' to be used by the superpowers against each other in the world politics, especially in the conflict zone and this bad boy also has its wicked interests behind partnering with these states. Earlier, the US partnered Pakistan and, now, Russia seeing its turn to use Pakistan. China has already been using Pakistan for its interests. Therefore, Lord Palmerston's (former Prime Minister) and Henry

Kissinger's (former US Secretary of State) similar arguments in context of the Britain and the US respectively become more relevant that there are no permanent friends or enemy in the world politics, but, the national interest are permanent. And their observation led to the interpretation that: "Our friends must serve our interests; therefore, they will remain our friends. And at the same time we have no problem sleeping with our enemies as long as it serves our interests. Our past friends may become our enemies as today's enemies potentially become our future friends." Each actor involved in Afghanistan trying to protect its individual interests rather working for the interests of people of Afghanistan as a whole. In the direction of writing a success story for Afghanistan, it has suggested that:

> Both Afghanistan and the US will achieve an 'honorable and enduring outcome' to the Afghan conflict if the Afghan administration under Ghani continues to purge corruption, initiate and speed up a wide range of reforms in the government, and, by the same token, the US continues supporting Afghan security forces. In the meantime, on the external front, the US must continue taking strong action against Pakistan to eventually force it to change its policy towards Afghanistan.[136]

The solution to the Afghan war was not a straight-jacketed that brained by the US alone. There was a need of the collective cooperation of all the superpower states that were expecting to accomplish their national interests in terms of peace and stability in Afghanistan that to be established especially by eliminating terrorism and its roots. Therefore, the US, without keeping away the ego of hegemony and the most powerful state, should have talked to other states like Russia, China, Iran, Pakistan and no doubt with India and the states of the Central Asian region. The other states also should have pondered in positive way for the sake of the well-being of the Afghan people and should have sidelined their personal enmities and mindsets of cold war politics. In fact, all these states were divided into groupism and rival politics that hampered early and well-thought peace process in Afghanistan. There was a need of attitudinal change among all the states looking at and thinking of flushing out the Afghan quagmire. However, the major challenge in the peace establishment in Afghanistan was the hard core rivalry between the US on one side, and Russia, China, Iran and even Pakistan on the other side. And both the sides seemed to be showing recalcitrance and not ready to compromise for the sake of good. Further adding fuel into antagonism, the then US Secretary of State Mike Pompeo called Russia, China and Iran as the "Bad Actors".[137] The complication of the US position against the Taliban, the anti-US states favouring the Taliban, and ignoring and failing to talk to Afghan's legitimate government further led to create more dilemmas in Afghanistan. However, it was rightly stated that "No internationally-led negotiations will work unless there is a consensus among Afghans, both those backing and opposing the government, to pursue a negotiated peace rather than continued conflict."[138]

As stated earlier, the US was never been ready to talk with the Taliban directly and always urged the Afghan government to take part in, but, later in July 2018, the Trump administration directed its top diplomats to seek direct talks with the Taliban with the hope of initiating negotiations with them to end the longest war. This attitudinal change brought significant shift in the US's foreign policy towards Afghanistan. In fact, the Taliban had already urged to talk to the US. Therefore, in search of required possibilities and congenial situation, the US senior diplomat, Secretary of State Mike Pompeo visited Kabul and Alice G. Wells, the top diplomat for the region, visited Afghanistan and Pakistan to lay the groundwork for the direct talks with the Taliban.[139] In fact, as argued, these efforts of the US were aimed at prevailing upon the Afghan's leadership that the talks with the Taliban were "not a replacement for negotiations with the country's coalition government", but aimed at the breaking of the ice and pave the ways for those talks, as "the previous Afghan government felt left out of peace efforts during the Obama administration, it resisted direct talks."[140] However, in July 2018, the Taliban engaged in their first direct contact with the US officials in a discussion about the future plan of the peace talks on Afghanistan in Qatar, where the Taliban has maintained a political office since 2013. This was considered as the most remarkable effort towards the prolonged war in Afghanistan. This meeting was held between a group of the Taliban and Alice Wells, a US top diplomat for South Asia. Regarding this meeting, one of the Taliban officials said that "the environment was positive and the discussion was useful." But it has stated that the US official had not confirmed and even not denied about the meeting that took place in Qatar as Alice Wells was also in Doha at that time. However, the US stated that "the United States is exploring all avenues to advance a peace process in close consultation with the Afghan government."[141] Even for that matter during this meeting it was said that "the Taliban want to solve their problems with the Americans to end the invasion."[142]

Privatization of the Afghan War?

By learning the fruitless results and increasingly debilitating security situation in Afghanistan, as has argued earlier, the Trump administration had pondered major changes in the US foreign policy in context of its engagement with the Afghan government, its stand on the Taliban and also the policy approach towards the other powers in the region that remained engaged in the conflicts directly or indirectly. And one of such major policy initiatives, as has been believed, of Trump administration was that of the "privatization of the Afghan war". The US administration, its think tanks and the scholars had debated this. However, in fact, it has reported that very few policy makers in administration and the American Congress supported the idea, whereas Pentagon openly expressed its opposition to the idea. However, Trump denied any such plan.[143] Erick Prince, the former US Navy Seal and former head of the Blackwater Private Security Council, had used his mind for the creation of an idea of outsourcing or privatizing the Afghan war, and he called this scheme as "A Strategic Economy of Force."[144] In fact, it has reported that "Plans to privatize the war proposed by two businessmen with ties to the White House have become a linchpin of the debate. Prince proposed to send private contractors to Afghanistan instead of US troops, and have the entire operation overseen by a viceroy," and it was held as "the only credible option for Afghanistan, dismissing the other options of withdrawing completely or using contractors or paramilitaries with a minimal US counterterrorism presence."[145] On privatizing or outsourcing of war, C. Raja Mohan argued that "While the outrage against outsourcing the Afghan war is real, the tragic reality is that the growing role of private armies is very much part of the modern hybrid wars."[146] For this proposal, Prince suggested the sending of 5500 contractors to Afghanistan to work with the Afghan National Security Forces (ANSF), and the appointment of a "viceroy" to oversee the entire exercise in Afghanistan, and the mentors of these contractors would be from the US, Britain, Canada, and South Africa.[147] Besides, it has reported according to Prince that "a small army of 6000, backed by 2000 US Special Forces, and by a private air wing of 90 planes could make a big difference to the battlefield situation," and this operation would cost the US treasury a small fraction of the current bill for running the Afghan war."[148] According to Prince, this endeavour would have cost just $4 billion a year and "working with a small force in Afghanistan would reduce the US dependence on Pakistan for logistics and allow Washington to mount some real pressure against Rawalpindi."[149] However, the major problem that outsourcing of war would have been the problem of sense of responsibility and accountability, and that would have led to the increasing violation of human rights and the danger of civil liberties.[150] The former President of Afghanistan Karzai opposing the privatization of the Afghan war, stated, "I vehemently oppose the proposal to the US government to outsource its war in Afghanistan to private security firms. This would be prolonging and intensifying the bloodshed in Afghanistan and a blatant violation of our national sovereignty and constitution."[151] However, with the changing circumstances and the failure of its ambition to win a war in Afghanistan by force, the US, having learnt the situation, eventually decided and opened direct talks with the Taliban. Without doubt, the US administration exhibited its commitment not to undermine the legitimacy of the Kabul government at any cost.

The US President, surprisingly, further in December 2018 by taking the unusual stand on Afghanistan, decided to withdraw its about 7000 out of 14,000 troops from Afghanistan, which indicated the end of prolonged American's military intervention in Afghanistan. The war in Afghanistan was held as the longest one in the American history. In fact, Trump's decision of slashing of troops shocked and surprised the diplomats and officials in Afghanistan, who had been engaged in ending the conflicts by having contacts with the Taliban and also the international stakeholders.[152] This decision was preceded by a three-day meeting between the US envoy Khalizad and the Taliban members in Abu Dhabi in December 2018 and Khalizad had called the talks as productive. In fact, at the same time, the Trump administration had decided to pull the troops from Syria. Unfortunately, Trump's decision would have further increased the violence and conflicts in Afghanistan as the Taliban had already occupied and controlled larger part of the Afghan territory. In fact, the US Defence Secretary James Mattis had advised against the withdrawal and who had to face Trump's anger, and as a result, Mattis had to resign. In fact, Trump's decision could be seen through the prism of "America First Policy" as he had earlier raised the question during 2016 presidential elections that how the US was benefiting from spending money and blood in Europe and Asia. He had criticized the US military intervention in Afghanistan as extremely expensive and politically foolish. Furthermore, it has believed that Trump's this act would have further encouraged the militants like the Taliban and the Islamic States in Afghanistan and Syria respectively. This decision optimally premised major potential to affect the security and the political stability in Afghanistan. However, this was seen as a good indication in terms of Taliban's inclination towards the negotiation for peace. In this context, Graeme Smith, a consultant for the International Crisis Group, believed that "This could nudge the political process toward serious discussion of peace. A partial withdrawal could send a useful message to all sides."[153] However, in January 2017, Zamir Kabulov, the Special Representative to the Russian President for Afghanistan, feared that "if Trump decides to withdraw the contingent, then everything will collapse."[154]

However, after the declaration of the slashing of troops by the Trump administration, and even the prevailing peace talks between the US and the Taliban, an attitudinal change in the Taliban's behavior was experienced and they seemed to be unpredictable in terms of their relations with the US. Urging the US to exit from the Afghanistan, on 27 December 2018, the

Taliban warned the US that they would face the consequences of the same fate as the Soviet Union which had to leave Afghanistan in 1989, if they did not leave the Afghan land. The Taliban spokesman Zabiullah Mujahid said hinting the US, "Take heed from the Soviet defeat in Afghanistan and abandon thoughts of testing the mettle of the already proven Afghans," and he further said that the future relations between the US and the Taliban should be based on "sound diplomatic and economic principles rather than conflict."[155]

Failure of the American War

Without doubt, the American war in Afghanistan failed. Even for that matter, Trump's new aggressive Afghan policy of 2017 that unveiling a "fight to win" strategy proved to be ineffective bringing no fruitful results. According to Nicholas Grossman, "A simple win-loss dynamic is the wrong way to think about the war. America's not in Afghanistan to win. It's there to hold the line."[156] Further Crossman stated:

> America's aim was no longer democratic nation-building, as in the era of George W. Bush.... There was no ideal end state in view. But the US had no choice but to stay in order to prevent jihadist groups filling any future vacuum, as happened in Iraq; to keep the Iranians and Russians out; and to keep Pakistan honest, stable, and in the US column. As the death toll mounts and the elected government weakens, the sum of America's shrunken Afghan ambition appears to be: hang on in there—and fingers crossed.[157]

Therefore, by learning its failure in the US's tactics and strategy against the Taliban, President Trump eventually decided to seek direct peace talks with the Taliban. Since 2001, none of the American administrations, but the Trump administration, for the first time, pondered on an alternate policy stand towards the conflicts.[158] In context of its longer period and failure of war, it has believed that "Afghanistan's toxic mix of state collapse, civil conflict, ethnic disintegration and multisided intervention has locked it in a self-perpetuating cycle that may be simply beyond outside resolution."[159] According to the Washington-based Pew Research Centre, forty-nine percent of the Americans have opined that the US war in Afghanistan failed.[160] It has argued that "in the absence of a holistic US strategy, Afghanistan risks becoming one large training ground and weapons testing site for the American armed forces."[161]

With its failure in war against the Taliban, the US began negotiations with the Taliban to end its prolonged war in Afghanistan. Eventually, the US and other international forces left Afghanistan in August 2021 permanently.

Notes and References

1. Karl Eikenberry, The American Calculus of Military Intervention, *Survival*, Vol. 56, No. 3, Jun-July 2014, p. 264, pp. 264-71.
2. Larry P. Goodson and Thomas H. Johnson, US Policy and Strategy Toward Afghanistan After 2014, US Army Strategic Studies Institute and US Army War College Press, Carlisle, PA, October 2014, p. 2.
3. Katherine Harvey, Afghanistan, The United States, and The Legacy of the Afghanistan's Civil War, 5 June 2003, EDGE, https://web.stanford.edu/class/e297a/Afghanistan,%20the%20United%20States.htm, accessed on 23 February 2018.
4. Goodson and Johnson, October 2014, p. 2.
5. Katherine Harvey, 2003.
6. *Ibid.*
7. *Ibid.*
8. *Ibid.*
9. *Ibid.*
10. Dhananjay Tripathi, The US Role in Afghanistan: A Critical Overview, in Rajen Harshe and Dhananjay Tripathi ed. *Afghanistan Post 2014: Power Configurations and Evolving Trajectories*, Routledge, New Delhi, 2016, p. 78.
11. *Ibid.*, p. 81.
12. Steve Coll, *Directorate S: The CIA and America's Secret Wars in Afghanistan and Pakistan, 2001–2016,* Allen Lane, New Delhi, 2018, p. 117.
13. Dhananjay Tripathi, 2016, p. 84.
14. *Ibid.*
15. Taliban in Afghanistan, Council on Foreign Relations, 17 February 2018, https://www.cfr.org/interactives/global-

conflict-tracker?co=C042701#!/conflict/taliban-in-afghanistan, 19 February 2018.

16. Paul D. Miller, The US and Afghanistan After 2014, *Survival*, Vol. 55, No. 1, 2013, pp. 1, 87-102.
17. Leonid Gusev, The US Interests in Afghanistan and Central Asia, *New Eastern Outlook*, 27 March 2012, https://www.rbth.com/articles/2012/03/27/the_us_interests_in_afghanistan_and_central_asia_15276, accessed on 8 March 2018.
18. *Ibid.*
19. *Ibid.*
20. *Ibid.*
21. *Ibid.*
22. *Ibid.*
23. Rajen Harshe and Dhananjay Tripathi, 2016, p. 82.
24. Meghan Keneally, Why the US got involved in Afghanistan—and why it's been difficult to get out, abc news, Aug 21, 2017, http://abcnews.go.com/US/us-involved-afghanistan difficult/story?id=49341264, accessed on 13 March 2018.
25. Paul D. Miller, 2013, p. 90.
26. Ashley J. Tellis, Jeff Eggers, US Policy in Afghanistan: Changing Strategies, Preserving Gains, May 22, 2017, http://carnegieendowment.org/2017/05/22/US-policy-in-afghanistan-changing-strategies-preserving-gains-pub-70027
27. Rajiv Dogra, *Durand's Curse: A Line Across the Pathan Heart*, Rupa, New Delhi, 2017, pp. 198-99.
28. *Ibid.*, p. 199.
29. Goodson and Johnson, October 2014, p. 16.
30. Steve Coll, 2018, pp. 270-73.
31. *Ibid.*, p. 271.
32. *Ibid.*, p. 272.
33. *Ibid.*, p. 277.
34. *Ibid.*, p. 278.
35. Catherine Lutz and Sujaya Desai, US Reconstruction Aid for Afghanistan: The Dollars and Sense, Watson Institute for International Studies, Brown University, 5 January 2015.
36. Michel Chossudovsky, The War is Worth Waging: Afghanistan's Vast Reserves of Minerals and Natural Gas, Global Research,

22 August 2017, https://www.globalresearch.ca/the-war-is-worth-waging-afghanistan-s-vast-reserves-of-minerals-and-natural-gas/19769, accessed on 13 March 2018.

37. *Ibid.*, also see Michel Chossudovsky, America's War on Terrorism, Global Research, Montreal, 2005, see also Michel Chossudovsky, Heroin is "Good for Your Health": Occupation Forces support Afghan Narcotics Trade, Global Research, April 29, 2007.
38. M. Ashraf Haidari, Afghanistan in 2017: Achievements and Challenges, *The Diplomat*, 28 December 2017, https://thediplomat.com/2017/12/afghanistan-in-2017-achievements-and-challenges/, accessed on 21 April 2018.
39. Goodson and Johnson, October 2014, p. V.
40. Douglas C. Lovelace, Jr. in Foreword, Goodson and Johnson, October 2014.
41. Quoted in C. Lutz and S. Desai, 2015.
42. US Relations with Afghanistan, US Department of State, Office of the Special Representative for Afghanistan and Pakistan, Fact Sheet, January 3, 2017, https://www.state.gov/r/pa/ei/bgn/5380.htm, accessed on 6 March 2018.
43. Rakesh Sood, 2018.
44. The US War in Afghanistan, 1999-2018, https://www.cfr.org/timeline/us-war-afghanistan, accessed on 5 March 2018.
45. Leonid Gusev, 27 March 2012.
46. Kiran Dhillon, Afghanistan is the Big Winner in US Foreign Aid, *Time*, 31 March 2014, http://time.com/43836/afghanistan-is-the-big-winner-in-u-s-foreign-aid/, accessed on 6 March 2018.
47. Ann M. Simmons, US foreign aid: A waste of money or a boost to world stability? Here are the facts, *Los Angeles Times*, 10 May 2017, http://www.latimes.com/world/la-fg-global-aid-true-false-20170501-htmlstory.html, accessed on 6 March 2018.
48. C. Lutz and S. Desai, 2015.
49. US Relations with Afghanistan, US Department of State, Office of the Special Representative for Afghanistan and Pakistan, Fact Sheet, January 3, 2017, https://www.state.gov/r/pa/ei/bgn/5380.htm, accessed on 6 March 2018.
50. US Aid to Afghanistan has Largely been Wasted and Stolen, Report Says, by VICE News, October 14, 2015, https://news.

vice.com/article/us-aid-to-afghanistan-has-largely-been-wasted-and-stolen-report-says, accessed on 8 March 2018.

51. Tellis and Eggers, for details see, Special Inspector General for Afghanistan Reconstruction (SIGAR), *Quarterly Report to the United States Congress*, Washington, DC: SIGAR, January 30, 2017, p. 4.
52. US Aid to Afghanistan has Largely been Wasted and Stolen, Report Says, by VICE News, October 14, 2015.
53. Goodson and Johnson, October 2014, p. 6.
54. Security Assistance Monitor, https://securityassistance.org/afghanistan, accessed on 12 April 2018.
55. John F. Sopko, SIGAR, Reconstructing the Afghan National Defense and Security Forces: Lessons from the US Experiences in Afghanistan, Virginia, September 2017.
56. *Ibid.*
57. Bilateral Security Agreement, https://www.afghanembassy.us/document/bsa/, accessed on 31 January 2019.
58. *Ibid.*
59. Kabul signed a similar agreement with NATO on September 30 to allow 4,000 to 5,000 additional troops—mostly from Britain, Germany, Italy, and Turkey—to stay in Afghanistan in a noncombat role after 2014. For details see, Charles Recknagel, Explainer: Key Points in US-Afghan Bilateral Secureity Agreement, 30 September 2014, RadioFreeEurope, RadioLibrary, https://www.rferl.org/a/explainer-bsa-afghan-us-security-agreement-bsa/26613884.html, accessed on 31 January 2019.
60. US Relations with Afghanistan, US Department of State, Office of the Special Representative for Afghanistan and Pakistan, Fact Sheet, January 3, 2017, https://www.state.gov/r/pa/ei/bgn/5380.htm, accessed on 6 March 2018.
61. *Ibid.*
62. *Ibid.*
63. James Griffiths, Who are the key players in Afghanistan?, CNN, 19 September 2017, https://edition.cnn.com/2017/08/26/asia/afghanistan-pakistan-india-china-russia-us/index.html, accessed on 7 February 2018.
64. John S. Sopko, 2017.
65. Security Assistance Monitor, 12 April 2018.

66. This is a revised text of a paper published earlier, for details see Vinod Khobragade, The Afghan Turmoil: US's New Policy and India's Options, *South Asian Journal of Socio-Political Studies*, Vol. XIX, No. 1, June-December 2018, pp. 5-11.
67. C. Raja Mohan, Privatising the Afghan War, *The Indian Express*, 28 August 2018, p. 7.
68. Julie Vitkovskaya, four things to know about America's war in Afghanistan, *The Washington Post*, August 24, 2017, https://www.washingtonpost.com/news/checkpoint/wp/2017/08/24/what-you-need-to-know-about-the-longest-conflict-in-u-s-history-the-war-in-afghanistan/?utm_term=.8897a5d517ea, accessed on 7 March 2018.
69. Tim Lister, Carnage in Kabul adds to US challenges in Afghanistan, CNN, January 29, 2018, https://edition.cnn.com/2018/01/28/middleeast/us-afghanistan-challenges-intl/index.html, accessed on 20 April 2018.
70. M. Ashraf Haidari, 2017.
71. Anthony H. Cordesman, Telling the Truth about the War in Afghanistan, Centre for Strategic & International Studies, 12 September 2018, https://www.csis.org/analysis/telling-truth-about-war-afghanistan, accessed on 20 February 2019.
72. Damir Marusic and Andrew Bernard, The "New" Afghanistan Strategy, *The American Interest*, 22 August 2017, https://www.the-american-interest.com/2017/08/22/new-afghanistan-strategy/, accessed on 13 March 2018, also see Jeremy Herb, Five key pieces of Trump's Afghanistan plan, CNN, 22 August 2017, https://edition.cnn.com/2017/08/21/politics/trump-afghan-plan-five-things/index.html, accessed on 10 April 2018.
73. Eikenberry 2014, p. 265.
74. Taliban in Afghanistan, Council on Foreign Relations, 17 February 2018.
75. Jeremy Herb, Five key pieces of Trump's Afghanistan plan, CNN, 22 August 2017, https://edition.cnn.com/2017/08/21/politics/trump-afghan-plan-five-things/index.html, accessed on 10 April 2018.
76. *Ibid.*
77. *Ibid.*
78. Tim Lister, 29 January 2018.
79. Varghese K. George, Trump links India's Afghan role to trade surplus, *The Hindu*, 23 August 2017, p. 12.

80. Ahmad Murid Partaw, Will Pakistan Change its Strategic Calculus towards Pakistan?, *Foreign Policy Journal*, 2 September 2017, https://www.foreignpolicyjournal.com/2017/09/02/will-pakistan-change-its-strategic-calculus-toward-afghanistan/, accessed on 26 April 2019.

81. Devirupa Mitra, While India, Afghanistan Hail Trump's South Asia Strategy, Questions Remain on What It Really Means, *The Wire*, 22 August 2017, https://thewire.in/170067/india-afghanistan-pakistan-donald-trump/, accessed on 7 September 2017.

82. *Ibid.*

83. *Ibid.*

84. Varghese K. George, No Role for India in Afghanistan: Abbasi, *The Hindu*, 22 September 2017.

85. Mubashir Zaidi, US-Pakistan Impasse Continues, *The Hindu*, 4 September 2017, p. 12.

86. Sajjad Hussain, Pakistan reassessing ties with US: Defence Minister, *The Indian Express*, 15 September 2017, p. 10.

87. Varghese K. George, Don't Treat Pakistan as a Whipping Boy: Asif to US, *The Hindu*, 6 October 2017, p. 12.

88. *Ibid.*

89. Jim Molan, Trump's Afghan Policy: Best in 16 Years, 28 August 2017, https://www.lowyinstitute.org/the-interpreter/trump-afghanistan-policy-best-16-years, accessed on 28 September 2017.

90. Rakesh Sood, Afghanistan, on a slow Fuse, *The Hindu*, 25 Janaury 2018, p. 8.

91. Lalit Jha, Pak Military's ops helping US's efforts against terrorism: Mattis, *The Indian Express*, 16 March 2018, p. 10.

92. Tom Hussain, 'Gray-listing' pushes Pakistan further into China's orbit, *Asian Review*, 6 March 2018, https://asia.nikkei.com/Politics-Economy/International-Relations/Gray-listing-pushes-Pakistan-further-into-China-s-orbit, accessed on 7 March 2018.

93. M. Ashraf Haidari, 28 December 2017.

94. Javid Ahmad and Bharath Gopalaswamy, India has feature role in Trump's new Afghan plan, *The Hill*, 1 September 2017, http://thehill.com/blogs/pundits-blog/foreign-policy/348898-india-has-feature-role-in-trumps-new-afghan-plan

95. PTI, India shares US's concerns over Pakistan giving safe havens to terrorists: Indian ambassador to US, *The Economic Times*, 1 September 2017, http://economictimes.indiatimes.com/news/defence/india-shares-uss-concerns-over-pakistan-giving-safe-havens-to-terrorists-indian-ambassador-to-us/articleshow/60323277.cms, accessed on 20 September 2017.
96. Geeta Mohan, India welcomes US President Donald Trump's new Afghanistan strategy and tough stand on Pakistan, *India Today*, 22 August 2017.
97. Varghese K. George, 12 September 2017.
98. C. Raja Mohan, The Trump Discontinuity, *The Indian Express*, 24 August 2017.
99. Joy Mitra, Afghanistan: Case for Indian Military Assistance, *South Asian Voices*, 15 June 2017, https://southasianvoices.org/case-for-indian-military-assistance-to-afghanistan/, accessed on 26 August 2017.
100. Yashwant Raj, US says India's security concerns in Afghanistan same as Pakistan's, *Hindustan Times*, 7 September 2017.
101. C Raja Mohan, *ibid.*, 24 August 2017.
102. *Ibid.*
103. Kallol Bhattacharjee, India Welcomes Trump's New Afghan Policy, *The Hindu*, 22 August 2017.
104. Sreemoy Talikdar, Donald Trump's Afghanistan policy presents India a chance to increase sphere of influence in South Asia, *FirstPost*, 23 August 2017, http://www.firstpost.com/world/donald-trumps-afghanistan-policy-presents-india-a-chance-to-increase-sphere-of-influence-in-south-asia-3965687.html, accessed on 19 September 2017.
105. Javid Ahmad and Bharath Gopalaswamy, 1 September 2017.
106. *Ibid.*
107. Vidya Ram, India should not Fall for US Designs, *The Hindu*, 5 October 2017, p. 12.
108. Editorial, *The Hindu*, 25 September 2017, p. 8.
109. C. Raja Mohan, New Foray into the Great Game, *The Indian Express*, 26 September 2017, p. 9.
110. Devirupa Mitra, 22 August 2017.
111. PTI, Afghan Leader at UN Urges Dialogue with Pakistan, *The Indian Express*, 21 September 2017, p. 10.

112. Suhasini Haidar, India Plans to Train Afghan Police Officers, *The Hindu*, 23 September 2017, p. 10.
113. Vidya Ram, 5 October 2017.
114. Robert Burns, US: Victory in Afghanistan possible by facilitating Taliban reconciliation, *The Indian Express*, 14 March 2018, p. 12.
115. As the US Troops Withdraw, *The Hindu*, 30 January 2019, p. 12.
116. Successes and Challenges in Afghanistan and Pakistan, US Embassy in Afghanistan, 5 August 2015, https://af.usembassy.gov/successes-challenges-afghanistan-pakistan/, accessed on 20 April 2018.
117. M. Ashraf Haidari, 2017.
118. Quoted by Eikenberry 2014, p. 268, for details see, Mark McNeilly, Sun Tzu and Art of Modern Warfare, Oxford University Press, Oxford, 2001.
119. Afghanistan: Growing Challenges, International Crisis Group, 30 April 2017, https://www.crisisgroup.org/asia/south-asia/afghanistan/afghanistan-growing-challenges, accessed on 19 April 2018.
120. Taliban in Afghanistan, Council on Foreign Relations, 17 February 2018.
121. Afghanistan: Growing Challenges, International Crisis Group, 30 April 2017, https://www.crisisgroup.org/asia/south-asia/afghanistan/afghanistan-growing-challenges, accessed on 19 April 2018.
122. Tim Lister, 2018.
123. Julie Vitkovskaya, 2017.
124. M. Ashraf Haidari, 2017.
125. Julie Vitkovskaya, Four things to know about America's war in Afghanistan, *The Washington Post*, August 24, 2017, https://www.washingtonpost.com/news/checkpoint/wp/2017/08/24/what-you-need-to-know-about-the-longest-conflict-in-u-s-history-the-war-in-afghanistan/?utm_term=.66b471ca9e1b, accessed on 5 April 2018.
126. *Ibid.*
127. Daniel L. Davis, *The National Interest*, 31 May 2017, http://nationalinterest.org/blog/the-skeptics/americas-afghan-mission-no-longer-serving-its-purpose-20932, accessed on 5 April 2018.

128. John R. Bass, Pakistan source of 'significant challenges' in Afghanistan: US, *The Times of India*, 15 September 2017, https://timesofindia.indiatimes.com/world/pakistan/pakistan-source-of-significant-challenges-in-afghanistan-us/articleshow/60527596.cms, accessed on 21 April 2018.
129. Deepening Democracy, *The Hindu*, 31 January 2019, p. 12.
130. Ayesha Siddiqa, Carrot to Stick, *The Indian Express*, 5 September 2017, p. 8.
131. M. Zaidi, 4 September 2017.
132. Ayesha Siddiqa, 5 September 2017.
133. Khaled Ahmed, Like Cold War, *The Indian Express*, 16 September 2017, p. 9.
134. Sajjad Hussain, China, Russia assures support to Pak after Trump Criticism, *The Indian Express*, 14 September 2017, p. 10.
135. Erin Cunningham, While the US wasn't looking, Russia and Iran began carving out a bigger role in Afghanistan, *The Washington Post*, 13 April 2017, https://www.washingtonpost.com/world/asia_pacific/with-us-policy-in-flux-russia-and-iran-challenge-american-power-in-afghanistan/2017/04/12/f8c768bc-1eb8-11e7-bb59-a74ccaf1d02f_story.html?noredirect=on&utm_term=.e5aca38d6f57, accessed on 21 April 2018.
136. Aziz Amin Ahmadzai, *The Diplomat*, 2017.
137. Pompeo Promises a New Democratic Order, *The Hindu*, 5 December 2018, p. 12.
138. International Crisis Group, April 2017.
139. Mujib Mashal and Eric Schmitt, White House Orders Direct Talks with Taliban, *The Hindu*, 17 July 2018, p. 12.
140. *Ibid.*
141. Kathy Gannon, Taliban, US Hold Useful Peace Talks in Qatar, *The Indian Express*, 29 July 2018, p. 15.
142. *Ibid.*
143. C. Raja Mohan, 28 August 2018, p. 7.
144. Rosie Gray, Erik Prince's Plan to Privatize the War in Afghanistan, *The Atlantic*, 18 August 2017, https://www.theatlantic.com/politics/archive/2017/08/afghanistan-camp-david/537324/, accessed on 31 August 2018.
145. *Ibid.*

146. *The Indian Express*, 28 August 2018.
147. Rosie Gray, 18 August 2017.
148. C. Raja Mohan, 28 August 2018.
149. *Ibid.*
150. *Ibid.*
151. Privatization of Afghan War against the National Sovereignty, TOLO News, 12 August 2017, https://www.tolonews.com/afghanistan/privatization-afghan-war-against-national-sovereignty-karzai, accessed on 31 August 2018.
152. Agence France-Presse, US to Withdraw Troops from Afghanistan, *The Hindu*, 22 December 2018, p. 12.
153. Quoted by Ruchi Kumar, Chaging Peace in the Middle of War, *The Hindu*, 23 December 2018, p. 6.
154. Julia Gurganus, Russia's Afghanistan Strategy, *Foreign Affairs*, 2 January 2018, https://www.foreignaffairs.com/articles/afghanistan/2018-01-02/russias-afghanistan-strategy, accessed on 16 January 2019.
155. Amid Talks, Taliban Urge US to Exit Afghanistan or Face Defeat, *The Indian Express*, 28 December 2018, p. 9.
156. Simon Tisdall, The US and Afghanistan: can't win the war, can't stop it, can't leave, *The Guardian*, 1 May 2018, https://www.theguardian.com/world/2018/may/01/the-us-and-afghanistan-can't-win-the-war-can't-stop-it-can't-leave, accessed on 20 February 2019.
157. *Ibid.*
158. Tanisha M. Fazal and Sarah Kreps, The United States Perpetual War in Afghanistan, *Foreign Affairs*, 20 August 2018, https://www.foreignaffairs.com/articles/north-america/2018-08-20/united-states-perpetual-war-afghanistan, accessed on 20 February 2019.
159. *Ibid.*
160. *The Economic Times*, 11 October 2018, https://economictimes.indiatimes.com/news/defence/49-americans-say-us-mostly-failed-in-afghanistan-poll/articleshow/66161849.cms, accessed on 20 February 2019.
161. Simon Tisdall, 1 May 2018.

3

Russia: The Strategic Re-Involvement

Introduction

The Soviet Russia (USSR) had intervened in Afghanistan in 1979, and its proxy possession of Afghanistan brought multiple alternations inside Afghanistan including the inception of the anti-Soviet forces to send them back. But, despite the anti-Soviet inner public opinion which lasted for the longer period, the significance of Russia for Afghanistan and vice-versa is more relevant even today. Soviet Russia provided largest chunk of the aid (of the total by all countries included together), to Afghanistan in its early years of reconstruction, and "by 1973, it was estimated that the Soviet Union had lent close to a billion dollars to Afghanistan," and, "this accounted for 60 percent of all the civilian foreign aid reaching Afghanistan."[1] However, the internationalization of Afghanistan crisis has been considered from the Soviet intervention. Before the Soviet Union, the British also had proactively engaged with Afghanistan for its objectives. As mentioned earlier, Afghanistan was held as the buffer state between the Soviet Empire and the British Empire, and on the "Buffer State" position of Afghanistan, it was stated that "Contemporary Afghanistan...had become a true buffer state in exactly the way that England desired."[2] However, some scholars have described the Great Game between the British and the Soviet as just a "power-play against the rival power in the...Central Asia.... And for Britain...this rivalry was simply one of many pressing strategic concerns that extended around the globe."[3] It has believed that "...the British occupied Afghanistan in order to create a pro-British buffer state able to withstand the onward march of Russian influence...(but)...the British were baffled and defeated in their attempts to transform Afghanistan into the desired agent of British influence...."[4]

The involvement of Soviet Russia in Afghanistan, after long time since its great game with Britain, as reported, was considered since 1955 when it had provided military training and material to Afghanistan, and as has believed, in 1960, the Soviet's had grabbed the opportunity to make an alliance with Afghanistan on the issue of Pashtunistan when Pakistan had engaged in alliance with the US. And further during the skirmishes between Afghanistan and Pakistan in 1961, Pakistan had shut down the borders between them, because of which, Afghanistan had to export all its goods via the USSR, and that led to Afghan's fall under the Soviet influence.[5] Further, in the 1973, a third of active troops, against the Afghanistan's King Zahir, was trained on Soviet soil. This coup, as reported, was initiated by the former Prime Minister of Afghanistan, Mohammed Daud who had support of the People's Democratic Party of Afghanistan (PDPA), which was founded in 1965 based on the Marxist/Socialist ideology.[6] However, the Daud government could not run successfully and ended in disaster, and a small group of Soviet-trained Afghan officers (anti-Daud faction) had occupied the control of the Afghan government on 28 April 1978, and declared the establishment of Democratic Republic of Afghanistan, and subsequently, Daud and his family was executed. Nur Taraki was made the President of Afghanistan who started the programmes of land redistribution, changed the status of women, and also the destruction of the old social order in Afghanistan. However, the internal strife in Afghanistan between anti- and pro-Soviet factions continued, and Afghanistan faced armed revolts in the entire country. Taking the cognizance of the situation there, as a result, the Soviet involvement in Afghanistan began since April 1978. Further, in September 1979, Taraki's Prime Minister, Hafizulluah Amin, a dissent, seized the control of government killing Taraki. But Amin's rule reached to chaos as he could not run efficiently.[7] In this context, it was stated that the Soviet leaders "had hoped that a rapid and complete military takeover would secure Afghanistan's place as an exemplar of the Brezhnev Doctrine, which held that once a country became socialist, Moscow would never permit it to return to the capitalist camp."[8] Afghanistan was facing civil wars between the pro-Soviet faction and the Islamic insurgents. The internal situation in Afghanistan was grappled with severe hostility and the Islamic insurgents were dominating to control the power. During this time, as reported, Soviet Russia sent its combat troops to three places: Kabul, Bagram Air Base outside of Kabul and the airbase at Shendan to the West.[9] Consequently, the Soviet military intervention provoked the US under President Carter to supply non-lethal aid to Islamic insurgents who were well known as Afghan mujahedeen. In fact, after the execution of the pro-Soviet leader, the Soviets resentment observed heightening, and consequently, the Soviet started assembling its forces near the Afghan borders. In fact, during this time, due to lack of strong leadership, the Afghan Army could not provide required basic security to the government of the day against the Islamic insurgents who were approaching to Kabul. The USSR President Leonid Brezhnev believed intervention as an only option to stop chaos in Afghanistan.

The Soviet Intervention

On 25 December 1979, the Soviet Union sent about 1,00,000 troops into Afghanistan that led to immediate possession of the complete military and political establishments of Afghanistan, and also maintained a friendly and socialist government in Afghanistan by suppressing the prevailing civil war there. This was reported as the first event during the cold war that the Soviet Union made military intervention in a country outside the Eastern Bloc.[10] In fact, this was, as believed, the second Soviet intervention in Afghanistan as the Soviet had a failed covert operation in 1929.[11] The Soviet forces in Afghanistan killed the leader of the Islamic insurgents and set up a new government making Babrak Karmal as a head who became Soviet's puppet giving the Soviet further opportunity to continue its domination in Afghanistan till 1988. In fact, justifying its intervention, the Soviet Russia stated that "the Soviet army's mission was to establish advantageous conditions to prevent possible actions by the governments of neighbouring countries against Afghanistan."[12] However, Soviet intervention was globally condemned especially by the US-led countries (NATO), as a part of cold war politics and they also started maneuvering for the withdrawal of the Soviet Union from Afghanistan under West's containment of communism policy. It has reported that

> By January 1, 1980, the Soviets had injected at least 50,000 men and 200 aircraft into Afghanistan along with a wide variety of armored vehicles, heavy artillery, and sophisticated anti aircraft gun indicating they may have expected resistance from the Afghan air force in addition to the Afghan Army. Another four Soviet motorized infantry divisions (approximately 50,000 men) were concentrated north of the border and constitute a reserve force which could be transported quickly to the south to augment Soviet occupation forces if the necessity should arise.[13]

In fact, "the Soviet plan was to stabilize the situation, strengthen the Afghan army, and withdraw the bulk of Soviet forces within three years," however, the Soviet occupation of Afghanistan lasted for about ten years and "over 525,500 officers, sergeants, soldiers and support staff of the Soviet armed forces served in Afghanistan."[14] But the Soviet forces had to face tough fight from the Mujahedeen as the Afghan's national army was not capable enough for fighting against the Mujahedeen. It has believed that the military leadership was recommended for the withdrawal, but the Soviet Russia had been facing leadership crisis to take appropriate decision. However, with the change in leadership in the USSR, and when in March 1985 Gorbachev came in power, he decided to withdraw its forces from Afghanistan, and consequently, withdrawal began in 1988 and completed in February 1989. In this invasion, "the Soviet forces killed 1.3 million people and forced 5.5 million Afghans to leave the country as refugees."[15] Further, according to another source, during the Soviet involvement for about ten years of brutal conflict in Afghanistan, it was estimated that "one million civilians...90,000 Mujahedeen fighters, 18,000 Afghan troops, and 14,500 Soviet soldiers" were killed.[16]

Consequently, the USSR's Afghan mission fetched no success. According to the former Soviet Ambassador to America, Anatoly Dobrynin, "the Soviet decision to invade Afghanistan was a gross miscalculation."[17] Further when Soviet Russia withdrawn, Afghanistan was left in a shattered situation only to fall its power in the Taliban's control, which, by grabbing major opportunity, consolidated terrorism in the country and also provided training base for Osama bin Laden. It was reported that

> By 1982, the Mujahedeen controlled 75% of Afghanistan despite fighting the might of the world's second most powerful military power. Young conscript Russian soldiers were no match against men fuelled by their religious belief. Though the Russian army had a reputation, the war in Afghanistan showed the world just how poor it was outside of military displays. Army boots lasted no more than 10 days before falling to bits in the harsh environment of the Afghanistan Mountains. Many Russian soldiers deserted to the Mujahedeen. Russian tanks were of little use in the mountain passes.[18]

Furthermore,

> The Soviet Union left Afghanistan in a humiliating 1989 defeat after a war that killed at least 15,000 Red Army soldiers fighting in the name of Communism against mujahedeen insurgents backed by the United States. The war devastated Afghanistan, killing at least one million citizens, ravaging its agriculture and creating a crippling refugee crisis that is still taking its toll on the country today. The Soviet invasion is largely seen as the beginning of the violence, and chaos in Afghan still live in, the start of what they are now calling their forty years of war.[19]

The American President Carter, because of cold-war rivalry, held the Soviet intervention in Afghanistan as "the greatest threat to peace since World War II,"[20] or a "grave threat to peace" and a "blatant violation of international rules of behavior."[21] Furthermore, after the Soviet invasion, due to increasing tensions between America and the Soviet Union, in 1983, the American President Reagan also had called the Soviet Union as "Evil

Empire".[22] However, "the Soviet war in Afghanistan in effect marked the end of empire. And it contributed to a decline in communist ideology and geopolitical conviction in Moscow," and was held as "the bankruptcy of the communist system."[23]

With this development, as has mentioned earlier, the US, China and Pakistan had supplied arms and support to the Afghan rebels against the Soviet forces in Afghanistan. Pakistan had sent seven army divisions to the Afghan border by mid-January 1980. China had infiltrated its "900 agents in Afghanistan near its 85 km-long border in Wakhan to arm and support the Maoist Shola-e-Javed group to fight against the Soviet's troops."[24] However, the Soviet invasion in Afghanistan was seen both the ways: success or failures. But mostly, according to the observations, it was a failure. Braithwaite stated the factors of Soviet's failure in Afghanistan that:

> There force was too small to hold the ground; they were unable to seal the frontier with Pakistan; the rebels received massive foreign aids from Pakistan, US, China, Saudi Arabia, Iran; governmental and popular will collapsed inside the Soviet Union; the Soviet aim of transforming Afghan society was unrealistic—most Afghans were determined not to accept what was an offer; and the Mujahedeen had the time, while the Soviets had only the watches.[25]

After the Soviet invasion, Pakistan along with the United States compelled Afghanistan to become a graveyard for the Red Army, and subsequently, forced Soviet withdrawal. On the other side, over the 1990s, Russia along with India and Iran supported the Northern Alliance against the rebellion groups backed by Pakistan and Saudi Arabia—first, Gulbuddin Hekmatyar's Hezb-i Islami (HIG) and later the Afghan Taliban.[26] In fact, it has stated that "the pernicious legacies of the 1979-1988 Soviet War in Afghanistan also ensure that Russian troop deployments are likely to be met with fierce public resistance" and, as has stated that the Russian public's apathy towards political crises in the Middle East and South Asia was an enduring consequence of Moscow's ill-fated military intervention in Afghanistan.[27] As has mentioned by Digg what William Odom had observed on the

Soviet invasion in Afghanistan that: "The most significant effect of the war in Afghanistan was the loss of the Soviet military's image of invincibility. Earlier interventions in Eastern Europe had quickly restored communist rule; but almost 10 years of fighting failed to achieve that in Afghanistan."[28]

Russia's Interests in Afghanistan

Russia's re-involvement in Afghanistan after the collapse of the Taliban regime in 2001 increased the debates amongst many experts of international relations that: What Russia is looking for in Afghanistan again? In fact, Russia's interest in Afghanistan is not new, but, in the 19th century Soviet Russia had extended its imperial expansion in the Central Asian region. During this time, Britain had also extended its empire in India, and the competition and conflicts for imperial expansion between the Soviet Russia and Britain has been well-known in the world history as a Great Game. The Soviet Russia had feared the British expansion in Central Asia, a very significant region close to its Southern border, that the British had been posing threats to its territory. As quoted by Sir Rodric Braithwaite, in 1838, General Perovski formulated the British threat in the words that "If the British succeed in establishing themselves in Kabul it would be only a step for (them) to reach Bukhara; Central Asia would be subjected to their influence, our Asian trade would be ruined, they might arm...our Asian neighbours against us, and supply them with powder, weapons and money."[29] And after this it has believed that British attacked the Soviet Russia twice. By controlling Kabul, British had to achieve its objectives in the region against the Soviets that of the controlling of Afghan's foreign policy and the de-influencing of Soviets in Kabul, though by conspiracy.[30] However, it has believed that "after the series of the successful campaigns in Central Asia in the 1860s," the Soviet Russia "reached to the borders of Afghanistan 50 years after the British."[31]

After the long time, Soviet Russia re-entered Afghanistan in 1979 and stayed there for a decade. Since its withdrawal from Afghanistan and its disintegration in 1991, which later came to be known as Russian Federation, Russia further appeared returning back in Afghanistan with a new grand strategy in the region. It has also observed that Russia had supported the US's attack on the Taliban Regime in Afghanistan in 2001 and indulged in toppling down of the Taliban regime. Because of the Taliban's terrorist activities and 9/11 incidence, in fact, perhaps Afghanistan has been the only place in the world, where the US and Russia did not clash against each other as the rivals of the cold-war politics.[32] And further, it was the Obama administration, when both Russia and the US had reached to adequate cooperation in Afghanistan. During this time "Moscow allowed US and NATO forces to transport equipment and supplies through Russian territory, sold Russian Mi-17 helicopters to US-supported Afghan forces, and worked with the United States to curb opium production and stem the wider drug trade."[33] The Russian support to the US's war on terror in Afghanistan was premised on its struggle against Islamic fundamentalism which had entered in its territory through the Afghan soil. Even for that matter Russia wanted to be the US partner against the war on terror, especially against the Taliban. Russia had a plan to curb the Islamic Fundamentalism with the help of the US-led forces in the Central Asian region, as a result, Russia allowed the US-led NATO forces to set up military bases close to Russian territory in the Central Asia to launch attacks against the Taliban. But, the US could not defeat the Taliban and the US war against the Taliban stretched towards the Afghan-Pakistan border. The US war in Afghanistan remained failed and unaccomplished. Moreover, since longtime both Russia and the US had largely common objectives in Afghanistan especially "preventing chaos and the reemergence of the safe havens for terrorists."[34] Therefore, both appeared working together during this time to fight against the Al-Qaeda. However, the rivalry between them has been discernibly eternal.

Subsequently, after the collapse of the Taliban regime, Russia learnt that the Western forces led by the US in Afghanistan seemed to be lasting long that developed Russia's skeptical perception making the atmosphere of distrust in the region. Therefore, during Russian-Afghan Forum in Moscow on 14 May 2009, Russia criticized "the western troops indirectly for their ineffective control of poppy cultivation and drug-trafficking....

The growth of drug production in Afghanistan coincided with the increase in the number of foreign armed forces, and that most of the drug cartels were located in the areas under US and NATO responsibility."[35] Therefore, with this observation, Russia's involvement in Afghanistan remained in tact. Further, Russia learnt that the US strategy failing in Afghanistan, and Russia was confident that the US was not going to leave the base, and established bilateral relations with the Central Asian countries as well in view of procuring, along with other interests, the oil and energy resources. Therefore, Russia "realized very early that promoting its development strategy to exploit Afghanistan's natural resources and intensify cross border trade required significant investments in the extension of Afghanistan's transportation and communication infrastructure."[36] Moreover, Russia realized that the US's war on terrorism or Islamic fundamentalism was hypocritical.[37] As a result, Russia decided its own strategy towards the stability of Afghanistan, and with the changing direction of the wind, Russia established links with the Taliban. In fact, while Asia was becoming the centre of world power politics, Russia, one of the major global powers, could not abstain from the developments in international politics especially in its volatile hinterland as a neutral power in the region. Therefore, since when the US President Obama had declared the withdrawal of the US-led international forces from Afghanistan by December 2014, Russia seemingly started relooking its foreign policy towards Afghanistan with broader specifically well-defined objectives in the war-torn country to be accomplished in 'the post-2014 Afghanistan'. Moreover, "Russia is a key player in combating the threats associated with drugs and radicalism."[38] However, among all other major foreign policy objectives towards Afghanistan, Russia's special interests are to 'Stabilize Afghanistan', to maintain 'Regional Hegemony' especially in Central Asia, and "Russian fluctuations towards Afghanistan since 2001 stemming from changes in its perceived interests and its prioritization of these two objectives," and to re-seeking 'Global Strategy.'[39] Further, according to the analysts, Russia had three-fold evolving strategy in Afghanistan that to "bolster regional security cooperation, provide limited direct support to the Afghan Government in the form of training, weapons and resource, and continue indirect support to the remaining ISAF forces."[40] However, its three-fold strategy remained unaccomplished. It has stated that

> Russian interests vis-à-vis Afghanistan are driven by threats rather than by opportunities; Moscow does not hope much to gain from Afghanistan, but rather it seeks to prevent outcomes that would adversely affect the Russian Federation. The Kremlin's priorities may fluctuate, but the core issues guiding its policy remain constant. Moscow expresses four enduring concerns in Afghanistan: instability, drugs trafficking, US and NATO presence and international terrorism.[41]

According to the Security Council of Russia, there are main three security challenges to the country: illicit drug trafficking, terrorism and illegal migration, and in this context, "the situation in Afghanistan is the prime source of the first threat and has a serious connection with the second and is possibly linked to the third one."[42] In fact, after 9/11, Moscow supported the US-led coalition in Afghanistan, which ousted the Taliban and brought back to power elements of the Northern Alliance that Russia had supported. The post-9/11 Afghan war and broader global war on terror also gave Moscow space to brutally crush the Chechen insurgency, which had been taken over by Salafi jihadists after Russia sidelined Chechen Sufi separatists. Russia also provided diplomatic and logistical support for a sizable US military presence in its backyard. From 2009 to 2015, Russia served as a supply route for the US and NATO forces through what was known as the Northern Distribution Network (NDN), which lessened Washington's dependence on Islamabad for the Pakistan-based ground lines of communication into Afghanistan.[43] Furthermore, according to Braithwaite, Russia's Afghan Policy has been driven by four main motives; "to ensure that the government in Kabul remained friendly to the Soviet Union; to limit, or if possible to exclude, American influence; to limit the effect of fundamental Islam; to interdict the drug traffic."[44]

Counter Terrorism and Security Interest: Russia perceives terrorist activities as security threat to its territory having border with the Central Asian countries. In fact, Russia, in its National Security Concept of 2000, had included terrorism as one of the primary threats to its national security, and according to this concept, as Russia viewed that the international terrorists had been "waging an open campaign to destabilize Russia," and this was hinted at the threat from the Taliban.[45] The Russian President Vladimir Putin sees Islamic States activities in the region especially in Afghanistan may put potential threat to Russian interests. Russia perceived the main sources of its security threats from terrorism in Central Asia, the presence of the US in Central Asian states and Afghanistan, and the Taliban which was active in Afghanistan and Pakistan, and importantly, the lateral entry of the ISIS in Russia's security threat panic.[46] Unlike Iraq and Syria, Russia wants to contain the presence of the Islamic State in the Central Asian countries and in Afghanistan. In fact, Russia's 2013 Foreign Policy Concept considered the situation of Afghanistan a crisis, which coupled with the withdrawal of international forces posing a great threat to Russia and other CIS countries.[47] It has reported that in 2014, the ISIS expanded to Afghanistan, which Russia fears that may lead to its expansion especially in the north of Afghanistan and further into Central Asia and Russia. The Taliban and the ISIS militants remained engaged in fighting against each other across Afghanistan since the IS entered the country and both the militant groups tried seeking to establish dominance in the country in which Taliban emerged winning Afghans' power, and "Russia fears that Afghanistan may become another safe haven for the so-called Islamic State (IS) militant group after Iraq and Syria."[48] Russia saw the development of embryonic presence of the Islamic States militants in the Af-Pak region that has panic Russia that they may establish their links with the Central Asian dysfunctional forces.[49] By learning this, Russia adroitly felt the significance of the Taliban in its interests against the IS, so, without losing any chance, grabbed the opportunity to form relations with the Taliban. Even the Taliban also learnt the Russian antagonism to the Islamic States. Believing in the dictum of "befriending the enemy's enemy," as a result, both Russia and the Taliban came close to each other to counter the threat posed by the Islamic State. In fact, Russia established its relations with the Taliban in 2007 to discuss the issue of drug trafficking through Central Asian countries that share borders with Afghanistan. However, the present Russia's involvement in Afghanistan was premised, as reported, on the logic of the consolidation of footsteps of the US and also its failing policies in Afghanistan.[50] According to Russian Upper House Senator Alexey Pushkov, "the United States lost the war in Afghanistan due to Bush's reckless use of force and Obama's inability to end the war in a timely fashion."[51] Even Presidents Trump and later Biden also could not do any substantial except of leaving the mission unaccomplished. However, Russia justified its stand with the Taliban as an agreement just for peace establishment in Afghanistan. And Russia believed that "the group (Taliban) is focused on gaining power over territory within Afghanistan, and is therefore a threat to Afghanistan's government but not a danger beyond the country's borders," and therefore, both Russia and the Taliban have common interest of defeating the Islamic States which has been operating from Afghanistan and Pakistan.[52] Given the developments in the region, Russia regularly made contacts with the Taliban and also organized meetings with China, the Taliban and Pakistan to discuss the Afghan issues. Surprisingly, Afghanistan government was not included in these meetings. According to Michael Kugelman, an expert at the Washington-based Woodrow Wilson International Center for Scholars, "Russia is taking a risk by turning to the Taliban... Russia is strengthening a non-state actor that is a formidable rival of IS, a terrorist group that worries Russia a whole lot."[53] However, earlier, Russia was against the US-led NATO's "efforts to engage with or even to 'buy off' the Taliban, considering this to ultimately imply a return to power of the Taliban."[54] Even for that matter during the US intervention in Afghanistan in 2001, as has mentioned earlier, Russia had also supported the stringent actions against the increasing Taliban-dominated insurgency in and around Afghanistan. However, Russia reversed its stand on the Taliban. In December 2016, the Russian Foreign Ministry made it public that Russia has been engaged with the Taliban in the field of "intelligence sharing" for their common "fight against the Islamic State," and has believed that "Russia's regional collaboration with Iran and Turkey on Syria, which have brought it some success, suggest it may look to pursue a similar approach in Afghanistan by bringing Iran, China, and Pakistan together."[55]

Narco-Terrorist Threat: Afghanistan is also considered as the source of threat to Russia in terms of narcotics.[56] Afghanistan produces the largest amount of opium in the world and its production gradually mushroomed near to record despite the presence of the US-led International Forces. It has blamed that the US administration has deliberately ignored the curbing of the production of opium in Afghanistan as it was not much affected by the use of the drugs or the problem of drugs addiction in America, and consequently, was never interested in curbing drug trafficking. Afghanistan supplies narcotics to the Central Asian countries and through which it reaches to Russia. Russia is the largest consumer market of the opium, and Afghanistan supplies about 90 percent of the heroin to Russia which it considers a major problem for the Russian society. The drug trafficking runs from the Northern Afghanistan (stronghold of earlier Northern Alliance) to Russia.[57] It has reported that "Russia consumes around a fifth of the world's illegal opiate supply and is afflicted by a heroin addiction epidemic."[58] About 70,000 people dies every year due to illicit drug use.[59] Therefore, Russia sees the curbing of narco-terrorist threats in its foreign policy towards Afghanistan. In this direction, Russian policymakers believed that "the Taliban can be a better partner than Afghanistan's National Unity Government" in curbing or fighting against narcotics threat, as in fact, opium is one of the largest sources of the Taliban's income.[60] And therefore, Russia engaged with the Taliban, however, it has stated that Russia cannot justify its engagement with latter solely on the plea of elimination of opium from Afghanistan. In fact, it has been crystal clear that the Taliban would never stop supporting opium production there as opium generates large chunk of its income about $400 million annually. Moreover, Russian meetings and ties with the Taliban since 2007 have not resulted in the reduction of opium reduction. Therefore, for this, only a stable and powerful government of Afghanistan holds the capability of addressing the challenge of narcotics in Afghanistan, and not the Taliban.[61] Moreover, besides, it has also stated that "Even if a primary goal behind Russia's ties with Taliban is sincerely fighting the Islamic State, Moscow is making a strategic mistake, since the Taliban cannot eliminate ISIS by themselves", as, in fact, in the past, most of the ISIS fighters in Afghanistan were the members of the Taliban, therefore, the possibility was held that more Russian-backed Taliban might be joining the Islamic State later in the future. Therefore, "Russian support to the Taliban will only further deteriorate the security in Afghanistan."[62]

Russia's Energy Policy in Eurasia: Central Asia is enriched with vast reservoir of hydrocarbons, and the region also serves as the avenue for the international energy communication. In terms of Russia's energy and hydrocarbon ambitions in the Eurasian region, Afghanistan holds a very significant place in Russia's foreign policy. But, Russia sees the consistently prevailing Afghan problem putting specific impediments in its ambitions in the region. Afghanistan is called as the 'Potential Energy Corridor' since 1991. In fact, Russia wanted to dominate the region and not to allow any other power to be settled in its backyard to challenge its hegemonic position in the region.[63] Besides, Russia has also substantial economic interest in Afghanistan. And therefore, keeping all the economic interests in mind, Russia has tried to put optimum efforts to normalize the civil war and the influence of other major powers, especially its rival powers, the USA, and to transform the conflicting situation in Afghanistan into a congenial ambience.

The Great Powers Game: The Russian perspective in Afghanistan vested in the Kautilya's dictum of 'befriending enemy's enemy'. The Russian standing with the Taliban directly indicated that Russia was undoubtedly intervening Afghanistan against the US as the US policy in Afghanistan was focused on 'the elimination of the Taliban'. As usual, the old cold-war rivalry, as observed, appeared taking place in and around Afghanistan. The fact of the matter is that Russia, China, Iran, Pakistan, and the Taliban were standing in tandem against the US presence in the region generally and Afghanistan particularly. Initially, when the US intervened in Afghanistan, Russia had some positive expectations in favour of its strategic interests, but, Russia had to suffer from the delusion. According to Arif Rafiq, "Surprisingly, Afghanistan is emerging as another arena in which Moscow is pointedly working at odds with Washington's interests. Indeed, recent moves by Russia now represent a pivot toward Afghanistan, posing a set of challenges that have been unanticipated by US observers of the region."[64]

Furthermore, the trilateral dialogue between Russia, China, and Pakistan over the Afghanistan issue was held in December 2016. However, this dialogue provided no space to the other major actors in the region, neither even Afghanistan, the US and nor India. The joint statement of the trilateral dialogue was to talk with the Taliban and the concerns over the Islamic States presence in Afghanistan and the region. In fact, Russia has embraced Pakistan's partnership in the region as against India's painful relations with Pakistan that has further increased India's concerns raising doubts over the future of India-Russia relations. Pakistan had been the US's cold-war ally, however, the developments can be seen from the perspective that there are no permanent friends and enemies in the international politics, only national interest matters. Accordingly, Russia-Pakistan-China equation can be seen. In broader sense, Russian peeping into Afghanistan was largely based on long-term presence of the US there, which had potential of threat to Russia as its policy makers perceived.

In the post-2014, in fact, Russia proactively involved in Afghanistan because of the US failure in winning over the Taliban. That might have been the happy moment for Russia, but, with the declaration of New Afghan Policy by the US President Donald Trump on 22 August 2017, it further increased the Russian panic. Trump declared of pouring more troops in Afghanistan to 'kill or defeat the Taliban'. Consequently, Russia became more concern and active in the region, however, this time, not alone but together with China and Pakistan, of course, consolidating relations with the Taliban. In fact, earlier "Russia has long been prepared for the ISAF withdrawal"[65] from Afghanistan, but that went in vain. Moreover, it has also analyzed that the US presence in Afghanistan also boosted Russia's interest. As it has felt that everything would collapse in Afghanistan if the US troops were withdrawn from the conflict zone.[66] In this context, it has opined that

> Even though Kremlin officials have frequently criticized Washington's handling of the Afghan security crisis and have urged the US to withdraw from Afghanistan, a closer examination of Russia's strategic interests reveals that Trump's new Afghanistan strategy could help consolidate Russia's role as a major stakeholder in Afghanistan. Therefore, Russian policymakers are likely to grudgingly accept Trump's decision to maintain and selectively expand Washington's military presence in Afghanistan for the foreseeable future.[67]

Further, it was held that the US New Afghan Policy "to expand counterterrorism operations in Afghanistan aids Russia's efforts to stabilize the country in two critical ways":

> First, Trump's decision to maintain a US military presence in Afghanistan allows Russia to influence the security situation in Afghanistan through diplomatic pressure on Washington, rather than through the deployment of its own military personnel. Second, Russian policymakers believe that an expanded US military presence in Afghanistan will prevent the Taliban from further expanding its territory and steer the Taliban towards embracing Russia's vision for a political resolution of the Afghanistan war.[68]

In other words, with the US presence and its military expansion in Afghanistan, Russia wished to influence the Taliban and the situation inside Afghanistan to accomplish its strategic interests. However, as has stated earlier, Russia and the Taliban regularly sat together for making a counter strategy against the US presence as an obstacle in their objective. By supporting the Taliban, Russia intended to put major impediments to the US and its ally's interests in the region. Besides, Russia also wishes to expand its influence beyond the Central Asian region especially covering Afghanistan and Pakistan. Further, by establishing close relations with Pakistan, Russia had a plan to establish network with the Taliban. In September 2016, in view of consolidating partnership, the Russian and Pakistani Special Forces conducted their first-ever joint military exercise in the north of Pakistan. Pakistan also has been supporting the Taliban since its establishment. In fact, Pakistan has been notorious, around the world, for its support to the militant groups. However, it has predicted that henceforth, Russia's ties with the Taliban may dilute the international criticism of Pakistan and both would share the burden of.[69] It has also believed that "ISIS's growing presence in Afghanistan could force Moscow to deploy military personnel to the war-ravaged country."[70] However, on this issue, it was expressed that

> A Russian military intervention in Afghanistan is likely to command little popular support, unless there is a major terror attack on Russian soil that can be demonstrably linked to instability in Afghanistan. Therefore, Putin's Afghanistan strategy remains premised on influencing Washington's Afghanistan policy through indirect means, instead of deploying Russian military personnel to Afghanistan. A key element of Russia's indirect pressure strategy in Afghanistan is credibly invoking the threat of a military retaliation or counter-deployment if Washington's Afghanistan strategy fails to accommodate Moscow's security concerns. The Trump administration's desire to avoid Russia-US proxy war in Afghanistan could convince the US military to address issues of strategic importance to Russia as it attempts to resolve Afghanistan's political crisis. By threatening a military retaliation, Russian officials believe that they can convince the US military to aggressively crack down on the traffic of unmarked planes that provide weapons to ISIS and step up efforts to curb the flow of illegal drugs into the CIS region. As the Trump administration is seeking to prevent revenues from Afghanistan's illegal drug trade from reaching the Taliban and to combat terrorism in Afghanistan, Russia's indirect pressure strategy could eventually provide a foundation for tactical cooperation on issues of shared importance.[71]

Russia's Diplomatic Relations

After the British departure from Afghanistan, in 1955, the Soviet Russian President Khrushchev had visited Afghanistan and told there that the Americans had planned to establish military base there in Afghanistan. In fact, after the British left the region, Soviet Russia perceived that America might be filling the vacuum in the region that posing threat to its influence and interest in the region.[72] However, with these developments, during the mid-1970s, the Soviet Russia had become the most important country to cultivate relations with Afghanistan, followed by India, to put pressure on Pakistan over the issue of Pashtunistan.[73] After the Indo-Soviet Friendship Treaty in 1971, Afghanistan also became dependent on the Soviet Union for the military and economic support. Subsequently, in 1978, the Soviet-Afghan Treaty of Friendship was signed. This 20-year "treaty of friendship, good neighborliness and cooperation," was signed by Soviet President Leonid Brezhnev and Afghan Prime Minister Noor Mohammad Taraki in a Kremlin ceremony. According to treaty, both the states agreed that they would have mutual economic, military, and technical aid and that both the countries also would continue to develop cooperation in the military field on the basis of appropriate mutual agreements between them. In fact, it has stated that this treaty helped the Soviet Union to achieve dominance over the Afghan government under Taraki and strengthened its influence in the volatile and struggling Afghanistan. However, this treaty and thereafter developments made the Western bloc led by the US uncomfortable, as they observed the expansion of the Soviet Union and its ideology. In this context, it was stated that

> The strong Moscow influence has upset Western strategists, worried about the impact on troubled Iran to the west, as well as on the other Persian Gulf states whose oil is vital to the West. The Afghan developments also are seen as a threat to Pakistan to the east, which itself is plagued by a protracted government crisis. The Afghans and Pakistanis have long contended over Baluchistan in southern Pakistan. The Taraki government could give covert aid to a leftist separatist Baluchi movement, which could in turn contribute to destabilization of the power balance in the Arabian Sea area. The Russians since czarist times have eyed the area for a possible warm water port. East-West

> maneuvering and influence in the remote, landlocked country of hill tribesmen and nomadic shepherds dates to the last century, when Britain sought to blunt those expansionist Russian aims."[74]

In fact, this treaty was seen as the dependence of Afghan leaders on the Soviet Union for the ideological, economic, and military support, and also the Soviets eagerness to "exploit the opportunity in a country with borders that front directly on nations in the Western camp." The friendship treaty specifically declared that the Soviet Union "respects the policy of nonalignment" of the Taraki government. However, Taraki repeatedly stressed that he had been pursuing a policy of neutrality.[75] After the long period of Soviet intervention about more than two decades, Russia found re-seeking to play significant role in Afghanistan in terms of economy and military cooperation. However, in fact, during the 1990s, especially against the Taliban Regime, Russia extended its efforts in building anti-Taliban alliance of the Afghans. Further, after the overthrow of the Taliban, Russia signed an agreement with the Transitional Afghan government led by Hamid Karzai in December 2002 to provide military and technical assistance. And from 2002 to 2005, it has believed that Russia's military and technical assistance to Afghanistan was reported more than $200 million.[76] During his first visit to Russia from 20-21 January 2011 after a long time by any Afghan President, while addressing the Russian Diplomatic Academy in Moscow, President of Afghanistan, Hamid Karzai stated, "Russia is a great political, economic and military power. In the past years our bilateral relations have significantly strengthened. We see Russia as a neighbour and important partner and want to develop good ties with this partner."[77] This was held as the positive step towards the building of healthy relationship between them after the long experiences of various bilateral differences since the Soviet withdrawal in 1989. Further, strengthening the bilateral relations between them, the Russian Ambassador to Afghanistan, Andrey Avetisyan said in February 2011 that "Russia and Afghanistan may not share common border these days but we are still neighbours very close to each other, and I dare say, understanding each other better now, like the two old friends who may part, come through difficult times but keep thinking about each other and eventually get together again."[78]

Moreover, the then President of Russia Dmitry Medvedev also exhibited honest gesture in rebuilding bilateral relations with Afghanistan. On Medvedev's gesture of friendliness towards Afghanistan, it was believed that "Russia is picking up from where the former USSR left in terms of resuming economic and military assistance to Afghanistan. He talked of reviving some of old Soviet-era projects, rather than initiating new ones, and that to mainly in the northern parts of the country."[79] In fact, appreciating Soviet Union's model and constructive role and its investment in Afghanistan, Hamid Karzai as a President stated that the Soviet money went to the right place and they were efficient in spending their money through the government of Afghanistan. Further, the Russian President Vladimir Putin stated, "I am certain that friendly ties and co-operation between Russia and Afghanistan in the future will add to the goodness and welfare of our people."[80] However, Russia has confined its involvement in Afghanistan to multilateral diplomacy, and the arms sales to disparate political factions. By and large, Russia's increased involvement in Afghanistan includes business investment proposals, diplomatic outreach, cultural programs, and financial and military support for the central government, power brokers in the north, and the Taliban. In 2014, it reopened a cultural center in Kabul.[81] In fact, Russia sought re-establishment of engagement with Afghanistan by using various means such as NATO-Russia Council, the SCO, Engaging Pakistan, and emphasis on coordination between the NATO and CSTO (Collective Security Treaty Organization) and other available means.[82]

Economic Aid and Reconstruction

After the World War II, Soviet Russia had provided $3.5 million loan for the infrastructure development such as construction of roads, and others including a grain elevator, a mill and a bakery in Kabul in 1954. By renewing the Soviet-Afghan treaty in 1955, the USSR got major opportunity to enter in the economic and political sphere of Afghanistan. In fact, Soviet

Russia was seeking economic cooperation with Afghanistan by freeing it from the influence of the Western capitalist powers, and to increase its self-sufficiency. For this, the Soviet Russia "tried to influence Afghan's economic production and foreign trade by inducing a deviation of commodity flows towards the USSR," moreover, "a loan of $100 million given to Afghanistan in 1956...."[83] In fact, the engagement between Soviet Russia and Afghanistan was based on "strategic, economic and ideological motivations and understanding...."[84] The Soviet Russia provided considerable budget support and economic assistance, and by this means, the Soviet Russia established itself as the most important trade partner of Afghanistan.[85] For the purpose of development of economic sectors in Afghanistan keeping its interests in mind, Soviet Russia started the construction of the road networks and highways and bridges connecting different parts of the country mostly in the northern and eastern provinces. During 1960s, Soviet Russia helped Afghanistan in modernizing the Naghlu Hydro Power Plant in the Kabul province and also the building of small power generation facilities in other provinces in Afghanistan. In fact, the Soviet Union had significant economic engagement with Afghanistan before 1978 and, by 1978, had built Afghanistan's main roads, and had provided more than $1.2 billion to Afghanistan as an economic aid, and it has also reported that Soviet Russia became the third largest economic aids provider to Afghanistan by 1978.[86] Moreover, in 1978, there were about 2000 Soviet technical and economic experts and advisers in Afghanistan.[87] However, during 1970s and 1980s, the Soviet Union's engagement in the transport and communication sectors was decreased. But Soviet developmental assistance in other various sector remained continued during the period of its invasion in Afghanistan. The Soviet Russia assisted in installing and constructing the extraction machinery and mechanism and pipeline networks for the natural gas in the country and "until 1980s, the USSR successfully maintained a monopoly on the surveying and exploration of mineral deposits in Afghanistan."[88] In fact, the USSR's engagement with Afghanistan in terms of industrialization and other infrastructure development and irrigation or "irrigation complex" and agricultural research was at the larger extent, and, as a result, Afghanistan became dependent on Russian "technology, spare parts, technical education and knowledge."[89] Besides, Russia also had opportunity to contribute in the reconstruction of Afghan's Salang Tunnel. Between 1955 and 1979, the USSR had provided economic and military assistance worth of $2 billion, and military advisors and training to Afghanistan.[90] Further, it has reported that after the formation of the PDPA government in 1978 and the Soviet intervention in 1979, "dramatically changed Soviet strategic objectives and the corresponding economic policies."[91] However, the Soviet assistance to Afghanistan remained continued till 1992 even after its withdrawal from Afghanistan in February 1989. Further, due to its disintegration that creating the "Russian Federation", and the resuming and escalation of the civil war in Afghanistan, the Russian investment and infrastructure projects in Afghanistan suffered heavily.[92] The domestic situation in Afghanistan deteriorated further with the emergence of the Taliban and its war with the opposition forces in the country. The agricultural fields started to be used for poppy cultivation. It has reported that even after the end of the Taliban regime, during the period 2004-07, poppy was cultivated on the lands that was prepared by the Soviets for the irrigation projects.[93] After, in fact, its disintegration, Russia avoided to pay much attention towards the newly independent Central Asian countries to escape from the economic burden and other responsibilities. However, with these changes, Russia observed new developments in the region bordering Russia. For example, the increasing cultivation of poppy and new drug-trafficking route through the Russian territory was emerged that affecting or posing the health threat to its society, and, other was the threat to the Central Asian countries from the Islamic Extremism of Uzbekistan.[94] And in such a critical situation, only Russia had a capacity to deal with. Therefore, with the increasing activities of the Taliban, as stated earlier, Russia supported the Northern Alliance against the Taliban during the 1990s.

Russia's experiences in the developmental work in Afghanistan have been substantial and commendable, but, as has mentioned earlier, Russia had to face many problems, and found inactive in developmental activities during the Taliban regime. However, after the incidence of 9/11, and thereafter the US intervention, Russia involved in the international developmental activities in Afghanistan and made optimum efforts to re-emerge as an important player in Afghan's economic needs, and significantly encouraged the developmental programmes in Afghanistan. Russia provided humanitarian assistance to Afghanistan after the post-Taliban period and also extended support to the anti-Taliban government there. But, it has observed that Russia especially after the post-Taliban period did not substantially engage at the larger extent in infrastructure development of Afghanistan, and perhaps, remained as a lesser donor country as compared to others. Afghanistan also did not create much space for Russia as compared to the role of Soviet Russia which was proactively engaged there. For example, Afghanistan awarded contract of its largest Aynak copper reservoir to China, and not to Russia. However, by learning its poor involvement in Afghan's reconstruction activities, it seems Russia has been making major efforts to get involved proactively as the other major powers also have recorded deep engagement in Afghanistan's reconstruction. Along with the bilateral agreement, Russia has been seeking "to enter more and more multi-lateral large scale projects with regional balance."[95] Furthermore, by 2010, as an initiative of economic cooperation, both the countries had a trade worth of $500 million.[96] During 2010 London Conference, Russia's delegation proposed to reconstruct and modernize more than 140 facilities that had been built by the Soviet administration as a developmental assistance, and later in 2011 Boon Conference, Russia showed its readiness to make large investment in Afghanistan, especially in TAPI gas pipeline project and the Central Asia South Asia (CASA)-1000 (electricity energy) transmission pipeline project.[97] "In 2011, Russia became Afghanistan's most important provider of mineral oil products," and in 2007, Russia was "the biggest creditor" to Afghanistan,[98] and "Russia had written off about 90 percent of the Soviet-era debt, totaling $11.1 billion."[99] In 2012, Russia and Afghanistan reached to an agreement to build a construction material plant in Kabul.[100] Moreover, in 2012, both the countries had meeting and agreed on the formation of the Russian-Afghan intergovernmental commission for trade and economic cooperation.[101] In fact, after the waves of the US troops withdrawal, Russia started relooking at the "the relics of the Soviet occupation and promoting its own political and cultural prowess" by promoting its investment in Afghanistan.[102] The Russian government focused 140 Soviet-era projects aiming their rehabilitation and reconstruction. Moreover, the Kabul House Building Factory, the country's largest manufacturing facility, was the first to receive assistance in 2013-14: $25 million for new equipment. Moscow also spent $20 million to renovate the Soviet House of Science and Culture, which was constructed in 1982. Moreover, as a soft power policy, in the direction of its revival in Afghanistan, Russia doubled the number of scholarships that it had offered to the Afghan students. Besides, Russia contributed a big library of Russian literature in Cultural Center and offered language courses.[103] "Russia is a major supplier of oil to Afghanistan and accounts for 13 percent of all imports into the country," and it has also been hoped that Afghanistan would receive further investment from Russian companies as they have participated in the implementation of energy and transports projects, and the majority of the Afghan's energy facilities were constructed with the assistance from USSR and the Russian companies have taken the responsibilities of modernizing them.[104]

Moreover, in March 2016, it has reported that Russia planned to support Afghans housing sector. In fact, though the Soviet Russia was more active in Afghanistan, at present, "Russia is still one of Afghanistan's important political interlocutors, trade partners (fifth highest export destination) and key suppliers of defence equipment (including MI-17 helicopters, AK-47 rifles and ammunition)."[105] Russia has aimed to establish links with the Afghan people by means of pushing forward its soft power in terms of economic investment. On October 30, 2017, a delegation of Russian businessmen visited Afghanistan "to negotiate with the Afghan government over an expansion of Russian investments in Afghanistan's agriculture, transport, and mining sectors", further "to increase the annual trade turnovers" between both the countries. By this, Russia aimed to deepening its links with

Afghanistan. It has also believed that "Russia's investments in Afghan economic development initiatives and military assistance provisions to Kabul are part of a broader strategy to rebrand Russia's image in Afghanistan." Further, it has believed that by means of economic development investments, Russia has been seeking to improve its image there and to gain public support for its involvement.[106] It has rightly stated that "More the relations between Afghanistan and Russia flourish and develop, the better it is for Afghanistan's security and economy as it will pay the way for Afghans to live a better life."[107]

Russia's Defence/Security Cooperation

"The core of the Soviet strategy to strengthen the Afghan regime was to rebuild and increase the capabilities of the Democratic Republic of Afghanistan (DRA) security forces, and therefore, military aid was the most important aspect of Soviet assistance."[108] From the period 1968 to 1979, Soviet's total aid to Afghanistan was $695 million and, "in 1980, only the military aid was valued at $370 million, and the military aid gradually increased until 1984 that reaching to 366.3 million rubles."[109] In fact with this, further, it has believed that the military aid was held as one of the major reasons of the Soviet's involvement in Afghanistan before 1978, and it has reported that from 1979 to 1986, its direct military aid increased by seven times, especially to build the Afghan army. Besides, it was further increased in 1988 at the time of Soviet's withdrawal and that year Soviet had provided military aid of about four billion rubles, and it has believed that this military aid had achieved its objective of increasing the capacity of the Afghan security forces to provide adequate security to the government of the day.[110] Further between 1985-88, military aid to Afghanistan increasingly reached to 1692 million rubles, especially to increase the Afghan army's capacity as of the transferring of responsibility by the Soviet after its withdrawal, and later between 1988 and 1989, major increase in the military aid was reported that reached at 3972 million rubles.[111] In fact, the objective behind providing huge military aid to Afghanistan was "to maintain the military balance after the Soviet troop's withdrawal."[112] However, after the collapse of the USSR, Russia faced its limitations to cut off its military and economic aids to Afghanistan. And after that, even Afghanistan also faced multiple difficulties in sustaining its security mechanism because of the increasing consequences of the civil war. As compared to the Soviet's military assistance, Russia's assistance was very meager. Furthermore, in December 2002, both Russia and Afghanistan signed an agreement on military and technical assistance, and between 2002-05, Russia's military assistance to Afghanistan was reported as of $200 million, in which Russia delivered airport maintenance equipment, a missile defence system to protect the Kabul airport, communication equipment, trucks repair equipment, spare parts and manuals, but in 2005 and thereafter, Russia suspended its military assistance to Afghanistan.[113] However, further in 2008, Russia resumed its supply of weaponry to the Afghan's national Army, and this action represented a pivotal point in Moscow's approach.[114] In this context, it has argued that

> Since 2008, Russia's participation in Afghanistan has been more active and constructive, albeit comparatively marginal. Its policy still displays inconsistencies, which stem from Moscow's seeming inability to reconcile its foreign policy and security priorities. Russian interests vis-à-vis Afghanistan are driven by threats rather than by opportunities; Moscow does not hope to gain much from Afghanistan, but rather it seeks to prevent outcomes that would adversely affect the Russian federation.[115]

By 2009, Russia realized the necessity of more "aggressive strategy" in Afghanistan rather a passive strategy given the increasing problems in Afghanistan and their repercussion near the Russian borders, and therefore, in this direction, Russia started searching opportunities to have practical cooperation with the NATO.[116] Keeping its proactive approach intact, Russia maintained the Northern Distribution Network for the required supplies to Afghanistan vie Russia and Central Asia. Moreover, Russia also "agreed to ISAF request for broadening the rail transit options for non-lethal material through Russia including the reverse transit vehicles and equipment back through Russia to Europe."[117] Furthermore, Russia "opened its airspace to the US Air Force...to fly from the US territory over the North Pole and across Russia to Afghanistan."[118] By this way also, Russia contributed in the Afghan's war. Further in 2010, Russia provided 20,000 Ak-47 rifles to Afghanistan and about 225 Afghan police officers were trained in Russia and hundreds of special officials were given training to deal with the menace of drugs. Furthermore, Russia agreed to arrange fund for the maintenance of the Soviet-era Afghan helicopters and special training to the Afghan technicians.[119] Moreover, in 2012, Russia opened NATO supply hub in its territory for the transit of non-lethal equipment and personnel to Afghanistan.[120] That showing its keen interests in resolving the Afghan problem. In this context, it has argued that he increasing supplies were "going through Russia puts Moscow in an optimal position across three interconnected policy areas. The supply routes support stabilization efforts in Afghanistan, improve Russia's position in Central Asia, and create a NATO dependency on Russia that could potentially be used as leverage."[121] The increasing war and violence in Afghanistan had created much concern for Russia and its southern neighbours bordering Afghanistan for the deteriorating condition. This led Russia to increase its cooperation with Afghanistan. Moreover, the consecutive failure of the dialogues between the Afghan government and the Taliban also further added the force in Russia's concerns. Therefore, in this direction, Russia underlined its strong determination to strengthen security cooperation with its long-time partner Afghanistan. In April 2013, a high-ranking official of the Russian government, Sergei Koshelev, the head of the International Co-operation Department of the Russian Defence Ministry, proposed the idea of creating Russian 'maintenance bases' in Afghanistan for Russian-made military equipment widely used by the Afghan armed forces. But, this was speculated as and if Russia making re-entry by deploying its military forces in Afghanistan which had created controversy in Afghanistan. However, by denying such speculation, the Russian Foreign Ministry stated that: "Moscow's position, that a return of the Russian military to Afghanistan is impossible, remains unchanged."[122] In September 2013, the Russian President Vladimir Putin said, as quoted by Tracy German, "Although there had been a decline in a Russian-Afghan economic relations, Russia would continue to support Afghanistan's army…supplying some times of weapons…as well as ammunition and…training specialists at Russian military academies."[123] In fact, Afghanistan asked Russia for assistance in supplies, services, and training for its military and police, and Russia also decided to assist Afghanistan in reinforcing its military capacities of its government forces. The Afghan government consistently made efforts to get Russia's military assistance and also to have more military cooperation from Afghanistan's regional and international allies. However, Russia appeared exhibiting its reluctance in re-indulging in Afghan's conflicts by playing direct role in fighting against the Taliban insurgency. Besides, Russia and Afghanistan made agreement on the maintenance and repairs of Russia and Soviet era produced helicopters and other military hardware in Afghanistan. In fact, it has argued that Russia's military and technical assistance to Afghanistan was hindered by the US sanctions.[124] Moreover, India has also discussed with Russia regarding the Russian military assistance to Afghanistan.

The 2014 declaration of withdrawal of its forces by the US administration under Obama increased Russia's diplomatic inclination towards Afghanistan, and this led them to come together after long time further to strengthen their bilateral relations. Subsequently, in 2015, both Russia and Afghanistan signed security treaty, and in February 2016, Russia supplied 10,000 Kalashnikov rifles/AK-47s rifles and millions of rounds of ammunition to the Afghan government, and also committed to provide more Russian military and economic aid. In fact, Russia was abstained from engaging with Afghanistan in terms of military supply since the US-led intervention, however, Russia provided logistical support for the reconstruction of the war-torn Afghanistan.[125] In context of Russia's military supply to Afghanistan, the then Afghan National Security Adviser Mohammad Haneef Atmar expressed, "This important donation is from an important friend of Afghanistan in a crucial time for Afghanistan and the region."[126] By and large, Russia established closer ties with the Afghan government in a bid to help shaping the developments on the ground, especially, its military aid and economic investment in the country. On bilateral engagement in the military sphere, it has stated that the "reflecting their historical ties, Russia and Afghanistan have a technical-military agreement, and Russia trains and provides weapons to Afghan civilian, military and policy specialists, in addition to upgrading Soviet-era infrastructure."[127] In February 2017, the Foreign Minister of Russia, Sergei Lavrov after meeting with the Afghanistan Foreign Minister Salahuddin Rabbani in Moscow stated that "Afghanistan is a long-time and close partner of Russia. Today, we reaffirmed our interest in further developing cooperation in political, military, socio-economic and humanitarian spheres."[128] However, the Russian Foreign Minister stressed for the compulsive inclusion of the Taliban in a constructive dialogue to find a solution to the security crisis in Afghanistan. In fact, Afghanistan, by understanding the significance of Russia in assisting its military development and security set up, was approached Russia for the military equipment and the military training for its forces. Russia also promised such assistance to Afghanistan.

The Tripartite Bonhomie: Russia, Taliban, and Pakistan

With the paradigmatic shifts in and around Afghanistan, Russia has effectively made alliance with its former enemy, the Taliban in Afghanistan, and has declared its contacts with them. In fact, Moscow has been maintaining contacts with the Taliban since 2005. It has alleged that Russia shared intelligence with the Taliban, and also provided arms to them, and it has also believed that Russia has been in contact with some Afghan warlords in the north.[129] Moreover, the Russian President Vladimir Putin and the former leader of the Taliban had a meeting in September 2015 to discuss the mutual cooperation and collaboration to fight against the Islamic State and even, Russia established contacts with the Taliban under Mullah Haibatullah Akhundzada, the current leader of Taliban.[130] Russia's support to the Taliban, in fact, carried many implications for the future of Afghanistan. Russia-Taliban engagement has potentially weakened the central government in Afghanistan resulting in the creation of very critical situation, just like Syria. In Syria, Russia has been supporting the notorious government of President Bashar al-Assad, but in

Afghanistan, by supporting the Taliban, Moscow has discarded the success of the legitimate government in Kabul backed by the international community.[131] Moreover, by spreading confusion since 2016, it can be observed that "Russia has been conducting annual joint military drills with Pakistan along the Afghan border," and therefore, some Afghans had expressed their concerns that "Afghanistan once again may become a geopolitical battlefield between the two great powers, this time the United States and Russia."[132] Regarding the Russian posture of collaborating or strengthening its ties with the Taliban decorated with its specific interests can be observed as what Samuel Ramani describes

> The United States' increasingly aggressive efforts to rollback the Taliban's territorial expansion also benefit Russia's interests, even though Russia has strengthened its diplomatic and military partnership with the Sunni extremist organization in recent months. Containing the Taliban's territorial reach furthers Moscow's long-term interests, as stagnant progress or defeats on the battlefield could convince the Taliban's senior leadership to accept Russia's proposals for a political resolution of the Afghanistan war. The Trump administration's new Afghanistan strategy is also appealing to Russian policymakers, as Moscow remains concerned about the Taliban's links to terrorist networks. Russian security services routinely arrest individuals on Russian soil suspected of colluding with the Taliban, and the Russian Supreme Court designated the Taliban as a terrorist organization since February 2003.[133]

Furthermore,

> If the United States increases its pressure on Pakistan to give up its links to the Taliban, Washington could help preserve Russia's balancing strategy in South Asia. As India views the Taliban as an instrument of Pakistani power projection in Afghanistan, New Delhi is likely to strengthen its economic and security cooperation with Kabul to stymie the Taliban's path to military victory. Had Trump failed to pressure Pakistan on its links to regional terror networks, Moscow might have been forced to unilaterally

> distance itself from Islamabad to reassure New Delhi of its continued reliability as a security partner. This scenario could have been damaging for Russia's security, as Pakistan maintains close links to Sunni extremists in Chechnya, and can retaliate against Russia if Moscow-Islamabad ties become strained over Afghanistan. By contrast, if Trump's Afghanistan strategy is implemented in full and US-Pakistan security cooperation increases, Russia will likely be able to avert a potential diplomatic conflict with Pakistan.[134]

As has observed earlier, the possibility of Afghanistan becoming the safe sanctuary of the ISIS militants compelled Russia to bring shifts in its Afghanistan policy. During the 'Heart of Asia' conference held in Amritsar on December 5, 2016, Russia's special envoy to Afghanistan, Zamir Kabulov, held the ISIS as more dangerous than the Taliban. Further, on December 8, 2016, the Russian Ambassador to Afghanistan stated on the possible IS threat and Russia-Taliban ties that their concern was that "Daesh not only threatens Afghanistan, but it is also a potent threat to Central Asia, Pakistan, China, Iran, India and even Russia. We have ties with the Taliban to ensure the security of our political offices, consulates and the security of Central Asia."[135] As reported by James Griffiths, according to Rand Corporation analyst Seth Jones, "Russia has increased its contacts with the Taliban and provided limited support out of concern that US military forces may withdraw from the region; as part of a broader strategy to increase Russian influence across the globe; and to weaken Islamic State."[136] In fact, over the objections and criticisms towards Russian linkages with the Taliban, Omar Nessar, the Director of the Moscow-based Center for Contemporary Afghan Studies (CISA), stated that "All regional and world powers have established contact with the Taliban; whether it is Pakistan, Japan, China or Iran, all countries have the right to contact the Taliban. Why shouldn't this also apply to Russia?"[137] However, it is criticized that Russia's material support to the Taliban, northern Afghanistan has become the yard of bloody battle.

Russia, besides the Taliban, also established proximity with Pakistan over the Afghanistan developments. In this context, Samuel Ramani expressed that a shared willingness to embrace the

Taliban and the suspicions about the US role (in Afghanistan), has brought both Russia and Pakistan together.[138] In fact, historically, Russia and Pakistan had distrustful relationship as the latter was the US's allies during the cold war period and Russia has always supported India against Pakistan. In fact, both Russia and Pakistan appeared playing joint role with others in stabilizing/de-stabilizing the situation in Afghanistan. Even for that matter, for the first time in the history of Russia-Pakistan relations, Russia in September 2016 sent troops to Pakistan for a joint military exercise that has demonstrated the increasing proximity between them. However, Russia justified it as the military cooperation with Pakistan aiming at the fight against the ISIS. This development has definitely confused India and that has heightened its concerns. As a result, because of their some common interests, Pakistan has consistently supported and advocated Russia's constructive role in Afghanistan. There are two reasons for this development as identified by Ramani; "First, Pakistani policymakers have strongly supported Russia's willingness to cooperate with the Taliban. Second, Russia has countered US efforts to contain Pakistan's influence in Afghanistan by diplomatically engaging Pakistan and accommodating Islamabad's views on the stabilization of Afghanistan."[139] By and large, Russia has joined the larger alignment with China and Pakistan in Afghanistan and the Taliban as well. However, Russia does not have its a sizable citizens in Afghanistan to be protected there and even its engagement with the Taliban had no impact on the level of violence in Afghanistan. But, Russia explicitly rejected the claims that Moscow engaged and used Taliban to fight the Islamic State's faction ISKP in the region. It has believed that "the Afghan Taliban has a narrow national focus on reinstating a puritan system in Afghanistan whereas the Islamic State is considered a transnational threat with a continental agenda."[140]

In fact, since last few years, a significant change in Russia's approach towards Afghanistan and the region around it has been observed. Russia has discarded the US allegations that it has been involved in weapons supply to the Taliban. However, Russia has acknowledged that it has opened up communication channels with the Taliban and also has tried to facilitate peace talks for the better future of Afghanistan. In a Raisina Dialogue, 2018, which was held in Delhi, Russian Deputy Minister for Foreign Affairs Igor Morgulov stated that the Islamic State has been the principal threat to Afghanistan and the region, and that threat would affect Russia also. Besides, Morgulov raised the questioned that "how its fighters had been brought into northern Afghanistan in unmarked helicopters when the airspace is under US control." However, the US by rejecting Russia's justification, questioned Russian and Iranian motives in weakening the legitimate Afghan government by extending recognition to the Taliban, the major obstacle in peace process in the country.[141] However, eventually it was the US administration which entered an agreement with the Taliban to pull out the US's forces from Afghanistan that finally offered wider space for the Taliban to come back in Afghan's power in August 2021.

Russia's Peace Initiatives

After very long time, Russia aimed at to re-play a big role in Afghanistan which has been witnessed by its calling of two regional meetings: the first was held in December 2016 and the other in February 2017. For the second time, Russia hosted a conference on Afghanistan in Moscow which was an expanded representation of six countries: Russia, Iran, China, India, Afghanistan, and Pakistan. Interestingly, a key player in Afghanistan, the United States, which still maintained the large number of troops there to support the Afghan government's counter-insurgency efforts kept out of the meetings. However, on its part, the US contemplated an increase in its military commitment as indicated by its commander in Afghanistan, Gen. John Nicholson who advocated to the Senate Armed Services Committee that "a few thousand" more NATO trainers are needed to break the stalemate against the Taliban.[142] However, with welcoming the Russian efforts towards peace and security in Afghanistan, India also raised concerns over the Russia-led talks with the Taliban. India's External Affairs Ministry stated that "We underlined that it is up to the government of Afghanistan to decide whom to engage in direct talks."[143] Moreover, Russia's extension of cordial hands to the Taliban for peace talks had some reasons as of the marginalization of Russia in January 2016 when a Quadrilateral Coordination Group (QCG) was formed with the participation of the United States, China, Pakistan, and Afghanistan to advance the peace process in Afghanistan and to talk to the Taliban on peace process also. Therefore, in reply to this and to exhibit its responsibility to play proactive role, Russia organized a trilateral meeting along with China and Pakistan to discuss the Afghanistan issues which was later supported by Iran also. Further, Russian Foreign Minister Sergey Lavrov, during his visit to Afghanistan in February 2017, had announced the calling of an international meeting for a peace process with the participation of Russia, Afghanistan, Pakistan, China, Iran, and India, and discarding invitation to the United States or any NATO member.[144]

On Russia's efforts in securing an Afghan peace deal, which something Washington had been trying to do repeatedly but failed every time is considered that that would be a major victory for Russia, serving many purposes. In this context, it has argued that

> First, any peace negotiation is payback to the Americans for their role in Moscow's crushing defeat in Afghanistan (which in itself was revenge for the catastrophic Vietnam War). Second, Moscow could add any deal to its growing list of foreign policy achievements, which perfectly suits Putin, who is looking to maintain his grip on power despite nationwide protests spurred by corruption among high-ranking officials.... Third, a Moscow-brokered peace may actually do what it promises and restore a semblance—or at least hope—of respite to a situation that is increasingly spinning out of control.[145]

In fact, Russia favoured official peace talks with the Taliban and also shared cordial relations with the Afghan government, but Russia was confident in China and US-mediated peace talks with the Taliban. In April 2017 (Moscow Format, discussed in the last chapter), Russia hosted an international conference on Afghanistan with the representatives from Afghanistan, China, India, Iran, Pakistan, and Central Asian Republics. In fact, the US was also invited but did not participate.

Notes and References

1. Katherine Harvey, Afghanistan, The United States, and The Legacy of the Afghanistan's Civil War, 5 June 2003, EDGE, https://web.stanford.edu/class/e297a/Afghanistan,%20the%20United%20States.htm, accessed on 23 February 2018.
2. Christian Tripoli, Grand Strategy and the Graveyard of Assumptions: Britain and Afghanistan, 1839-1919, *The Journal of Strategic Studies*, Vol. 33, No. 5, October 2010, p. 707.
3. *Ibid.*, p. 708.
4. *Ibid.*, p. 709.
5. Bijan Omrani, The Durand Line: History and Problems of the Afghan-Pakistan Border, *Asian Affairs*, Vol. 40, No. 2, 2009, pp. 177-95.
6. In 1967, the PDPA had a split into two factions: one led by Babrak Karmal who had supported Daud, and another faction led by Marxist leader Nur Taraki who had allegiance to the USSR.
7. Paul Dibb, The Soviet Experiences in Afghanistan: Lessons to be Learned?, *Australian Journal of International Affairs*, Vol. 64, No. 5, 2010, p. 496.
8. The Soviet Invasion of Afghanistan and the US Response, 1978-1980, Office of the Historian, https://history.state.gov/milestones/1977-1980/soviet-invasion-afghanistan, accessed on 25 February 2019.
9. James Phillips, The Soviet Invasion of Afghanistan, 9 January 1980, The Heritage Foundation, http://www.heritage.org/europe/report/the-soviet-invasion-afghanistan, accessed on 20 October 2017.
10. *Ibid.*
11. Tim Bird and Alex Marshall, *Afghanistan: How the West Lost its Way*, Orient Blackswan, New Delhi, 2012, p. 10.
12. Paul Dibb, 2010, p. 496.
13. James Phillips, 1980.
14. Paul Dibb, 2010, p. 496.
15. *Ibid.*, pp. 497-98.
16. Alan Taylor, The Soviet War in Afghanistan, 1979-1989, The Atlantic, 4 August 2014, https://www.theatlantic.com/photo/2014/08/the-soviet-war-in-afghanistan-1979-1989/100786/, accessed on 20 October 2017.

17. Paul Dibb, p. 498.
18. C.N. Trueman "Russian invasion of Afghanistan" historylearningsite.co.uk. The History Learning Site, 9 March 2015. 16 Aug. 2016, accessed on 20 October 2017.
19. Amie Ferris-Rotman, Dj Vu: Why is Russia Back in Afghanistan?, *Haaretz*, 4 May 2017, https://www.haaretz.com/world-news/europe/.premium-explained-what-s-russia-doing-back-in-afghanistan-1.5467373, accessed on 6 February 2018.
20. Paul Dibb, p. 503.
21. Phillips, *The Heritage*, *ibid*.
22. Paul Dibb, p. 504.
23. *Ibid*., p. 505.
24. Avinash Paliwal, *My Enemy's Enemy: India in Afghanistan from the Soviet Invasion to the US Withdrawal*, HarperColins Publishers India, Noida, 2017, p. 49.
25. Sir Rodric Braithwaite, The Russian in Afghanistan, *Asian Affairs*, Vol. 42, No. 2, 2011, p. 227.
26. Arif Rafiq, Russia Returns to Afghanistan, *The National Interest*, 12 January 2017, http://nationalinterest.org/feature/russia-returns-afghanistan-19040, accessed on 16 October 2017.
27. Samuel Ramani, Why Russia Wants the US to Stay in Afghanistan, *The Diplomat*, 23 August 2017, https://thediplomat.com/2017/08/why-russia-wants-the-us-to-stay-in-afghanistan/, accessed on 11 October 2017.
28. Paul Dibb, p. 505, for details see William E. Odom, *The Collapse of the Soviet Military*, Yale University Press, New Haven, 1998.
29. Sir Rodric Braithwaite, 2011, p. 215.
30. *Ibid*.
31. *Ibid*.
32. Masood Saifullah, Why is Russia so interested in Afghanistan all of a sudden?, *DW*, 3 January 2017, http://www.dw.com/en/why-is-russia-so-interested-in-afghanistan-all-of-a-sudden/a-36989680, accessed on 10 October 2017.
33. Julia Gurganus, Russia's Afghanistan Strategy, *Foreign Affairs*, 2 January 2018, https://www.foreignaffairs.com/articles/afghanistan/2018-01-02/russias-afghanistan-strategy, accessed on 16 January 2019.

34. *Ibid.*
35. Andrei Dorre and Tobias Kraudzun, Persistence and Change in Soviet and Russian Relations with Afghanistan, *Central Asian Survey*, Vol. 31, No. 4, December 2012, p. 435.
36. *Ibid.*, p. 428.
37. Natasha Kuhrt, Afghanistan's Significance for Russia: Regional or Global Strategy, Russian Analytical Digest-80, 2010, pp. 5-8.
38. Nikolay N. Gudalov, Developments in Afghanistan after 2014: A perspective from Russia and its possible role in Rajen Harshe and Dhananjay Tripathi (ed) Afghanistan Post-2014, Routledge, New York, 2016, p. 150.
39. Scott Bohn, Russia's Afghanistan Policy: An Irresolute Strategy for an Uncertain Future, *Comparative Strategy*, Vol. 33, No. 3, 2014, pp. 205-21.
40. *Ibid.*, p. 206.
41. *Ibid.*, p. 211.
42. Nikolay Gudalov, 2016, p. 154.
43. Arif Rafiq, 12 January 2017.
44. Sir Rodric Braithwaite, p. 217.
45. Scott Bohn, 2014, p. 207.
46. For details, see Debendra Mahalik, Terrorism in Central Asia: Security Implications for Russia, *Journal of International Studies*, Vol. 2, 2012, pp. 133-47.
47. Scott Bohn, p. 214.
48. Masood Saifullah, 3 January 2017.
49. Arif Rafiq, 12 January 2017.
50. Masood Saifullah, 3 January 2017.
51. Samuel Ramani, Why Russia Wants the US to Stay in Afghanistan, *The Diplomat*, 23 August 2017, https://thediplomat.com/2017/08/why-russia-wants-the-us-to-stay-in-afghanistan/, accessed on 11 October 2017.
52. Gurganus, 2018.
53. Masood Saifullah, 3 January 2017.
54. Natasha Kuhrt, 2010.
55. Hashim Wahdatyar, Four Reasons Russia Increasingly Favors the Taliban in Afghanistan, *The Diplomat*, 14 February 2017,

https://thediplomat.com/2017/02/4-reasons-russia-increasingly-favors-the-taliban-in-afghanistan/, accessed on 17 October 2017.

56. Natasha Kuhrt, 2010.
57. *Ibid.*
58. Arif Rafiq, 12 January 2017.
59. Hashim Wahdatyar, 14 February 2017.
60. *Ibid.*
61. *Ibid.*
62. *Ibid.*
63. Kaneshko Sangar, Afghanistan's Significance for Russia in the 21st Centaury, Interests, Perceptions and Perspectives, *Politics in Central Europe*, Vol. 12, No. 1, 2016, pp. 69-82.
64. Arif Rafiq, 12 January 2017.
65. Nikolay N. Gudalov, 2016, p. 154.
66. Samuel Ramani, 2017.
67. *Ibid.*
68. *Ibid.*
69. Hashim Wahdatyar, 14 February 2017.
70. Samuel Ramani, 2017.
71. *Ibid.*
72. Sir Rodric Braithwaite, 2011.
73. Avinash Paliwal, 2017, p. 37.
74. Kevin Klose, Soviet Signs Treaty with Afghanistan, *Washington Post*, December 6, 1978, https://www.washingtonpost.com/archive/politics/1978/12/06/soviets-sign-treaty-with-afghanistan/20bf658b-a229-44e7-a08b-70e92fd488c0/?utm_term=.d3e7db693f2a, accessed on 23 October 2017.
75. *Ibid.*
76. Vishal Chandra, Russia's Growing Afghan Re-Engagement, *Strategic Analysis*, Vol. 35, No. 4, July 2011 (pp. 552-58), p. 552.
77. *Ibid.*
78. *Ibid.*
79. *Ibid.*, p. 553.
80. Kevin Seiff, Russia Hopes Infrastructure Projects will Build Bridges in Afghanistan, *The Guardian*, 7 April 2014, https://

www.theguardian.com/world/2014/apr/07/russia-afghanistan-investment-kabul-karzai, accessed on 21 January 2019.

81. Julia Gurganus, 2018.
82. Vishal Chandra, 2011, p. 556.
83. A. Dorre and T. Kraudzun, 2012, p. 427.
84. *Ibid.*
85. *Ibid.*
86. Anton Minkov and Gregory Smolynec, Economic Development in Afghanistan During the Soviet Period, 1979-89: Lessons Learned From the Sovieet Experience in Afghanistan, Defence R&D Canada, Center for Operational Research and Analysis, Technical Memorandum 2007-35, August 2007, p. 3. This report was downloaded and accessed on 21 January 2019.
87. *Ibid.*
88. A. Dorre and T. Kraudzun, 2012, p. 432.
89. *Ibid.*
90. Tracy German, Russia and Afghanistan: The Long Shadow of History, in Harsh Pant, 2016, p. 122.
91. A. Minlkov and G. Smolynec, 2007, p. 3.
92. A. Dorre and T. Kraudzan, p. 433.
93. *Ibid.*, p. 434.
94. *Ibid.*, p. 435.
95. A. Dorre and T. Kraudzun, 2012, p. 437.
96. Vishal Chandra 2011.
97. A. Dorre and T. Kraudzun, 2012, p. 437.
98. *Ibid.*, pp. 437-38.
99. Vishal Chandra 2011, p. 553.
100. Nikolay N. Gudalov, 2016, p. 162.
101. Tracy German, 2016, p. 124.
102. Kevin Seiff, 7 April 2014.
103. *Ibid.*
104. Tracy Germany, 2016, p. 124.
105. Patryk Hugeil, Russia's Greater Involvement in Afghanistan: International Aspects, *The Polish Institute of International Affairs*, 13 June 2017, https://www.pism.pl/publications/bulletin/no-57-997, accessed on 21 January 2019.

106. Samuel Ramani, Russia's Soft Power Push in Afghanistan, *The Diplomat*, 29 November 2017, https://thediplomat.com/2017/11/russias-soft-power-push-in-afghanistan/, accessed on 21 January 2019.
107. Tracy German, 2016, p. 124.
108. A. Minkov and G. Smolynec, 2007, p. 4.
109. *Ibid.*
110. *Ibid.*, p. iii.
111. *Ibid.*, p. 4.
112. *Ibid.*, p. 5.
113. Vishal Chandra, 2011, pp. 552-53.
114. Scoot Bohn, 2014, p. 211.
115. *Ibid.*
116. *Ibid.*, p. 212.
117. *Ibid.*
118. *Ibid.*
119. Vishal Chandra, 2011, p. 554.
120. Scott Bohn, p. 212.
121. *Ibid.*, pp. 212-13.
122. Thomas Ruttig, From Point Zero to 'New Warmth': Russian-Afghan relations since 1989, 8 August 2014, https://www.afghanistan-analysts.org/from-point-zero-to-new-warmth-russian-afghan-relations-since-1989/, accessed on 25 October 2017.
123. Tracy German, 2016, p. 124.
124. Moscow and Kabul agree on maintenance of Russian helicopters in Afghanistan, Russia Beyond, 7 December 2016, https://www.rbth.com//news/2016/12/07/moscow-and-kabul-agree-on-maintenance-of-russian-helicopters-in-afghanistan_654299, accessed on 6 February 2018.
125. Waslat Hasrat-Nazimi, Russia's New Role in Afghanistan, DW, 2 March 2016, http://www.dw.com/en/russias-new-role-in-afghanistan/a-19087432, accessed on 25 October 2017.
126. Catherine Putz, From Russia with Bullets: Moscow Gifts Kabul 10,000 AK-47s, *The Diplomat*, 24 February 2016, https://thediplomat.com/2016/02/from-russia-with-bullets-moscow-gifts-kabul-10000-ak-47s/

127. Tracy German, 2016, p. 123.

128. Russia Stresses Stronger Security Cooperation with Afghanistan, *Iran Daily*, 7 February 2017, http://www.iran-daily.com/News/177220.html?catid=3&title=Russia-stresses-stronger-security-cooperation-with-Afghanistan, accessed on 2 February 2018.

129. Said Sabir Ibrahimi, Can Russia Help Bring Peace to Afghanistan?, *The Diplomat*, November 02, 2018, https://thediplomat.com/2018/11/can-russia-help-bring-peace-to-afghanistan/, accessed on 5 November 2018.

130. Hashim Wahdatyar, 14 February 2017.

131. *Ibid.*

132. Said Sabir Ibrahimi, Can Russia Help Bring Peace to Afghanistan?, *The Diplomat*, November 02, 2018, https://thediplomat.com/2018/11/can-russia-help-bring-peace-to-afghanistan/, accessed on 5 November 2018.

133. Samuel Ramani, 23 August 2017.

134. *Ibid.*

135. Manabhanjan Meher, Russia's Policy Shift towards Taliban and Pakistan, IDSA Comment, Institute for Defence Studies and Analysis (IDSA), https://idsa.in/idsacomments/russia-policy-shift-towards-taliban-and-pakistan_mmeher_010317, accessed on 4 January 2018.

136. James Griffiths, Who are the key players in Afghanistan?, CNN, 19 September 2017, https://edition.cnn.com/2017/08/26/asia/afghanistan-pakistan-india-china-russia-us/index.html, accessed on 7 February 2018.

137. Waslat Hasrat-Nazimi, 2 March 2016.

138. What's Driving Russia-Pakistan Cooperation on Afghanistan?, *The Diplomat*, 9 May 2017, https://thediplomat.com/2017/05/whats-driving-russia-pakistan-cooperation-on-afghanistan/, accessed on 4 January 2017.

139. *Ibid.*

140. Said Sabir Ibrahimi, 2 November 2018.

141. Rakesh Sood, Afghanistan, On a Slow Fuse, *The Hindu*, 25 January 2018, p. 8.

142. Manabhanjan Meher; also see General sees Russian meddling in Afghanistan, need for more troops to fight Taliban, *Washington Times,* February 9, 2017.

143. *Ibid.*, also see Moscow Six-Party Talks on Afghanistan Commit to 'Red lines' on Taliban Engagement, *The Wire*, February 16, 2017.

144. Hashim Wahdatyar, 14 February 2017.

145. "In a poll released last month by the independent Levada Center, the majority of Russians surveyed felt Putin's greatest achievement was the military and foreign policy; a decade ago, his management of the economy was viewed as his greatest strength..." for details see Amie Ferris-Rotman, *Haaretz*, 4 May 2017.

4

Pakistan: The Dysfunctional Neighbour

Introduction

The territorial disputes basically shape the relations between/ amongst the states having common borders. Generally, as has observed over the years, the states that have common or contiguous land border always seemingly confront each other for the protection of their national interests such as strategic and economic interests, changing power relations in the world politics, and to preserve their respective state sovereignty on the assumption of the threat from each other when the states have legacy of bilateral/multilateral animosity. Mostly, states believe that the neighbouring hostile state(s) try to interfere in each other's domestic affairs to destabilize the political order in terms of gaining something leverages over the others. In fact, the major wars amongst the European great powers also had been, among others, for the territorial expansion, however, mostly in the non-European territories. In this context, Paul Hansel explained that "contiguous states face higher risks for war."[1] ".... Since expansionism and territorial disagreements between states are traditionally regarded as the most common sources of war."[2] The territory of the state is much valuable for the reservoir of natural resources, and importantly as a historical homeland or cultural commonness and the individual state's claims over these territories lead to produce severe violence and wars. It has stated that "historical claims are often relate to cultural claims, because the greater the cultural importance of the territory, the stronger the historical claims to it. Historical claims are strong when the territory in the question is the claimant group's homeland" because that "includes both priority and duration and expresses the ultimate case of man-land symbiosis."[3] Certainly, in this direction, the relations between Pakistan and Afghanistan have historically been tense and incessantly continuing without exhibiting any possibility of normality in a recent future. The cross-border infiltration, refugees, drug trafficking, militant groups, and disputes over counterterrorism policy and dialogue with terrorist groups have been the regular contributing factors to take forward the entrenched trust deficit, confrontations and the weakening of the bilateral relationship between the two neighbours. As has observed, "mutual suspicion surrounding the contentious Afghanistan-Pakistan border and Islamabad's long record of interference in Afghan politics have continued to divide Kabul and Islamabad, diminishing the prospect of cooperation between the two capitals."[4] The US scholar of international affairs Vanda Brown describes the Afghanistan-Pakistan structure of relationship and perceptions as:

> Yet Afghanistan's location at the crossroads of the Middle East, Central Asia, and South Asia has for centuries made a friendly neighborhood elusive. Although religious, ethnic, economic, and cultural ties between Afghanistan and Pakistan run deep and wide, the two countries have frequently been at odds with one another. During the Cold War, Afghanistan became a battleground in the global conflict between the Soviet Union and United States, with Pakistan as a key US ally supporting the anti-Soviet mujahidin. Pakistan has long been a difficult and disruptive neighbor, seeking leverage in Afghanistan, hoping to limit India's influence there, and cultivating radical groups within Afghanistan as proxies. Despite a decade of US attempts to bring Islamabad and Rawalpindi (the seats of Pakistan's government and military establishment, respectively) on board with its efforts in Afghanistan, Pakistan continues to be ensnared in—while also augmenting—Afghanistan's instability. Pakistan fears both a strong Afghan government

> closely aligned with India, potentially helping encircle Pakistan, and an unstable Afghanistan that becomes—as has already happened—a safe haven for anti-Pakistan militant groups and a dangerous playground for outside powers.[5]

In the South Asian region, it will not be an exaggeration to state that Pakistan has always been the rogue and recalcitrant state among all the others. However, Pakistan more smartly demonstrates itself as a peace loving and a state against the violence and terrorism. But, most of the states within and outside the region know the dysfunctional nature of Pakistan, and perhaps Pakistan has become much obstinate and behaves like a devil man because of the supports it has been receiving initially from the US and now from China and Russia. In context of Pakistan's engagement with Afghanistan, it has always been destructive and dysfunctional against the interest of the Afghan's non-Taliban government. In other words, Pakistan always believed and adopted the "double dealing" mode in context of its policy towards Afghanistan. For instance, Pakistan supported, participated, and engaged in alliance with the US intervention in Afghanistan and military action against the Taliban regime, and on the other hand, Pakistan's military establishment, the ISI, permitted the visits of many Taliban military commanders in Pakistan and also provided asylum to them in its territory.[6] However, historically, the Pakistan-Afghanistan relations have always been characterized by mutual mistrust and are viewed in terms of security dimensions, despite both the countries share close ethnic, linguistic, religious, and economic affinity. In fact, generally as observed in most of the Third World countries that the countries with common or close social and cultural interlinking have mutual conflicts, ethnic wars, and confrontations due to common and porous borders, and therefore, the case of Afghanistan-Pakistan relations can be seen through the prism of complexity. Moreover, before the 1978 coup d'état in Afghanistan, both were indulged in propaganda war against each other as "Afghanistan sought to discredit Pakistan as a creature of colonialism and an artificial state, while Pakistan recurrently imposed punitive sanctions on the Afghan economy by closing the transit trade crossing with Afghanistan."[7] It has argued that Afghanistan's peaceful future hinges on the regional environment especially the role of Pakistan in Afghanistan and its relations with the Taliban. As long as Pakistan keeps friendly relations with the Taliban and plays dysfunctional role against the legitimate Afghan government, it can be indication that Afghanistan will not come out from the turmoil and difficulties created by the Taliban with the support from Pakistan. On Afghanistan and Pakistan complications, Vanda Felbab-Brown further argued that

> An unstable Afghanistan threatens Pakistan, complicating the latter's ability to refurbish its weak state and economy and suppress dangerous internal militancy. But in the absence of dramatically improved relations with India, Pakistan is likely to prefer an unstable Afghanistan to a strong Afghanistan closely aligned with India. Pakistan thus retains an interest in not liquidating its long-term relationship with the Afghan Taliban and the Haqqani network, a policy that exacerbates Afghan instability.[8]

Furthermore, Vanda Felbab-Brown identified that

> Pakistan's policies toward both militant groups and Afghanistan are determined as much by incompetence, inertia, and a lack of capacity as by calibrated duplicitous manipulation. Crucially, Pakistan's willingness to accommodate Afghanistan-oriented militant groups is motivated by a fear of provoking militants to incite violence in Punjab and threaten the core of the Pakistani state instead of focusing externally. This paralyzing fear persists despite Pakistan's desire to defeat Tehrik-i-Taliban Pakistan.[9]

As has believed, "successive governments in Pakistan, particularly, the military regimes, have institutionalized and perpetuated negative constructs of existential threat perceptions from outside, disseminated systematically through formal school curriculum and educational textbooks based on tailor unscientific interpretations of history and culture of the region."[10] The international community has always been aware and critique of Pakistan's relations with the terrorism especially in the South Asian and

Af-Pak border region. In other words, Pakistan has adopted the policy of sponsoring to terrorist activities as its foreign policy means to accomplish its national interest especially towards its enemy states or zone of interests. And India and Afghanistan are such two countries where Pakistan explicitly applies terrorism-laden policy. In case of Afghanistan, Pakistan has been playing the double game that inclining more towards the Taliban and working disastrously against Afghanistan as a whole. Pakistan's hand seems to be omnipresent in the Afghan turmoil since the inception of the Afghan war. However, the fact of the matter is also that "No solutions to the problem of Afghanistan can come without Pakistan's support."[11]

Pakistan was an ally (non-NATO) of the US during the cold war and post-cold war period as Pakistan's common border with Afghanistan provides a vital rout for the US's supplies into Afghanistan. Significantly, during the decade of 1980s, "Pakistan was the base for the Saudi-America alliance behind Mujahidin...Pakistan also serves as the major logistical line for the NATO forces in Afghanistan. Over 80% of the supplies coalition forces depend on to survive arrive via Pakistan from the port of Karachi."[12] Besides, it has also been, as stated, a major route for terrorist groups and funding, particularly the Haqqani Network and, however, Pakistan has also been a major victim of terrorism and believed in '*Bad and Good Terrorism*'. Depicting Pakistan's internal fractured structure, Vanda Felbab-Brown stated that Pakistan has been already hallowed out because of "its administrative structures having undergone a steady decline since independence," and "major macroeconomic deficiencies have increased, and deep poverty and marginalization persist amid a semi-feudal distribution of power, often ineffective and corrupt political leadership, internal social and ethnic fragmentation, and compromised security forces."[13]

Pakistan's Interests in Afghanistan

In fact, mostly it has analyzed that Pakistan's rivalry and security competition with India has been main driver of Pakistan's foreign policy in Afghanistan and also its supports to the Taliban there. Besides this, there are more factors identified in this context.

"Pakistan's policy is the result of not only its enduring rivalry with India, but also of historically rooted domestic imbalances within Pakistan, and Islamabad's contentious and distinct relationship with Afghanistan," and these domestic imbalances are: "the militarized nature of foreign policy making, ties between military institutions and Islamic networks, and the more recent rise of grassroots violence—have either contributed to Pakistan's accommodation of the Afghan Taliban or tempered its interest in expelling the movements leadership."[14] In general, Pakistan's key interests in Afghanistan before the US intervention in Afghanistan had been identifies as "the creation of a durable peace with an Afghan government that is pro-Pakistan; the repatriation of Afghan refugees from Pakistan soil; access into Central Asian Markets and a safe route for the oil and gas pipeline from Turkmenistan to Arabian sea."[15] However, by and large, Pakistan has multiple interests in Afghanistan looking at its common border and the major issues of confrontations between them.

Security Interests: Pakistan's interests, no doubt, are vested in stability in Afghanistan. The instability in Afghanistan definitely, as perceived by Pakistan, leads to increasing security concerns of Pakistan too. To its contrary, however, it has also stated that "Peaceful Afghanistan not in Pakistan's interests."[16] Pakistan nurtures some specific security concerns as it sees; *first*, in its East, India is an immediate neighbour with which Pakistan has historical hostility since its independence in August 1947; Pakistan has always been expecting a weak government in Afghanistan as it fears that a strong government in Afghanistan which will have very close and strong relations with India, and India will have strong opportunity to encircle Pakistan. A weak government in Afghanistan would offer more opportunities to Pakistan to further strengthen its influence in Afghanistan. In fact, Pakistan's interest in Afghanistan remained to control and to influence the domestic political equations in Afghanistan through weak and unstable government. In this context, Vanda Felbab-Brown argued, "Pakistan has long been difficult and destructive neighbor, seeking leverage in Afghanistan, hoping to limit India's influence there, and cultivating radical groups within Afghanistan as proxies."[17] In fact, it has also argued that

> Pakistan does continue its patronage of the Taliban and terrorists of all hues, it does so due to its dire need to defend itself against Indian influence in Afghanistan. It is unclear whether this logic arises from a defense of the underdog—where Pakistan is clearly so much smaller than India, or simply from the acceptance that there is nothing much that the US can do to get Islamabad to stop assisting terrorists.[18]

Second, in its West, the prolonged Afghan war could spare Pakistan from casting its repercussions. Even in its West, Pakistan cannot afford an instable Afghanistan. In other words, Afghan's war spillovers in western Pakistan that posing security threat to Pakistan. As a result, Pakistan's two hundred thousand soldiers are fighting war on terrorism in the western region.[19] In this context, Samran Ali reported

> Pakistan maintains that TTP and Indian Intelligence agency, RAW are using Afghanistan as a base for terrorist activities in Pakistan. India uses Afghanistan for providing training and military support to Pakistani TTP and Baloch insurgents to carry out subversive activities.... A stable and friendly Afghanistan can help eliminate support to TTP and Baloch insurgents from Afghanistan resulting in improving security in Balochistan province.[20]

Until 1979, both Afghanistan and Pakistan had cordial relations because of their economic and religious-ethnic commonalities, but with the changing circumstances, Pakistan's perceived concern was that the increasing Delhi-Kabul engagement would probably lead to two-prong war against Pakistan that further leading to the destruction and division of its territory and also would pose major security threats. Moreover, the Soviet invasion in Afghanistan further had complicated Pakistan's security parameters. Therefore, by perceiving the probable security challenge due to India's increasing influence and engagement in Afghanistan, Pakistan adopted the policy of "Strategic Depth" against India in Afghanistan and exploited Afghan territory by supporting the Taliban.[21] In fact, it was stated that "the Pakistani military doctrine behind the concept of strategic depth suggests transforming Afghanistan into a client or subservient state that is beholden to the Pakistani security establishment."[22] Further in 2010, justifying Pakistan's military doctrine in Afghanistan, Gen. Ashraf Parvez Kayani argued, "Pakistan wanted strategic depth in Afghanistan, but (did) not want to control it,"[23] and also stated that the peaceful, friendly, and stable Afghanistan would help Pakistan in protecting it from the security problem from its western border. However, in context of Pakistan's strategic depth doctrine, Cassidy argued that Islamabad's incessant application of "Islamist proxies in Afghanistan to pursue its quixotic notion of strategic depth has killed any strategy or momentum for the US-led coalition in Afghanistan, and also threatens Pakistan, because some of the same Islamist militants that Pakistan cultivated have turned on and attacked Pakistan."[24] In other words, by and large, the strategic depth doctrine of Pakistan turned as to be a fiasco. According to Umair Jamal as General Naseerullah Babar (who was central to Pakistan's attempts to navigate the newly available potential economic opportunities in Central Asian region, while negating the military dimension of 'strategic depth') said, "the talk about strategic depth is nonsense.... We realized that Afghanistan is a perfect corridor for goods from Central Asia. Those countries needed an Asian outlet, especially for oil and gas. We wanted to take advantage of that."[25]

Economic Interests/Trade and Business with Central Asian Countries: In the recent years, the Central Asian countries have become a hub for the major countries around the world for its affluent energy resources which are still untapped. They are indulged in a race to exploit these resources by establishing gas and oil pipelines in and around the region. Importantly, Pakistan also seeking an opportunity to engage in a trade with the Central Asian countries and has been trying to reach out there for trade. But, the major challenge in Pakistan's this interest to be achieved is that Pakistan has no common and direct borders with these countries, and, Afghanistan, geographically, separates Pakistan and the Central Asian countries. Therefore, Afghanistan offers a strategic opportunity to Pakistan. Keeping this in mind, Pakistan wants a stable Afghanistan which will provide a more feasible route to the region. Moreover, China's OBOR/BRI project in

Afghanistan also offers multiple opportunities to Pakistan for its robust economic growth. The CPEC, worth of about $48 billion, which is the part of BRI promises to connect Central Asia with South Asia and beyond through Afghanistan and Pakistan. Besides, the TAPI pipeline also is very useful for Pakistan as it provides energy resource for its economic revitalization. Furthermore, the port of Gwadar is situated on the coast of Pakistan which has been held as most suitable gateway to connect with the energy rich Central Asian countries. China has provided huge investment to build and modernize this port in view of having feasible access in the Central Asian region and in the Arabian Seas and also towards the other ocean routes to reach to the Europe. As it provides valuable asset in terms of Pakistan's economic interest, however, to reach to the Central Asian region from this port, Afghanistan creates the blockades. Therefore, as it was said, "Afghanistan is no longer a corner where nodes of terrorist networks can be hidden. It is a strategically situated route for the transport of Central Asian oil and a place of strategic importance for the regional players."[26] However, by and large, Pakistan's economic interests are hinges on the peaceful and stable Afghanistan.

Mitigation of Indian Influence: The prolonged tension between Pakistan and Afghanistan led to the increasing influence of India in Afghanistan. Afghanistan, during the non-Taliban regime, sought to be abstained from its trade dependence on Pakistan due to the bilateral tensions between them over the years by establishing cordial relations with India. Moreover, the common public opinion about India amongst the Afghan people has grown positively. As a result, India became a more attractive option for Afghanistan to trade with instead of Pakistan. In fact, Pakistan's foreign policy and its actions in Afghanistan were shaped by the relations with its rival India. Pakistan fears an Indian-dominated or closely allied Afghanistan would leave it encircled and vulnerable in any potential future conflict. And therefore, to marginalize India's influence, Islamabad always seeks a weak Kabul government dominated by a pliant and supportive Taliban so that Pakistan can maintain 'strategic depth' against an Indian invasion if any takes place in future. Pakistan also seeks the guarantee of safe haven for the terrorists it supports and to counter and prevent India from projecting its power in South Asian region. Pakistan also believes that India supports the separatist in Balochistan, and therefore, Pakistan seeks to obstruct India's ability to support separatists there. As a result, it has stated that Pakistan would not change its policy towards Afghanistan and its alliance with India as long as India poses an existential threat. The fact also is that Pakistan's military plays a central role in setting Pakistan's Afghan policy. However, with the re-establishment of Taliban government in August 2021, Pakistan's ecstasy mounted and emerged more powerful as compared to India's interests in Afghanistan. India found in perplexing situation since then.

Bilateral Disputes

The Durand Line and the Issue of Pashtunistan: The Durand Linc (2560 kms) has become a bone of contention between Pakistan and Afghanistan since long period. This line divided the Pashtun tribal belt between two countries under the 1893 Durand agreement. In fact, Pakistan recognizes the Durand Line as its legitimate western border, but Afghanistan has never agreed to it as an international border. This border has created problems as the militants easily and freely use it to cross because of the missing bilateral cooperation between the two states. And Pakistan perceives through this border that the militants may potentially pose security threat to it. Therefore, Pakistan seeking an agreement with Afghanistan to resolve the border dispute between them. In fact, when Afghanistan rejected Pakistan's borders claims in the post-1947 period after the British departure, Pakistan, in return, adopted punitive policy, and according to Nunan, Pakistan "turned an iron cage into a house of sand" and began constraining Afghans by "punishing them with blockades for aspiring to unite with their brethren and dreaming about Pashtunistan."[27] Consequently, this constraints led to cutting off Afghan's traditional connectivity with the Indian subcontinent that creating difficulties for the Afghan economy.

In 1955, Afghan Loya Jirga declared that "it does not in any way regard the areas of Pashtunistan as part of the territory of

Pakistan, unless and until the people of Pashtunistan desire it and consent thereto."[28] It has believed that during the departure of the British from Indian subcontinent especially the Indian Empire in 1947, Afghanistan had put forward the proposal for reviewing the border, but, the request in this regard was refused. Consequently, Afghanistan pushed forward a call for an independent Pashtunistan that to be carved out of Pakistan. But, Pakistan was against this call as it has always felt Afghanistan's support for Pashtunistan as a threat to its national security. Therefore, with the aim for Pashtunistan, it has believed that during the 1950s and 1960s, Afghanistan sponsored a Pashtun separatist movement in Pakistan's North-West Frontier Province (NWFP), which has been known as, at present, Khyber Pakhtunkhwa (KPK). Furthermore, in 1979, the Afghan Prime Minister, Hafizullah Amin, explicitly stated Kabul's aspiration for a 'greater Afghanistan'. The Durand Line, however, he said, 'tore us apart'.[29] In fact, Afghanistan wanted an independent Pashtunistan without losing its own territory, but at the cost of Pakistan's territory. According to Omar Sharif, chair at the American Institute of Afghan Affairs, Pakistan believed that the Afghan's demand for independent Pashtunistan was not genuine as it was not ready to include the Pashtuns of Afghan side in the greater Pashtunistan, but was supporting it to include the Pashtuns living in the Pakistan's territory. This definitely assured Afghan's deliberate policy towards disintegration of Pakistan's territory.[30] However, Pakistan spoiled Afghan's Pashtunistan ambition.

Balochistan Secessionist Movement: There has been a prolonged insurgency of Balochistan people in Pakistan due to which Pakistan has deployed its thousands of soldiers in the Baloch region. Pakistan has been pledging that India and Afghanistan are dysfunctionally engaged in supporting the Balochistan's Secessionist Movement against the interests of Pakistan. It has believed that "Kabul began to provide material assistance and refugee status to several thousand Baloch guerrillas, reinforcing pre-existing Pakistani efforts to establish greater proxy influence in Afghanistan" and as a result, Pakistan created an "Afghan Cell" to establish contacts with the anti-government leaders in Afghanistan.[31] However, in fact, Pakistan has failed to provide substantial evidences to prove India's involvement in Balochistan Secessionist Movement. In this context, Umair Jamal and Yaqoob Khan Bangash reported that

> ...from Pakistan's perspective, Indian involvement cannot be disregarded entirely. It cannot be argued that India's interest in Afghanistan is entirely humanitarian. India's proactive involvement in Afghanistan, especially close to the Pakistan border, definitely makes Pakistan sensitive. The claim is not without historical justification as Pakistan has been dismembered before and that too with the help of Indian intervention.[32]

According to them as analysts argued, "...even if India is involved in inflaming insurgency in Balochistan it is because of Pakistan's involvement in Kashmir for similar purposes and India is just returning the favour by playing a tit-for-tat spy game with Islamabad," nevertheless, "there exists a serious territorial problem for Pakistan which sits next to Afghanistan."[33] Besides, the CPEC project has been facing the major hurdles because of the problem of peace and stability in the region, as a result, to taste the fruits of benefits that probably will emanate from the CPEC project, Pakistan needs strong strategic actions in the region. Therefore, Pakistan has been struggling to see normalcy in the region.

Repatriation of the Afghan Refugees: At present, it has reported that Pakistan hosts about 1.4 million registered and 1.1 million unregistered Afghan refugees in its territory and Pakistan seems to be unable to host them for longer time due to its meager resources. Therefore, Pakistan believes in repatriating these refugees back to Afghanistan, but, the US seemed unwilling for this action. In this context, Nancy Izzo Jackson, the US Deputy Assistant Secretary in the Bureau of Population, Refugees, and Migration Situation, justified the US stand by stating that "Afghan's situation has not been conducive for their return, and also clarified that it has been the combine responsibility of the US and Afghan government to make conducive environment for the Afghan's refugees to return to their homes in Afghanistan.[34] On

Pakistan's hosting of Afghan refugees, Zahid Nasrullah Khan, Pakistan's Ambassador to Afghanistan expressed

> We are facing specific security and economic challenges due to the presence of refugees we are hosting for the last 40 years, so there is a concern that refugees must return. It's very important to cut this umbilical cord which got created in 1979 between Afghanistan and Pakistan. We have 1.27 million refugees and around 1.5 million undocumented Afghans, out of which we have documented around 300,000 and we have issued them Afghan citizen cards on the arrangement that eventually Afghanistan would give them Afghan passports and they would return to their country. So that large mass of the population of Afghanistan has to return; however their return has to be voluntary, gradual, and dignified. Further he also said about the bilateral proposal to resolve the refugee problem between two countries that; Pakistan and Afghanistan will work out a practical plan which would ensure the safety and well-being of the refugees in Afghanistan and would take into consideration the capacity of the Afghan government to honorably resettle the refugees. Currently they have nothing to come [home] to in Afghanistan. This was the reason behind the deadline extensions.[35]

Diplomatic Engagement

Since the independence of Pakistan in August 1947, both Pakistan and Afghanistan have strained bilateral relations. Afghanistan had expressed its vote against the admission of Pakistan in United Nations Organization in 1948 because of their disputes over the Durand Line.[36] Besides, Afghanistan had called for independent Pashtunistan, and in 1949, Pakistan inadvertently had conducted air attack on Afghan territory.[37] And this was followed with the repudiation of all the boundary treaties made with the British by a *Loya Jirga*, a great council in Kabul, and extended support to the idea of an independent Pashtunistan, and also had urged that "all the people in those areas should be given a referendum and the right to vote to join Afghanistan."[38]

In 1950, there was an incursion into the tribal areas by Afghan forces disguised as tribesmen. These were repulsed by Pakistan Pashtuns. Pakistan stopped Afghan imports for three months. In 1954-55, the government of Pakistan decided to change the country's administrative structure.... Afghanistan saw it as the tribal areas being taken away from their potential influence. There were riots at the Pakistani Embassy in Kabul, Pakistani consulates and counter-demonstrations in Pakistan. There were military calls-ups and mobilisations. There was no war, but diplomatic relations became frosty in the extreme.[39]

Despite similarity of religious and ethnic commonness, their relationship had been grappled with the various disputes. Besides, both the countries had frequently engaged in the demands of closing down of their embassies and other diplomatic offices in each other's countries. Further in 1961, they faced skirmishes leading to the shutting down of borders between them. "Since 1959 Pakistan had repeatedly protested to the Afghan Government against its persistent harassment of officials and the staff of Pakistani missions and consulates in Afghanistan," and the Afghan officials were engaged in dysfunctional activities in their consulate in Pakistan.[40] Both the states have consistently exhibited anguished against each other. After the 1978 coup d'état, Pakistan's involvement was actively intensified in Afghanistan. In most of the cases, it has observed that both the countries have strained and antagonistic relations that developed because of the Taliban factor and other issues of national interests like border disputes and the ethnic order across the borders. The fact that mostly believed is that Pakistan has always been trying to peep and disturb the domestic order of Afghanistan by every possible way, and, as a result, Pakistan is also blamed for forcing instability and violent order in Afghanistan. Therefore, Afghanistan never relied on Pakistan's bluffs as a peace-loving and responsible neighbour striving to extend its optimum helping efforts to create a peaceful and stable situation in Afghanistan. In other words, both the states have mostly experienced the mutual trust deficit in their bilateral relationship. The mutual blame game and accusations and counter-accusations have been the routine practice between them. Pakistan's army, as reported by many, plays very dysfunctional role in Afghanistan. However, in fact, on the Pakistan-Afghanistan relations, during a meeting with the US officials and when he was asked about Pakistan's role in Afghanistan, General Kayani of Pakistan stated that his goal was "a peaceful, friendly and stable Afghanistan." He stated further that "I have no desire to control Afghanistan. Anyone who wants to control Afghanistan is ignorant of history, since no one has ever controlled it."[41] It has argued that Kayani's answer "a peaceful, friendly and stable Afghanistan" became the common answering phrase to the question asked by the international community on Pakistan Army's aims and goals amidst the Taliban's revival.[42] However, both the countries have been engaged in making failing attempts for the bilateral rapprochement.

After the overthrow of the Taliban regime by the US in 2001, Pakistan perceived major opportunities to play a comprehensive role in Afghanistan. The US and Pakistan had been the natural alliance since very long time and the presence of the international forces led by the US in Afghanistan, as perceived, could avail opportune situation for Pakistan to accomplish its interests in and around Afghanistan. Pakistan's President General Pervez Musharraf, under the US pressure declared its position against the Taliban government and withdrew its support to it, and also provided facilities for the US-led military operation against the Al-Qaeda and the Taliban in Afghanistan. However, Pakistan's stand against the Taliban was hypocritical and was not genuine. Pakistan's this policy-stand towards the US intervention in Afghanistan was described by its Foreign Minister Abdul Sattar as "a [y]es-but approach [that] would allow Pakistan tactical flexibility," and in this context, he said, "[W]e agreed that we would unequivocally accept all US demands, but then we would express our private reservations to the US and we would not necessarily agree with all the details."[43] After 2001, "the official relationship between Pakistan and Afghanistan has been largely characterized by latent acrimony and persistent distrust surrounding the subject of the Afghan Taliban."[44] Further, Hamid Karzai, a pashtun leader, got an opportunity to become the first President of post-Taliban Afghanistan in 2001 under the security umbrella of the US-led forces. As a result, learning the vitality of this opportunity, President Karzai, in the direction of making comprehensive development and progress of Afghanistan, started his honest and hard efforts by approaching the world leaders and also given priority to the better relations with the neighbouring countries like Pakistan and Iran. President Karzai who remained in office for the longer time since 2001 also made number of official and diplomatic visits to Pakistan and mostly discussed on the extremism and the terrorism. Further, the reconstitution of the Taliban movement in 2003 by using Pakistan's territory to launch insurgency against Afghanistan was surfaced. This led to increase pressure on Pakistan by the Afghan government and the international community for cooperation to act against the Taliban militants, but Musharraf and his administration denied the presence of the Taliban men in Pakistan. Since then the issue of terrorism and extremism remained the worst bone of contentions between them. As a result, on this issue, the security forces of both the countries exchanged of small amount of arms firing across the borders and such clashes continued for several months.[45] However, to normalize the relations, in August 2004, President Karzai visited Pakistan and discussed the most troubling issues of terrorism and economy with President Musharraf in Islamabad. The common statement of their meeting stated that both the leaders "reiterated their common commitment to fight terrorism." Moreover, the meeting between two indicated that "the two neighbours would strengthen capability and co-operation in the field of intelligence and the forces on the ground".[46] On 6 September 2006, Pakistan President Musharraf visited Afghanistan with high level delegation and met President Karzai, and both the leaders discussed the need of honest cooperation and coordination to fight the menace of extremism and terrorism, and also reassured each other that their territory would not be allowed to use for the terrorist activities across the borders. Moreover, on 27 September 2006, both the leaders met in a tripartite meeting in the presence of then US President George Bush at the White House. But, during this meeting Musharraf blaming Karzai called him "Ostrich", who doesn't want to tell the world about the real facts in Afghanistan for his own personal reason. This had further fueled the negative repercussion on bilateral relations.

However, further, in December 2007, both Musharraf and Karzai met again in Islamabad signaling improvements in their relations and also tried to mend the differences and called for the greater cooperation in fighting terrorism across their borders, and also to build their mutual confidence amid accusations against each other that none had been doing enough positive sincerely. In fact, despite multiple meetings with Pakistan's President, Karzai did not stop blaming Pakistan for harbouring the Taliban and militant's training camps in its territory, while Musharraf blamed lawlessness and government's failure to rule against insurgency in Afghanistan. However, this meeting offered better opportunity to both the leaders to work together against the menace they had been facing.[47] During this time, Musharraf said that "the two intelligence agencies on both sides must cooperate more strongly if we are to deal with terrorists and extremists more effectively." In fact, before visiting Pakistan, it has reported that in an interview to CNN in December 2007, Karzai criticized the Madrasas in Pakistan making major controversy between two as he said that "closing the religious schools was a key to ridding Afghanistan of terror groups like the Taliban."[48] Musharraf, further making efforts to balance the relationship, said, "I think we have developed very strong understanding of each other's problems and we look forward to cooperation and coordination in all fields for our mutual benefit."[49] Besides, on the other hand, Karzai said, "The meeting was productive in all aspects.... There is reduced activity on the Afghan side...," but further he added, "unfortunately, there is an increased activity now on the Pakistani side. (We both) discussed the issue of Swat and South and North Waziristan, and the issues of terrorist activities in Afghanistan. We discussed Helmand. We discussed other parts of Afghanistan."[50]

Despite the end of military administration and the establishment of civil administration after the resignation of Musharraf in August 2008 to avoid impeachment, politics in Pakistan further faced some democratic uncertainties. However, in March 2008, Yousuf Raza Gilani of Pakistan Peoples Party (PPP) became Prime Minister of Pakistan, who remained in office till his removal April 2012 by the Supreme Court on the charges of contempt of court. After Musharraf, Asif Ali Zardari became President of Pakistan in September 2008, who also tried to seek cooperative relations with Afghan government, but Pakistan's Afghan policy was firmly controlled by Rawalpindi, headquarter of Pakistan's Army.[51] In March 2010, Karzai revisited Pakistan and met Prime Minister Gilani. During this meeting, both the leaders focused on the need of mutual cooperation for the stability in the region for the good of their countries. Moreover, Pakistan also raised concerns over India's presence in Afghanistan. And, to assuage the people of Pakistan over the increasing unrest over India's presence in Afghanistan, maintaining balanced approach, Karzai said, "Afghanistan does not want proxy war between India and Pakistan."[52] The significant development between the two countries was the setting up of the Joint Commission in January 2011 to seek peace with the Taliban, and further, in April 2011, Gilani visited Afghanistan. During this time, both the leaders agreed to add the military and intelligence officials to the joint commission. In a joint news conference with Karzai, Gilani held this visit as "one of the most historical and unprecedented meetings, because all the stakeholders were with us," and further said, "I have assured President Karzai that Pakistan strongly supports an Afghan-led and Afghan-owned process for reconciliation and peace,"[53] Besides, Gilani said, "We both are suffering, we are brothers, we are neighbours, we should fight a common enemy. Therefore we should have a greater cooperation between both countries," and "There should be no blame game, because we want to stop terrorism."[54] By and large, during this meeting, both the countries had discussions over various issues including bilateral relations, regional security, terrorism and cross-border infiltration. Furthermore, in October 2011, Ustad Mohaqiq, member of Wolesi Jirga and the Chairman of Commission on Law and Justice of Wolesi Jirga, met Gilani. During this meeting, Gilani said, "There can be no peace without peace in Afghanistan," and also said, "We want to see independent, prosperous and stable Afghanistan. My government will support any solution which will not destabilize Pakistan as was the case last time when this country had to host three million Afghan refugees."[55]

Further in July 2012, Pakistan's new Prime Minister Raja Parvez Ashraf visited Afghanistan and discussed with the Afghan leaders to advance the Afghan reconciliation process and he also promised the Afghan leaders to help arrange meetings between Afghan and Taliban representatives. Moreover, Britain's visiting Prime Minister David Cameron, Raja Pervez Ashraf and Hamid Karzai together in Kabul agreed to resume meetings of the two-track Peace Commission. Here in Kabul, while talking to the reporters, Ashraf said, "Pakistan is playing the role of facilitator.... If Pakistan can facilitate in any manner, we will do it.... Let me assure you that Pakistan does not support any terrorists. It is not in our interest and we cannot afford it."[56] However, even during Ashraf's visit, Afghan officials kept criticizing Pakistan for its involvement in terrorist activities across the border, and Pakistan also denied all the charges. In fact, Ashraf also could not complete his term and vacated Prime Minister's post on 24 March 2013. Again on 5 June 2013, Nawaz Sharif became the Prime Minister of Pakistan for the third non-consecutive term. It has stated that when Karzai visited Pakistan in August 2013 and met Sharif, the result was disappointing as usual. His visit to Pakistan was said to be ended with muted disappointment and both the leaders failed to move any agreement over the issues of the Peace Talks with Taliban and the insurgent's sanctuaries in Pakistan, and even Prime Minister Sharif showed no passion to deal the Taliban peace talks. However, during this meeting, it was argued that "Pakistan did offer economic assistance to its neighbour in rebuilding the country," but it was also reported according to many analysts that "Sharif cannot do much to bail out Karzai," and "the real power lies at Pakistani military headquarters in Rawalpindi, which exerts influence over the Taliban," as "the Taliban is the Pakistani army's biggest leverage in the landlocked country, providing an advantage against India's growing engagement and influence in Afghanistan."[57] In context of the failures of agreement between two countries, "the problem is that Afghanistan's expectations are higher than Pakistan's ability to deliver. Had Islamabad been really powerful and in control of the Taliban it could have solved its own internal problems and contained the growing menace of insurgencies in its own country."[58] By and large, both the leaders, especially Pakistan could not resolve peace problem with the Taliban. However, concluding his visit, Karzai invited Sharif to Afghanistan. Further in the last week of November 2013, Prime Minister Shariff visited Afghanistan to hold talks with Karzai on the peace process with the Taliban. In fact, before leaving to Afghanistan, Sharif said to the reporters that "peace in Afghanistan is a priority for Pakistan and all efforts would be taken to accomplish that."[59]

In November 2014, to improve the strained relations, new Afghan President Ashraf Ghani visited Islamabad as soon as he assumed power in Kabul and met Sharif. During this visit, both the leaders watched cricket match together and also visited the General Headquarters of the Pakistan Army in Rawalpindi to meet Army Chief Raheel Sharif. This was the first visit to Pak's Army Headquarter by any Afghan President in the decades that showing the gesture of building cooperation between two countries. During his visit to Pak's Army Headquarter, Ghani extended surprising "appreciation" for Pakistan's counter-terrorism efforts assuring Afghan's "cooperation to jointly curb the menace of terrorism." In fact, his visit was aimed at strengthening political, security, and economic cooperation between two countries. Moreover, Ghani's visit to Pakistan was described as "a great opportunity for both sides...to reset their...relations.... The political will exists in Kabul and Islamabad to open a new chapter in ties, as peace in Pakistan means peace in Afghanistan."[60] In fact, bilateral diplomatic efforts were undertaken to normalize the strained relationship between two countries that erupted because of the mutual accusations and blames by the officials of both the sides regarding the hidden sanctuaries and support to the Taliban across the borders of both the countries. Further, after a month of Ghani's visit to Pakistan, however, both the states could not abstain from playing the blame game and started further their mutual allegations and counter-allegations. The fact as has observed that each of the two countries indulged in accusing of extending support to proxies and groups that creating instability and proactively carrying out terrorist attacks on the other side of the Durand Line. Besides, Afghanistan stayed accusing Pakistan of propping up and providing sanctuaries to the Afghan Taliban on its territory, and vice versa. In fact, while Tehrik-i-Taliban Pakistan (TTP) was responsible in carrying terrorist attacks in Pakistan, and Pakistan blamed Afghanistan of providing safe havens to TTP in its soil. Therefore, in May 2015, Sharif along with his military chief visited Afghanistan to talk with the Afghan leaders on the peace issue.

Moreover, the Taliban violence in Afghanistan further threatened traditionally disturbed bilateral relationship between them. The high-level visits and subsequent meetings between the leaders of two countries aimed at promoting cordial relations between the two countries, promoting better understanding and to identify the areas where both the countries can establish cooperation. Moreover, it was also stated that "Pakistan is doing all it can to promote the peace and reconciliation process in Afghanistan that is Afghan-owned and Afghan-led, and... ill continue with this policy."[61] But, in the mid-2015, both the states further experienced mistrust because of the terror attacks in Afghanistan. Besides, Ghani learnt that the Taliban leader Mullah Omar had dead in the hospital in Karachi, which revealed that Pakistan had role of hosting the Taliban in its territory. As a result, undermining Pakistan's role as a facilitator for the peace talks, Ghani said, "We hoped for peace, but war is declared against us from Pakistan territory".[62] However, subsequently in December 2015, President Ghani also visited Pakistan for global conference where he received grand welcome (which is generally offered to the leaders like President of China and not for the leaders of the next door country) by Sharif and his team, and, this development was portrayed that Pakistan was very serious to mend the frayed relationship between them. In fact, it has argued that Ghani was warned by the Afghan leaders even not to smile there in Pakistan. However, criticizing Pakistan for being inactive against taking actions against the sanctuaries for the Taliban in their soil, Ghani in his speech there said, "We are fighting on behalf of all of you, but we are the ones who are suffering some of the worst atrocities."[63] Anguished with Pakistan's incessant role against Afghanistan, despite many bilateral visits and meetings between the leaders of both the countries, while addressing a joint session of Afghan's two houses of parliament in April 2016,

Ghani "threatened to lodge a formal complaint against Pakistan at the United Nations,"[64] and stated that "If we do not see a change, despite our hopes and efforts for regional cooperation, we will be forced to the UN Security Council and launch serious diplomatic efforts."[65] In fact, Ghani had called Pakistan to make attempts to bring the Taliban for the negotiations for peace and also to take military actions against the militant groups active against Afghanistan from its territory.

While addressing a speech in International Peace Conference on Kabul Process that was held in June 2017, Afghan President Ghani singled out Pakistan for its military's alleged support to the Afghan Taliban that has undermined the security and stability in Afghanistan. However, these allegations were countered by Pakistan as baseless. In this context, Pakistan side stated that "the onus of setbacks and failures in Afghanistan should not be blamed on Pakistan. Mere rhetoric of blaming others to hide their failures in Afghanistan will not solve the problem…instead of blaming Pakistan, Afghanistan needs to look inward and identify the real issues."[66] However, while criticizing Pakistan in Peace Conference, Ghani also highlighted Pakistan's "legitimate interests" in Afghanistan and Kabul's willingness to address Islamabad's concerns, and stated, "we recognize that Pakistan has legitimate regional security interests and we have offered the appropriate guarantees of neutrality."[67] It has also stated that due to non-cooperative behavior and blame game between two countries, Ghani denied the visit of Pakistan's civilian and military leaders to Afghanistan. In fact, Ghani's hard stand against Pakistan could not bring any positive change rather worsening the situation further. And making them worst, the Afghan President called Pakistan as "the Centre of the Taliban" due to increasing and incessant attacks on Afghan people and the government establishments in various parts of the country. Ghani said that the list of the individuals engage in terrorist activities and their networks has been shared with Pakistan and also demanded Pakistan immediately to take "clear and specific actions" and not just to give "mere commitments." Contrarily, Pakistan never accepted any accusation declaring them baseless. Pakistan stated, "Blaming Pakistan for security lapses inside Afghanistan is unfair, especially when such large spaces and support to these elements is available within the country."[68]

On 6 April 2018, Pakistan's Prime Minister Shahid Khaqan Abbasi visited Afghan capital, Kabul, aiming to ease tensions between them. Abbasi, during this visit, met with President Ghani, Chief Executive Officer Abdullah Abdullah, and other senior Afghan officials. The reviving peace talks with the Taliban, the return of Afghan refugees who are now in Pakistan, and the exchange of prisoners were high on the agenda of the meeting between Ghani and Abbasi. In fact, ahead of his trip, Abbasi said that "nobody wants peace in Afghanistan more than Pakistan because we are the most affected" by terrorism. Even after his visit, the blame game between two countries remained continue. However, the end of the blame game was said to be agreed upon during the 6 April 2018 meeting in Kabul between Ghani and Abbasi under the Afghanistan-Pakistan Action Plan for Peace and Solidarity (APAPPS). The seven principles in the Action Plan included: "undertaking action against irreconcilable and fugitive elements" on both sides; denying territories to anti-state groups or individuals (on either side); creating a joint supervision, coordination, and confirmation mechanism through Liaison Officers (LOs) for the realization of the agreed actions; avoiding land and air violations of each other's territory; and avoiding the public blame game by using the cooperation mechanisms to respond to mutual contentions and concerns. However, despite, Abbasi's visit to Kabul and mutual agreement on the APAPPS, since 6 April 2018, both the Islamic State of Khorasan Province (ISKP) and the Afghan Taliban continued their attacks in Afghanistan indicating that they were not happy and agreed to the meetings between the leaders of two countries. Moreover, when Ghani declared ceasefire, a high-level security delegation led by Afghanistan's National Security Advisor Muhammad Hanif Atmar visited Islamabad and held meetings and discussions with high ranks Pakistani officials."[69] Furthermore, Pakistan's Army Chief, Qamar Javed Bajwa visited Kabul on 12 June 2018, with a plan aiming how to build trust and avoid mutual blame game over terrorism. During this visit, both the countries also significantly, discussed the area of intelligence cooperation.

By and large, however, both the countries could not bring any fruitful change in their bilateral relations in positive way. In fact, the main hurdle between their bilateral relationships was the use of terrorism as a foreign policy mechanism to accomplish dysfunctional interests by Pakistan for which, as Afghanistan believes, Pakistan providing safe havens for Afghan Taliban. And vitally, no one was ready to act on curbing the menace of terrorism and extremism perhaps because the matter might be beyond their capacity to deal with, lack of political will or the lack of strong leadership which could act strongly and honestly, some might be wishing of status quo.

Positively, amidst incessant bilateral tensions, the military and intelligence officials of both the countries met in Pakistan and agreed to enhance the joint efforts to counter terrorism. The Afghan delegation was led by Hanif Atmar, the Afghan President's national security adviser. On the bilateral cooperation between Afghanistan and Pakistan against the terrorism and other required areas, on 28 May 2018, Pakistan Army's statement came out that both the sides reached to the agreement to fast-track the formulation of working groups, especially on bilateral security cooperation, and to undertake measures that would assist both sides in reduction of violence at the hands of terrorists. Both the sides also assured each other that they would not allow terrorist outfits to use their territory against each other. In fact, almost in every meeting between the leaders and officials of both the sides, the subjects of security cooperation, peace, stability, mutual friendship, and trusts have been discussed and deliberated, but, since a long-time, both the states failed to reach to the hope of any positive change in their bilateral relations. Instead, confrontations appeared permanent between them, and perhaps their confrontations indicated the end of hostility only when either of two perishes.

The new Prime Minister of Pakistan, Imran Khan, who came in power in August 2018, was considered as the next hope for the progress in tense relations between two, and he also hinted positively and promised new and fruitful relations. But, it was seen that Khan's cordiality with the ISI and Pakistan's military headquarter would decide the future plan of the foreign policy towards Afghanistan and the fate of its relationship with the Afghan Taliban as Khan is under major influence of the military of Pakistan. The Pakistan Army has always been keen in peeping into the developments in the domestic politics of Afghanistan. And therefore, Imran Khan also didn't appear confident to do anything positive for the stability in and out of Afghanistan. Until date, no Pakistan's Prime Minister could do anything viable in resolving the bilateral deadlocks and no one could cease to support the Afghan Taliban against the government in Kabul. Prime Minister Khan may also follow the legacy of his predecessors. However, he celebrated the recent victory of the Taliban against the democratically elected government of Afghanistan.

Role in Reconstruction of Afghanistan

The fact is that Pakistan has always been blamed by Afghanistan for anti-Afghan role by supporting the Taliban economically, materially, and strategically and also indulged in playing dysfunctional game to destabilize Afghan's political order. However, it has believed that Pakistan engaged in Afghanistan in positive way also. The media and even the governments in and around Afghanistan, and even Pakistan have not highlighted Pakistan's engagement in reconstruction role in Afghanistan. In fact, Pakistan has also worked in humanitarian activities for the people of Afghanistan. In this context, Pakistan Ambassador Zahid N. Khan counted Pakistan's reconstruction assistance to Afghanistan:

> We have done a number of projects. We have opened a kidney center in Jalalabad, we have built a school and a hostel here in Kabul, and we have built another state-of-the-art hospital, Jinnah Hospital.... We have built a complete unit in Kabul University and in Mazar-i-Sharif we have built a university. But besides these, what we have added to the human capital of Afghanistan is tremendous. We have been giving them for the last three years 3,000 scholarships and from 2018, we have dedicated 200 specialized scholarships only for women. We have been giving them training in plant protection, in operating their

> kidney centers, and all besides that, a large number of Afghan students, around 100,000, are studying in Pakistan. In Brussels we pledged $500 million to do other projects for socio-economic development. We have invited the Afghan government to hold a meeting with us so there can be a need assessment and according to that we are willing to do other projects here.[70]

Pakistan has extended assistance to Afghanistan in various capacities such as a state-of-the-art Allama Iqbal Faculty at Kabul University which has already been completed. The building of Sir Syed Science Faculty Block in Nangarhar University, Jalalabad, the structure of Liaqat Ali Khan Engineering Faculty in Balkh University, Mazar-i-Sharif by the assistance of Pakistan. Moreover, Rehman Baba High School in Kabul, and on the same campus, hostel for 1000 students are constructed. Pakistan has also donated buses for the students of Kabul University. A sprawling Jinnah Hospital Complex with ten towers in Kabul, which is said to be the provider of the most modern health facility in the country, a 200-bed Nayeb Aminullah Khan Logari Hospital in Logar and, the civil work on Nishtar Kidney Hospital in Jalalabad are contributed by Pakistan. Pakistan also took the responsibility to train the Afghan doctors, paramedics, and technicians to run this facility. It has also reported that Pakistan donated mobile field hospitals and ambulances to several provinces. The construction of Torkham-Jalalabad Road in eastern Afghanistan was completed with the help of Pakistan's assistance. Moreover, Pakistan provided assistance to build three intra-city roads in Jalalabad and also provided earth-moving and road building machinery to various provinces in Afghanistan, and, further, Pakistan also "donated 50 buses for public transportation, cash assistance to the Afghan government and food packages to the needy and school supplies to students in large numbers."[71] Pakistan extended its assistance to many other major projects that including two eye hospitals, limb centre at Badakhshan, two Nuclear Medical Centers in Kabul and Jalalabad. Moreover, Pakistan has committed US$330 million for reconstruction and assistance projects in Afghanistan. Even for that matter, Pakistan also constructed several industries in Afghanistan after 2001. State-owned National Bank of Pakistan

(NBP) was the first foreign bank to operate in Afghanistan after 9/11 and two private Pakistani banks were also started in Afghanistan after the NBP. The telecommunication industry of Afghanistan was developed and run on the manpower provided by Pakistan and the Afghans got trained in Pakistan. State-owned Pakistan International Airlines (PIA) pioneered the opening of Afghanistan to international air traffic. Arianna Afghan Airlines uses Pakistan's civil aviation training facilities.[72] It has argued that Pakistan had planned to enhance Kabul's connectivity to the world by improving its road links and developing rail connections with Afghanistan. Many doctors, nurses and other medical supporting staff were provided training by Pakistan.

Furthermore, according to Masood Khalid, Pakistan's Ambassador to China, Pakistan's development assistance to Afghanistan reached to US$1 billion and this assistance boosted investment in infrastructure, education, health, agriculture, and capacity building of Afghan professionals. Pakistan has also made contribution in education by extending 6,000 fully funded scholarships to Afghan students while 100 seats were reserved for women annually. Besides, in the 2018, around 750 Afghan students joined Pakistani universities to pursue their education in Pakistan.[73] Khalid, further said, "Pakistan is also assisting Afghanistan in capacity building in the fields of agriculture, banking, railways, military and diplomacy. Multiple Afghan agricultural professionals have undergone training in Quarantine and Plant Protection in Pakistan," and besides this, it was promised to "provide 20 fully funded scholarships to officials of Afghan Ministry of Agriculture, Irrigation and Livestock to pursue their professional studies at Faisalabad Agricultural University."[74]

Economic Engagement

Interdependency between the states over the trade and business is the significant feature of the present-day bilateral or multilateral relations. And for this, as Richard Cooper stated, "the trend towards economic interdependence between countries will require substantial changes in their approach to foreign policy...."[75] Though both the countries have been envisaging the dilemma of terrorism and extremism and the mutual blame for the proxy wars against each other, the fact is that Pakistan is Afghan's largest trading partner, while Afghanistan is Pakistan's second-largest export destination. However, the fact is that the trade between them has always been in favour of Pakistan that creating trade deficit for Afghanistan as it always remained just as a consumer state for Pakistan's products. Afghanistan is a landlocked country and, as a result, it has to be heavily dependent on the other countries, especially the neighbours, for trade with the world especially through the sea and the land routes. In fact, such type of geographical location has always created troubles to such countries in their trade relations with the world. Therefore, in view of this, such landlocked countries started demanding access to the trade routes of the world. So, by understanding such type of the problems, the United Nations Convention on the Law of the Seas, in 1864, facilitated the landlocked countries the right of access to and from sea without taxation of traffic through transit states. Therefore, according to this law of the seas, Pakistan signed a Transit Route Agreement with Afghanistan on 2 March 1965 (Afghanistan Pakistan Transit Trade Agreement—APTTA). This agreement allowed both Afghanistan and Pakistan to grant and guarantee to each other the freedom of transit through their respective territories.[76] Further, in 2010, the APTTA was redesigned "to allow the transit of Afghan exports through Pakistan to the Wagah border with India, and to the seaport cities of Karachi and Gwadar," and because of this, Pakistan's transportation vehicles are allowed to send its products to entire Afghanistan. Moreover, this agreement also contributed in forming a joint chamber of commerce. Further, in July 2012, both the countries agreed to extend the APTTA to Tajikistan, a first step towards "the establishment of a north-south trade corridor."[77] It has, however, also stated that, despite, Afghanistan has access through Karachi port, it has learnt, according to the Afghan traders, that the administration in Pakistan creates problems while passing through, and Pakistan uses this transit route to pressurize Afghanistan. Besides, it has also stated that in context of India-Afghanistan trade, Pakistan allows the passage of Afghan's trucks or other trading vehicles to India, but, does not allow the vice versa. However, despite redesigning of the trade agreements in 2010 and 2012 to strengthen trade relations and to facilitate the Afghan transit trade route through Pakistan, however, the bilateral trade has been facing the problem of functioning or implementation of it because of the security, stability and other economic factors between them. In fact, healthy and peaceful economic cooperation and adequately improved trade and transit facilities between them have optimum potential to help connect South Asia with the Central Asian countries. For this purpose, even, as has observed by the analysts, the investors from Pakistan seem to be eager to start their business and investments in Afghanistan and in the Central Asian region. Significantly, Afghanistan offers a trade route for Pakistan to access in the Central Asian region. Besides, Afghanistan is also dependent on Pakistan for its outreach especially to connect the South Asian region.

When Hamid Karzai became the President of Afghanistan, he focused on extending economic and trade bilateral relations with Pakistan, and as a result, as has reported, the trade volume between Pakistan and Afghanistan rose from $20 million in 2002 to over $700 million in May 2004, which increased further, however, except only a decline in the year 2006-07. Besides, the bilateral trade risen up to US$2509 million in the year 2010-11.[78]

Trade between Pakistan and Afghanistan has increased substantially, from $0.83 billion in FY06 to $2.1 billion in FY13. Pakistan supplies the largest share of total Afghan imports, at 24.3 percent as of FY13, but this share has declined since 2011 because many factors related to security and stability in the region. Afghanistan's total reported exports are currently equivalent to only 5 percent of total imports, with exports amounting to $363.70 million in FY13.... Pakistan is the largest export destination, accounting for 32.2 percent of all Afghan exports; even without direct transit access, India forms the second-largest destination for Afghan exports, at 27 percent of the total.[79]

President Ghani, in November 2014, while on a visit to Pakistan beholden Afghan's optimum potential to function as a land bridge between Pakistan and Central Asia, and also expected favour from Pakistan for Afghan's trade with India, but, as has stated earlier, Pakistan discourages the trade between Afghanistan and India. However, Ghani decided to improve Afghan-Pakistan "bilateral trade to $5 billion by 2017." Besides, "Pakistan in turn agreed to take measures to clear 95 percent of Afghan goods imported under the transit trade agreement within twenty-four hours, and to lower tariffs and charges for port and storage facilities." It has reported that in 2016-17, the Afghan's total international trade was reported at just over $7 billion, out of which some $ 6.5 billion as imports and around $596 million as exports. The fact was that during this period, only three countries, namely Iran, Pakistan, and China contributed around half of Afghanistan's total imports, each exporting goods worth more than $1 billion to the country. However, further, Ashraf Ghani, after elected as President, planned to look other alternatives and made efforts to enhance Afghan's trade with India, Iran, China, and Central Asian countries.[80] As has observed, because of the tense relations between two, Pakistan's trade with Afghanistan declined and Afghan's trade with India and Iran increased. With the increasing India-Afghanistan trade, Pakistan lost almost half of its trade with Afghanistan and found losing its footprints in Afghanistan. According to Zubair Motiwala, chairman of Pakistan-Afghanistan Joint Chamber of Commerce and Industry, "Pakistan's trade with Afghanistan has slumped to $1.2 billion from $2.7 billion over the last two years." Further he said, "Delhi has been providing various items at subsidized rates to penetrate into the Afghan market and the Indo-Afghan air corridor with a 75% rebate has played a vital role in boosting bilateral trade between Delhi and Kabul."[81] According to the Pakistan Bureau of Statistics, the country's exports to Afghanistan fell to $1.271 billion in FY17 from $1.437 billion in the previous year. Exports in the first quarter of 2017-18 stood at $319 million.[82] Further, according to Zahidullah Shinwari, president of the Sarhad Chamber of Commerce and Industry (SCCI), the strained relations between Islamabad and Kabul are to be blamed for the 80% drop in the volume of bilateral trade, which has dropped from its high of between $2.5-$3 billion to a mere $500 million in 2018.[83] According to the statistics of 2017, trade value between the two countries dropped by $1 billion USD to $1.5 billion

USD. In 2015, the trade between them was $2.5 billion USD. The Commerce Ministry of Pakistan admitted that frequent closures of the Pak-Afghan border had also contributed to the steady decline in exports to Afghanistan. The other factor behind the trade decline between them was that of the diversion of Afghan trade to Iran.[84] As has reported, the bilateral trade volume was $1.6 billion during 2014-15, $1.22 billion during 2015-16, $1 billion during 2016-17. Till April 2018, the bilateral trade volume between Pakistan and Afghanistan was reported just to $930 million the lowest so far. In fact, it has argued that the imposition of regulatory duty on imports, the return of US and NATO forces from Afghanistan have affected the bilateral trade to this low point.[85]

However, to dilute the pressure of dependence for trade route on Pakistan, Afghanistan started seeking alternate routes, and in this direction, Afghanistan, India, and Iran have finalized a draft for a new transit trade agreement aimed to allow Afghanistan's land route through Iran's Chabahar port, in the Gulf of Oman that connecting Afghanistan to the Persian Gulf, and on the other side, allowing the passing of goods from India and other South Asian countries into Afghanistan and Central Asia. As a result, Pakistan seemed to be more jealous and anguished after looking at India's possible strong hands to influence Afghanistan, and even Afghanistan wished, though alternate trade partners, directly or indirectly, to flush Pakistan's dream to influence and pressurize situation in Afghanistan.

Pakistan-Taliban Nexus

While having discussion with Dave Smith, the retired colonel deployed by the Defense Intelligence Agency of the US, the former Director of the ISI, General Mahmud Ahmed, in context of future prospects for security in Pakistan and Afghanistan, in May 2007, said, "Religious extremism is spreading...Military force won't work. Military force won't work in Afghanistan, either.... If the intent is to stabilize Afghanistan, the Taliban were and are the best solution," and also said that the solution to the problem in the region or in Afghanistan was the withdrawal of the American forces from Afghanistan.[86] It is firmly believed that "Pakistan is the single biggest supporter of Islamist militants that threaten Afghanistan."[87] As quoted by Robert Cassidy, according to the Department of Defense Report, 2017, *Enhancing Security and Stability in Afghanistan*,

> Certain extremist groups—such as the Taliban and the Haqqani Network—retain freedom of movement in Pakistan.... The externally supported Haqqani Network remains the greatest threat to Afghan, US, and coalition forces.... Afghanistan faces a continuing threat from this externally supported insurgency and the highest regional concentration of terrorist groups in the world.[88]

During 1980s and 1990s, Pakistan supported Sunni Islamic Pashtun elements including the Taliban even before and during the Taliban's rule (1996-2001) in Afghanistan and also exploited the Afghan territory as a part of Strategic Depth policy.[89] It has believed that

> Pakistan has been intimately associated with the Taliban since its birth in the mid-1990s and the ISI played major role by extending support to Mullah Omar when he founded the organization in Kandahar and the ISI also had provided training to Omar even before in the 1980s in one of its training camps where the mujahedin were trained that had fought the forces of Soviet occupation in Afghanistan. And as stated, Pakistan (along with Saudi Arabia and the United Arab Emirates) had extended legitimate recognition to the Taliban's Regime in Afghanistan in 1996.[90]

When the Taliban had seized power in Kabul in 1996, the Pakistan and its ISI supported the Afghan's power in their hand and also had supplied intelligence and material assistance to use against their opposing forces, ensuring the friendly government that controlled most of Afghanistan.[91] In fact, relationship between Pakistan and Afghan Taliban had become more significantly stronger, which Bruce Riedel described as "complex and complicated nexus":

> Without doubt, Pakistan and its intelligence service, the Inter-Services Intelligence Directorate of the army (ISI), have more influence over the Taliban than any other country or intelligence service. It provides critical safe

> haven and sanctuary to the groups' leadership, advice on military and diplomatic issues, and assistance with fund raising. But its influence is not complete, and whether it could persuade the Taliban to settle for a political settlement in Afghanistan, is unclear at best.[92]

In context of neighbourhood foreign policy especially towards India and Afghanistan, as mentioned earlier, Pakistan's foreign policy premised on the terrorism as its determinant factor. In case of Afghanistan, Pakistan applied policy of supporting Taliban as a means in accomplishing its policy objectives in Afghanistan. Even for that matter, Pakistan, in some cases, also used Afghanistan against India's outreach to the Central Asian region. Pakistan very cleverly felt that its objectives in the region especially against its enemy states could not be born without adopting the method of supporting terrorism, and, as a result, Pakistan believed in. Till the US invasion in Afghanistan in 2001, Pakistan was indulged in providing military support and training to the Taliban regime in Afghanistan such as the sending of hundreds of defense advisers and war experts "to run its tanks, aircraft and artillery, thousands of Pakistani Pashtuns to man its infantry and small units of its Special Services Group commandos to help in combat with the Northern Alliance," moreover, it has also believed that Pakistan supplied the oil that was required for the Taliban's war machines.[93] In fact, despite the UNSC's resolutions prohibiting all the countries around the world not to provide any kind of aid to the Taliban as of its asylum, but Pakistan provided it to the Al-Qaeda and Osama bin Laden. Moreover, it was also reported by the 9/11 Commission, "the ISI had mid-wifed the alliance between Mullah Omar and bin Laden, so it was no surprise that Pakistan ignored the UN."[94] However, after 9/11 incidence, the American military intervention in Afghanistan toppled the Taliban regime, which consequently, defeated the Taliban and they ran out of the Afghan territory and received asylum in Pakistan especially in Baluchistan, where the Taliban leader Mullah Omar himself hidden and settled. However, he began rebuilding his Taliban in exile from Pakistan and by 2004, as it has observed, resumed the war inside Afghanistan. For this, Pakistan extended all critical help and assistance to them to strengthen further. As a result, however, it has argued that without Pakistan's assistance, the Taliban would never have recovered and rebuilt its strength.[95] Moreover, according to the NATO study report published in 2012,

> ISI support was critical to the survival and revival of the Taliban after 2001 just as it was critical to its conquest of Afghanistan in the 1990s. It provides sanctuary, training camps, expertise and help with fund raising. Pakistani officers have been killed on the battlefield in Afghanistan operating under cover with Taliban forces.... The ISI is thoroughly aware of Taliban activities and the whereabouts of all senior Taliban personnel.[96]

Pakistan has always extended its support for survival and revival of the Taliban in Afghanistan. However, it has mostly reiterated that Pakistan has been the victim of terrorism and its people and the soldiers have laid their lives either as a victim of terrorism or fighting against the terrorism. But, Pakistan is also notorious for its support to the terror outfits in the region and it's assertiveness in these activities. Pakistan has been considered as in intact with state sponsor terrorism. Pakistan has extended and assisted the raising of required infrastructure for the terrorism. In fact, it has believed that "Pakistan's struggle against seeping religious radicalization, mindless sectarian violence, frequent suicide bombings, unraveling of ethnic fault lines, and a growing culture of socio-religious intolerance, which it has so assiduously tried to export to both Afghanistan and India," would further potentially shake the stability of Pakistan, however, unless the country's leadership, political or military, rationally promote adequate and positive structural shifts and reforms within the country.[97] However, the analysts believe that Pakistan extended its support to the Taliban because of the "fears of Indian domination in Afghanistan," and that "it is easier to buy Pakistan's line, and hopefully get it to cooperate on the ground," and Pakistan would lose its significance there in Afghanistan, as a result, however, "the vested interests within Pakistan will never allow a neutral and peaceful Afghanistan.... For Pakistan, persistence palpably pays."[98] Furthermore, Tara Kartha narrated Pakistan's dysfunctional role in Afghanistan as:

> First, Pakistan began this whole bloody...cycle of war in Afghanistan, well before the US was aware of it as anything more than a largish spot on a map. Prime Minister Zulfikar Ali Bhutto thought it a good idea to support a group of jihadis as early as 1977-78, to send a message to Kabul that it had better recognize the "Durand Line" as a border, or else. As may be recalled, the Durand Line was imposed on Afghanistan by the British, long before Pakistan came into existence. Bhutto apparently thought it a good idea to invoke the "Islam card" to overcome Pashtun nationalism, probably hoping that religious fervor would dampen ethnic loyalties. Therefore the brutal fact is that the US, didn't start this jihad inspired seemingly endless war. Pakistan did. Second, as Afghanistan deteriorated into chaos following the exit of the Soviets in 1989, it was the then Interior Minister of Pakistan, Naseerullah Babar who virtually created the Taliban, and provided the wherewithal and military advice to push it quickly into Kabul. Babar publicly claimed credit for this achievement, leaving no room for any doubt as to who's was the hand that fuelled the jihadi fire. Islamabad could not possibly have had India in mind when taking this decision. At the time, Indian presence was almost completely absent, as was any interest in Afghanistan's travails.... So the Taliban phenomenon was conceived, aided and abetted by Pakistan for its own reasons, which was to dominate and degrade a neighbouring country.[99]

In fact, Pakistan wanted the US to be engaged in Afghanistan so that to sustain its interests and objectives elsewhere in the region. Terrorism is part of Pakistan's diplomatic trade and it has optimized Afghan's instability by providing "intelligence, weapons and protection to the Afghan Taliban and the Haqqani network."[100]

Pakistan-US Cooperation in Afghanistan

Since its independence in August 1947, Pakistan was militarily engaged with the US in viewing the possible security threats emanating from India and elsewhere. In 1954, both the countries signed a mutual defense assistance agreement and became the cold war allies against the Soviet-led Communist bloc and also since then, the flow of the US's military aid started to move in Pakistan. However, because of the democratic failures and subsequently military rules and wars with India imposed the US sanctions that led to the tensions between them that further creating fluctuations in their bilateral relationship. However, with the Soviet's intervention in Afghanistan in 1979, and the prevailing cold war between the US and Soviet Russia, the intelligence and military agencies of both the US and Pakistan further came closer.[101] From this development, actually, Pakistan grabbed an opportunity to regain its relationship with the US to advance its interests in the region. The US was also keenly interested to have the country like Pakistan for its interests against the Soviet Russia. During the US's strategy aiming for the withdrawal of the Soviet forces from Afghanistan and to compete and to eliminated the Soviet military presence in Afghanistan, the US used Pakistan as a frontline state and poured and channeled weapons to combat the Soviet forces through Pakistan.[102] It has believed that during the period of Zia-ul-Haq as the President (1978-86), Pakistan perceived the Soviet invasion in Afghanistan in terms of exploiting the US's resources such as economic and military support and to achieve its material objective, Pakistan made its bases available for the US forces to fight and sabotage the Soviet presence in Afghanistan and making them to withdraw from Afghanistan. Moreover, Pakistan supported the US's support to the Mujahedeen groups to fight against the Soviet forces in Afghanistan and provided its soil for their asylum. The Mujahedeen are said to be financed by Saudi Arabia and armed by the US through Pakistan's ISI. Therefore, eventually, the coalition of the US, Pakistan, Saudi Arabia and the Mujahedeen imposed pressure on the Soviet forces to withdraw from Afghan soil.[103] These countries covertly supported the Mujahedeen till Soviet's withdrawal in 1988. In fact, military cooperation between Pakistan and the US remained the most significant feature of their bilateral relationship. However, during Pakistan's nuclear weapons programme in 1998 (to balance India's Nuclear Weapon programme in 1998 which was launched by then India's Prime

Minister Atal Bihari Vajpayee), the US had put sanctions on it. But, they could not abstain away from each other for longer time, and after the 9/11, terrorist attack, their relations saw again paradigm shift and became, since then, the strong partners once again. After 9/11, the US attack on Afghanistan forced the Al-Qaeda and the Taliban leaders to cross the Afghan border entering Pakistan, and, Pakistan provided them asylum and since then, Pakistan became the headquarter of the terrorism with further increasing of more terrorist groups. In fact, since then the Bush administration started major war on terrorism. Even for that matter, the US made Pakistan its partner in war on terrorism. In fact since the 9/11, Pakistan had been the major recipients of the US's foreign military assistance. But, Pakistan since then did nothing fruitful in the eradication of terrorism rather supported it further. As a result, the US started raising the questions on Pakistan's credibility over its role in war against terrorism. By learning and understanding Pakistan's foul game in the US mission against terrorism, President Trump pulled tight string against the US's funding and military assistance to Pakistan. However, Pakistan blamed the US and criticized Mr. Trump's New Afghan and anti-Pakistan policy that was declared in August 2017 (for details see chapter on the US Role in Afghanistan). In this context, Mushahid Hussain, Chairman of the Pakistan Senate Defense Committee, wrote for CNN that the country was "an abiding and favorite scapegoat for US failures in Afghanistan."[104]

However, despite Trump's harsh policy, Pakistan's approach towards the terrorism remained unchanged. In fact, earlier, Pakistan enjoyed the military and economic support from the US to gain its interests in the region especially against Afghanistan and India, and later, after its detachment with the US led by Trump, however, a recalcitrant Pakistan further consolidated partnership with China. As both Pakistan and Afghanistan had prolonged tension between them, in 2016, President Ashraf Ghani said that the Taliban would not survive a month without Pakistani support, and Pakistan would not be capable to support the terrorists without, earlier the US and now, China's support. Surprisingly, further, with the increasing tensions with the US, recently, Pakistan has also formed healthy relations with Russia, and, Russia has also grabbed that opportunity against the US By and large, it seems that the new alliance of Pakistan, Russia, and China and even Iran may potentially alter the regional politics in South Asia and in and around Afghanistan. Moreover, despite the US's suspension of military aids and the economic and other sanctions, Pakistan does not seem to stop providing safe havens to the extremists in its soil. It has observed that "US military aid to Pakistan also decreased by 60 per cent between 2010 and August 2017, without a significant impact on Pakistan's behavior."[105] And the reason behind this as Vanda Felbab-Brown stated that

> Pakistan fears an unstable Afghanistan would become a safe haven for anti-Pakistan militant groups and a dangerous playground for outside powers, even though this has already happened; Pakistan bets that the Taliban will maintain significant power and perhaps even obtain formal political power in Afghanistan one day and does not want to alienate it; Pakistan further fears that targeting Afghanistan-oriented militant groups would provoke retaliation in Pakistan's Punjab heartland; Pakistan's lack of full control over the militant groups it has sponsored; and Pakistan is also afraid of a strong Afghan government aligned with India, potentially helping to encircle Pakistan.[106]

Further, on 1 September 2018, the Trump administration has decided to cancel $300 million aid to Pakistan on account of latter's lack of decisive actions in support of American strategy in the region. In fact, before Trump, President Obama had authorized drone attacks on Pakistan safe havens. Further, Pakistan's new Prime Minister Imran Khan "repeatedly blamed Islamabad's participation in the US led anti-terror campaign for the surge in terrorism on home soil over the last decade and has vowed to rebalance Islamabad's relationship with Washington."[107] As has believed, "Pakistan is at war with itself as well as with the rest of the world. Unless Pakistan's military-jihadi complex is completely dismantled, it will continue to pose a threat to the world."[108] By and large, despite its domestic fumbling and pathetic economic and political situations, Pakistan in its foreign policy domain appearing to be successfully surging forward by means of using fox's mind.

Notes and References

1. Hansel, Paul R. "Territory: Theory and Evidence on Geography and Conflict" in *What Do We Know about War?* Edited by John A. Vasquez, pp. 57-84. Lanham, MD: Rowman and Littlefield, 2000.
2. Tuomas Forsberg, Explaining Territorial Disputes: From Power Politics to Normative Reasons, *Journal of Peace Research*, Vol. 33, No. 4, November 1996, pp. 433-49.
3. Brian Taylor Sumner, Territorial Disputes at the International Court of Justice, *Duke Law Journal*, Vol. 53, 1779, 2004, pp. 1789-90.
4. Khalid Nadiri, Pakistan's Choices in Afghanistan: Old Habits, New Consequences, in Harsh V. Pant (ed.) *Afghanistan's Regional Dilemmas: South Asia and Beyond*, Orient Blackswan, New Delhi, 2016, p. 22.
5. Vanda Felbab-Brown, Pakistan's Relations with Afghanistan and Implications for Regional Politics, Brookings Report, 14 May 2015, https://www.brookings.edu/research/pakistans-relations-with-afghanistan-and-implications-for-regional-politics/, accessed on 16 June 2018.
6. Khalid Nadiri, p. 21.
7. *Ibid.*, p. 22.
8. Vanda Felbab-Brown, 14 May 2015.
9. *Ibid.*
10. Vishal Chandra, *The Unfinished War in Afghanistan*, IDSA & Pentagon Press, New Delhi, 2014, p. 188.
11. Moeed Yusuf, Decoding Pakistan's 'Strategic Shift' in Afghanistan, SIPRI, May 2013, p. 1.
12. Bruce Riedel, Pakistan's Role in the Afghanistan War's Outcome, 20 May 2010, Brookings, https://www.brookings.edu/opinions/pakistans-role-in-the-afghanistan-wars-outcome/, accessed on 28 July 2018.
13. Vanda Felbab-Brown, NBR Report #55, 2016, p. 125.
14. Khalid Nadiri, 2016, p. 22.
15. Christopher Budihas, What Drives Pakistan's Interests in Afghanistan?, The Land Warfare Papers, The Institute of Land

Warfare, Association of the United States Army, No. 82, April 2011, p. 6.

16. Tara Kartha, Peaceful Afghanistan not in Pakistan's Interests: The Truth and Lies Behind Islamabad's Interference in Kabul, *FirstPost*, 1 May 2017, https://www.firstpost.com/india/peaceful-afghanistan-not-in-pakistans-interest-the-truth-and-lies-behind-islamabads-interference-in-kabul-3416080.html, accessed on 31 July 2018.
17. Vanda Felbab-Brown, Pakistan's Relations with Afghanistan and Implications for Regional Politics in Mapping Pakistan's Internal Dynamics: Implications for State Stability and Regional Security, The National Bureau of Asian Research, NBR Special Report#55, Washington, February 2016, p. 125.
18. Tara Kartha, 2017.
19. Samran Ali, Afghanistan's Stability, Pakistan's Interests, *The Nation*, 26 February 2018, https://nation.com.pk/26-Feb-2018/afghanistan-s-stability-pakistan-s-interest, accessed on 31 July 2018.
20. *Ibid*.
21. Moeed Yusuf 2013, SIPRI, p. 1; Pakistan has designed the military doctrine of Strategic Depth against and to marginalize the Indian influence in Afghanistan. The Policy is about" (1) a physical concept seeking to incorporate use of Afghan territory as a part of Pakistan's war-fighting plans vis-à-vis India; (2) Treating Afghanistan as Pakistan's backyard in order to keep all Indian influence out of Afghanistan; and (3) Using Afghan territory as the forward base for Pakistan's sub-conventional pro-military strategy in Indian Kashmir during the 1990s. For details see, A. Pande, *Explaining Pakistan's Foreign Policy: Escaping India*, Routledge, London, 2011, pp. 1-87, also see, Lt Col Khalid Masood Khan detailed 'The Strategic Depth Concept' as "Strategic depth, in Military terms, refers to the internal distance within a state from its Forward Defended Localities (FDLs) or the distance from the frontline to its centre of gravity or Heartland, its core population areas or important cities or industrial installations. It refers to the consideration relating to the vulnerability of the centre of gravity of a country to the enemy's onslaught in case of war as against the capability provided by the space available within the territory to halt enemy's advance, counter attack and restore the balance. Militarily, a country having more strategic depth

is considered to be at a greater advantage as compared to the one having lesser space. Strategic depth is a geographical factor, which naturally strengthens the defense capability of a country and on the other hand places great challenges on the aggressor; it reinforces the natural capacity to absorb a military aggression from the defender's point of view, and also burdens the aggressor with the problem of maintaining a long logistical tail. Thus the strategic depth of a country is directly proportional to its national security, especially in case of hostile neighbors. In military history, Russia is considered to be a classic example" of Strategic depth, *The Nation*, 16 October 2015, https://nation.com.pk/16-Oct-2015/the-strategic-depth-concept, accessed on 3 August 2018. Besides, for further theoretical understanding and geographical studies, refer, Ahmet Davutoglu, "Strategic Depth", 2001.

22. Anand Arni and Abhimanyu Tondon, The Genesis of Pakistan's "Strategic Depth" in Afghanistan, *Fair Observer*, 2 June 2014, https://www.fairobserver.com/region/central_south_asia/the-genesis-of-pakistans-strategic-depth-in-afghanistan-88910/, accessed on 3 August 2018.
23. *Ibid.*
24. *Ibid.*
25. Umair Jamal, What are Pakistan's Economic Interests in Afghanistan?, *Asia Times*, 22 December 2016, http://www.atimes.com/pakistans-economic-interests-afghanistan/, accessed on 1 August 2018.
26. *Ibid.*
27. Timothy Nunan, *Humanitarian Invasion: Global Development in Cold War Afghanistan*, Cambridge University Press, 2016.
28. Jayant Prasad, The Travails of Afghanistan: A Contemporary History, *The Wire*, 5 June 2017, https://thewire.in/books/the-travails-of-afghanistan-contemporary-history, accessed on 4 August 2018.
29. Jamal and Bangash, 2016.
30. Christopher L. Budihas, p. 4.
31. Khalid Nadiri, 2016, p. 23.
32. Understanding Pakistan's Strategic Interests in Afghanistan, *The News*, 17 January 2016, http://tns.thenews.com.pk/understanding-pakistans-strategic-interests-afghanistan/#.W2FWxbh1iCl, accessed on 1 August 2018.

33. Jamal and Bangash, 2016, *ibid.*
34. Samran Ali, 2018.
35. Maija Liuhto, Amb. Zahid Nasrullah Khan on Afghanistan-Pakistan Relations, *The Diplomat*, 23 May 2018, https://thediplomat.com/2018/05/amb-zahid-nasrullah-khan-on-afghanistan-pakistan-relations/, accessed on 6 August 2018.
36. In fact, Afghanistan had claimed that with the partition of British India in August 1947, all the agreement with that country became null and void. For details see, Ahmad Shayeq Qaseem, Afghanistan-Pakistan relations: border controversies as counter-terrorist impediments, *Australian Journal of International Relations*, Vol. 61, No. 1, 2007, pp. 65-80.
37. Bijan Omrani, The Durand Line: History and Problems of the Afghan-Pakistan Border, *Asian Affairs*, Vol. 40, No. 2, 2009, pp. 177-95.
38. *Ibid.*
39. Bijan Omrani, 2009.
40. Pakistan: Relations with Afghanistan, The Round Table; *The Commonwealth Journal of International Affairs*, Vol. 52, No. 205, 1961, online 2008, p. 81.
41. Steve Coll, Directorates, Allen Lane, New Delhi, 2018, p. 351.
42. Steve Coll, 2018, *ibid.*
43. Khalid Nadiri, 2016, p. 25.
44. *Ibid.*, pp. 27-28.
45. *Ibid.*, p. 28
46. Karzai, Musharraf Unite on Terror, BBC News, 24 August 2004, http://news.bbc.co.uk/2/hi/south_asia/3589492.stm, accessed on 9 August 2018.
47. Salman Masood and Carlotta Gall, Karzai in Pakistan to mend ties, *The New York Times*, 27 December 2017, https://www.nytimes.com/2007/12/27/world/asia/27pakistan.html, accessed on 9 August 2018.
48. Karzai, Musharraf talk Terror, CNN, 26 December 2007, http://edition.cnn.com/2007/WORLD/asiapcf/12/26/karzai.pakistan/index.html?iref=nextin, accessed on 9 August 2018.
49. Masood and Gall, 27 December 2007.
50. *Ibid.*
51. Khalid Nadiri, 2016, p. 29.

52. Salman Masood, Karzai Meets with Top Officials in Pakistan, *The New York Times*, 11 March 2010, https://www.nytimes.com/2010/03/12/world/asia/12karzai.html, accessed on 21 August 2018.
53. Qaiser Butt, Bridging Trust Deficit: Afghanistan, Pakistan Upgrade Peace Commission, *The Express Tribune*, 17 April 2011, https://tribune.com.pk/story/150241/afghan-peace-plan-pm-military-brass-to-set-off-on-mission-kabul/, accessed on 21 August 2018.
54. *Ibid.*
55. There can be no peace without peace in Afghanistan, *Dawn*, 21 October 2011, https://www.dawn.com/news/667939, accessed on 21 August 2018.
56. Mirwais Harooni, Afghanistan, Pakistan to Resume Talks on Afghan Peace, Reuters, 19 July 2012, https://uk.reuters.com/article/afghanistan-trilateral/afghanistan-pakistan-to-resume-talks-on-afghan-peace-idINDEE86I0FI20120719, accessed on 23 August 2018.
57. Sanjay Kumar, Karzai's 20th Trip to Pakistan: Was it Different From the First?, *The Diplomat*, 29 August 2013, https://thediplomat.com/2013/08/karzais-20th-trip-to-pakistan-was-it-different-from-the-first/, accessed on 10 August 2018.
58. *Ibid.*
59. *The Economic Times*, Nawaz Sharif Leaves for Kabul on Day-long Visit, 30 November 2013, https://economictimes.indiatimes.com/news/politics-and-nation/nawaz-sharif-leaves-for-kabul-on-day-long-visit/articleshow/26625344.cms, accessed on 10 August 2018.
60. Salman Masood, Afghan President Out to Ease Relations on Visit to Pakistan, *The New York Times*, 14 November 2014, https://www.nytimes.com/2014/11/15/world/asia/afghanistan-pakistan-ashraf-ghani-nawaz-sharif.html, accessed on 10 August 2018.
61. Ayaz Gul, Pakistan's Sharif Visits Afghanistan as Taliban Ramps up attacks, VAO News, 12 May 2015, https://www.voanews.com/a/pakistan-afghanistan-sharif-ghani-abdullah/2762992.html, accessed on 10 August 2018.
62. Harsh V. Pant, *Afghanistan's Regional Dilemmas: South Asia and Beyond*, Orient BalckSwan, New Delhi, 2016, p. 3.

63. Rod Nordland and Mujib Mashal, Afghan President Recieves Unexpected Welcome in Pakistan, *The New York Times*, 9 December 2015, https://www.nytimes.com/2015/12/10/world/asia/afghanistan-pakistan-ashraf-ghani-visit.html, accessed on 11 August 2018.
64. Harsh V. Pant, 2016, p. 3.
65. *Ibid.*, pp. 3-4.
66. Umair Jamal, Does Afghanistan Seeks Rapprochement with Pakistan?, *The Diplomat*, 10 June 2017, https://thediplomat.com/2017/06/does-afghanistan-seek-rapprochement-with-pakistan/, accessed on 6 August 2018.
67. *Ibid.*
68. Ayaz Gul, Ghani says Afghan Taliban Centered in Pakistan, VOA News, 2 February 2018, https://www.voanews.com/a/afghan-president-pakistan-taliban/4236002.html, accessed on 9 August 2018.
69. Daud Khattak, Are We Finally Seeing a Breakthrough in Afghanistan-Pakistan Relations?, *The Diplomat*, 15 June 2018, https://thediplomat.com/2018/06/are-we-finally-seeing-a-breakthrough-in-afghanistan-pakistan-relations/, accessed on 6 August 2018.
70. Maija Liuhto, 23 May 2018.
71. Pakistan's Role in Afghanistan's Reconstruction, *Pakistan Today*, 15 October 2011, https://www.pakistantoday.com.pk/2011/10/15/pakistan%E2%80%99s-role-in-afghanistan%E2%80%99s-reconstruction/, accessed on 7 August 2018.
72. *Ibid.*
73. Pakistan's development assistance to Afghanistan reaches 1 Billion US$: Envoy, *The Nation*, 15 June 2018, https://nation.com.pk/15-Jun-2018/pakistan-s-development-assistance-to-afghanistan-reaches-1-billion-us-envoy, accessed on 8 August 2018.
74. *Ibid.*
75. Richard Cooper, Economic Interdependence and Foreign Policy in the Seventies, *World Politics*, 24 (2), 1972, p. 159.
76. Ruzia Sultana, Pakistan, Afghan Economic Relations: Issues and Prospects, *Pakistan Horizon*, Vol. 64, No. 1, January 2011, pp. 21-37.
77. Husain and Ilahi, 2015.

78. Ajmal Rahimi, Opinion: Afghanistan-Pakistan bilateral trade analysis, *Afghanistan Times*, 12 February 2018, http://afghanistantimes.af/opinion-afghanistan-pakistan-bilateral-trade-analysis/, accessed on 13 August 2018.
79. Ishrat Husain; Muhammad Ather Elahi, The Future of Afghanistan-Pakistan Trade Relations, Peace Brief, United States Institute of Peace, 17 August 2015, https://www.usip.org/publications/2015/08/future-afghanistan-pakistan-trade-relations, accessed on 13 August 2018.
80. Ajmal Rahimi, 12 February 2018.
81. Dipanjan Roy Chaudhary, Indo-Afghan ties hit Pakistan's economy, *The Economic Times*, 8 March 2018, https://economictimes.indiatimes.com/news/politics-and-nation/indo-afghan-ties-hit-pakistans-economy/articleshow/63208883.cms, accessed on 13 August 2018.
82. *Ibid.*
83. Bilateral Trade Between Pakistan, Afghanistan has dropped by $2b, *The Express Tribune*, https://tribune.com.pk/story/1616577/2-bilateral-trade-pakistan-afghanistan-dropped-2b/, accessed on 13 August 2018.
84. Ajmal Rahimi, 13 August 2018.
85. Shahid Shalmani, Pakistan, Afghan Trade on decline in recent years, *Arab News*, 4 June 2018, http://www.arabnews.com/node/1314951/world, accessed on 13 August 2018.
86. Steve Coll, 2018, p. 281.
87. Robert Cassidy, Pakistan: Graveyard of Strategy, Modern War Institute, 31 January 2018, https://mwi.usma.edu/pakistan-graveyard-strategy/, accessed on 4 August 2018.
88. *Ibid.*
89. Moeed Yusuf, SIPRI, May 2013, p. 1.
90. Bruce Riedel, Pakistan, Taliban and The Afghan Quagmire, Brookings, 24 August 2013, https://www.brookings.edu/opinions/pakistan-taliban-and-the-afghan-quagmire/, accessed on 26 February 2018.
91. Bruno and Bajoria, 2008.
92. Bruce Riedel, 2018.
93. *Ibid.*
94. *Ibid.*

95. *Ibid.*
96. *Ibid.*
97. Vishal Chandra, 2014, p. 188.
98. Tara Kartha, 1 May 2017.
99. *Ibid.*
100. Vanda Felbab-Brown, Commentary: Why Pakistan Continues to Provide Safe Heaven for the Afghan Taliban, Channel News Asia, 13 Jan 2018, https://www.channelnewsasia.com/news/asia/commentary-why-pakistan-continues-to-provide-safe-haven-for-the-9842316, accessed on 29 August 2018.
101. Greg Bruno and Jayshree Bajoria, US-Pakistan Military Cooperation, Council on Foreign Relations, 26 June 2008, https://www.cfr.org/backgrounder/us-pakistan-military-cooperation, accessed on 28 August 2018.
102. Rajen Harshe and Dhananjay Tripathi, *Afghanistan Post 2014: Power Configurations and Evolving Trajectories*, Routledge, New Delhi, 2016, p. 23.
103. *Ibid.*
104. James Griffiths, Who are the key players in Afghanistan?, CNN, 19 September 2017, https://edition.cnn.com/2017/08/26/asia/afghanistan-pakistan-india-china-russia-us/index.html, accessed on 7 February 2018.
105. Vanda Brown, 13 Jan. 2018.
106. *Ibid.*
107. Agence France-Presse, US to Cancel $300 mn aid to Pak, *The Hindu*, 3 September 2018, p. 12.
108. Harsh V. Pant, *Afghanistan's Regional Dilemmas: South Asia and Beyond*, Orient Blackswan, New Delhi, 2016, p. 12.

5

Iran: The Spoiler?

Introduction

Islamic Republic of Iran (IRI) and Islamic Republic of Afghanistan (IRA) share long common settled border of about 936-km in length and a long history of bilateral relations. Besides, Iran plays a very important role as a political and cultural factor in and around Afghanistan. About 25 percent population of Afghanistan is Shiites which is also as in Iran. Because of this, any ethnic clash in Afghanistan or Iran affects the domestic situation both the countries. The analysts of international politics observed that Iran has played very significant role in the turmoil situation in Afghanistan since the Soviet intervention. And, in February 1979, Iran had Islamic Revolution[1] that was the result of popular uprising led by Khomeini (this uprising was against the US-supported government of Mohammad Reza Shah Pahlavi who ruled from 1941 to 1979) that bringing some changes in Iran's policy towards Afghanistan. During the Soviet occupying of Afghanistan, Iran had created the "ideological sphere of influence" inside Afghanistan by empowering the Shiites, and later created the "political sphere of influence" by unifying the Dari/Persian speaking minorities. Moreover, Iran also created the "sphere of resistance" by supporting the Northern Alliance in Afghanistan and further creating of "economic sphere of influence" by engaging in the reconstruction of Afghanistan.[2] By this observation, it seems that the role and engagement of Iran in Afghan conflict has been held much conspicuously complex and has been changing according to the changing circumstances in and around Afghanistan. In fact, Iran also has been wishing a stable Afghanistan with a friendly and congenial government that protecting the rich diversity of Afghanistan. In terms of security and economic development of Afghanistan, Iran's position has been considered more strategic and significant. However, despite the other factors, the US involvement in Afghanistan in the post-9/11 incidence made Iran's policymakers more concerned and uncomfortable viewing the historical enmity between Iran and the US Therefore, the US presence in Afghanistan became vital factor in Iran's Afghanistan policy. It has observed that Iran developed a security centric and bi-layered foreign policy to safeguard its national interests in and around Afghanistan. Earlier, Barnett R. Rubin stated that the overall Iranian role had been to work closely with the US to bring Karzai into power, however, the Iranians believed that the main threat to them was an American attack to overthrow their government, they might do anything it takes to make the United States and its allies uncomfortable there.[3] By and large, the certain issues such as the presence of the US and the NATO forces in Afghanistan, drug trafficking via Iran, the presence of Afghan immigrants in Iran and internal conflicts and tensions in Afghanistan especially the rise of the Taliban and the Islamic State (IS) are severe issues putting major implications on Iran's national security interests and the bilateral relationships between Afghanistan and Iran.

Besides, Iran sees Afghanistan as a focus point for its "Look to the East-Grand Strategy," which mainly focuses on the increased energy and economic relations between Iran and the eastern countries in the Asia especially China, India, and Japan.[4] However, Iran recently adopted the policy of supporting the Taliban to achieve its foreign policy interests in Afghanistan that making its image negative when the question of fight against terrorism emerges. It has believed that Iran played very important role in Bonn process-2002 that produced the Constitution of Afghanistan.[5] The foreign policy of any state hinges on its internal and external environment and the national interests, and, so, Iran's foreign policy is also shaped by its national interest in the international domain. Moreover, the foreign policy of Iran is mostly shaped by the external factors such as the prestige and international standing of the country. For example, the Western countries like the US and its regional alliances such as Israel and Saudi Arabia termed Iran as a "rogue state".[6] Therefore, by learning such an anti-Iran mindset by others, Iran has formulated its foreign policy towards the West and its immediate regional powers. In fact, according to the analysts of international studies, Iran has also adopted the anti-West policy by proactively supporting the organizations like Hezbollah and Hamas, refusing to recognize Israel as a legitimate state and mushrooming the nuclear weapons and also not abiding by the international laws and norms.[7] According to Bruce Koepke,

> Iran's foreign policy since 1979 Islamic Revolution has been shaped by Ayatollah Ruhollah Khomeini's ideology and Islamic solidarity, and strongly influenced by the country's relations with the United States as well as by the wider geopolitical changes in its region. Iran's policy on Afghanistan over three decades has been broadly constructive and often generous, albeit not consistently transparent. Its Afghanistan strategy is complex and multifaceted but also adaptable and quite pragmatic.[8]

Iran's new policy which was shaped by the Khomeini's ideology and the staunch opposition to the US, was pragmatic.[9] Further, since when Afghanistan came under the influence of the external military forces, Iran's policy under Ahmadinejad (2005-13) adopted dual mode of its policy: support to the President Karzai and his government, and opposition to the US and its NATO allies in Afghanistan. In fact, as has argued, the main objective of Iran's Afghan policy was the Islamic solidarity, support for Shia co-religionists and Dari-speaking ethnic minorities in northern and western Afghanistan and Iran's economic interests and ambitions to assert its position as a regional power.[10] Besides, it has also stated that the international events and developments also shaped Iran's Afghanistan policy especially the sanctions imposed by the US on its nuclear program.[11]

Iran's Interests in Afghanistan

Afghanistan has always been a vital factor in Iran's foreign policy since Iran's Islamic Revolution of 1979. Afghanistan's geopolitical location is of immense value for Iran. As a neighbouring state, Iran has to deal many things with the Afghan government. Afghanistan also offers vital strategic space for Iran's multiple strategic objectives and interests and also in terms of culture, ideology, language, and civilization. Both the states have historical religious (Islam) and cultural (Persian) relationship. As a result, Iran has always been seeking to accomplish its interests in Afghanistan by the means of geo-cultural set up. Iran has always supported the groups of its cultural lineages in the domestic politics of Afghanistan subsequently to create, as stated earlier, a 'sphere of influence' in Afghanistan.[12] Moreover, Iran has specific geo-economic interest in Afghanistan which it is striving to accomplish by involving there. Afghanistan offers a major market for the Iranian products that are now dominated in some of the Afghan provinces, and Afghanistan is also a very congenial place for Iranian investment. In fact, it has believed that Iran wants to establish economic partnership with Afghanistan on the assumption that the post stability situation in Afghanistan would offer more benefits to Iran. Furthermore, energy is the important factor of Iran's economic interests in Afghanistan as it is very important point for Iran to increase and maintain its economic and energy relations with the Asian countries, and moreover, to maintain peace and stability in the region especially in Central Asia. Because, Iran feels its economic interest depends on the stability in the region.[13] Afghanistan is held as "energy hub" as it is located at the centre of a triangle of producing countries such as Iran, Qatar, and Turkmenistan. Moreover, Afghanistan offers Iran with a corridor to China. Iran is also developing its sea port Chabahar that would provide Afghanistan an access to the sea.[14] By and large, Iran's interests in Afghanistan include the factors such as "increased influence, trade and investment, drug trade, Sunni militancy (in the form of the Taliban, Al-Qaeda and more recently DAISH) and foreign presence (vis-à-vis US-led NATO forces in the country)."[15] Besides, Iran's foreign policy sees its national and regional security, geo-political interests and to influence the domestic politics in Afghanistan.

Iran's National Security: As the world powers intervened in Afghanistan (Soviet invasion of 1979 and the US intervention in 2001), their presence and influence in Afghanistan increased the security panic and concerns of the neighbouring countries of Afghanistan. And therefore, as an Afghan's neighbour, Iran also felt a serious security threat to its national security and interest. By creating its sphere of influence by any means in Afghanistan, Iran has always been seeking to prevent the entry of great powers politics in and around Afghanistan.[16] According to Iran, the foreign forces in Afghanistan have been spreading extremism in the region. Iran perceived that the presence of the US forces as a Washington's strategy to strengthen its own strategic position in Central and South Asia, as well as the Persian Gulf, at the expense of Iran's national and security interests.[17] In fact, the most pressing concerns of all had been the US presence, earlier in its west in Iraq and in east in Afghanistan since 2001 to till very recent (2021). Besides, it has also reported that "the US recently had a military presence in Oman, the UAE, Turkey, Israel, Turkmenistan, Kyrgyzstan, Pakistan, Georgia, Azerbaijan, as well as in Afghanistan demonstrates a notion of encirclement for Tehran, which in turn fuels the rejectionist themed ethos of the IRI's regime."[18] Therefore, elimination of foreign forces from its hinterland has been Iran's main foreign policy objective. According to Iran, Taliban-ruled Afghanistan was not compatible with the security interests of Iran, and had expected the elimination of Saddam Hussain from Iraq and the Taliban probably from Afghanistan by the US forces would dilute Iran's security threat perception in the region. However, now, Iran sees the US as a security threat. In fact, it has argued that during the Karzai government since 2001, Iran's policy was seen ambiguous as of supporting to the Afghan government, and on the other hand, covertly supporting and extending military assistance to the Taliban insurgency. Iran realistically exhibited opportunism in case of its national security.[19] Since then, Iran tried to destabilize the US-led mission without toppling the Afghan government of Karzai of the day. During this time, Iran was completely against the regaining of Afghan control by the Taliban. In fact, to protect its national security interests from the US and its allies such as Israel and Saudi Arabia, Iran has extended measured support to the Taliban insurgency in

Afghanistan. By and large, Iran followed the policy of overt and peaceful cooperation with the national government, and covert support to the Taliban in Afghanistan. Moreover, Iran felt that the US has been supporting the anti-Iranian Balochi insurgents to disturb the Iranian territorial integrity. The Baloch insurgents are predominantly Sunni Muslims (an ethnic group scattered in Iran, Pakistan and Afghanistan). These insurgents or nationalists have been seeking the integration of the Baloch dominated province in southeast Iran and the Pakistan territory. Some of the Pakistani Baloch call the Iranian Baloch province as "West Balochistan." The Pakistan's Southwest Baloch-dominated province has emerged as the source of instability to the Iranian government.[20] Consequently, the Balochi insurgency along with the traditional tensions between Iran and Afghanistan (river water disputes, drugs trafficking and the question of Afghan refugees in Iran) has encouraged Iran to provide military assistance to the Taliban.[21]

Security from Drugs Trafficking: The severity of the drugs problem in Iran has been depicted as

> Iran's drug problem has become a national epidemic… the poor as well as the affluent, the secular as well as the pious, to an assortment of hard drugs including crystal meth, painkillers, synthetic hallucinogens and heroin and opium trafficked from neighboring Afghanistan. No walk of society is immune. Even the sons of Islamic clerics….[22]

Iran provides a transit route for 'opium trade', about 60 percent, especially the heroin that is produced in Afghanistan extending towards Turkey and Europe especially western. Even the transit countries are also the consumer states, as a result, Iran also has been facing the problem of drug addiction among the younger generation that costing the economic and social life of the Iranian society. It has reported that about 2.8 million people in Iran are consuming drugs that trafficking from Afghanistan, and, as a result, the UN called Iran as one of the worst addiction crises in the world, affecting people from all walks of society.[23] However, Iran has been spending robustly for the war on drugs in its eastern border with Afghanistan to get rid of, but could not win yet. It has alleged that along with the criminals and drugs peddlers, the

Iranian officials are also said to be involved in the mushrooming of drugs supply chain from eastern borders to western borders of Iran.[24] As Afghanistan is the world's largest source of the drug or opium producer about 90 percent of the world's production, and as reported, Iran as "the main conduit to get it out." It has reported that since the US invasion in 2001, the opium production rapidly surged in Afghanistan. Despite Iran's border guards have long been fighting the drug traffickers crossing from Afghanistan, but Iran's Revolutionary Guards and the Taliban have both benefited from the illicit trade, exacting dues from traffickers.[25] According to one of the Iranian diplomats as quoted by Haji-Yousefi, "by emphasizing the regional solution, Iranian policy in Afghanistan aimed at helping the establishment of an independent and stable government in that country", which, as Yousefi opined that could "lead to returning of Afghani refugees residing inside Iran to their homeland, reducing Afghanistan's rampant drug trade, and increasing bilateral economic cooperation as well as border exchanges."[26] In fact, it has held that "Iran is on the front line in the war against narcotics and that Iranian antidrug forces are reputed to be some of the best in the world…their work accounts for 80 percent of the opium and 25 percent of the heroin intercepted worldwide."[27] Moreover, the Iran government has started comprehensive policy by establishing rehabilitation centers for the treatment of the addicted Iranians. Iran has also been held as an important active partner in the efforts of UNODC (United Nations Office on Drugs and Crimes). Iran was also engaged in Iran-Afghanistan-Pakistan tripartite sessions on drugs control, and also agreed in 2008 on the joint plan against the cross-borders drugs trafficking especially from Afghanistan. Besides, Iran is said to be one of the forerunners to campaign against the drugs trafficking that has been emanated from Afghanistan.[28] However, contrarily, Iran has established contacts with the Taliban militants who are said to be responsible for growing and trading rampantly the production of opium and heroin in Afghanistan. Iran is also accused for "participating in drug trafficking with the Taliban."[29] Both Iran and the Taliban are benefiting from drug trafficking. According to the UNODC, "$28 billion worth of heroin and opium is annually trafficked from Afghanistan to

Western Europe, and Iran's drug problem has become a national emergency."[30] However, by and large, Bruce Koepke argued that

> Iran's attempts to strengthen its influence in Afghanistan to secure regional security and geopolitical interests will, in turn, be shaped by US relations, radical Sunni insurgency-generated border instability, possible Taliban reintegration, the narcotics industry, nuclear negotiations, and potential ongoing sanctions. Constructive Iranian-Afghan cooperation could catalyze international engagement on broader political concerns, but continued US presence and/or Taliban resurgence could create unpalatable future scenarios for Iran. All political issues and policies, however, will remain tied to Iran's nuclear issues.[31]

Bilateral Disputes

Afghan Refugees in Iran: Among many, the refugee issue is also very critical between the bilateral relations between Iran and Afghanistan. The incessant war and rampant poverty in Afghanistan forced the Afghan people to be scattered across the globe for survival, and, millions of these Afghans are living and many grown up in refugee camps especially in Iran and Pakistan and some are working as labours in states of Persian Gulf region. Iran has been providing asylum to millions of Afghan refugees which were influx in Iran after the war that caused because of the Soviet invasion, civil war and later the Taliban control of Afghanistan. However, because of the refugee problems, both Iran and Afghanistan have tensions. It has also believed that Iran showed much liberal and generous approach towards Afghan refugees allowing them to live and work within Iranian society and they are said to be living as "immigrants" rather than refugees.[32] But despite its generousness towards them, Iran has been concerned for their burden in financial terms as they are accessing and benefiting the Iranian welfare and other systems that are intended to be enjoyed by the Iranian citizens, and therefore, all these are increasing the delivery costs that increasing financial burden on the Iranian exchequer. Therefore, it has alleged that to escape from this excessive burden, Iran adopted the "forced repatriation of Afghan refugees from Iran."[33] According to Iran's

Statistical Center, there are more than 95 percent of migrants in Iran originated from Afghanistan and their number exceeds 1500,000. Moreover, there are many illegal Afghani in Iran that has created and presented the problem of social services.[34] It has reported that "Two million undocumented Afghans and a million Afghans with refugee status already lived in Iran."[35] However, it has estimated that only about 950,000 Afghan refugees are United Nations registered, as the Iranian authorities have not provided legal asylum to all the Afghan refugees.[36] According to Akram Khatam, a human rights activist, "the social stage is still not set for a change towards the way Afghan migrants are viewed publically in Iran," however, it has seen that the Iranian's "attitudes toward Afghan migrants are headed in a positive direction"...and "Iranians, particularly the younger generation, are extending sympathy toward Afghan migrants for the hardships they have gone through. More and more Iranians are standing behind Afghan migrants in asserting their rights."[37] However, the Afghan origin students are still meeting with unequal treatment by the Iranian administration. The Afghan students in Iran have major challenges of education and jobs opportunities. However, to abridge inequality with the Afghan students, the Iranian leader Ayatollah Ali Khamenei called the Iranian officials to register and provide equal education to the Afghani students across the nation.[38] The millions of Afghani people living in Iran are said to be homeless and shelterless which is considered as the major problem for the Iranian administration. The Iranian government is also accused for "severe maltreatment of Afghans, including summary deportations, physical abuse at the hands of security forces, limited job opportunities outside menial labour, and restricted access to education."[39] According to Patricia Gossman, an Afghanistan senior researcher for Human Rights Watch (HRW), "Afghans face discrimination in several areas, including restrictions on travel and freedom of movement, legal barriers to claiming asylum and limited access to humanitarian aid, among other things."[40] However, condemning the accusations made against Iran over the Afghan refugees and defending Iran, Masoud Hamyani stated

> Iran has been hosting millions of Afghan refugees for almost four decades. Presently, 11 per cent of the total population of Afghanistan dwells in Iran. This has been a great source of income and repatriation of millions of dollars to their own country annually. Also, Iran is bearing a huge spending annually for the education of more than 3,80,000 Afghan refugee children in Iranian schools and 17,000 Afghans in universities at different levels. Importantly, 77,000 undocumented Afghan children were allowed to enroll in Iranian public schools based on a decree issued by Iran's Supreme Leader. To cite an example, three Afghan students, including a girl, have attained top ranks in Iran's highly-competitive nationwide university entrance exam for a Master's degree....[41]

Furthermore, it has also stated that some Afghan refugees in Iran are also poured into the battlefield of Syria. The Iranians are providing 10-years living permit to unauthorized Afghan refugees on the condition if they go to Syria to fight in a war.[42] On the Afghan refugee's battlefield role in Syria, Ali M. Latifi very aptly reported

> The Fatemiyoun Division (formerly Brigade), a militia of Shiite Afghan refugees, was formed around early 2014 and trained by both the Revolutionary Guards and Hezbollah veterans. Its strength has been estimated at 8,000 to 14,000 men. The Iranian authorities maintain the fighters are volunteers. The initial recruits to the Fatemiyoun Division were initially Shiite Hazara Afghans, who settled in Iran after the Soviet occupation, after the civil war in the early 1990s and the subsequent Taliban rule. Their recruitment had echoes of how Pakistan—the other major host of the Afghan refugee population—recruited the Sunni Pashtun Afghan refugees and their children to form the Taliban in the mid-1990s.... In the past few years, Iranians have expanded recruitment to undocumented Afghans.... Apart from the refugees' economic anxiety and precarious legal status, the Iranians exploit the Shia faith of Afghan refugees to recruit them to fight for the Assad regime in Syria. Iranian propaganda framed the Syrian war to these

> refugees as a Shiite struggle for the defense and protection of the faith and its holy sites. The fighters have little or no knowledge of the political-security context into which they are marching.... They do not speak Arabic, most of them have never been beyond Afghanistan or Iran, many are barely literate, most are devout Shiites. Iranians and Mr. Assad's forces used the Afghan recruits as the first-wave shock troops (the first in any operation)...the Afghans being sent to fight the most difficult battles, and speak about heavy casualties among Afghan fighters and the eventual victory after multiple assaults. They (Iran administration) never make a show of the Iranian fighters who die in Syria, only the Afghans...hundreds of Afghans killed in Syria in Qom. It is their way of trying to convince the Iranian people that only Afghans, and not Iranians, are dying in Syria.[43]

Human Rights Watch also confirmed above information by stating that, "Iran has been recruiting thousands of Afghan refugees to fight in pro-government armed groups in neighbouring Syria. Many had been coerced into fighting, while some had been deported to Afghanistan as punishment for refusing" and many others were "offered residency papers and financial incentives in exchange for taking up arms in Syria." However, Iran's foreign ministry has denied all such allegations and claimed that the refugees have volunteered to fight in Syria out of political or religious convictions.[44] However, despite all the allegations, the UN has praised the Iranian government for taking intensive care of the Afghan refugees. The UN High Commissioner for Refugees in Tehran, Sivanka Dhanapala said, "The leadership demonstrated by the Iranian government has been exemplary in hosting refugees and keeping borders open."[45] In fact, the Iran administration has complained that the excessive presence of Afghan refugees has created myriad problems in the Iranian social order. According to the Iranian officials, "The refugees put a strain on Iran's economy by competing with Iranian citizens for scarce jobs, while weakening the economy by consuming and using Iran's heavily subsidized goods and services...(they) might also pose security risks because of their illegal status in the country."[46]

However, highlighting their significance in Iran, it has argued that

> The presence of Afghan refugees in Iran provided Tehran with a unique opportunity to train an indigenous Afghan force that was to be relocated to Afghanistan at the opportune moment. This policy permitted Iran to create a sophisticated network inside Afghanistan, reinvigorating indigenous organizations, and creating new, disciplined forces, similar to Lebanese Hezbollah. Iran established training centres in...(various) cities in Iran, where members of the Afghan Shi'i organizations received military training for six months."[47]

Water Dispute: The issue of river water sharing of the Harirud and Helmand rivers has posed major challenge and confrontations in the bilateral relations between the two countries. Both these rivers pass through Afghanistan to flow in Iran. In fact, both countries have dispute over the trans-boundary waters of these rivers since, as has been reported, 19th century. The problem of disagreement between two has affected the livelihood of the people of both the sides. In view of resolving the water conflicts, in 1973, both the countries signed an agreement, and according to this agreement, Iran paid some amount of money to Afghanistan, and Iran could receive water of 850 million cubic meters of water of Helmand River from Afghanistan. However, subsequently, the coups d'état in 1973, later the Soviet invasion in 1979 in Afghanistan, and also the Islamic Revolution of Iran in 1979 marginalized and devalued this agreement further only to invite the confrontations between both the countries.[48] After this, because of the instability in Afghanistan and the Taliban's control of Afghan's power between 1996-2001, both the countries could not find an opportunity to come across the table to resolve the issues of water disputes between them. Furthermore, after 2001, President Karzai and his successor Ashraf Ghani started construction of the dams on the rivers. The construction of Salma dam on Harirud by India, development of Kajaki dam and construction of Kamal Khan dam on Helmand River have been among the most important of those projects.[49] It has, however, stated that "the development of hydro-electric power such as through the Salma hydro-electric dam along the Harirude, is also likely to heighten tensions between the two countries, as the dam will likely to affect the amount of water available to Iran," and "Afghanistan has plan to build 21 dams in the different parts of the country, some of them on rivers that flow downstream to Iran."[50] The Iranian Republic President Hassan Rouhani, as a result, raising its concerns in a conference held on 3-5 July 2017, in Tehran (International Conference on Combating Sand and Dust Storms) criticized "…Afghanistan for implementing these dam building projects, noting that the Islamic Republic could not remain indifferent to construction of Salma, Kamal Khan and Kajaki dams in Afghanistan."[51] Afghanistan also reacted sharply on Rouhani's criticism.

Diplomatic Engagement

In 1919, Iran had extended formal diplomatic recognition to the Afghan government and since then both had normal relations, however, except in the years 1962 (tensions on the issue of Hirmand River which is still prevailing as recently Afghan government has blocked the flow of Hirmand water that entering in the Iranian territory. Hirmand is in Afghanistan territory), 1979 (Soviet intervention) and the Taliban regime 1996. In fact, during the Taliban regime, Iran-Afghanistan diplomatic relations were tense and hostile as, in 1997, Iran had rejected the Taliban regime and had extended support to the Northern Alliance (along with India and Russia). Besides, the Taliban had started violence against the Shia's in Afghanistan and also had its hands in killing of Iran's diplomats in Mazar-e-Sharif in 1998 in reaction to Iran's support to the Northern Alliance. Iran discarded to offer recognition to the Taliban governments during this periods.[52]

Till its Revolution in 1979, the Shah's government kept watch on the political developments in Afghanistan with a view to alter or manipulate the conditions in favour of Iran. Further, it has also argued that the USSR's Ambassador to Iran had discussed with Iran's Ayatollah Khomeini about the Soviet mission of intervention on the request of Afghan government.[53] However, Iran was the first country to oppose the Soviet invasion in Afghanistan in 1979, and had expressed strong sympathy for the Afghan Muslim's suffering. Iran believed that communism was more dangerous that was predictably seen spreading in Afghanistan, and the immediate consequence of the Soviet's invasion was the influx of more than two million Afghan refugees in Iran and about same number to Pakistan. Even for that matter, however, Afghanistan had also held Islamic revolution of 1979 as dangerous to Afghan's interest, as a result, showing its negative approach to Iran. This development had damaged the diplomatic relations between Afghanistan and Iran.[54] Iran felt Soviet's presence in Afghanistan as a threat to its security and sovereignty, and even after that the US presence in Afghanistan since 2001 increased Iran's security concerns. Therefore, to normalize its security concerns in the region that emerged because of the big powers presence, it has stated that Revolutionary Iran was "acting idealistically rather than realistically in its foreign policy regarding Afghanistan...aimed at preparing the ground for the Soviet withdrawal as well as securing its status and central role in the post-occupation state through supporting different Afghan groups affiliated to Tehran such as Shiites.[55]

During the Soviet-Afghan war, Iran sent "the Islamic Revolutionary Guard Corps (IRGC) forces to provide training and support to Shi'a groups in an effort to export Islamic Revolution in Afghanistan."[56] Further, after the withdrawal of the Soviet forces from Afghanistan, the pro-Soviet government in Afghanistan lasted just for about two years and thrown out of the power in 1992, and the Mujahedeen government occupied power in Kabul (1992-96). During this time, Iran's foreign policy was said to be baffled because of the growing civil wars there in Afghanistan as the different Afghan groups started conflicting amongst themselves (and also because of the meddling of the warlords like Soviet Russia, the US, Pakistan, and Iran). Such conflicting situation increased Iran's concerns, and, as a result, Iran tried to normalize the turmoil situation in Afghanistan and also to establish agreements amongst the fighting groups by conducting various meetings. However, Iran had officially supported the Mujahedeen government. But despite, multiple efforts, Iran could not stop civil war in Afghanistan.[57]

After the Soviet withdrawal and the fall of the Najibullah government in 1992, Iran's involvement in Afghanistan increased at the larger extent. It has argued that with the end of war with Iraq in 1988, a more stable Iran could spend its resources to spread its influence in Afghanistan. From 1992 to 1996, Iran extended its support not only to the Rabbani government in Kabul but also to the various Mujahedeen groups fighting with each others to control the power, and simultaneously provided assistance to the dissident groups fighting against the government as well. This exhibited Iran's flexible and dual policy in Afghanistan. However, after the Taliban's control of power in Afghanistan on 26 November 1996, Iran supported the Northern Alliance against the Taliban regime.[58] In fact, Taliban's controlling of Afghanistan was condemned by many states including India, Iran and others and felt it as a threat to peace, stability and security in and around Afghanistan, and even the ideologically different countries in and out of the region. However, Pakistan, Saudi Arabia, and the UAE had supported and extended official recognition to the Taliban government. During this time, the major conflict was persisted between "the Sunni fundamentalist Mujahedeen, the group from which the Taliban emerged and the United Islamic Front for the Salvation of Afghanistan or Northern Alliance", and "the Taliban continued gaining ground in this conflict as it controlled 75 per cent of the country by 2001."[59] Iran held the Taliban government as a severe threat to its national security and posing major challenges to Iran's foreign policy towards Afghanistan and beyond especially its 'look to east policy.' The Taliban's actions were held against Iran. In this context, it was stated that Taliban "not only targeted the Islamic nature of the Islamic Republic of Iran, but also was a threat to its Iranian nature." Besides, the support that Taliban had received from Pakistan, Saudi Arabia and others, had heightened Iran's serious concerns. The massacre of Shiites in Mazar-i-Sharif (about 2000 Shiites)[60] and the killings of eight Iranian diplomats and one journalist and the captive of the 50 Iranians by the Taliban compelled the Afghan-Iran relations in critical and bad situation that forcing Iran and Afghanistan on the brink of war in September 1998. Further, Iran's Supreme Leader, Ayatollah

Ali Khamenei, accused Pakistan for supporting the Taliban in capturing Bamiyan after the Mazar-i-Sharif. The Taliban had massacred hundreds of Hazara ethnic group of the Bamiyan. As a result, Khamenei had mobilized Iranian force of "70,000 that composed of Iranian Revolutionary Guards and Iranian military forces, along the Iran-Afghanistan border."[61] However, "war between the two countries was averted when the Taliban, after the threat of war by Iran and under the pressure of the United nations, returned the bodies of the murdered diplomats and sent the captive Iranians home," and Iran had perceived the captive of its nationals as a national humiliation.[62] This incidence was admitted by the Taliban leader Mullah Mohammad Omar that the Taliban soldiers had either intentionally or unintentionally killed the diplomats.[63] In this context, the spokesperson of the IRGC vehemently argued that "the Taliban and the main agents responsible for this horrific crime must know that they shall never be immune to the tumultuous anger of the Islamic corps."[64] In fact, in the late 1990s, the Taliban deliberated anti-Shiite program that provoked the war with Iran. During the Afghan civil war, the Taliban had aimed to cleanse northern Afghanistan of Shiite Hazaras.[65] By and large, during the Taliban regime, Iran-Afghanistan relations were mostly strained and tense. Iran along with India and Russia was emerged as one of the strong supporters of the anti-Taliban movement on the common assumption that "a fundamentalist Sunni Islamic government in the region would have a negative impact on regional security and stability, limiting trade and investment in the newly independent Central Asian States."[66]

The fact was that, being a regional power and neighbour, Iran has a strategic stake in Afghanistan and always wished to develop its sphere of influence in Afghan administration and politics, and therefore, to maintain the domestic situation in Afghanistan congenial for its interests, Iran focused on keeping all the options open and putting its enemies away from dominating Afghanistan. In this context, the former CIA officer Robert Baer stated that "Afghanistan has long been a source of instability and strategic interest for Iran.... Under both the Shah and Ayatollah Khomeini, Iran demonstrated that it will take almost any measure to keep western Afghanistan out of the hands of its enemies", and in 1996, for instance, Iran 's National Security Council took decision in an emergency meeting to invade Afghanistan to capture Herat to prevent Taliban's movement near Iran's border, however, the Taliban threat was diluted and Iran aborted the plan of invasion, but the decision was "evidence of Iran's commitment to keep that part of Afghanistan at least neutral."[67]

Furthermore, gradually, Iran emerged as the main foreign supporter to the Northern Alliance which was main domestic rival of the Taliban, besides, Iran also tacitly cooperated with the United States in overthrowing the Taliban in 2001. "Although Iran originally viewed the Taliban as an ideological threat, geopolitical dynamics post-9/11 changed Tehran's original calculation."[68] Therefore, it has argued that "the Iranian main foreign policy goal during the reign of Taliban was to support the anti-Taliban coalition inside Afghanistan, on one hand, and to participate in regional and international meetings held for the resolution of crisis in Afghanistan, on other hand."[69] Consequently, in terms of protecting its domestic and external interests, Iran extended military assistance to the anti-Taliban forces in Afghanistan. In fact, "Iran stressed that the Taliban control over Afghanistan is not legitimate and would put the regional peace and security at risk.... Taliban was not only a regional threat for Iran but a global threat...."[70] And Iran's future global threat prediction of the day came in reality in terms of deadly 9/11 incidence. As has mentioned, Iran provided support to the US against the Taliban. Subsequently, the 2001 US invasion in Afghanistan offered major opportunities for Iran to spread its influence in Afghanistan. Therefore, with this objective, "the IRI was influential in taking part in the December 2001 Bonn Agreement which was aimed to promote national reconciliation, lasting peace, stability and respect for human rights in the country [Afghanistan]."[71] In other words, Iran played very constructive role during Bonn process which produced Afghan's Constitution based on democratic principles.[72]

After the US intervention in Afghanistan, Iran's foreign policy concerns especially its national security could not be normalized, though the Taliban's threat saw some normalization with the

US presence in Afghanistan near its eastern border. In fact, not only the US presence in its neighbourhood, but the problem of stability in Afghanistan and in the region was also the matter of Iran's security concerns. However, Tascano termed the Iranian role in Afghanistan as "spoiler" and wanted "to create difficulty in order to sell facility."[73] After the overthrow of the Taliban regime and the control of Afghanistan by the Northern Alliance, the internal disputes on the question of who will be the leader of new government in Afghanistan emerged because of the ethnic identity, as the Northern Alliance was dominated by the Dari-speaking Tajiks and about 40 percent population of the Pashtuns in Afghanistan. However, this deadlock was cleared with the help of Iran. The Iranian leaders could convince the leaders of the Northern Alliance to support the leadership of the Pashtun leader Hamid Karzai for the post of the Afghan President. During this time, Iran emerged as the major troubleshooter in Afghanistan by garnering support for Karzai.[74] And, "Iran continued to demonstrate its support for the Post-Taliban government in Afghanistan in February 2002 by expelling Karzai's opponent Gulbuddin Hikmatyar."[75] According to Will Fulton, "The fragile political and security situation in Afghanistan, however, has provided the Islamic Republic with an opportunity to extend its political, economic, and military influence. Iran has attempted to take advantage of this opportunity by building ties with the Karzai government...", besides, "while at the same time supporting the Taliban insurgency through its Qods Force", and "Iran has also extended its ideological influence in Afghanistan through channels like the Imam Khomeini Relief Committee."[76]

In a summit that was held in David Camp, 6-7 August 2007, Afghan President Karzai, in the presence of US President George W. Bush, had appreciated Iran as "a helper and solution", and further stated that "Iran has been a supporter of Afghanistan, in the peace process that we have and the fight against terror, and the fight against the narcotics in Afghanistan".... "They (Iran and Afghanistan) had very, very good, very, very close relations".... "We will continue to have good relations with Iran. We will continue resolve issues, if there are any, to arise."[77] Further during Iranian President Mahmoud Ahmadinejad's visit to Afghanistan, on 14 August 2007, welcoming him, Karzai held their relationship as historic and friendly, and stated that since Bonn Conference 2002, Iran had been helping Afghan people in their efforts of "security, counterterrorism, reconstruction and improving people's life." Moreover, the Iranian President expressed that Iran and Afghanistan are "two brother nations with common interests, cultures and histories...we are neighbours whose relationship cannot be bound by any restrictions; neighbours are the natural allies," and subsequently, both the countries signed six bilateral cooperation agreements.[78] However, by believing in the method of by hooks or by crooks, Iran also made attempts to influence the Afghan politics by giving cash amounts to President Karzai's office, several members of parliament and other officials, according to the report which was revealed in 2010. In a press conference, President Karzai himself confessed that Iran provided from 500,000 to 700,000 Euros to his office once or twice a year, and he also said that Afghan would keep it asking Iran for such cash. Karzai described these cash as official aids, which he received similarly from the US administration also.[79] However, Shukria Barakzai, an Afghan lawmaker and a chair of the Defence Committee in the Afghan Parliament, stated that Iran had spent millions of dollars expanding its influence in Afghanistan. Criticizing "Iran as a cancer," she further stated, "It has affected all the Afghan government and nongovernmental bodies. They are everywhere: in the higher-education system, working with the media, working with civil society."[80]

Above all, it has observed that Iran maintained its diplomatic engagement with Afghanistan by the means of "an overwhelming economic presence, both in trade and investment, the growth of important routes of trans-frontier communication, political influence over local authorities, the active presence of Iranian intelligence"[81] especially in the Herat province and Kabul of Afghanistan. In other words, Iran's "soft power" including Iranian culture is significantly prevailing in Afghanistan's few regions.[82] However, by and large, Ray Takeyh writes in the book titled *Hidden Iran: Paradox and Power in the Islamic Republic,* "[F]or Tehran the issue in Afghanistan has not been ideological conformity but stability."[83] In this context, Toscano pointed out that

> Iran's Afghan policy is not ideological, nor is its inspired by religious priories, but aims more at guaranteeing security, increasing political influence and seizing economic advantage...Afghanistan offers Iran, and more specifically the Iranian regime, an opportunity for breaking out of its isolation by becoming a part of a regional and global arrangement for its management after the International Security Assistance Force (ISAF) pull-out.[84]

In Afghanistan, in fact, Iran's main objective has been to make sure that any foreign forces that are deployed should leave eventually, and that any Afghan government of the day in power would not, at least, threaten its interests, and, should be friendly or aligned with them, and for this order, Mohammad Reza Bahrami, the Iranian Ambassador stated, "We are responsible.... A strong accountable government in Afghanistan has more advantages for strengthening our relations than anything."[85] Gradually, the leaders of Iran and Afghanistan started and engaged in many diplomatic visits to consolidate their bilateral relations for mutual cooperation on various issues of common interest. In July 2013, Iran-Afghanistan Agreement was signed to allow Afghanistan access to Chabahar Port. Further in December 2013, Karzai visited Tehran and strengthened his friendly relationship with newly elected Iran President Rouhani through a strategic Iran-Afghanistan Agreement.[86] The political engagement between both the countries was seen at the highest level when the Foreign Minister of Iran Javad Zarif visited Afghanistan in January 2015 and later, in April 2016, the Afghan President Ashraf Ghani also visited Iran. President Ghani, during this time, in his meetings with the Iranian leaders like President Rouhani and supreme leader Ali Khamenei, discussed the issues such as economic, security, and cultural ties, and more importantly, the issue of Afghan Refugees in Iran was in the centre of the meetings. Further in January 2016, the Chief Executive Abdullah Abdullah also visited Iran with the hope of creating better future for cordial relations and cooperation. He discussed various issues with the Iranian leaders. The important issues that were focused in these meetings were strengthening of economic relations and also the major development of cooperation between Iran, India, and Afghanistan on the joint project of the Chabahar port. Besides, providing of education to the Afghan refugees in Iran, joint fight against terrorism and extremism, and the focusing on the completion of Iran-Afghanistan railway network as early as possible.[87] However, further in July 2017, the Iran-Afghanistan relationship observed deteriorating, when Iran's President Hassan Rouhani criticized "Afghanistan's water management and irrigation projects for causing environmental damage in Iran."[88] As has been argued by Masoud Hamyani,

> The Iran-Afghanistan relations have not been influenced by any third party and...both the sides are negotiating a strategic partnership through the establishment of five committees on different issues.... Iran remains committed to its undertakings and respect the Afghan sovereignty, independence, territorial integrity and national unity. Tehran values its cultural-historical ties with Kabul, has always supported peace, stability and security, and has been there to support its neighbour's socio-economic development. Nothing shall change this.[89]

Economic Engagement

Iran holds prominently the strategic significance in multi-ethnic Afghanistan and also is considered as a key factor in Afghan's economic and security structure. Iran's engagement with Afghanistan has been major in economic terms and also intended officially to influence the Afghan administration by means of economic help. Iran was said to be the first country that started extending assistance to Afghanistan in the reconstruction of its destroyed infrastructure, and ruined and crippled economy. Iran allocated and provided hundreds of millions of dollars as grants, loans, and investment for the development projects and also extended the technical and vocational training facilities in Afghanistan. In fact, main objective of Iran remained to establish a sphere of economic influence in Afghanistan. Iran is a major economic partner of Afghanistan and has assisted Afghanistan economically to establish stability and peace there as Iran's national interests in and through Afghanistan hinges on the internal situation and stable government in Afghanistan. Earlier, in 1975, the Shah of Iran had offered Afghanistan $2 billion over a ten year period and early in the same year $400 million on easy terms.[90] Furthermore, with the removal of the Taliban, Iran increased its economic engagement in Afghanistan. As a result, in the Donor Conference (Tokyo) in 2002, Iran, a major economic player, had pledged $560 million (about 12 percent of total $4.5 billion assistance) for the reconstruction and development of roads, energy, infrastructure, and schools in Afghanistan, which was the largest amount of any non-Organization of Economic Cooperation and Development (OECD) state.[91] And later in London Conference-2006, Iran assured $100 million to Afghanistan. Iran also spent $50 million per year between 2007 and 2013 for the better future of Afghanistan.[92] As stated, Iran has always been keenly interested in stability in Afghanistan, as a result, always participated in most of the conferences on the Afghan mess that helped in having friendly relationship with the Karzai government resulting in the strengthening of the economic relations between two countries. As mentioned earlier, "in October 2010, (Karzai) acknowledged that his office accepted about $2 million per annum from Iran."[93] During this time, Iran had set its export of $500 million annually to Afghanistan, besides, its commitment to the reconstruction of infrastructures in the country. For example, the multimillion dollar plans to secure power supply of Afghan western regions with the help of Turkmenistan, and to secure the natural gas supply of Herat.[94] According to Milani, during 2002-03, Iran's export to Afghanistan was only about $120 million; however, it increased rapidly later since 2002 because of the infrastructure development such as the roadways and lower tariffs. In 2005, the annual value of the trade was reported to be $250 million.[95] Between 2001 and 2002, about half of Afghan's total exports went to Iran, and about 70 percent of Afghan's total foreign trade came through Iran.[96] Iran remained the ninth biggest non-US country to pledge funds for Afghanistan in the 10 years since the end of the Taliban regime; between 2002 and 2012, Iran had pledged $1000 millions.[97]

Iran "exports a variety of critical goods to Afghanistan—including food, medicine, and oil provides $50 million in annual anti-narcotics aid. Bilateral trade more than doubled between 2011 and 2013."[98] Iran's exports to Afghanistan increased from $497 million in the March 2005-06 fiscal year and reaching to $2.87 billion in the fiscal 2012-13, and the trade; total imports and exports, between two countries increased from $ 193.49 million in 2008 to $525.19 million in 2012,[99] but the exports decreased slightly in the fiscal 2013-14, however, it further bounced back to $3 billion in 2016-17. And Afghanistan's exports to Iran have been reported as little as a dozen million dollars on average over the years, which peaked at $32 million in the fiscal 2013-14. In 2014, the volume of trade between both was close to $2.4 billion, out of which $2.3 billion was the export of Iranian goods to Afghan. It has also stated that Iran also "hopes to include Afghanistan in its plan to, by 2025, export 80 billion cubic meters (bcm) of natural gas annually to Asian and European countries."[100] In the year of March 2016-17, Iran's exports at $3 billion and Afghanistan's at $10 million were reported.[101] According to Afghanistan Chamber of Commerce and Industries (ACCI), "Iran was Afghanistan's biggest trade partner in the last solar year—March 2017 to 21 March 2018—and exported goods to the value of over $1.98 billion. The ACCI stated, "trade volume between Afghanistan and Pakistan was $1.2 billion in the same time, and $1 billion with China. Now Iran is our biggest (trade) partner."[102] Mohammad Reza Bahrami, the Ambassador, stated that more than $400 million Iran has invested to help Afghanistan access ports on the Persian Gulf,[103] and Afghanistan imports the goods of this worth from Iran every year. In fact, most of Iranian economic investment was focused in the Herat region of Afghanistan and has been rightly spent on the infrastructural development such as transportation, roads and bridge construction, education, agriculture, power generation, and telecommunication projects. The transportation links between Iran, Afghanistan, and Central Asian region was also significant of Iran's investment in Afghanistan. Moreover, Iran also helped Afghanistan in rebuilding its radio and television infrastructures.[104] Iran also allocated about $43 million for a

123 kilometer "Golden Transit Route" linking Herat in western Afghanistan to the Dogharoun region in Iran which has already completed.[105] Besides, Iran has undertaken the biggest project of Railway route worth of $75 million[106] by joining the Herat and Iran which was said to be completed by 2017. Moreover, Iran is also the largest exporter or supplier of electricity power to Afghanistan, especially in the western provinces.[107] Besides, "since the two neighboring countries have a lot in common with regard to language, religion, culture, history and literature, Iranian cultural products such as books, music, films and software applications are very popular among the Afghan people."[108] However, "Afghanistan's main imports from Iran are construction materials, food and fuel...Iran holds a 22% share ($2.5 billion) from Afghanistan's $11.5 billion consumer market."[109]

Importantly among many recent developments, Iran's Chabahar project offers great opportunity to Afghanistan to have full access to the open seas and the international water, and, to facilitate this access, Iran provided Afghanistan's public and private sectors with sufficient facilities and preferential treatment to utilize this port and "among the 500 companies licensed to operate in Iran's Chabahar, 165 are reportedly Afghan" and "Iran has provided special incentives to Afghan investors at Chabahar."[110] As reported, "Iran is offering an 80% discount in export tariffs and a 75% discount on import duties to Afghan traders using Chabahar...(as) Afghanistan is a major destination for Iranian exports."[111] And therefore, the Afghan Foreign Ministry called on the US administration to exempt the Iran's port city Chabahar from a new wave of economic sanctions against Iran.[112] This Iranian port city is vital in terms of Afghans economic interests. Through this port, Afghanistan will have various economic opportunities beyond the South and Central Asian region. Even since Ashraf Ghani became President of Afghanistan, both Iran and Afghanistan engaged in various economic cooperation. Both the countries have signed MoU for cooperation in the field of exploration and exploitation of mines in Afghanistan and to export it around the world. Even for that matter, Afghanistan exempted custom duty for the

Iranian investors in Afghanistan. Iran's export to Afghanistan is considered as 40 percent of Afghan's total imports.[113]

In 2011, Iran and Afghanistan Agreement was signed for the export of oil products, and according to this agreement, Iran aimed "to export one million tons of various oil products—including 600,000 to 700,000 tons of diesel; 250,000 to 300,000 tons of gasoline; and 100,000 tons of jet fuel per year."[114] Iran supported the export of oil products to neighboring Afghanistan, and it was argued that the government-sponsored lawful shipments would help to contribute to checking trans-border smuggling. And for this, Iran's assistance to Afghanistan in the exploration of crude oil and natural gas topped the negotiations between two countries. Further in October 2015, both the countries through bilateral agreement decided the extension of training to Afghan staff in the gas industry, and both the countries also agreed on to provide Iran's technical services to Afghanistan in its oil and gas industries. It has reported that "Iran exports 3 million liters of gasoil per day to Afghanistan which is planned to increase in a bid to curb smuggling to its eastern neighbor where it is sold at multiple prices."[115] By March 20, 2018, Iran exported 10,000 tons of diesel to Afghanistan (and Iraq), and Iran also planned to export 8,000 tons of diesel from the northern city of Sari to neighboring Afghanistan by late June 2018.[116] The objective behind Iran's economic strategy in Afghanistan has been to put efforts for the stability in Afghanistan and to throw away the American presence there. As has stated earlier, in fact, Iran perceived the US presence in Afghanistan as a threat to its multiple interests in and around Afghanistan, as a result, Iran criticized the US-Afghanistan Strategic Partnership Agreement (SPA) of 2012 that provided framework for US-Afghan relations even after 2014 drawdown. Iran pleaded that such arrangement was against the traditional neutrality of Afghanistan in South and Central Asia that leading to develop distrust in the regional states relations.[117]

Defence/Security Cooperation

In the field of security, Iran-Afghanistan has lesser security engagement and the supply of weapons except in some cases.

During the first Taliban regime, Iran provided military assistance to the Northern Alliance in Afghanistan. However, during the period of democratically elected government in Afghanistan, it has alleged that Iran provided arms and funds to the Taliban. In context of bilateral security arrangement, furthermore, in August 2013, the MoU was signed between heads of National Security councils of both Iran and Afghanistan (President Rouhani and President Karzai respectively). The 2013 agreement emphasized expanded bilateral cooperation on military, intelligence, and economic issues. In fact, significantly, this agreement was primarily a security agreement which emphasized on the cooperation in military training, combating terrorism and organized crime, and even referenced joint military exercises. Through these exercises, according to the agreement, both the countries were expected to come together to "fight against the shared threats of terrorism, narcotics and others." The 2013 agreement also provided for intelligence sharing between the two countries on "developments in the field of threats for national security...including in Central, West and South Asia."[118] Since the 2013 MoU, relations between them have been largely stable. The agreement makes the commitments pertaining to the issues such as: "Cooperation and coordination between the intelligence organs...to fight insurgency, Expansion of trade and commerce, Facilitation of tourism and trade...Trilateral cooperation between High Secretariat of National Security of Iran, Advisor Office of National Security of Afghanistan, and Secretariat of National Security of India and Russia."[119]

Further, on 15 December 2015, Iran and Afghanistan signed MoU to "improve cooperation on border security and counter narcotics operations as well as the prevention of illegal border crossings."[120] However, on Afghan's security cooperation with the other states, Ghani, however, reassured the Iranian President Rouhani that Afghan's such security accords would not pose any threat to Iran and its interest in and around the region or elsewhere. In May 2018, Iranian Police Commander Brigadier General Hossein Ashtari in a meeting with his Afghan Defense Minister Lieutenant General Tariq Shah Bahrami urged that Iran and Afghanistan should boost security in their joint borders and exchange information on fighting drug trafficking, organized crimes and terrorist groups, and, Afghan's defense minister also said that Afghanistan needs Iran's support in fighting outlaws, terrorist groups and drug traffickers, and that Iran and Afghanistan share similar stance on fighting Daesh (ISIS) and called for two countries' teamwork against common threats.[121]

Iran-Taliban Engagement

Masoud Hamyani, Third Secretary, Press Division, Embassy of Iran (New Delhi) argued that

> Based on the request of the Government of Afghanistan and in order to provide intelligence coverage, maintain security of the eastern borders of Iran and insecurity prevailing on the common border due to the weakness of foreign and Afghan forces, the Islamic republic of Iran has initiated limited contact with the Taliban faction. Tehran has used its limited contact to encourage and convince the Taliban to bring them to the negotiation table. It is crystal clear that almost all key players on the ground have their own relations with the Taliban aimed at encouraging them to join the peace process.[122]

Afghanistan emerged an area of more geopolitical competition than cooperation for Iran and other states which moved together in Afghanistan against the presence of the US. It has seen that Iran joined Russia and Pakistan against the presence of the US in Afghanistan and also established links with the Taliban. In fact, according to Amin Tarzi, "The current support provided to the Taliban is...coordinated with Russia despite overall strategic differences between the two countries' long-term priorities...(and) the Taliban has found a sympathetic ear in Moscow, potentially inducing the re-internationalization of the Afghan conflict," and Zamir Kabulov, Russia's special envoy to Afghanistan, said, "Taliban interests objectively coincide with ours."[123] Even for that matter, the US overtly alleged Iran for providing weapons and other aids to the Taliban. However, Iran's alleged support to Taliban was considered because of the increasing violence in the relatively peaceful south-western province of Afghanistan, besides, the forced repatriation of Afghan refugees from Iran.[124] Iran, like Russia and China, also urged the US to leave Afghanistan. And therefore, encouraged and indulged in the activities against the US. In fact, Afghanistan was seen as the platform for the Russia-Iran cooperation against the US. However, though both Iran and Russia nurtured common interests in Afghanistan, but both also have their specific interest for which both may indulge in competition against each other in the future. In other words, Iran and Russia came together only in a campaign against the US presence in Afghanistan.

Till the Taliban came back in power second time in August 2021, Iran's Afghan policy was principally based on the hedging against both the USA and possibly stretching the Islamic State (ISIS) in and around Afghanistan. As of the US allegations, Iran tacitly supported the Taliban, despite its antagonism to the Taliban's brand of Islam and determined political opposition to them during the 1996-2001. When the Taliban had occupied power in 1996, Iran's supreme leader Khamenei had termed them as "a disgrace to Islam."[125] However, especially to hurt and sabotage the US mission in Afghanistan, particularly by the Islamic Revolutionary Guard Corps with a view of teaching a lesion to the US, some factions of the Iranian state extended support to the Taliban activities, despite, its support to the Afghan government and its US-led reconstruction after the 9/11 attacks. In fact, earlier it was said that Iran and the Taliban were not much cordial especially after the incidence of the Mazar-i-Sharif in 1998. And this incidence had become the cause of war between Iran and the Taliban, because of which, as has reported, Iran had deployed about two lakh soldiers close to Iran-Afghan border against the Afghan regime of the day, however, the war did not occur.[126] And subsequently, Iran had taken opposite stand and supported the anti-Taliban opposition. In fact, Iran's support to the US intervention in Afghanistan was timely and temporary that was emerged out of the necessity or its policy towards the US intervention in Afghanistan which apparently was pragmatic and relevant according to the realist perspective. However, with the expansion of the US-led NATO campaign in Afghanistan, Iran started extending support to the Taliban to bleed the Americans and their allies by raising the cost of the intervention so that compelling them to leave the country unsuccessfully in frustration. Otherwise, it was believed that "Shiite Iran and strictly Sunni Afghan factions particularly the Taliban make natural enemies, and that their mutual perceptions and respective ideological nuances mark a great divide in the regional polity."[127] However, with the changing circumstances and new regional and global transformations, Iran and the Taliban came closer by organizing meetings and conferences, though some of them said to be secret and open as well. Shelala, Kasting, and Cardsman stated that the Taliban delegation visited Tehran in early June of 2012 as mentioned in one of the reports and it was also reported that they were invited by the Iranian side as an independent political system and they had discussions on very important issues. Besides, in 2011, a Taliban contingent attended the conference that was held in Tehran, and in 2013, however, the Iranian officials and the Taliban had meeting that, as said, reflected the development in their relationship.[128] However, the Iranian Foreign Ministry had denied any such meeting with the Taliban.

In fact, subsequently with changing developments, the Iran-Taliban relationship became apparent, as in this context, Alireza Nader and Joya Laha observed, that "Although Iran has traditionally backed Tajik and Shi'a groups opposed to the Taliban, its enmity with the United States and tensions over the nuclear program have led it to provide measured support to the Taliban, which espouses an avowedly anti-Shi'a and anti-Iranian ideology."[129] Their observation was much relevant in context of increasing Iran's support to the Taliban as Iran's enmity with the US aggravated further. In this context, it was argued that

> Iran currently provides measured support to the Taliban, perhaps as a way to signal to the United States that it can increase its support in the event of hostilities. Potential US or Israel military actions against Iran's nuclear facilities could result in more significant Iranian aid to the Taliban, including the provision of advanced explosively formed projectiles and surface to air missiles.[130]

The strengthening bonhomie between Iran and the Taliban apparently seen in the decision of the US President Donald Trump's threatening approach and pulling out of nuclear deal with Iran. In fact, Trump's offensive gesture forced Iran to increase its support to the Taliban activities in Afghanistan especially against the US. However, despite Iran's support to the Taliban, there seemed absolute absence of Iran's wish that the Taliban to be back in power. In fact, with the passing of time, a section of Taliban leadership wanted to re-establish cordial relations with a very significant neighbour Iran. Moreover, with Iran's increasing proximity with the Taliban, the Iran-Afghan government relations were seen increasingly tense. The Afghan government in November 2016 forwarded the allegations that Iran has been harbouring and supporting the Taliban leaders and involved in provocation of violence in Afghanistan. This development, as a result, fuelled Iran-Afghanistan tensions. Moreover, contrary to the US allegations, Iran also accused the US of supporting the Islamic State militants in Afghanistan to fuel regional terrorism and threatening the neighbouring countries, and, the US helicopters have been transporting the IS militants from eastern Afghan to unknown locations. While speaking and addressing the gathering of diplomats, scholars, and journalists in Islamabad, the Iranian Foreign Minister Mohamad Javad Jarif made the allegations that

> We see intelligence, as well as eyewitness accounts, that Daesh fighters, terrorists, were airlifted from battle zones, rescued from battle zones, including recently from the prison of Haska (Meyna).... This time, it wasn't unmarked helicopters. They were American helicopters, taking Daesh out of Haska prison. Where did they take them? Now, we don't know where they took them, but we see the outcome. We see more and more violence in Pakistan, more and more violence in Afghanistan, taking a sectarian flavor.[131]

Furthermore, on Iran-Talban nexus, Samuel Ramani wrote:

> Since 2002, the Iranian military has forged alliances with Sunni insurgent groups that aim to liberate Afghanistan from US forces. The Iranian government has justified these partnerships by arguing that a large US troop presence on Iran's borders poses a threat to Iran's security. In light of this border security argument, Iran's military cooperation with

> the Taliban has been most extensive in the three western provinces of Afghanistan that border Iran.[132]

As has argued, "Iran believes its influence over Afghanistan will be maximized through a more gradual shift toward a political settlement."[133] Besides, the IRQC, since 2015, has been supplying arms and extending training to the Taliban in the western region of Afghanistan especially "to ensure that an anti-US, pro-Iran buffer zone is created on Iran-Afghanistan border. Iran's desire for a durable sphere of influence in western Afghanistan is much more likely to be fulfilled through military rather than diplomatic means…."[134] Mohsen M. Milani argued that "while Iran has been guilty of extremism and adventurism in some critical aspects of its foreign policy, its overall Afghan policy has contributed more to moderation and stability than to extremism and instability."[135] From this, it was crystal clear that Iran assisted the Taliban.[136] As reported by Will Fulton, according to the State Department's 2009 Country Reports on Terrorism,

> Iran's Qods Force has arranged arms shipments to select Taliban members, including small arms and associated ammunition, rocket propelled grenades, mortar rounds, 107mm rockets, and plastic explosives since at least 2006, and provided training to the Taliban in Afghanistan on small unit tactics, small arms, explosives, and indirect fire weapons…. The Islamic Republic's strategy thus far has been to disrupt attempts at creating a stable security environment while exerting its influence in the Afghan political sphere.[137]

As reported, the Afghan officials stated that Iran conducted an intensifying covert intervention, provided local Taliban insurgents with weapons, money, and training and also provided Taliban commanders sanctuary and supplied fuel for their trucks and also padded Taliban ranks by recruiting among Afghan Sunni refugees in Iran. Besides this they further said, "the regional politics have changed…. The strongest Taliban here are Iranian Taliban," and "Iran and the Taliban—long-time rivals, one Shiite and the other Sunni—would seem to be unlikely bedfellows…. Iran has sent squads of assassins, secretly nurtured spies and infiltrated police ranks and government departments, especially in western provinces."[138] As said by one of the Afghan officials, "Iran's support of the Taliban is aimed in part at disrupting development projects that might threaten its dominance. The Iranian goal, they contend, is to keep Afghanistan supplicant."[139] As reported by Fatemeh Aman (2017),

> Iran is sending weapons on helicopters to help the Taliban destabilize Afghanistan. Iran is sabotaging Afghan markets to promote Iranian goods, stealing Afghanistan's water, attempting to bomb Afghan dams, and even participating in drug trafficking along with the Taliban...Afghan media, even the most credible, are filled with reports about 'Iranian terrorists' in Afghanistan's cities...many Taliban commanders who conduct terrorist attacks in Herat own houses in Iran.[140]

Iran was also blamed for sabotaging the Salma Dam by providing economic and military assistance to the Taliban. As has believed, between 2007 and 2011, international forces in Afghanistan intercepted Iranian arms shipments destined for the Taliban.[141] However, rejecting all the allegations, Iran described them as "a conspiracy to sabotage Iran-Afghan relations."[142] In fact, it has stated that whether Iran assisted the Taliban economically and military was held as a "speculation," but Iran, no doubt, has increased its profile and influence in the region in view of the strong presence of the US in its neighbourhood, remains the fact of the story.[143] Further, the changing political developments, regime changes and the American peeping in the neighbourhood region heightened the Iranian insecurity. And all these factors determined the Iranian foreign policy and strategies towards in and around Afghanistan. Till 2010, as reported, Iran was strongly opposed to any kind of negotiation between the Afghan government and the Taliban, however, surprisingly, from 2011, Iran extended its support to the peace talks and even offered to host the meetings between the two.[144] In July 2012, Iran permitted the Taliban to open its office in Zahedan in Eastern Iran province, and, in December 2016, Iran invited the Taliban leaders in Islamic Unity Conference in Tehran.[145] Furthermore, in 2016, Iran Ambassador to Afghanistan Mohammad Reza Bahrami in Kabul confirmed that Iran has established communication ties with the Taliban to gain control of the intelligence information and also stated that Iran had been always ready to help Afghan government on peace process with the Taliban.[146] However, in 2015, after the US accusation on Iran's Support to the Taliban, Bahrami had rejected this accusation. He stated, "Iran and Taliban do not have any relations. In Iran's security strategy, there is no interpretation in connection with terrorist groups and any connection with these groups are against Iran, the region and outside the region."[147] Factually, while justifying connection with the Taliban, Masoud Hamyani pitched the Iranian stand that

> In Iran's security strategy, there is no interpretation of connecting with terrorist entities dividing them into good and bad terrorists. Therefore, any relationship with the Taliban is against the security and the national interest of Iran, the region and the outside region. There is a strong belief that we share a number of threats and interests with Afghanistan. Iran continuously seeks long lasting and comprehensive relations with the Central Government in Kabul....[148]

Siegfried O. Wolf, on the Iran-Taliban nexus, argued and alleged that Iran was not only the part of the so-called Axis of Evil, it was the epicenter of it and being largely portrayed as a state that was an irrational actor, extremely guided by an ideology, on track to acquire nuclear weapons by any means, and additionally, Iran was characterized as a state which was one of the prime supporters of terrorism worldwide, the 'invisible hands' behind all kinds of insurgencies, destabilizing not only the Middle East but its South Asian neigbourood as well.[149] Further on 26 December 2018, Iran met with the Afghan Taliban, which was, as believed, announced by Ali Shamkhani, secretary of Iran's Supreme National Security Council, during his visit to Afghanistan. In this regards, he stated that "the Afghan government has been informed of the communications and talks carried out with the Taliban, and this process will continue," and further on security matters, he said, "the Islamic Republic has always been one of the primary pillars of stability in the region and cooperation between the two countries will certainly help in fixing Afghanistan's security issues of today."[150] This was the first time, as believed, that the talks between Iran and the Taliban were confirmed. On 30 December 2018, Afghan Taliban visited Tehran for a second round of peace talks to end the prolonged conflicts in Afghanistan. The spokesman of Iran's Foreign Ministry Bahram Ghasemi told that the Taliban delegation was present in Tehran and the lengthy negotiations were held with the Iran's deputy Foreign Minister Abbas Aragchi. He further stated that Iran's policy priority towards the Afghanistan was "to help facilitate negotiations between Afghan groups and the Afghan's government."[151] Moreover, the Taliban discussed Afghanistan's "post-occupation situation, restoration of peace and security in Afghanistan and the region" with Iran during this meeting between them. In fact, Iran also making a more concerted and honest open push for the peace in Afghanistan ahead of the probable drawdown of the US troops.[152] However, Iran expressed concerns over probable increasing of violence in Afghanistan and its repercussions in Iran after the US declaration of the slashing of its half of the troops in Afghanistan. By and large, as has been pointed out that the Iran-Taliban cooperation aimed at "primarily a function of Iran's desire to hamper US efforts in Afghanistan, and have little to do with shared interests between Iran and the Taliban. Any conceivable Iranian collaboration with the Taliban...should be viewed as a symptom, rather than a driver, of broader US-Iranian competition."[153]

Iran-US Hostility and Afghanistan

Iran and the US as rivals are well known to the entire world, and, as a result, "competition with Iran has played a role in US decision-making, but has not been a key driving force."[154] In fact, since the Islamic Revolution, Iran, and the US indulged in major antagonism. The Khomeini's ideology shaped the Iran's policy against the US in the region. According to Morgane Colleau, "the US-Iran institutionalized enmity has often acted as a coercive social fact on policy makers, embedded as it is in individual and collective consciousness, reutilized practices of containment and deterrence, and structures of legitimacy."[155] However, both the states also had cooperation in case of Afghanistan and others since 2001 as Iran had supported the US attack on the Taliban regime in Afghanistan in 2001. Besides, it has mentioned that "the officials from the United States and Iran had meetings to topple the Taliban" and these meetings were came to be known as the "Geneva Contact Group," however, it was stated that though the United Nations and other states like Germany and Italy had extended political cover to these meetings, the main focus of these meetings was the Iran-US cooperation in Afghanistan.[156] Moreover, Iran provided reliable intelligence about the Taliban to the US by providing maps showing Taliban's positions in Afghanistan and also arrested and deported hundreds of Al-Qaeda and Taliban militants who had crossed into Iran for sanctuary.[157] It has also reported that Iran had offered military training to 20,000 Afghan soldiers "as part of a US-led program to rebuild Afghanistan's army."[158] According to Hillary Mann Leverett (former Director for Iran and Persian Gulf Affairs at the National Security Council in the George W. Bush Administration), "Iran hoped and anticipated that tactical cooperation with the United States would lead to a genuine strategic opening between our two countries."[159] However, despite Iran's support which was though vested in its interests, in January 2002, the US under Bush administration had labeled Iran as a part of "axis of evil" (along with the other so-called evils; North Korea and Iraq. In Iraq, the US perhaps performed its most ambitious job and had also maneuvered the plan to do same in Iran, but failed.). In 2003, Iran had made "a formal offer to open comprehensive negotiations with Washington, but it was ignored by the George W. Bush administration. Afghanistan had been one of the agenda points."[160] In this context, Christensen stated

> In spring 2003, Iran sent 'a grand bargain' proposal to the US through Swiss Embassy. Iran offered to stop backing Hamas and Hezbollah, acknowledge the state of Israel, cooperate on Afghanistan and give IAEA full access to its nuclear program. In return Iran asked for American security guaranties—a recognition of Iran's legitimate security interests in the region with according defense capacity-lifting of sanctions and the right to peaceful nuclear programme.[161]

However, this could not move forward in the positive direction as the US had not responded. Furthermore, President Bush taking jibe at Iran while delivering his State of the Union address on 31 January 2006, described Iran as "a nation now held hostage by a small clerical elite that is isolating and repressing its people. Iranian government is defying the world with its nuclear ambitions, and the nations of the world must not permit the Iranian regime to gain nuclear weapons."[162] The then President of Iran Ahmadinejad also vehemently reacted that leading to the development of estrangement and diplomatic mutual mistrust. In fact, mutual distrust has been a perpetual history of Iran-US relationship. During August 2007 meeting with Karzai, the US President George W. Bush also expressed his mistrust regarding Iran by stating that "I would be very cautious about whether the Iranian influence in Afghanistan is a positive force.... (However, it is) up to Iran to prove to the World that they are the stabilizing force as opposed to destabilizing force."[163] However, "the US State Departments each annual report on international terrorism since early 1990s has described Iran as the leading or most active state sponsor of terrorism."[164] Consequently, the relations between Iran and the US led to further deterioration. Iran also had held the US presence in its very close neighbourhood as threat to its national security and fear of the US attack. The US tried to marginalize the Iranian national interests in and around the region. This clearly exhibits the open confrontation between Iran and the US and also in some cases both seemed to be competitors in Afghanistan. Unfortunately, in Afghanistan's picture, cooperation between Iran and the US faded rapidly both started posing against each other. The US and the NATO criticized Iran for its support to "the Taliban elements as a part of its continuing effort to counter and undermine the American endeavour in Afghanistan. Iran's alleged support to the Taliban was also coincided with the growing violence in some of the relatively peaceful south-western part of Afghanistan."[165] In fact, "the US viewed Iran's relations with Afghanistan in terms of zero-sum game; a gain for Iran is a loss for the US."[166]

In March 2012, the Obama administration had organized, the US-GCC Strategic Dialogue that aimed against Iran and to contain and marginalize Iran's power/influence in the region. Further, in view of normalizing bilateral relations, since 2013, President Rouhani of Iran and the US President Obama moved forward towards each other. Both the administrations developed historical telephonic communication and also had various formal meetings. It was "for the first time since the early 1980s, track I diplomacy was reportedly at the forefront of US-Iran contacts."[167] In other words, both the states indicated the possibility, at the high level of both sides, to meet and discuss the hard issues like the nuclear one. As a result, subsequently, Iran and the US along with the UK, Russia, France, Germany, and China (or P5+1 and Iran) agreed on the Iran nuclear deal (Joint Comprehensive Plan of Action in July 2015) that increased the confidence building measures between the two countries. By making Iran the part of this deal, Obama could successfully prevail upon the Iranian leaders to give up or suspend its nuclear ambition in return for the lifting of the sanctions imposed by the international community and this deal further opened new opportunities for the bilateral relations between the US and Iran. Subsequently, after this deal, it was believed that Iran must be confident then that the US might not be using Afghan soil to attack Iran, and, Iran could start thinking positive about the US. This could alleviate the tensions between both Iran and the US to short extent. Significantly, Obama's efforts could bring both the states close to each other to increase mutual trust and solidarity. Obama's "call for engagement included no preconditions, no threats, and used the language of honesty and mutual respect."[168] But, with this development between the US and Iran, the regional powers such as Israel and the Saudi Arabia, which had been the United States' traditional allies, felt uncomfortable and got upset with the Obama administration. President Obama, by creating Iran-US proximity, in fact, tried to restore the balance in the region which was fumbled due to the revolts in Arab World and the civil wars in the region.[169] Both Iran and the US seemingly had the common interests in Afghanistan such as the promotion of peace and stability and discouraging any sort of the Taliban and IS's extremism. Moreover, Iran was thinking that if the US withdraws from Afghanistan in 2014 as declared by Obama,

Iran would get more opportunities in Afghanistan by stepping in view of filling the power vacuum. But, this could not happen and that further anguished Iran to move opposite to the US. Therefore, because of its increasing security concerns with the US incessant presence in Afghanistan, it has reported that Iran tried "to derail the US Afghanistan Bilateral Security Agreement (BSA), signed in September 2014 that allowed the United States to maintain troops in Afghanistan even after 2014. It prohibits the United States from launching military action against other countries from Afghanistan."[170] However, realizing its limited power to compete with the US, Iran adopted the other option of collaborating with the powers like Russia and China, and even extending support to the Taliban on the plea of bringing them on the negotiation table or for the peace talks, mainly to counter and weaken the influence and presence of the US forces and its allies in Afghanistan. By and large, it can be argued that Afghan territory provided Iran to sabotage the US's regional interests although at the lower level or may not be.

The US President Donald Trump, after Obama's diplomatic engagement with Iran, adopted harsh and differently negative approach towards Iran that further re-imposed the bilateral old hostility and posed himself and the US against Iran. This can be very explicitly observed that Trump did not mention about the role of a major country Iran in the new Afghan and South Asian strategy which he announced in August 2017. Therefore, by learning the approach of the US generally and Trump's particularly, Iran further started strengthening Taliban by equipping and sponsoring their insurgency across Afghanistan. According to Aziz Amin Ahmadzai "any strategy that doesn't deal with Pakistan is not a strategy that will bear fruit. Killing each mosquito individually and ignoring its pond is not solution," and therefore, "Ignoring the role Iran can and will play definitely undermine Afghan, the US, and international community efforts in the fight against radicals and extremist groups in Afghanistan and in the region is shortsighted.[171] However, rather depicting the picture of cooperation between them, unfortunately, Trump pulled the US out from the six nations JCPOA or nuclear deal on 8 May 2018. Trump called "Iran Nuclear Deal" as "the worst deal ever" in the American history of international relations. On Trump's efforts of reversing the rapprochements with Iran by his predecessors, Stanly Johny stated

> Mr. Trump sees Iran through the establishment's foreign policy prism. He wants US policy to swing back to America's traditional allies, Israel and the Sunni Arab world. They saw the nuclear deal and the subsequent opening up of the global economy for Iran as further helping Tehran consolidate its position in West Asia at a time when its already spreading its influence through a Shia corridor. Mr. Trump doesn't have broader regional stabilisation strategy. Rather, in his worldview, Iran has to be a rolled back for the US's traditional allies to assert themselves even more strongly in the region. He dumped the nuclear deal not to force Iran to renegotiate it, but to provoke and isolate it instead.[172]

Ironically, the increasing antagonistic development between the US and Iran pushed a stumbling block in accomplishing the set objectives in Afghanistan. It is crystal clear that mutual rivalry amongst the states involved in crisis resolution worldwide have adversely affected the stable and peaceful order in the world, and so, the peace process in the failed states like Afghanistan would be lingering until the constructive cooperation amongst the major states come up. The global leaders like the US and the regional leaders like Iran needed to understand rationally. However, the US made major efforts to stabilize Afghanistan by a war against the Taliban and other terrorist groups that looking into enter Afghan mess, but, the US could not end the war in Afghanistan due to mutual rivalry between/amongst the regional countries involved there including Iran. Furthermore, the US also asked the other countries even including India to bring oil imports from Iran to Zero and end the engagement with Iran in view of 'Isolating Iran.' On the incessantly prevailing Iran-US psychological warfare or hostile episode, Stanly Johny reported, "The cornerstone of Donald Trump's West Asia policy is Israel's security. The containment of Iran is the subplot."[173] Furthermore, Pakistan also complicated the issues in Afghanistan and also posed threats to the Iranian security by supporting the militancy in Iran's Sistan and Balochistan province and also the support to the Sunni extremism in Afghanistan. Furthermore, adding fuel in their hostility, in April 2019, the US declared the IRQC as a terrorist group.

However, despite allegations for the Taliban links and the well-defined rivalry with the US, Iran's main priorities in Afghanistan as its immediate neighbour are "fighting against terrorism, assisting restoration of peace and security, deterring the menace of drug cultivation and trafficking, housing refugees, and playing a constructive role in rebuilding Afghanistan."[174] In fact, as has stated, Afghanistan offered important space to Iran's policy makers, but, the Iranian leadership appeared very slow in readjusting its strategic outlook, keeping Iran's Afghan policy hostage to its hostility towards the US.[175] According to Bruce Koepke, "Successful negotiations would build confidence and allow more constructive Iranian regional engagement, a boon for future Afghan democratization, security and economic integration."[176]

Notes and References

1. Its slogan was "Neither East nor West. Only Islamic Republic", Amir Kamel, Iran in Afghanistan: Rejecting Foreign Presence in Harsh V. Pant (ed.), *Afghanistan's Regional Dilemma: South Asia and Beyond*, Orient Blackswan, New Delhi, 2016, p. 134.
2. For details, see Mohsen M. Milani, Iran's Policy Towards Afghanistan, Government and International Affairs Faculty Publication Paper 106, *Middle East Journal*, Vol. 60, No. 2, Spring 2006, pp. 235-56
3. Vishal Chandra, *The Unfinished War in Afghanistan, 2001-2014*, IDSA, Pentagon Press, New Delhi, 2015.
4. Kayhan Barzegar, Iran's Foreign Policy in post-Taliban Afghanistan, *The Washington Quarterly*, Vol. 37, Issue 2, 2014, pp. 119-37.
5. Sumitha Narayan Kutty, Iran's Continuing Interests in Afghanistan, *The Washington Quarterly*, Summer 2014, pp. 139-56.
6. Morgane Colleau, The Kaleidoscope of Iran's Foreign Policy in the Context of Profound Regional Upheavals in Robert Mason (eds.), *Reassessing the Order and Disorder in the Middle East:*

Regional Imbalance or Disintegration, Rowman & Little Field, London, 2017, p. 89.

7. *Ibid.*
8. Bruce Koepke, Iran's Policy on Afghanistan: The Evolution of Strategic Pragmatism, Stockholm International Peace Research Institute (SIPRI), September 2013, p. 2.
9. *Ibid.*
10. *Ibid.*
11. Bruce Koepke, Iran's Relations with Afghanistan's National Unity Government in Amin Saikal (ed.), *The Arab World and Iran, Middle East Today*, Palgrave Macmillan, New York, 2016, p. 148.
12. Haji-Yousefi, 2012 p. 63.
13. Barzega, 2014.
14. Toscano, 2012.
15. Amir Kamel, p. 132.
16. Haji-Yousefi, 2012, p. 63.
17. Kayhan Barzegar, 2014.
18. Amir Kamel, 2016, p. 133.
19. Roberto Toscano, Iran's Role in Afghanistan, CIDOB Policy Research Project, Barcelona Centre for International Affairs, 2012.
20. Alireza Nader and Joya Laha, Iran's Balancing Act in Afghanistan, Occasional Paper, National Defense Research Institute, RAND, 2011.
21. *Ibid.*
22. Ramin Mostaghim and Shashank Bengali, Iran's growing drug problem: 'No walk of society is immune', *Los Angels Times*, Dec. 19, 2016, http://www.latimes.com/world/la-fg-iran-drug-addiction-2016-story.html
23. Bethan McKernan, Number of Drugs addicts in Iran doubles in six years, *Independent*, 26 June 2017, https://www.independent.co.uk/news/world/middle-east/iran-tehran-drug-addiction-opium-heroin-afghanistan-taliban-a7809046.html, accessed on 22 June 2018.
24. Tascano, 2012.
25. Carlotta Gall, In Afghanistan, US Exists, and Iran Comes in, *The New York Times*, 5 August 2017, https://www.nytimes.

com/2017/08/05/world/asia/iran-afghanistan-taliban.html, accessed on 10 May 2018.

26. Haji-Yousefi, 2012, p. 69.
27. Robert Czulda, The Defensive Dimension of Iran's Military Doctrine: How Would They Fight?, *Middle East Policy*, Vol. XXIII, No. 1, Spring, 2016, p. 94.
28. Nasser Saghafi-Ameri, The Afghan Drugs Problem: A Challenge to Iran and International Security, *Iranian Review of Foreign Affairs*, Vol. 1, No. 2, Summer 2010, pp. 213-35.
29. Fatemeh Aman, Worsening Relations between Iran and Afghanistan?, Lobe Log, 11 August 2017, https://lobelog.com/worsening-relations-between-iran-and-afghanistan/, accessed on 22 June 2018.
30. *Ibid.*
31. Bruce Koepke, 2016.
32. Tascano, 2012.
33. Vishal Chandra, 2015, p. 193.
34. Shirin Shakib, How can Iran Educate a Million Afghan Refugees? DW, 22 September 2017, http://www.dw.com/en/how-can-iran-educate-a-million-afghan-refugees/a-40640770, accessed on 21 June 2018.
35. Ali M. Latifi, How Iran Recruited Afghan Refugees to Fight Assad's War, *The New York Times*, 30 June 2017, https://www.nytimes.com/2017/06/30/opinion/sunday/iran-afghanistan-refugees-assad-syria.html, accessed on 21 June 2018.
36. Patrick Strickland, What are Afghan Refugees leaving Iran?, 17 May 2016, https://www.aljazeera.com/indepth/features/2016/05/afghan-refugees-leaving-iran-160511103759873.html, accessed on 21 June 2018.
37. Shirin Shakib, 2017.
38. *Ibid.*
39. Patrick Strickland, 2016.
40. *Ibid.*
41. Masoud, Hamyani, Pioneer, 2018.
42. Ali M. Latifi, 30 June 2017.
43. *Ibid.*
44. Patrick Strickland, 2016.

45. Bethan McKernan, Iran's Exemplary Refugee Hosting Efforts Praised by UN, *Independent*, 16 March 2017, https://www.independent.co.uk/news/world/middle-east/iran-refugee-resettlement-efforts-exemplary-un-praise-united-nations-a7633621.html, accessed on 21 June 2018.
46. Track Persia, 2017.
47. Track Persia, Iran's Afghanistan multi-track policy since the success of the Islamic Revolution, 18 February 2017, http://www.trackpersia.com/irans-afghanistan-multitrack-policy-since-islamic-revolution/, accessed on 23 June 2018.
48. Amanollah Shafaei, Building Dams on Rivers and Damming Iran's Relations with Afghanistan, *Iran Review*, 27 August 2017, http://www.iranreview.org/content/Documents/Building-Dams-on-Rivers-and-Damming-Iran-s-Relations-with-Afghanistan.htm, accessed on 20 July 2018.
49. *Ibid.*
50. Shahrbanou Tadjbakhsh and Mohammad Fazeli, Iran and its Relationship to Afghanistan After the Nuclear Deal, Peace Research Institute Oslo, PRIO Paper, July 2016, p. 8.
51. Amanollah Shafaei, 2017.
52. Amir M. Hazi-Yousefi, Iran's Foreign Policy in Afghanistan: The Current Situation and Future Prospects, *South Asian Studies*, Vol. 27, No. 1, January-June 2012, p. 64.
53. Adam Tarock, p. 805.
54. Amir M. Haji-Yousefi, 2012, pp. 65-66.
55. *Ibid.*, p. 66.
56. Will Fulton, Afghanistan-Iran Foreign Relations, Critical Threats, 8 April 2010, https://www.criticalthreats.org/analysis/afghanistan-iran-foreign-relations, accessed on 11 July 2018.
57. Amir M. Haji-Yousefi, 2012, pp. 66-67.
58. Alireza Nader, Ali G. Scotten et al., *Iran and Afghanistan: A Complicated Relationship in Iran's Influence in Afghanistan*, Rand Corporation, 2014, p. 8.
59. Amir Kamel, Iran in Afghanistan: Rejecting Foreign Forces, in Harsh Pant edited, 2016, p. 134-35
60. Amir M. Haji-Yousefi, 2012, p. 67.
61. Joshua Levkowitz, 2017.

62. Adam Tarock, The Politics of the Pipeline: The Iran and Afghanistan Conflict, *Third World Quarterly*, Vol. 20, No. 4, 1999, pp. 801-20.
63. Douglas Jehl, 1998.
64. Will Fulton, 2010, also see Douglas Jehl, "For Death of Its Diplomats, Iran Vows Blood for Blood," *The New York Times*, September 12, 1998, http://www.nytimes.com/1998/09/12/world/for-death-of-its-diplomats-iran-vows-blood-for-blood.html, accessed on 11 July 2018.
65. Joshua Levkowitz, Iran's Taliban Gamble in Afghanistan, 17 May 2017, Middle East Institute, http://www.mei.edu/content/article/iran-s-taliban-gamble-afghanistan, accessed on 21 May 2018.
66. Nader and Scotten, 2014, p. 9.
67. Mir H. Sadat and James P. Hughes, US-Iran Engagement Through Afghanistan, *Middle East Policy Council*, Vol. XVII, No. 1, Spring 2010, http://www.mepc.org/us-iran-engagement-through-afghanistan, accessed on 3 July 2018.
68. Joshua Levkowitz, 2017.
69. Amir M. Haji-Yousefi, 2012 p. 67.
70. *Ibid*.
71. Amir Kamel, p. 137.
72. Sumitha Narayanan Kutty, Iran's Continuing Interests in Afghanistan, *The Washington Quarterly*, Vol. 37, No. 2, June 2014, pp. 139-56.
73. Toscano, 2012.
74. Nader and Scotten, 2014, p. 9.
75. Amir Kamel, p. 137.
76. Will Fulton, Afghanistan-Iran Foreign Relations, Critical Threats, 2010.
77. Chandra, 2015, p. 201.
78. *Ibid*.
79. Robert M. Shelala II, Nori Casting, and Anthony H. Cordesman, US and Iranian Strategic Competition: The Impact of Afghanistan, Pakistan, India and Central Asia, Center for Strategic and International Studies, Burke Chair in Strategy Report, 26 June 2013, p. 9, https://csis.org/files/

publication/130626_AfPak_Asia.pdf, accessed on 26 January 2019.

80. Ernesto Londoño Iran intensifies efforts to influence policy in Afghanistan, *The Washington Post*, January 4, 2012 https://www.washingtonpost.com/world/asia_pacific/iran-strives-to-play-spoiler-in-afghanistan/2012/01/01/gIQAZ6gCbP_story.html?utm_term=.dcbf9f7dade9, accessed on 10 December 2018.
81. Toscano, 2012.
82. Herat, an Afghan province, was considered as an integral part of Iran until 1857, and Dari, one of Afghanistan's two official languages, is a dialect of Iran's official language of Farsi. For details, see M. Kugelman, 10 July 2014, Foreign Policy. In the Herat region, Iran's influence in Afghanistan is most visible. As a part of Iran, Herat served as the capital of the Persian Empire in the early 15th century. When the British repelled Iranian advances toward Herat, Iran and the United Kingdom signed the Treaty of Paris in 1857. Although Iran abandoned its historic claim on Herat, it reserved the right, under Article VII of the treaty, to send forces into Afghanistan "if its frontier is violated." Since then, Iran has occasionally sought to keep Herat as a buffer zone. For a few years, Ismail Khan, the Tajik governor of Herat, helped Iran realize that goal. For details, Sajjan M. Gohel, Iran's Ambigous Role in Afghanistan, CTC Sentinel, Cambridge Terrorism Centre, March 2010, Vol. 3, issue 3, pp. 13-16, https://ctc.usma.edu/irans-ambiguous-role-in-afghanistan/, accessed on 10 July 2018; also see for details J.C. Hurewitz ed., *The Middle East and North Africa in World Politics: European Expansion*, 1535-1914, New Haven, CT: Yale University Press, 1975, pp. 341-43.
83. Ray Takeyh, *Hidden Iran: Paradox and Power in the Islamic Republic,* A Council on Foreign Relations Book, Times Books/Henry Holt and Company, New York, 2006.
84. Toscano, 2012.
85. Carlotta Gall, 5 August 2017.
86. Amir Kamel, 2016, p. 142.
87. Nihar Ranjan Das, Afghanistan's Relations with India and Iran: An Assessment of Ghani Period, Issue Brief, Indian Council of World Affairs, 27 July 2016.
88. Samuel Ramani, The Myth of an Iran-Russia Alliance in Afghanistan, *The Diplomat*, 25 October 2017, https://

thediplomat.com/2017/10/the-myth-of-an-iran-russia-alliance-in-afghanistan/, accessed on 3 May 2018.

89. Masoud Hamyani, Afghanistan-Iran Relations, *The Pioneer*, 29 June 2018, https://www.dailypioneer.com/columnists/oped/afghanistan-iran-relations.html
90. Adam Tarock, 1999, p. 804.
91. Amir M. Haji-Yousefi, 2012, p. 69; also see Mohsen M. Milani 2006, p. 251; Kugelman, 2014.
92. Shahrbanou Tadjbakhsh and Mohammad Fazeli, July 2016, p. 8.
93. Amir Kamel, p. 141.
94. Amir M. Haji-Yousefi, 2012, p. 69.
95. Milan, 2006, p. 251.
96. Amir Kamel, p. 138.
97. *Ibid.*
98. Kugelman, 2014.
99. Amir Kamel, p. 40.
100. Shahrbanou Tadjbakhsh and Mohammad Fazeli, July 2016, p. 8.
101. Ali Shirdelian, Iran-Afghan Economies Tied by One-Way Trade, *Financial Tribune*, 22 August 2017, https://financialtribune.com/articles/economy-business-and-markets/70824/iran-afghan-economies-tied-by-one-way-trade, accessed on 2 July 2018.
102. Iran is Afghanistan's Biggest Trade Partner, Afghan Online Press, 22 March 2018, http://www.aopnews.com/economic-news/iran-is-afghanistans-biggest-trade-partner-acci-deputy/, accessed on 4 May 2018.
103. Carlotta Gall, 5 August 2017, also see, The Iran-Afghan bilateral trade was reported to $2.8 billion in 2017, TOLO NEWS, 22 February 2017, https://www.tolonews.com/afghanistan/afghanistan-iran-trade-28-billion, accessed on 2 July 2018.
104. Mohsen M. Milani, 2006, p. 251.
105. *Ibid.*, p. 252.
106. Afghanistan, International Crisis Group, 6 July 2018, https://www.crisisgroup.org/trigger-list/iran-us-trigger-list/flashpoints/afghanistan, accessed on 13 July 2018.

107. Shahrbanou Tadjbakhsh and Mohammad Fazeli, July 2016, p. 8.
108. Ali Shirdelian, 22 August 2017.
109. Iran Biggest Trade Partner of Afghanistan in 2017-18, *Financial Tribunal*, 9 April 2018, https://financialtribune.com/articles/economy-domestic-economy/84309/iran-biggest-trade-partner-of-afghanistan-in-2017-18, accessed on 2 July 2018.
110. *Ibid.*
111. *Ibid.*
112. Afghanistan Wants Iran's Chabahar Port Exempted From US Sanctions, 24 June 2018, http://www.aopnews.com/us-afghanistan-relations/afghanistan-wants-irans-chabahar-port-exempted-from-us-sanctions/, accessed on 2 July 2018.
113. Nihar Ranjan Das, 27 July 2016.
114. Kayhan Barzegar, Iran's Foreign Policy in Post-Taliban Afghanistan, *The Washington Quarterly*, Vol. 37, No. 2, 2014, pp. 119-37, p. 121.
115. Islamic Republic News Agency, 17 October 2015, http://www.irna.ir/en/News/81803193, accessed on 26 January 2019.
116. Iran Daily, 22 May 2018, http://www.iran-daily.com/News/215530.html, accessed on 26 January 2019.
117. Kayhan Barzegar, 2014.
118. Ankit Panda, Iran, Afghanistan Approach Strategic Cooperation Pact, *The Diplomat*, 22 January 2015, https://thediplomat.com/2015/01/iran-afghanistan-approach-strategic-cooperation-pact/, accessed on 4 July 2018.
119. TOLO News, Afghanistan Signs Strategic Cooperation Agreement with Iran, 5 August 2013, https://www.tolonews.com/afghanistan/afghanistan-signs-strategic-cooperation-agreement-iran, accessed on 4 July 2018.
120. Bruce Koepke 2016, p. 155.
121. Islamic Republic News Agency, Iran, Afghanistan stress elevation of security cooperation, 14 May 2018, http://www.irna.ir/en/News/82915693, accessed on 26 January 2019.
122. Masoud Hamyani, Afghanistan-Iran Relations, *The Pioneer*, 29 June 2018, https://www.dailypioneer.com/columnists/oped/afghanistan-iran-relations.html, accessed on 6 July 2018.

123. For details see, Amin Tarzi, Iran, Russia, and the Taliban: Reassessing the Future of the Afghan State, Foreign Policy Research Institute, Program on the Middle East, 14 June 2017, https://www.fpri.org/article/2017/06/iran-russia-taliban-reassessing-future-afghan-state/, accessed on 19 July 2018, also refer, Javid Ahmad, Russia and the Taliban make Amends, *Foreign Affairs*, 31 January 2016, https://www.foreignaffairs.com/articles/afghanistan/2016-01-31/russia-and-taliban-make-amends
124. Vishal Chandra, 2015.
125. Janne Bjerre Christensen, Strained Alliances: Iran's Troubled Relations to Afghanistan and Pakistan, Danish Institute of International Studies (DIIS) Report, Copenhagen, 2011:03, p. 9.
126. Michael Kugelman, *Foreign Policy*, 10 July 2014.
127. Vishal Chandra, 2015, p. 194.
128. Robert M. Shelala II, Nori Casting, and Anthony H. Cordesman, 26 June 2013, p. 6.
129. Alireza Nader and Joya Laha, Iran's Balancing Act in Afghanistan, Occasional Paper, National Defense Research Institute, RAND, 2011.
130. *Ibid.*
131. Afghan Online Press, Iran Accuses US of Supporting IS in Afghanistan, 13 March 2018, http://www.aopnews.com/us-afghanistan-relations/iran-accuses-us-of-supporting-is-in-afghanistan-washington-denies-allegation/, accessed on 4 May 2018.
132. Samuel Ramani, 25 October 2017.
133. *Ibid.*
134. *Ibid.*
135. Mohsen M. Milani, 2006.
136. Tascano, 2012.
137. Will Fulton, 2010.
138. Carlotta Gall, In Afghanistan, US Exists, and Iran Comes in, *The New York Times*, 5 August 2017, https://www.nytimes.com/2017/08/05/world/asia/iran-afghanistan-taliban.html, accessed on 10 May 2018.
139. *Ibid.*

140. *Ibid.*
141. Michael Kugelman, The Iran Factor in Afghanistan, *Foreign Policy*, 10 July 2014, https://foreignpolicy.com/2014/07/10/the-iran-factor-in-afghanistan/, accessed on 2 July 2018.
142. *Ibid.*
143. Vishal Chandra, 2015.
144. Javid Ahmad, The Enemy of Iran's Enemy in Afghanistan, 21 June 2015, *Foreign Affairs*, https://www.foreignaffairs.com/articles/afghanistan/2015-06-21/enemy-irans-enemy-afghanistan, accessed on 13 July 2018.
145. Kenneth Katzman, Iran's Foreign and Defense Policies, Congressional Research Service-CRS Report, 7-5700, 18 July 2018, p. 47.
146. Iran Officially Confirms having Communication with Taliban in Afghanistan, Ariana News, 9 December 2016, https://ariananews.af/iran-officially-confirms-having-communication-with-taliban-in-afghanistan/, accessed on 19 July 2018.
147. Iranian Ambassador Disputes Claims of Tehran Supporting Taliban, TOLO News, 17 June 2015, https://www.tolonews.com/afghanistan/iranian-ambassador-disputes-claims-tehran-supporting-taliban, accessed on 19 July 2018.
148. Masoud Hamyani, 2018.
149. Iran-Afghanistan Relations: A Dangerous Balancing Act, *The Independent*, 11 May 2012, Dhaka, p. 25.
150. Agence France-Presse, Iran Held Talks with Taliban: Official, *The Hindu*, 27 December 2018, p. 12.
151. Afghan Taliban Visited Tehran for Talks, *The Indian Express*, 1 January 2019.
152. Agence France-Presse, Taliban Confirms Meeting Iran Officials, *The Hindu*, 2 January 2019, p. 12.
153. Robert M. Shelala II, Nori Casting, and Anthony H. Cordesman, 26 June 2013, p. 6.
154. *Ibid.*
155. The Kaleidoscope of Iran's Foreign Policy in the Context of Profound Regional Upheavals in Robert Mason (eds.), *Reassessing the Order and Disorder in the Middle East: Regional Imbalance or Disintegration*, Rowman & Little Field, London, 2017, p. 95.

156. For details see Kenneth Pollack, *The Persian Puzzle: The Conflict between Iran and America*, Random House, 2005, p. 346, cited from Chandra 2015, p. 199.
157. Cited from Chandra.
158. Michael Kugelman, 10 July 2010.
159. Greg Bruno and Lionel Beehner, Iran and the Future of Afghanistan, Council on Foreign Relations, 30 March 2009, https://www.cfr.org/backgrounder/iran-and-future-afghanistan, accessed on 13 July 2018.
160. Michael Kugelman, 10 July 2010.
161. Janne Christensen, 2011, pp. 10-11.
162. Ray Takeyh, 2006, p. 1.
163. Vishal Chandra 2015, p. 201.
164. Kenneth Katzman, 18 July 2018.
165. Vishal Chandra, p. 193.
166. Sumitha Narayanan Kutty, Iran's Continuing Interests in Afghanistan, *The Washington Quarterly*, Vol. 37, Issue 2, 2014, pp. 139-56.
167. Morgane Colleau, 2017, p. 96.
168. *Ibid.*
169. Stanly Johny, Proving the Hardliners in Tehran Right, *The Hindu*, 25 July 2018, p. 8.
170. Kenneth Katzman, 2018, p. 47.
171. Aziz Amin Ahmadzai, 2017.
172. Stanly Johny, 25 July 2018.
173. *Ibid.*
174. Masoud Hamyani, 2018.
175. Shahram Akbarzadeh, Iran's Policy Towards Afghanistan: In the Shadow of the United States, *Journal of Asian Security and International Affairs*, Vol. 1, Issue 1, April 2014, pp. 63-78.
176. Bruce Koepke, 2016, pp. 145-63.

6

China: From Low-Profile to Strategic Presence

Introduction

Throughout its history, China has regarded itself as the centre of the world. Proud of their brilliant culture and historical heritage, the Chinese have regarded their homeland as 'the centre of the civilized world'. The large territory, population, common language, and Confucian political, ethical, and social values they share, reinforce their 'great power images'. With the possible exception of India and Japan, no country in Asia could be compared with China, either politically, militarily or culturally. The military as well as cultural superiority and prosperity... further reinforced the...China's presumed influence in Asia. Consequently, China had established around itself a system of tributary states which were expected to be submissive and to pay at least some tribute to China. At any sign of hostility on their part, China was quite prepared to use force to cope with them.[1]

The Five Principles (Peace Principles) which have been considered as a major pillar in China's foreign policy even today, were originally conceived by India's first Prime Minister, Jawaharlal Nehru and China's first Premier, Zhou Enlai, in the Panchsheel Treaty, signed on April 29, 1954, which are: Mutual respect for each other's territorial integrity and sovereignty, Mutual non-aggression, Mutual non-interference in each other's internal affairs, Equality and cooperation for mutual benefit and Peaceful co-existence. In context of these principles, it was stated that "the principles originally represented a vision of international relations that was highly principled and not based on realism necessarily. After Mao Zedong declared that China had "stood up" after a century of humiliation in 1949, and thereafter, China needed to base its foreign policy around a set of principles that focusing its principled independence in world affairs, and "the Five Principles were borne of post-colonial solidarity and Chinese leaders embraced them for both their moral weight and strategic flexibility."[2] Beholding the significance of the five principles for the future Architecture of Asian Security, the Chinese President Xi Jinping declared that "The five principles that China initiated together with India... have become a basic norm governing state-to-state relations... China's peaceful development begins here in Asia, finds its support in Asia, and delivers tangible benefits to Asia."[3] China's Premier Li Peng in a speech at the 96th Inter-Parliamentary Conference on September 19, 1996 had stated elements of China's Foreign Policy that of: Maintaining independence, Maintaining world peace, Friendly relations and cooperation, Good-neighborly and friendly relations and Enhanced unity and cooperation with developing countries.[4] Further, China developed five principles of 'peaceful coexistence' which were mentioned in Defence White Paper 2006: "China maintains military contracts with other countries on the basis of Five Principles of Peaceful Coexistence, and develops cooperative military relations that are non-aligned, non-confrontational and not directed against any third party."[5] Caine and others laid down the five principles of peaceful coexistence as: Peaceful development is the inevitable way for China's modernizations; promoting world peace and development with China's own growth; developing by relying on its own strength, reform, and innovation; seeking mutual benefit and common development with other countries and building a harmonious world of substantial peace and common prosperity.[6]

However, Hao and Chou argued that China's foreign policy maker's agenda failed in strengthening its relations with neighbouring countries, and therefore, the Chinese leadership has been focusing the "policies center on the pursuit of central control through exercising administrative-military coercion, making the borderlands economically dependent, standardizing the cultural identity…"[7] China's relations with its neighbours such as Japan, South Korea, Philippines, Malaysia and others including India and Bhutan are fragile and distressful. In the direction of making its foreign policy successful, further Hao and Chao stated that

> China today is consolidating its land border and beginning to turn outward…China's action abroad is different from that of the United States. China does not take a missionary approach to the world affair, as moral is not China's concerns. The need to secure energy and raw materials in order to support the rising living standard of Chinese population is the primary motivation of Chinese outward-looking foreign policy strategy. To accomplish this task, China has pursued an omni-dimensional foreign relation strategy, not only to secure its relationships with major world powers but also to improve its relations with all neighboring countries including former rivals. Creating a peaceful external environment and gaining maximum economic benefits have become main concerns for Chinese leader. Internally, China has also tried to change its policy towards its borderland, making sure that border land provinces help to secure a stable relationship with neighboring states and also benefit from the inter-regional economic interaction.[8]

According to 18th Chinese Communist Party (CCP) Congress, which was held in November 2012, China's foreign policy states that "Peaceful Development is China's basic state policy, and win-win cooperation is a banner for China's friendly relations with other countries. To realize 'China dream', we must have a peaceful international environment. At the same time, the country will resolutely safeguard its national sovereignty, security, and core interests. The two policies are two pillars of Chinese diplomacy, and do not conflict with each other".[9] From the perspective of the realist theory of International Relations, Edward Freidman stated that "the strong do what they will; the weak do what they must. The PRC's post-2008 territorial expansionism in Asia which is experienced by neighboring governments as a threat to the sovereignty and future of China's Asian neighbors is but a recent instance of a ubiquitous reality," and therefore, "...the CCP's foreign policy is not premised on a principle of non-interference. The strong intervene and often prevail."[10] The global politics has been experiencing larger transformation with China's increasing economic and military power. The emerging China has disturbed the existing great powers and posed greater challenge to most powerful state of the world, the US. Moreover, along with the great powers, the regional powers also are panic with China's increasing leverage. The South Asian region, obviously, could not abstain from falling under the influence of China. However, China has declared among its smaller neighbours that "China's economic development and growing military might will not turn the country into a regional bully." But, China's posture or encroachment in the South and East China Sea appears to be interventionist, where, China seems failing to abiding by the five principles of peace. In fact, China believes and applies five principles when its interests are not being jeopardized, but, China poses itself tough if its interests tending to be fumbling. China has learnt that military use can cost heavy blot, and therefore, focused on the use of economic power and influence to frighten or coerce the others. However, though China has extended policy of peaceful development and cooperation with the neighbouring states, but it believes in what Xinhua invoked Confucius: "He who wants success should enable others to succeed." China's territorial expansionism in neighbourhood is more apparent. China has dared the small countries in the South China Sea, and even India, the South Asian superpower, is also not exempted. In other words, China's policy of cooperation and peaceful development seems applicable merely against the neighbours who succumb to China's influence. In fact, India and Pakistan have taken 'pride of place' in China's policy towards South Asia.[11] The China-Pakistan nexus against India is based on the Kautilya's dictum: befriending enemy's enemy. China has adopted aggressive policy towards the neighbouring states having common border and other disputes and regularly indulged in threatening them with tough or hard tactics and posture by making the plea of sovereignty violation by claiming others territory as its own. In such juncture, generally China does not talk about cooperation or peaceful settlement.

On China's policy, Michael Pillsbury analyzed that China has skillfully maneuvered the strategies to overtake all other world powers, including the USA.[12] China with over $3 trillion in foreign exchange reserves is liberally using its economic might to promote its influence around the world. In an article in the *Global Times*, Ding Gang, a senior editor with People's Daily, wrote, "...With the wheels of history turning into the 21st century, China has reinstated itself as the global economic centre."[13]

History of China-Afghanistan Relations

Afghanistan was historically absent in China's foreign policy. Since the formation of People's Republic of China on 1 October 1949, as stated, both the countries had no special features of relationship in terms of political, economic or security or any other. However, Afghanistan had extended official recognition to China on 12 January 1950, but failed in receiving quick official response from China.[14] And, since then, Afghanistan just played a peripheral role in China's foreign relations.[15] It has also believed that "the roots of China's Afghanistan Policy are based in nostalgia and a sense of civilizational change."[16] However, their relations began taking shape gradually as their formal diplomatic relations were established in 1955 with China's increasing concerns due to the US's economic and military assistance to Afghanistan.[17] Furthermore, besides, the US's assistance, China also observed the Soviet Union's increasing proximity with Afghanistan that compelled it to engage bilaterally with Afghanistan. In fact, China perceived that Soviet Union's increasing shadow in Afghanistan might have posed threats to Afghan's sovereignty and its own national interests. As a result, concerned with the multiple developments, China started focusing on Afghanistan, and in 1956, Afghan's cultural delegation had visited China and met Zhao Enlai, and after that Enlai also made visit to Afghanistan in 1957, and Afghan's head of the government Daud visited China in 1959. Further, in 1960, Enlai re-visited Afghanistan to signed a treaty of Friendship and Mutual Non-aggression.[18] According to the Chinese scholar, Shen Yu Dai, this treaty had "evoked the heritage of the Silk Road" of China.[19] During 1957 visit to Afghanistan, Enlai signed a trade agreement with Afghanistan signaling the inclination towards the improving of bilateral ties.

Both the countries further signed a border treaty and a protocol on border demarcation in 1965," besides, improving their ties, and both the countries also agreed on common border of 40 miles known as "Wakhan-Pamir Region," and made a joint declaration to support the "Five Principles of Peaceful Co-existence" and the "Ten Principles of the Bandung Conference of 1955", a Conference for the formation of the Non-Alignment Movement (NAM).[20] In fact, Afghanistan-China common border area which has been known as Wakhan Corridor is used by China as a buffer zone. The Wakhan Corridor which came into existence in 1895 was a byproduct of deal between Britain and Czarist Russia (Anglo-Russian Pamir Commission Report) intended "to divide their respective spheres of influence"[21] and "the two empires would not touch each other at any point."[22] Furthermore, "China has never moved forward with any plans to develop cross-border infrastructure, despite periodic requests from the Afghan side."[23] In fact, both the countries believed that the friendship agreement would "further consolidate the good-neighbourly relations between the two countries."[24] Moreover, after this period, both the countries started "reciprocal state visits and agreements on trade and economic cooperation, but, as believed, Afghanistan never emerged from the periphery of Chinese interests in the region."[25] This has believed that China's foreign policy towards Afghanistan during 1950-60 was focused on "aiding and abetting revolutionary and anti-imperialist struggle, in the process provoking a Sino-Soviet tussle for influence in the Third World."[26]

Furthermore, during the 1970s, with the changing domestic political uproar and disturbing situation, Afghanistan was observed reaching closer to Soviet Union. With the 1971 friendship treaty between the Soviet Union and India, China also came closer to Pakistan. During this time, Pakistan and Afghanistan had also major problem of disagreement over the issues of Pashtun, as a result, the China-Afghanistan relations were observed becoming more complicated. However, China remained abstain from aligning with Afghanistan when Afghanistan and Pakistan indulged in disputes, especially, to avoid rift in its relations with Pakistan.[27] Gradually, Afghanistan increased its proximity with the Soviet Union and later with India. In July 1973 coup d'état, Mohamad Daud occupied power in Afghanistan, and he was held as "the main architect" of Soviet-Afghanistan special relations. With this development, China faced major rise of Soviet's influence in Afghanistan and this development compelled China furthered its attention towards Afghanistan especially in terms of its security concerns, however, China had reluctantly extended official recognition to Daud Regime in Afghanistan.[28] Further, it has also reported that China had extended economic and military support to the Pashtun and Baluch dissidents in their struggle for autonomy against the Daud regime.[29] China's arms and ammunition support to the rebellions had started in early 1970s and that increased after 1979. When the Soviet Union intervened in Afghanistan in 1979 and stayed until 1988, Afghanistan was remained focused in China's policy for its security concerns. During this time, China was heavily concerned of "an acute risk of encirclement" by the Soviet Union's presence in Afghanistan or elsewhere in Asia. Besides, China was also afraid that "the building of long-term bases foreshadowed intentions for a permanent presence, which would help the Soviet Union gain a strategic edge over China and Pakistan."[30] China was also concerned that the Soviet Union could have reached to the Indian Ocean by entrenching its bases in Afghanistan. In this context, the then vice-premier of China, Geng Biao had stated that "If the Soviet's barbarous aggression goes unchecked, the next target is Pakistan."[31] However to counter the Soviet presence in Afghanistan, China put its involvement low in Afghan's development programmes, and China along with Pakistan, the US and Saudi Arabia had strategically provided required support to the Mujahedeen forces against the Afghan government which was supported by the Soviet Union. China's arms support to the Mujahedeen was financed by the US and Saudi Arabia and Pakistan had played the role of distributor of these weapons. It has also believed that "China also maintained direct relationships with certain Mujahedeen factions beyond the Pakistani channel."[32] During this time, China became more sympathetic towards Pakistan and both built very strong proximity after the Soviet invasion in Afghanistan. In other words,

Soviet-Afghan proximity created the China-Pakistan proximity and also adopted the dysfunctional state of affairs in war-torn Afghanistan for decades.[33] During 1980s, in fact, China adopted the periphery policy aiming to foster close bilateral economic and security relations with its neighbours and it also aimed at to "mitigate regional fears about China's rise" and also it has believed that China had perceived that by adopting this policy, "it would lead to a twenty-first century New Asianism, in which China would have central place.[34]

According to Michael Clark, "China's perception of Afghanistan as a source of potential threats to not only its security but also that of the wider Central Asian region was heightened sharply with the emergence of the Taliban as a force in the Afghan tumult in 1994, and their ultimate capture of Kabul in 1996."[35] It has also believed that like other countries, China also showed its unwillingness in supporting this regime and had halted its political relations and closed its embassy in Kabul.[36] But, according to the Afghan analyst, Malik Setiz, China had maintained unofficial relations with the Taliban government.[37] In fact, in general, from the mid-1990s, China focused on 'cooperation,' 'multilateralism,' and 'regionalism' and making them as a central features of China's "New Security Diplomacy" in order to counter its domestic political and social challenges.[38] And in the period between 1990 to 2001, China had formed a strategy to include Afghanistan peacefully in its "New Security Doctrine."[39] However, it had adopted a low profile foreign policy and its role in Afghanistan. It has also believed that China's policy towards Afghanistan in mid-1990s was largely negative or preventive, that was especially to prevent any spillover of Islamic terrorism in Xinjiang and to prevent other non-traditional threats like weapons and drug trafficking.[40] In the words of Andrew Small, China adopted "hedging policy" towards Afghanistan, and this policy "saw it quietly maintaining a relationship with the Quetta Shura, the Taliban's leadership council based across the border in Pakistan...China, despite external pressure—was careful to treat the Taliban as a political group rather than a terrorist entity, even going so far as to provide money and arms supplies."[41] In fact, China had learnt that it could not be abstained from the Taliban regime because of its security interest, and therefore, China again put Afghanistan in its foreign policy. Moreover, during this time, China's Xinjiang province envisaged the pervasive violence, and the cycle of repression and confrontation between the Chinese government and the people of Uyghur ethnic identity. And this was believed that China faced, for the first time, Islamic militancy in its territory, and the Taliban had provided its territory for the Uyghur militants to establish a network of training camps.[42] However, in December 2002, China with the support of Pakistan had established talks with the Taliban leader Mullah Omar not to allow its any group, especially the Uyghur militants, the use of Afghan territory against China. And in exchange, Mullah Omar "sought two things from China; formal political recognition and protection from U.N. sanctions." However, this deal benefited to none and neither side done anything satisfactory.[43] It has also reported that "even though the Taliban's alliance with Al-Qaeda posed serious security threats in light of the insurgency in the Xinjiang region, the Chinese continued its cooperation with the Taliban."[44] By and large, according to Andrew Small: "Its dealings with the Taliban enabled China to take care of its main security concerns; squeezing the safe havens for Uyghur militants, reducing the risk of China becoming a target for Islamic militants more broadly, and protecting Chinese personnel and assets in Afghanistan from attack."[45] Further, as quoted by Mohanty, as had observed by David Denoon, "China shifted from its aggressive posture and violent policy of the 1970s and 1980s where it was quite willing to use force, to a much more diplomatic route in the 1990s."[46] In 2001, China had supported the US's "Operation Enduring Freedom" against the Taliban, but without active participation. In fact, China believed that by contributing its troops in the US's intervention in Afghanistan, it had been held as a "subordinate partner" of the US-led alliance there, for which China was not willing to be. However, in the post-Taliban regime, as Bose and Panda argued: "In the case of China and Afghanistan, it may appear that structural constraints are a weak predictor of Chinese foreign policy given China's ideational emphasis on 'Third World' solidarity and its Five Principles. But while these dynamics have informed Beijing's foreign policy rhetoric in general, and bear a strong presence in official diplomatic interactions...China's push for cooperation with Afghanistan has hitherto been driven strongly by the logic of self-help."[47]

Chinese policy towards Afghanistan after 9/11 moved towards the growing political engagement and China believed in accommodating the interests of the Afghan government and the Taliban. Further, because of its prime location, Afghanistan emerged as a passage for China to move forward its "March West" strategy."[48] However, the fact that was argued that its role as stated was limited, and "unlike the Western powers, China was not interested in rebuilding Afghanistan politically or in altering its political structures, social patterns or ideological orientations," and "while China avoided participating in multilateral efforts in Afghanistan in the 2002-12 period, it maintained close ties with the Afghan government..." and signed the "Treaty of Friendship, Cooperation and Good Neighborly Relations with Kabul."[49] In the post-Taliban period, in terms of its economic, security, and political stability needs of interests that Afghanistan had been seeking was aids from the various countries, and China was also one of such countries that was picked up by Afghan's new leadership. However, China's role in Afghanistan has grown rapidly in recent years. As has believed, it was in the context of the US phased drawdown of its forces from Afghanistan from December 2014 and, subsequently and consequently, the further possibility of heightening of violence and chaos there in Afghanistan that putting its repercussions on Chinese territory and its interests of moving towards the Western countries strategically, China began peeping and stepping up its involvement in Afghan affairs in 2012.[50] China started looking at the strategic vacuum that was created after the US's decision of drawdown of its troops. Since this period, China's role in Afghanistan shifted from "low-profile presence to strategically proactive presence." By and large, since the drawdown of the US forces, the Asian giant China entered Afghanistan, though initially not militarily, but keeping security situation in its border areas or a probable security threat in its Xinjinag province. In fact, China's modus operandi in Afghanistan began with economy and gradually shifting into military, in the name of aids or security assistance. Though China's military involvement in Afghanistan is limited, its presence close to its border is apparent. In fact, in the post-2014, China adopted proactive foreign policy towards Afghanistan and began focusing robustly on its Belt and Road Initiative (BRI/OBOR) project through Afghanistan or Central Asia and the Middle East towards the West, integrating them all, so that to normalize the influence of the Western powers especially the US around its peripheral influence.

China's Interests in Afghanistan

China's foreign policy towards Afghanistan is driven with the specific interests and has been shaped by two tendencies: "the desire for security in Xinjiang and for geographical advantage—at different stages." "From 1991 to 2001, Beijing's Xinjiang calculus was very much the core driver in determining China's approach to Afghanistan, while from 2001 onwards a broader geopolitical calculus has emerged" which has been seen as OBOR.[51] However, since 2014, as has observed, China's concerns over the deteriorating security situation in Afghanistan have heightened. The fear of instability in its western province Xinjiang has directed China to focus on security issues while dealing with Afghanistan. However, along with the above-mentioned interests, Richard Ghaisy identified China's four interests in Afghanistan. First, mitigating safe havens for the Turkistan Islamic Party; secondly, gradually eroding the need for the US-North Atlantic Treaty Organization military presence in Afghanistan; thirdly, creating a "buffer" of stable states around China, and finally protecting the construction and transit security of its ambitious Belt and Road initiative.[52] By and large, China has, among others, two most important foreign policy interests in Afghanistan: first, to suppress the terrorism and Islamic extremism in its Xinjiang region, and second, China's BRI/OBOR project.

Though China and Afghanistan have a small common border of 90 kms, but, Afghan's east border with China's northwestern province, which is known as Xinjiang—China's largest autonomous administrative region, is major conflict zone grappled with terrorism and Islamic extremism which China sees as the major security concern. Uyghur in Xinjiang is the largest ethnic Muslim community and they regard themselves as culturally and ethnically closer to the central Asian countries. Han Chinese is the largest ethnic group in China, but is a minority in Xinjiang. However, the Uyghur and other Muslim groups are said to be the victims of Chinese marginalization policy that led to the emergence of extremism in the region. By and large, ethnic unrest led to the Uyghur Islamic extremism. Therefore, China believed, Xinjiang explicitly as "the frontline for the three evils of separatism, terrorism, and religious extremism," and as a result, "there exists the dangerous possibility of radical elements hailing from foreign lands using Afghanistan as a launch-pad to establish insurgent links with the already vulnerable Uyghur-inhabited areas of China."[53] China's Xinjiang region has borders with the other Muslim countries such as—Kazakhstan, Kyrgyzstan, Tajikistan, Afghanistan, and Pakistan. Keeping in mind the possible threats emerging from Uyghur Islamic community in the Xinjiang province, China wants to suppress any such extremism having connections with the other extremist groups in Afghanistan; the Taliban or even ISIS. China fears ethnic unrest in this region may pose difficulties in its outreach to the Central Asian region. In this context, it has argued that

> Afghanistan's instability affects China's own stability, particularly that of its terrorism-prone Xinjiang region. Members of the Turkistan Islamic Party, a Xinjiang-focused Islamic separatist group, have been apprehended in Afghanistan. China fears that an unstable Afghanistan will permit greater use of Afghan territory by the militants to plot attacks on Chinese territory and sustain the country's thriving drug industry. This can threaten social stability in China and the perceived ability of the Chinese government to protect the populace from harm. In addition, the Islamic State Khorasan (IS-K) branch threat in South Asia is growing. In Afghanistan, it is based in its eastern Nangarhar province, close to the border with Pakistan. IS-K has regional aspirations that include Central Asia and nearly stretch into China's western borders.[54]

In fact, "China's interest in Afghanistan are essentially negative—preventing instability from spreading to Xinjiang province; and preventing instability in Afghanistan from upsetting its relation with the larger regional environment in Central Asia,"[55] and for the success of its "March West Strategy," "Xinjiang is now viewed as China's backdoor into Eurasia, and new markets in Central Asia, Europe and the Middle East. Yet all this is dependent on shoring up the Party's control and stability in Xinjiang".[56]

Furthermore, China's One Belt One Road (OBOR) project, which has been held as the revival of old Silk Routes, is the biggest constellation of states of the 21st century. China is investing huge human and financial resources into the OBOR as a long-term vision for economic integration of the Eurasia and even beyond that towards Europe. The OBOR, which is renamed as the Belt and Road Initiative (BRI), is President Xi Jinping's vibrant grand strategy to make China the world's richest and most powerful nation in the world. Chinese President believes that the BRI and the Maritime Silk Road (MSR), much bigger and better connected, will be spread across the heartland of Central Asia down to the Indian Ocean, as well as across the Mediterranean and onwards into Europe. However, one of the major world powers India has shown reluctance in joining BRI. In the BRI Forum summit which was organized on 14-15 May 2017, Chinese President Jinping and the heads of 29 countries reaffirmed their commitment to build an open economy and ensure free and inclusive trade under the ambitious BRI. In this summit, President Xi said, "it is our hope through the Belt and Road development; we will unleash new economic forces for global growth, build new platforms for global development, and rebalance economic globalization so mankind will move closer to a community of common destiny."[57] President Xi pledged $124 billion for the new Silk Road, which aims to bolster China's global leadership ambitions by building infrastructure and trade links between Asia, Africa, and Europe and beyond. Besides, China-led Asian Infrastructure Investment Bank (AIIB), established in 2015 as a regional financing mechanism for OBOR, has an initial total capital of $100 billion. The objective of the

BRI is to develop ports, roads, railway lines and industrial parks basically to accomplish the tread and investment objectives of all the participating states. It has stated that China's manufacturing machine would move both surplus goods and low-paying jobs to less affluent nations, while pulling up its own economy to enter a higher-income market such as Europe. Further Ding stated on China's growth explosion that "...The BRI is by no means a one-way flow of wealth enabled by the exploitation of the empires. It aims to build an active economic and trade corridor and an interconnectivity network in Asia, Europe and Africa, via stimulating the potential of these regions, creating an unprecedented convergence effect," the official Chinese press agency, Xinhua has declared this as "the China solution for global economic revival."[58]

Afghanistan like other countries in the South Asian region also is of major significance in terms of China's interest to be fulfilled. In fact, this project is beneficial not only to China but Afghanistan also. This project has optimum potential to provide Afghanistan's need for infrastructure development and also for the use of potential vast natural resources. The geopolitical location of Afghanistan offers multiple opportunities to Afghanistan to become a core part of China's trade and investment network. Afghanistan has expressed strong interest in the BRI. As a result, in this direction, by deepening its political, economic, and military engagement in Afghanistan and also signing a memorandum of understanding on the BRI initiative in 2016, China has emerged as the player into region's great game.[59] However, the security and instability are identified as the major challenges in achieving the objectives of the BRI and further closer engagement and substantial Chinese investment. China wants the security in the areas where its investment is made in Afghanistan and especially in the $46 billion worth CPEC (China Pakistan Economic Corridor—connecting Pakistan's port Gwadar to China's Kashgar in Xinjiang region). China's BRI and Silk Road Economic Belt strategies offer optimum opportunities for both countries for mutual cooperation, which produce economic benefits to Afghanistan and also would boost the country forward. China's BRI strategy comprises the construction of railways and highways to connect Central Asia, South Asia, and the Middle East, and, Afghanistan is located at the geographical hub of these regions. However, if any unrest or civil war occurs, there would likely result in instability spilling over into nearby regions, making it difficult for the strategy to succeed. "...if it receives the financial backing it needs, the New Silk Road can support Afghanistan's access to energy markets, improve infrastructure and institutions to boost trade and transport, streamline customs and border operations, and increase people-to-people ties between Afghanistan and its neighbors".[60] However, any instability emanating in Afghanistan would constrain China's expansive infrastructural and connectivity ambitions. And to achieve the objective of security, China has tried to maintain better relations with almost all the stakeholders in Afghanistan. Therefore, Xinjiang's security situation and the BRI strategy have major potential for China's urgent need to secure a stable and peaceful Afghanistan. Moreover, it has also believed that to protect its security interests especially against the probably emerging threat from the Islamic State in Xinjiang, China has deployed its military near the Wakhan corridor specifically in "the Gorno-Badakhshan Autonomous Region (GBAO) of Tajikistan," the region that bordering the Afghan's Wakhan Tract and China's Xinjinag region. The major objective of China here believed as of "expanding the scope of their strategic and economic influence toward Central Asia."[61] On security concerns, Harsh V. Pant analyzed that

> Security concerns have prevented Chinese investment in Afghanistan from getting off the ground. China is interested in playing a lager role in Afghanistan, long seen as primarily a US responsibility after its 2001 invasion. China's Afghan policy is now feeling the pressure emanating from the withdrawal of Western troops and Taliban surge threatening to give a boost to Islamic militancy in China's western Xinjiang region.[62]

Diplomatic Engagement

In December 2001, China and Afghanistan re-established their bilateral diplomatic relationship after the end of the

Taliban regime. Besides, it has also believed that after Afghan President Hamid Karzai's China visit in 2002, China re-opened its embassy in Kabul which was shut down when the Taliban had occupied Kabul. China was also one of the first countries to extend official relations with the Karzai's new government. In December 2002, both had signed Kabul Declaration on Good Neighbourly Relations and according to this agreement, China assured its respect for the Afghan's territorial integrity and sovereignty.[63] Further, in 2003, President Karzai made two short visits to Beijing, but despite that no constructive improvement was seen in their relations, but just a demonstration of friendliness and cooperation in fight against the terrorism. Even for that matter, during this time, Afghanistan blamed China for its hidden relations with the Taliban and the supply of arms to them. In other words, China adopted the policy of "calculated accommodation" of both the Afghan government and the Taliban.[64] However, China's involvement in Afghanistan was observed as very meagre and it was also believed that "since 2001, China had adopted a hands-off policy towards Afghanistan, preferring the US to do most of the heavy lifting. It did not want a serious involvement in Afghanistan but it did not want a victory for the extremist either, given its negative impact on China's problems with Uyghur separatists in Xinjiang."[65] In fact, other than its security concerns, with its growing needs for energy and natural resources, and further opening up of Afghanistan's energy, mineral and raw materials to foreign investors, China grabbed opportunity to establish China-Afghanistan diplomatic ties. On the other hand, by learning the significance of China's assistance for its holistic development and to protect national interest, Afghanistan also offered wider space for China's soft intervention. During Afghan President Karzai's visit to China in March 2010, in a meeting with Chinese President Hu Jintao, both agreed to build a comprehensive cooperative partnership of good neighbourliness, mutual trust and friendship for generations. President Jintao, during this time identified five priority areas for both the countries that to strengthen overall bilateral ties by engaging in more regular meetings and exchanges, to promote further bilateral economic collaboration, to deepen cooperation in the humanities in the areas such as personnel training, education, culture, and public health, to enhance security and police collaboration by combating cross border organized crimes and the three evil forces of terrorism, extremism, and separatism and to coordinate each other in multilateral affairs.[66] Further in 2012, Karzai again visited China, and this visit was considered as more crucial as both China and Afghanistan jointly declared the establishment of strategic and cooperative partnership. The joint declaration focused the areas of future development by further strengthening the issues previously declared such as enhancing political mutual trust, economic cooperation, enhancing people-to-people exchanges, security cooperation in combating the three evils and illicit drug trafficking and multilateral collaboration, and moreover, Afghanistan was granted the status of observer member of the SCO.[67] Since the beginning of 2014, "China's Afghanistan diplomacy has become more positive, proactive, and dynamic."[68] As has believed, "by 2014, terrorism prevention and domestic stability began appearing more prominently on the Beijing-Kabul bilateral diplomatic agenda."[69] In the year 2014, high-level diplomatic exchanges were observed regularly. During a visit to Afghanistan in February 2014, Chinese Foreign Minister Wang Yi urged that "China would support Afghanistan in achieving smooth political, security, and economic transitions." With Ashraf Ghani becoming President of Afghanistan in September 2014, both China and Afghanistan experienced very positive and proactive diplomatic bilateral relations not only in terms of economic and investment, but in terms of security and military assistance also. In October 2014, in his first visit to China, President Ghani together with Jinping expressed their intention to deepen their strategic partnership and laid the foundation for strengthening relationship between them. During this time, China hosted a conference to discuss the peace process and reconstruction in Afghanistan, in which Ghani had rushed to participate and there he called on the Taliban to join the Afghan dialogue. China also supporting Ghani's call to the Taliban, urged them to "lay aside former enmity and join the political reconciliation process."[70] There, Ghani held China "as a strategic partner, in the short term, medium term, long term and very long term."[71] President Ghani in his speech said, "we count on the active engagement of the People's Republic of China in promoting peace, prosperity and stability in Afghanistan and in the region."[72] President Jinping on the other side held Ghani "as an old friend of the Chinese people with whom China prepared to work towards a new era of cooperation and to take development to a new depth."[73] By signing four agreements on trades and commerce, economic ties, humanitarian aid and travel permits for public servants, they also urged to work in the areas of politics, economics, security, and culture. Both the leaders declared jointly on combating against the Turkistan Islamic Movement. President Ghani also promised and agreed that "Afghanistan will not allow any activities that threaten China's (security) on Afghan territory".[74] In November 2014, China's domestic security Counsellor, Guo Shengkun, visited Afghanistan to discuss and to focus "primarily on guarding against and combating the terrorist forces of the East Turkistan Islamic Movement (Uyghur militant group), a separatist group from the Xinjiang Uyghur Autonomous Region in northwest China"...and both sides also discussed on the cooperation in the expansion of economic, trade, reconstruction, peace and security. Moreover, deputy chief of the PLA general staff, Lieutenant General Qi Jianguo, also travelled to Afghanistan as a special envoy of China's President. In fact, it has reported that before this, there had never been "so many high-level Chinese diplomatic, securities, and military officials visited Afghanistan in the span of one year".[75] Besides, after Ghani's visit in October 2014 "the Afghan government arrested and handed over 15 Uyghurs to China in February 2015". In this context, Ahmad Bilal Khalil stated, "These Afghan promises and the act of returning Uyghurs to China became bargaining chips meant to gain security assistance from Beijing, and to further persuade China to use its leverage on Pakistan to start direct talks with the Afghan Taliban".[76] In 2015, the two countries have marked the sixtieth anniversary of the establishment of diplomatic relations which was established in January 1955.

Further, by hosting, for the first time, the fourth Foreign Minister's meeting of the annual Heart of Asia-Istanbul process on 31 October 2014, an effort by the international community initiated in 2011 aiming to engage Afghan and its neighbours for peace and cooperation for rebuilding and reconstructing Afghanistan, China has boost up the process towards its aims signaling its keen interest for the reconciliation process that leading to develop new Afghanistan. During the Istanbul process in 2014, Chinese Premier Li Keqiang formalized the five suggestions that China believes Afghanistan should adopt that Afghanistan to be governed by the Afghan people; promoting political reconciliation; speeding up economic reconstruction; exploring new paths of development; and providing the Afghan government with stronger external support from the international community.[77] "China hopes that this support will encourage Kabul to develop friendly relations with its neighbors, will bolster Afghanistan's regional economic cooperation, and will help the country to enhance its own security capabilities."[78] During the state visit of the Chief Executive Officer (CEO) of Afghanistan H.E. Dr. Abdullah Abdullah to the People's Republic of China, seven bilateral cooperation agreements were signed between both the countries in May 2016. The agreement included: the Memorandum of Understanding (MoU) of OBOR, technical cooperation with a grant of RMB 500 million Yuan, the non-emergency humanitarian supplies with a grant of RMB 50 million Yuan, economic and technical cooperation, agreement between both the governments to initiate the feasibility study over the project of the low-cost housing for civil servants in Kabul, to build the integrated teaching building and the auditorium of Kabul University, and exporting of Afghan saffron to China.[79]

China's Role in Afghanistan

China's Vice Foreign Minister Wu Dawei laid down the principles regarding China's role in Afghanistan as quoted by Jingdong Yuan are

> ...First, China is committed to working together with the international community for political stability, social progress, economic development, and the improvement of people's livelihood in Afghanistan. Second, China supports the efforts to combat all forms of terrorism, with a special emphasis on addressing those root causes

that give rise to terrorism in the first place. Third, China would like to engage in various ways in the reconstruction process in Afghanistan. Fourth, China supports the United Nations to play a chief role in coordinating the efforts of the international community helping Afghanistan and China supports the Shanghai Cooperation Organization to actively join in the resolution of the Afghan problem. Fifth, as a friendly neighbor, China is committed to developing with Afghanistan a relationship of neighbourhood friendship and reciprocal cooperation on the basis of the Five Principles of Peaceful Coexistence.[80]

In fact, the fumbling economy, the fragile and debilitating security and diminishing stability situation compelled Afghanistan's elected government to seek multiple assistance from almost all the major powers including the US, China, India and (even Pakistan despite knowing its support to terrorism) to bring normality in Afghanistan and almost all these states, doubtfully Pakistan, kept supporting Afghanistan in lifting it out from the quagmire of violence. In this direction, China's proactive involvement in Afghanistan indicated that China made its conviction taking responsibility of freeing Afghanistan from the shackles of terror and violence. According to Paulo Casaca, founder and executive director of the Brussels-based South Asia Democratic Forum (SADF), "The Chinese diplomacy is very active all around the world, and it is only natural that Beijing pays special attention to countries at its borders, and particularly when a country like Afghanistan is so destabilized."[81] Before 2014, the China-Afghanistan relations remained largely normal, limited, and stable and sometimes ambiguous. In fact, China engaged with Afghanistan by supporting the US's operations against the Taliban regime in 2001. However, in the post-Taliban period, China emerged as the largest investor especially in the wider mines sector in Afghanistan, but China abstained from direct involvement in Afghan's internal conflicts. However, recently Afghanistan has become important destination of China's foreign policy. By extending its diplomatic engagement, China urged, as a responsible major power, to play very crucial role in the economic development, security advancement and peace and stability establishment in Afghanistan. China also contributed in the peace reconciliation process between the Afghan government and the Taliban, though failed, and even played as the role of mediator between Afghanistan and Pakistan. In fact, globally known fact is that Pakistan is under immense influence of China. And therefore, it is more confidently assumed that China can persuade Pakistan in maintaining just order in and around Afghanistan.

Economic Aids and Investment

Though, initially, China maintained low profile relations with Afghanistan, but had provided $28.5 million loan to Afghanistan in 1964 and this amount was to be increased to $44 million in 1972 with the aim of investing in the industrial projects. Moreover, China had completed Afghan's Parwan Irrigation project in 1976.[82] However, in fact, with the Saur Revolution in Afghanistan in 1973, as has mentioned earlier, Daud's regime reached closer to the USSR and China-Afghan relations were seen further marginalized and remained normal throughout the 1970s. Furthermore, during the Taliban regime, China initially stayed little away from Afghanistan as long as it could afford. But later, China tried economic engagement with Afghanistan. In this context, it has believed that "China was willing to buy peace with the Taliban. Just a few days before 9/11, China signed a Memorandum of Understanding on Economic and Technical Cooperation with the Taliban promising much needed economic assistance and investments to the republic. Of course, with the US-led war in Afghanistan, Beijing had to distance itself from Afghanistan."[83] From 1999 to 2001, China's Huawei Technologies and Zhongxing Telecom were reportedly involved in Afghanistan.[84]

With the changing circumstances and with the emerging needs for its national interests and foreign policy requirements, subsequently, economic diplomacy newly emerged as the core of China's foreign policy. China believes that economic development plays major role in establishing stability and peace in any failed state like Afghanistan. However, the American perception, as it was believed, was that without peace, economic development cannot take place in Afghanistan. Therefore, to establish peace and stability, China engaged with Afghanistan, initially, through the means of economic diplomacy. China extended major investment and developmental projects and economic support for myriad purposes. After the US Afghan intervention in 2001, China provided a grant of $15 million to Afghanistan on the signing of Financial and Mechanical Assistance Agreement with Afghanistan in 2003.[85] One of the Chinese companies grabbed a Mes Aynak Copper Mines project worth of $3.5 billion in 2008, which is considered as the largest in the investment history of Afghanistan,[86] however, this project was said to be facing huge security challenges. In December 2011, it has stated that the China National Petroleum Corporation signed a deal to develop oil fields and refineries in the Amu Darya basis. The deal was worth of $400 million investment which was held as the first such contract given by the Afghan government which was expected to yield about $7 billion in revenues for Kabul in the coming decades.[87] Since the launching of BRI project in 2013, China has been actively participating in Afghan's economic development in terms of investing billions of dollars in telecommunications such as wireless infrastructure, railways connecting Kabul to other major cities ($2.7 billion), construction of pipeline from Turkmenistan through Afghanistan and Tajikistan to Xinjiang.[88] In 2011, China provided free aid of $23.7 million to Afghanistan[89] and between 2001 and 2013, China has provided Afghanistan with a total of 1.5 billion yuan (approximately $240 million) of aid. In 2014 alone, China provided Afghanistan with 500 million yuan ($80 million) of aid and also pledged to provide an additional 1.5 billion yuan ($240 million) over the next three years. Besides, in addition, China had planned to provide 500 scholarships for Afghan students to study in China for five years and also the extension of training to 3,000 Afghan professionals in various fields, including counterterrorism, anti-drug trafficking, agriculture, and diplomacy.[90] Moreover, China's total investment in Afghanistan reached to $5.7 billion by 2014.[91] During May 2016 visit to China by the Afghan Chief Executive Abdullah Abdullah, President Jinping reassured him China's commitments to Afghan's reconstruction and development. Further during

President Ghani's visit to China in October 2016, Jinping witnessed the extension of cooperation and declared $320 million assistance to Afghanistan.[92] It has believed that China was expecting to extract $100 billion from this project. Besides this, "the China National Petroleum Corporation (CNPC) has also helped Afghanistan in setting up country's first commercial oil production site," and "China was expected to extract 1.5 million barrels of oil annually from 2013."[93] In January 2017, the Chinese company (China Road and Bridge Corporation) signed a deal with Afghan government worth of $205 million aiming to 178 km build roads and bridges connecting northern Mazar-i-Sharif city to Yakawlang in Afghanistan.[94] In terms of investment, it has stated that "a stable Afghanistan is critical for security in much of Asia and internationally, yet continued violence in the country has prevented key states from building the economic opportunities, and the transport links and energy trade with the region, that Afghanistan desperately needs. The United States, China, India and Pakistan all have proposed investment projects that could help Afghanistan…."[95] Moreover, "China is investing in a housing project worth $300 million that will fund 10,000 apartments in Kabul. As a part of OBOR, China is also improving its own connectivity to Afghanistan. The first train from China was linked to Hairatan in northern Afghanistan via Kazakhstan and Uzbekistan. By investing in railways, China is also weaving land-locked Afghanistan into an integrated economic system and reducing its dependence on transit routes through Pakistan."[96] However, Franz-Stefan Gady, a senior fellow at the East-West Institute, expressed "China has been seen as a 'free rider'-gaining economic benefits by exploiting the country's natural resources while not contributing to the political and military solution of the conflict. So it is not surprising that as Western engagement in the country diminishes, China gradually steps in to fill the void to secure its interests."[97] Pant also argued that "China did not make a significant attempt to project its economic power in Afghanistan,"[98] and if had China completed its vital economic projects there, "China would have largest direct economic stake in Afghanistan of any country."[99]

Defence/Security Cooperation

China's role in security issues with the international forces was close to none and was reluctant in providing so in the fear of heavy risks in Afghanistan. China has not extended any military aid in the past, only the limited humanitarian and economic assistance was provided. However, in a meeting between President Ghani and President Jinping, China offered military aid to Afghanistan, as has reported, only in terms of general training and non-offensive weapons. In May 2015, both China and Afghanistan signed the first Memorandum of Understanding regarding security relations and China's readiness to assist the Afghan police in terms of training and equipment. Afghanistan had expressed its interest in cooperation between two countries as both facing new security problems and challenges. Moreover, both the countries also signed agreements for cooperation to protect borders and to ensure security in the border regions, to limit illegal cross-border migration and to curb drug trafficking on the China-Afghan border. Further, for this purpose, China pledged to provide bullet proof jackets, demining equipments, armored police vehicles, and devices to search automobiles for security threats. It has also reported that in October 2015, both signed MoU on defense cooperation.[100] In a February 2016 visit to Afghanistan, General Fang Fenghui, a member of China's Central Military Commission (CMC) and chief of the CMC's General Staff, met top Afghan leaders and "for the first time in the history of Sino-Afghan bilateral relations," Fang extended his consent and agreed "to allocate 480 million yens ($73 million) to Afghan Security Forces," besides, he also "proposed quadrilateral cooperation against terrorism in the region, which threatens Chinese projects like CPEC and OBOR."[101] China believed that "Afghanistan is of great importance for the Chinese economic belt, but, terrorism is a big threat to the project, and hence China is stressing the fight against terrorism"...China also expressed its willingness in 2016 to "deepen cooperation with the Afghan military in the areas of counterterrorism intelligence, joint exercises, and personnel training in order to jointly protect regional peace, stability, and development"...Further, in May 2016, China stated that it "firmly supports Afghanistan to fight terrorism and will continue to provide support for the country to strengthen the construction of security capability."[102] By and large, China promised and extended multiple aids to Afghanistan for the modification of Afghan National Police. China, after having learnt the need of security and stability in terms of protecting its interest, also proposed security network in collaboration with Afghanistan, Pakistan, and Tajikistan to counter terrorism in the region. These countries are also said to be agreed for the four states counter-terrorism mechanism with specific aim of sharing intelligence and joint training. Therefore, in this direction, when Ashraf Ghani came in power, China slowly and gradually kept increasing its security relations with Afghanistan by providing financial-military aid and Chinese military equipments to support Afghan's anti-terrorism efforts.

Furthermore, China urged the extension of supporting Afghanistan to develop its defence and counterterrorism capacity. In this context, the Chinese Defence Ministry Spokesperson Wu Qian said during a press conference on 30 August 2018, "China and the international community are all supporting Afghanistan to strengthen its defence and counterterrorism building efforts."[103] "China will send at least one battalion of troops, along with weapons and equipment, to be stationed there and provide training to their Afghan counterparts."[104] Besides, it has also reported that China was helping Afghanistan to set up a mountain brigade in the country's north to boost counterterrorism efforts. However, China rejecting its forces in Afghanistan said that China would not deploy Chinese military personnel of any kind there in Afghan soil at any time. In fact, clearing its stand, China stated that it was neither setting up a military base in Afghanistan and nor sending troops to the strife-torn country Afghanistan.[105] However, in the areas of security cooperation, Wu said, "China and Afghanistan had normal military and security cooperation."[106] Moreover, on 6 September 2018, the Afghan Ambassador to Beijing stated that "China was all set to train Afghan soldiers on Chinese soil, in an effort to counter Islamic State (ISIS) and al-Qaeda militants attempting to infiltrate Xinjiang through the northeastern border of Afghanistan, the mountainous Wakhan Corridor." However, China had denied it.

But as believed, "China is very much in the process of building a military training camp in Wakhan itself, and intends to station at least one battalion of troops at the base, accompanied with requisite weapons and military equipment…."[107] However, according to the Afghan Ministry of Defense (MoD) as reported by Sudha Ramachandran,

> A new military base is being set up in the Badakhshan province with the Chinese extending financial support covering all material and technical expenses for this base, ranging from weaponry and military equipment to uniforms for soldiers. In addition to the military base, China is financing an Afghan mountain brigade that will operate in Badakhshan province near the border areas…So far, China's military role in Afghanistan is geographically limited. It is focused on Badakhshan province and restricted to the Afghan side of this province's border with China. China is unlikely to expand its role geographically as it does not want to get caught in the Afghan quagmire as did the Soviet Union and the United States.[108]

In fact, China has denied its any such military role there in Afghanistan and maintained that it has been engaged only in the "capacity building" in the Badakhshan province. However, China stated that both China and Afghanistan are engaged in "joint law enforcement operations" in border areas to prevent and fight terrorism.[109]

Peace Process and Mediation

China's increasing role in Afghanistan's peace and reconciliation process as a peace maker was seen as the significant issue of debates and discussions amongst the analysts especially its intentions or motives and its modus operandi in the war-ravaged country. China, in fact, by learning the significance of a peaceful and stable Afghanistan for its strategic and security concerns, believed and decided to be engaged in peace process of Afghanistan and exhibited its supporting position on Afghan's long-term peace and stability by means of, though limited economic, political, and diplomatic assistance.[110] Therefore, in this direction, in October 2014, ahead of the beginning of the drawdown of the US forces, China hosted the third Ministerial Level Istanbul Process or Heart of Asia Conference, which was held as a regional cooperation process aiming to support the peaceful and stable Afghanistan. In this conference, representatives of 14 countries reported their participation. In this conference, as quoted by Bose and Panda, China wanted to focus on "Peaceful reconstruction of Afghanistan, and build consensus of regional countries on strengthening cooperation on Afghanistan and jointly safeguarding security and stability in Afghanistan and the region."[111] Further, President Ghani's visit to China in 2014 has become important milestone in the bilateral ties between two states inviting China's major role in Afghan's peace process between the Afghan government and the Taliban. China, to accomplish this objective, along with Ghani, used its leverages with its all-weather friend Pakistan, and as a result, in July 2015, Afghan's High Peace Council delegation had met with the Taliban representatives in Islamabad.[112] China has also honestly shown its keen interests and made honest efforts in peace process by holding the bilateral as well as multilateral dialogues. In fact, China, perhaps, learnt to work on both the peace process and economic development simultaneously. It has also believed that China adopted 'flexible dealing' with the Taliban, "to ward off its subversive religious influence in Xinjiang," and "to facilitate Chinese operations in Afghanistan's mines" and therefore, in this direction, China facilitated negotiations between the Afghan government and the Taliban, and the secret meetings took place on 19-20 May 2015 in Chinese city Urumqi and on 5 June 2015 in Islamabad.[113] Significantly, China's contacts with the Taliban, as stated earlier, were facilitated by Pakistan. Moreover, China along with Afghanistan, the US, and Pakistan became the member of the Quadrilateral Cooperation Group which aimed at to establish peace and stability in Afghanistan by bringing the Taliban to the negotiation table and into the peace process. In January 2016, China's foreign ministry stated, "China supports 'the Afghan-led, Afghan-owned' reconciliation process, and stands ready to play a constructive role to that end.... On the premise of respecting Afghanistan's sovereignty and the will of all sides, China will work with all parties to support...peace talks inside Afghanistan."[114] Initially the Taliban had shown its reluctance to participate in the negotiation. However, the peace makers tried their best to convince the Taliban to be part of the peace talks. Without inclusion of Taliban, peace process had no value. China believed importance "to keep the effort alive, not least because it reduces mistrust between Afghanistan and Pakistan." However, further "in July (2016), a delegation of Taliban negotiators visited China, apparently to report on the situation in Afghanistan from their perspective." But, the Afghan government expressed concerns about China providing "a platform to those groups that are responsible for the killing of the people of Afghanistan." It is argued that "while China might make some progress towards a peace process with the Taliban, the actual danger of such bilateral meetings is that they might undermine the efforts of the quadrilateral group." In 2014, talks among China, Russia, and India took place, as did a second round of talks between China and Iran. In past years, China has also held bilateral talks on Afghanistan with India and Pakistan.[115] It is believed that China might have played major role by using the platform of SCO of which Afghanistan is an observer member since 2012 and "the Shanghai Cooperation Organization, a regional group that includes most of Afghanistan's neighbours and nearby countries, is an important multilateral platform for coordinating policies toward Afghanistan".[116] The SCO promotes regional cooperation on economics, politics, and security, and therefore, on these terms, the SCO had optimum potential to play crucial role in Afghan's peace process. However, even before the joining by Afghanistan, the SCO countries had created the "SCO-Afghan Plan" to deal with the various problems such as terrorism, drug trafficking and organized crimes.[117] Keeping in mind its national interests and volatile situation in its border region, China strove hard and perhaps honest multilateral and regional efforts to deal with Afghan's problems that ranged from tackling security and institutional capacities to improving border control, fighting criminal networks, and counterterrorism. China's multilateral and regional efforts "engage Afghanistan's neighbours in the country's development, but would still need larger common efforts to change the situation on the ground significantly."[118]

Further, despite diverse speculations, China continued the holding of bilateral and trilateral meetings on Afghanistan with other countries in the region. In fact, in early 2015, keeping the space of moving forward, China tried facilitating peace talks between the Ghani government and the Taliban. But, China's efforts made no progress because of continuously deteriorating relations between both Afghanistan and Pakistan on account of Taliban's incessant attacks in Afghanistan. Therefore, as China learnt that its efforts to convince and bring the Taliban on the negotiating table would be formidable unless Afghanistan and Pakistan form better link of relations, China believed and planned to include Pakistan also into its peace efforts with the Afghan government and the Taliban. And in view of this, China "engaged in several rounds of shuttle diplomacy between Islamabad and Kabul to put in place a trilateral crisis management mechanism."[119] For this, the first round of the China-Afghanistan-Pakistan Trilateral Strategic Dialogue was held in Kabul in February 2015. Moreover, in December 2017, China organized and hosted trilateral peace talks of these countries where they unanimously called on the Taliban to join the peace process so that to establish peace and stability in Afghanistan. In fact, as what China perceived, the Afghan President Ghani also, believing in the same line of perception, stated, "The problem fundamentally is not about peace with Taliban. The problem is fundamentally about peace between Pakistan and Afghanistan."[120] However, keeping this perception in mind, China formally initiated mediation to normalize tense relations between Afghanistan and Pakistan so that both to jointly counter the menace of terrorism and extremism and also to encourage them for the promotion of regional stability, peace and security. During his visit to Afghanistan and Pakistan in June 2017, China's Foreign Minister Wang Yi urged the leaders of two countries to develop effective counter-terrorism mechanism by increasing cooperation between the hostile neighbours. Yi expressed, "China sincerely wishes for Afghanistan and Pakistan to improve relations, rebuild mutual trust, strengthen cooperation, and achieve mutual safety and development.... As Afghanistan and Pakistan's mutual friend, China encourages them to establish a crisis prevention and management mechanism as soon as possible, to properly deal with any kind of sudden occurrence".[121] Yi while making an official statement expressed that "if required, China will be ready to observe and explain steps" to both the countries against terrorism and extremism.[122]

However, despite its assertive role in order to stabilize Afghanistan, China's involvement in Afghanistan could not abstain from the myopic perspectives. As has believed that the Chinese efforts in Afghanistan were aimed at restricting the US influence in the region, and further it has stated that "Russia's realignment in Afghanistan, forging a strategic partnership with Pakistan and China and engaging with the Taliban, seems to be geared by a single objective: to confront the US wherever it is possible".[123] Contrarily to this, Zhao Huasheng stated that China was not seeking to fill a void left by the withdrawal of US forces, but that it, in the future, could play a useful role in the reconciliation process between the Afghan government and the Taliban.[124] Further, according to Siegfried O. Wolf, a researcher at the University of Heidelberg's South Asia Institute, "Beijing is only trying to contain the crisis and not to resolve it. China is indirectly encouraging Pakistan to continue its state patronage of cross-border terrorism. At the same time, Beijing is supporting Pakistan's policy of fighting anti-state militants, especially those groups that could pose a threat to CPEC (the China-Pakistan Economic Corridor)".[125] Besides, it has also opined according to Afghanistan observers that Beijing sought Pakistan's assistance not only to help create peace in Afghanistan, but also to keep regional rival India at bay. Moreover, China's counterterrorism measures appeared to exclude the US and India as, it has believed that Chinese authorities have historically treated New Delhi as a geopolitical rival and India's increasing close ties with the US are also perceived as a threat to Beijing's interests, therefore, China preferred not to cooperate with India. Consequently, it appeared that Beijing has been trying to construct a new security bloc in Asia, however, by discarding the involvement of the Sino-Indian security cooperation.[126] Yet, on China's proactive role in peace making process, Pantucci stated that

> The main characterization of Beijing's efforts in Afghanistan remains hedging. China continues to engage through multiple regional and international formats. Either through international multilateral vehicles like the Shanghai Cooperation Organisation (SCO), the 'Heart of Asia' or 'Istanbul Process', the Conference on Interaction and Confidence-Building Measures in Asia (CICA); or through sub-regional groupings like hosting Pakistan-Afghanistan-China trilateral, bilateral engagements with India, Russia, the UK, Germany, the US or Pakistan focused on Afghanistan...or finally through Chinese instigated mechanisms focused on Afghanistan like the Quadrilateral Coordination Group (QCG made up of Afghanistan, Pakistan, US and China) or the Quadrilateral Cooperation and Coordination Mechanism (QCCM, made up of Afghanistan, Pakistan, Tajikistan and China).[127]

Furthermore, on peace and stabilization of Afghanistan, Ramachandran stated

> It has advantages that strengthen its hand in brokering talks between the Afghan government and the Taliban. It is not burdened by a negative historical legacy and hence its role as a facilitator has been acceptable to the government and the Taliban. More importantly, Beijing is Pakistan's closest ally. It can leverage its enormous influence over Islamabad to get it to support the peace process as well as to bring on board the Taliban. Besides, as a participant in groupings such as the Quadrilateral Coordination Group and the 6+1 Dialogue, China can bring ideas and expertise from these dialogues to its brokering efforts. In addition, China is in a position to offer powerful inducements —benefits of regional trade and economic development—to lure Pakistan and Afghanistan to the negotiating table and to co-operate and reach a settlement. And finally, while China is wary of the Taliban, it is not averse to doing business or cutting deals with them.[128]

In fact, Afghanistan needed assistance from entire world community especially the world and regional superpowers by making effective efforts that to promote investment, economic growth, good governance, stability and security in Afghanistan, which would have helped to further promote the regional peace and stability and the economic development of the region eventually. The most formidable task in Afghanistan was security which remained in danger because of Pakistan's state-sponsored terrorism, and, as recently revealed, Iran's support to Taliban and also Russian hidden involvement, though it was aimed against the US. The power game between the US and its adversaries in Afghanistan actually benefited to none except the Taliban, consequently, deteriorating the situation further. Therefore, in the direction of normalizing the situation in Afghanistan, the US tried to explore a new approach towards Pakistan. The potential responses under talks, as reported, included the expansion of the US's drone strikes, redirecting aids to Pakistan and perhaps eventually downgrading Pakistan's status as a major non-NATO ally.[129] However, China did not appear to signal such a strong stand against its all-weather friend Pakistan. In fact, China has its own interests in maintaining the just peaceful order in the region. But, both Afghanistan and Pakistan failed to contain the use of their land for the terrorist activities against each other and also both indulged in allegations for sponsoring terrorist attacks against each other that further aggrandized the trust deficit. However, China made hard efforts to normalize the tense relations. China's better diplomatic relations with both warring neighbours became better. The Afghan government was also interested to involve China in its peace-making process along with the other powers. China might have built some sort of pressure on or prevail upon Pakistan to be an honest neighbour ceasing its dysfunctional support against Afghanistan and to normalize its relations with Afghanistan so that to improve the life of the Afghani people by fastening the process of reconstruction. In fact, the urgent need was to ponder on how to end terrorism from Afghanistan. Thinking of establishment of peace-stability without the end of terrorism was just a chimera. In fact, it has believed that "China wants to preserve its growing economic profile in Afghanistan but is not interested in making significant political investment at the moment. It hopes it can rely on its 'all-weather' friend in Pakistan to meet its interests in Af-Pak."[130] However, as

Pant believed that major powers including China that have their vested interests in Central Asia "do not have much sympathy for Pakistan's desire to strengthen radical Sunni groups," and "China is as interested as the US and India in effective Pakistan action against the terror sanctuaries in North Waziristan."[131]

Notes and References

1. Leo Yueh-Yun Liu, *China's Basic Foreign Policy Objectives in China as a Nuclear Power in World Politics*, UK: Palgrave Macmillan, 1972, pp. 11-24, http://link.springer.com/chapter/10.1007%2F978-1-349-01426-2_2
2. Ankit Panda, "Reflecting on China's Five Principles, 60 Years Later," *The Diplomat*, 26 June 2014, http://thediplomat.com/2014/06/reflecting-on-chinas-five-principles-60-years-later/, accessed on 13 May 2017.
3. *Ibid.*
4. Embassy of the People's Republic of China in the United States of America," http://www.china-embassy.org/eng/zmgx/zgwjzc/t35077.htm, accessed on 12 May 2017.
5. R. Dellios, "The PRC's Governance Diplomacy in the Asia-Pacific Region" in Chow, E., W, Kao, S, S, F &, Yu, P., K-H. (ed.) International Governance, Regimes, and Globalization: Case Studies from Beijing and Taipei, Lanham, MD: Lexington Books, 2010, p. 98.
6. Caine, S.E. et al., "Discord or Harmonious Society: China in 2030". April 14, Occasional paper/Center for Strategy and Technology, No. 68, Washington D.C.: Government Printing Office, 2011, p. 54.
7. Yufan Hao and Bill K.P. Chou, China's Policies on Its Borderlands and the International Implications, Singapore: World Scientific Publishing Company, 2010.
8. *Ibid.*
9. Quoted in T.C.A. Rangachari, "China's Role in South Asia: A Indian Perspective," in Aryaman Bhatnagar and RitikaPassi (ed.) Neighbourhood First, Navigating Ties Under Modi, ORF-Global Policy, GP-ORF Series, Observer Research Foundation and Global Policy Journal, 2016, p. 86.
10. China's Non-Interference Policy: PRC Leaders and The Realist Perspective," China Policy Institute: Analysis, 31 March 2014,

https://cpianalysis.org/2014/03/31/chinas-non-interference-policy-prc-leaders-and-the-realist-perspective/, accessed on 13 July 2017.

11. Sithara N. Fernando, "China's Relations with Sri Lanka and Maldives: Models of Good Relations among big and small countries," China Report, 46, 3, Sage, 2010, p. 285.
12. The Hundred Year Marathon: China's Secret Strategy to Replace America as the Global Superpower, New York: Henry Holt and Co., 2015.
13. Ding Gang, B & R Provides More Balance in Globalization, *Global Times*, 10 May 2017, http://www.globaltimes.cn/content/1046290.shtml, accessed on 7 January 2019.
14. Andrew Small, China in Afghanistan Beyond 2014: A Growing Imprint in Harsh V. Pant, *Afghanistan's Regional Dilemmas: South Asia and Beyond*, Orient Balckswan, New Delhi, 2016 p. 106.
15. Jonathan Z. Ludwig, Sixty Years of Sino-Afghan Relations, *Cambridge Review of International Affair*, Vol. 26, No 2, 2013, p. 395.
16. Srinjoy Bose and Ankit Panda, Indian and Chinese Foreign Policy Imperatives and Strategies vis-à-vis Afghanistan, *India Review*, Vol. 15, No. 4, 2016 (pp. 379-406), p. 391.
17. Baisali Mohanty, China in Afghanistan: Security, Regional Standing, and Status, Observer Research Foundation, ORF Occasional Paper# 126, October 2017, p. 6.
18. Jonathan Z. Ludwig, 2013, p. 395.
19. Bose and Panda, 2016, pp. 391-92, for details, see Shen Yu Dai, China and Afghanistan, *The China Quarterly*, 25, 1966.
20. Baisali Mohanty, 2017, pp. 6-7.
21. Andrew Small, 2016.
22. Jonathan Z. Ludwig, 2013, p. 393.
23. Andrew Small, 2016, p. 105.
24. Quoted in Bose and Panda, 2016, p. 392.
25. Andrew Small, 2016, p. 106.
26. Baisali Mohanty, 2017, p. 7.
27. Jonathan Ludwig, pp. 395-96.
28. Baisali Mohanty, 2017, p. 7.

29. *Ibid.*
30. Andrew Small, p. 106.
31. *Ibid.*
32. *Ibid.*, pp. 106-07.
33. Shubhangi Pandey, China's Surreptitious Advance in Afghanistan, *The Diplomat*, 22 September 2018, https://thediplomat.com/2018/09/chinas-surreptitious-advance-in-afghanistan/, accessed on 31 December 2018.
34. Jeff Reeves, Does China's Afghan Foreign Policy Constitute a Grand Strategy?, *Defense Concepts*, Griffith University, Vol. 5, No. 4, 2011, p. 31, https://research-repository.griffith.edu.au/handle/10072/41362, accessed on 31 December 2018.
35. Michael Clark, One Belt, One Road and China's Emerging Afghanistan Dilemma, *Australian Journal of International Affairs*, Vol. 70, No. 5, 2016.
36. Syed Waqas Haider Bukhari, The Role of China in Economic Stabilisation and Reconstruction of Afghanistan, 2012, Margalla Papers, p. 30.
37. Rustam Ali Seerat, China's Role in Afghan-Taliban Peace Talks: Afghan Perspectives, Institute of Chinese Studies, Analysis, No. 33, August 2015.
38. Michael Clark, pp. 564-65.
39. Baisali Mohanty, October 2017, pp. 2-3.
40. Michael Clarke, 2016, p. 568.
41. Andrew Small, 2016, p. 109.
42. *Ibid.*, p. 107.
43. Andrew Small, Why is China Talking to the Taliban?, *Foreign Policy*, 21 June 2013, https://foreignpolicy.com/2013/06/21/why-is-china-talking-to-the-taliban/, accessed on 11 January 2019.
44. Baishali Mohnaty, p. 13.
45. Andrew Small, 2016, p. 109.
46. Baisali Mohanty, p. 13.
47. Bose and Panda, 2016, p. 392.
48. Zhao Hong, China's Afghan Policy: The Forming of the "March West" Strategy?, *The Journal of East Asian Affairs*, Vol. 27, No. 2, Fall/Winter 2013, pp. 1-29.

49. Sudha Ramachandran, Is China Bringing Peace to Afghanistan?, *The Diplomat*, 20 June 2018, https://thediplomat.com/2018/06/is-china-bringing-peace-to-afghanistan/, accessed on 31 December 2018.
50. *Ibid.*
51. Michael Clarke, 2016, p. 564.
52. Richard Ghaisy, Why Afghanistan's Stability is so Important to China, Diplomacy and Defence, *South China Morning Post*, 22 May 2017, http://www.scmp.com/news/china/diplomacy-defence/article/2095156/opinion-why-afghanistans-stability-so-important-china, accessed on 1 August 2017. Some of part of this chapter has been published earlier as: Reconstructing the Failed States: China's Role in Afghanistan, *South Asian Journal of Socio-Political Studies* (*SAJOSPS*), Vol. XVIII, No. 1, July-December 2017, pp. 5-12.
53. Shubhangi Pande, 2018.
54. Richard Ghaisy, 22 May 2017.
55. Bose and Panda, 2016, p. 394.
56. Anna Lipscomb, Culture Clash: Ethnic Unrest in Xingjian, US-China Institute, 19 September 2016, http://china.usc.edu/culture-clash-ethnic-unrest-xinjiang, accessed on 12 August 2017.
57. Ben Blanchard and Sue Lin Wong, China's New Silk Road Promises Trade and Riches...Reuters, https://uk.reuters.com/article/uk-china-silkroad-protectionism/chinas-new-silk-road-promises-trade-and-riches-with-president-xi-at-helm-idUKKCN18B06E, accessed on 7 January 2019.
58. Ding Gang, 10 May 2017.
59. Arushi Kumar, Why China's One Belt, One Road Matters for Afghanistan, *South Asian Voices*, 12 May 2017, Carnegie India, http://carnegieindia.org/2017/05/12/why-china-s-one-belt-one-road-matters-for-afghanistan-pub-69974, accessed on 12 August 2017.
60. Jennifer Staats, To Help Afghanistan, Leverage China's Investment, USIP, 6 June 2017, https://www.usip.org/blog/2017/06/help-afghanistan-leverage-chinas-investments, accessed on 7 August 2017.
61. Shubhangi Pandey, 2018.
62. Harsh V. Pant, 2016, p. 6.

63. Baishali Mohanty, October 2017, p. 17.
64. *Ibid.*
65. Harsh V. Pant, 2016, pp. 6-7.
66. Shamil Shams, What does China want to achieve in Afghanistan?, DW, 26 June 2017, http://www.dw.com/en/what-does-china-want-to-achieve-in-afghanistan/a-39406187, accessed on 1 August 2017.
67. Vishal Chandra and Ashok K. Behuria, Afghanistan Beyond 2014: The China Factor in S.D. Muni and Vivek Chadha (edited) *Asian Strategic Review*, Pentagon Press in collaboration with Institute for Defence Studies and Analysis: New Delhi, 2013, p. 38.
68. Zhauo Hausheng, 8 March 2015.
69. Bose and Panda, p. 398.
70. Harsh V. Pant, Afghanistan's Regional Dilemmas: South Asia and Beyond, Orient Blackswan, 2016, p. 6.
71. *Ibid.*
72. Quoted in Baishali Mohanty, October 2017, p. 19.
73. Harsh V. Pant, 2016, p. 6.
74. Ahmed Bilal Khalil, The Rise of China-Afghanistan Security Relations, *The Diplomat*, 23 June 2016, http://thediplomat.com/2016/06/the-rise-of-china-afghanistan-security-relations/, accessed on 3 August 2017.
75. Zhao Hausheng, What is Behind China's Growing Attention to Afghanistan?, Carnegie Endowment for International Peace, 8 March 2015, http://carnegieendowment.org/2015/03/08/what-is-behind-china-s-growing-attention-to-afghanistan-pub-59286#motivations, accessed on 4 July 2017.
76. Ahmed B. Khalil, 2016.
77. Zhao Hausheng, 8 March 2015.
78. *Ibid.*
79. Foreign Ministers of Afghanistan and China Sign Five Bilateral Cooperation Agreements, Ministry of Foreign Affairs, Islamic Republic of Afghanistan, 17 May 2017, http://mfa.gov.af/en/news/five-biliteral-agreements-signed-by-foreign-ministers-of-china-and-afghanistan-main, accessed on 18 August 2017.
80. Jingdong Yuan in Chris Ogden edited *New South Asian Security*, Orient Blackswan, New Delhi, 2016, p. 83.

81. Shamil Shams, 1 August 2017.
82. Jonathan Ludwig, 2013, p. 396.
83. Kemel Toktomushev, China's Military Base in Afghanistan, China and US Focus, 11 January 2018, https://www.chinausfocus.com/foreign-policy/chinas-military-base-in-afghanistan, accessed on 10 January 2019.
84. Baishali Mohanty, p. 13.
85. Noor Rahman Tahiri, Afghanistan and China Trade Relationship, Munich Personal RePEc Archive, 6 August 2017, MPRA Paper No. 82098, pp. 2-3, https://mpra.ub.uni-muenchen.de/82098/ accessed on 10 January 2019.
86. Lisa Curtis, China's South Asia Strategy, The Heritage Foundation, Congressional Testimony, 10 March 2016, http://www.heritage.org/research/testimony/chinas-south-asia-strategy, accessed on 19 July 2016.
87. Jingdong Yuan, 2016, p. 81.
88. *Ibid.*
89. Noor Rehman Tahiri, 2017, p. 3.
90. Zhao Hausheng, 2015.
91. Bose and Panda, 2016, p. 393.
92. Lisa Curtis, 10 March 2016.
93. Harsh V. Pant, 2016, p. 7.
94. Afghan Online Press, 9 January 2017, http://www.aopnews.com/reconstruction-and-development/chinese-firm-signs-contract-to-build-road-in-afghanistan/, also see, RaffaelloPantucci, 2017.
95. Jennifer Staats, 6 June 2017.
96. Arushi Kumar, 2017.
97. Shawn Snow, Chinese troops appear to be operating in Afghanistan, and the Pentagon is OK with it, *Military Times*, 5 March 2017, https://www.militarytimes.com/news/pentagon-congress/2017/03/05/chinese-troops-appear-to-be-operating-in-afghanistan-and-the-pentagon-is-ok-with-it/, accessed on 14 August 2017.
98. Harsh V. Pant, 2016, p. 7.
99. Quoted in Bose and Panda 2016, p. 393, for more details see GaoFei and Xiao Yu, What can the Shanghai Cooperation Organisation and China Bring to Post-2014 Afghanistan, Asian Perspective, No. 38, 2014, p. 525.

100. Ahmed B. Khalil, 2016.
101. *Ibid.*
102. *Ibid.*
103. Atul Aneja, No Troops to Afghanistan, *The Hindu*, 31 August 2018, p. 12.
104. *Ibid.*
105. *Ibid.*
106. *Ibid.*
107. Shubhangi Pandey, 2018.
108. Sudha Ramchandran, 2018.
109. *Ibid.*
110. Bose and Panda, p. 394.
111. *Ibid.*
112. *Ibid.*, pp. 393-94.
113. *Ibid.*, p. 397.
114. Shannon Tiezzie, China joins Afghanistan, Pakistan, and US for talks on Afghan Peace Process, *The Diplomat*, 12 January 2016, http://thediplomat.com/2016/01/china-joins-afghanistan-pakistan-and-us-for-talks-on-afghan-peace-process/, 19 August 2017.
115. Zhao Huasheng, 2015, *ibid.*
116. *Ibid.*
117. For details see, Meena Singh Roy, Role of the Shanghai Cooperation Organisation in Afghanistan: Scope and Limitations, Strategic Analysis, 34:4, 2010, pp. 545-61.
118. Angela Stanzel, 2016.
119. Sudha Ramachandran, 20 June 2018.
120. James Rupert, Afghan President: Pakistan is Why Peace with Taliban is Possible, United States Institute of Peace, March 25, 2015, https://www.usip.org/publications/2015/03/afghan-president-pakistan-why-peace-taliban-possible, accessed on 4 August 2017.
121. Shamil Shams, 1 August 2017, DW (DeutcheWelle).
122. Ayaz Gul, China Begins Mediation Bid to Ease Afghanistan-Pakistan Tensions, Afghan Online Press, 24 June 2017, http://www.aopnews.com/china-afghanistan-relations/china-begins-

mediation-bid-to-ease-afghanistan-pakistan-tensions/, accessed on 3 August 2017.

123. Shamil Shams, 1 August 2017, DW.
124. Zhao Huasheng, 2015.
125. Shamil Shams, 1 August 2017, DW.
126. *Ibid.*
127. Raffaello Pantucci, Commentary: China's expanding security role in Afghanistan, Reuters, March 1, 2017, http://www.reuters.com/article/china-afghanistan-securityrole-idUSKBN1683QY, accessed on 14 August 2017.
128. Sudha Ramchandran, 2018.
129. McMaster: Trump will no longer tolerate Pak support to militants, *The Indian Express*, 7 August 2017, p. 10.
130. Harsh V. Pant, Afghanistan's Regional Dilemmas, 2016, p. 5.
131. *Ibid.*, p. 12.

7

India: Yes to Soft Power, No to Hard Power

Introduction

Afghanistan's geopolitical position is strategically very important for India as it serves as India's gateway to Central Asian countries, and "it is seen as bridge connecting India, Central Asia and Iran." Though without sharing a common border practically, both India and Afghanistan have a prolonged historical and cultural links, however, their diplomatic relations have been seen only after India's independence and remained normal and warm throughout King Zahir Shah's reign till 1973. India held Afghanistan as an important neighbour and integral part of South Asian Community, and Afghanistan "looks at India as a potential counterweight in its relationship with Pakistan."[1] Pakistan has always been dysfunctionally active against both India and Afghanistan that brought both the countries together to build a strong bond of bilateral relationship. In fact, "following India's independence from Great Britain and Partition, Afghanistan saw India as an ally in its increasingly bitter and occasionally militarized dispute with Pakistan over the inclusion of ethnic Pashtuns in the new state of Pakistan."[2] Besides, India has always supported Afghanistan against the recalcitrant Pakistan. On Afghanistan-India-Pakistan trilateral dynamics, the renowned historian William Dalrymple, as quoted by Avinash Paliwal, argued that "hostility between India and Pakistan lies at the heart of the current war in Afghanistan."[3]

Looking towards India-Afghanistan current relations as both having harsh enmity with Pakistan, which is situated between two, Kautilya's dictum of 'befriending enemy's enemy' depicts the consolidated nature of bilateral ties. However, Paliwal and Pant see India's Afghanistan Policy "much more than either a proxy war against Pakistan or a desperate search for Central Asia's natural resources."[4] Emilian Kavalski sees Afghanistan as "one of the few places in the world where Indian foreign policy has been able to gain significant foothold and actually demonstrate New Delhi's capacity to exert influence", and for this development, the significant factors had been

> First, the perceived existential threat to India from failing statehood in Afghanistan is much more palpable than that from the Central Asian Republics; second, New Delhi and Islamabad seem to have been sparing over influence in Afghanistan; third, India does not have the same scruples about hurting Russian feelings as it has in Central Asia; and fourth, China has not been able to extend its outreach to the country to the same extent as it has done in the Central Asian States, which puts New Delhi and Beijing on more or less equal footing.[5]

By and large, however, India's foreign policy perspective towards Afghanistan steered the promotion of peace and peaceful co-existence, protection and maintenance of regional security and stability, mutual respect to territorial integrity and non-intervention in legitimate borders, extension of economic and cultural cooperation and reconstruction of New Afghanistan. India's foreign policy believes in the principles of Panchsheel while looking towards its relations with any country including its neighbours. India upholds the means of peace for resolving any matter of confrontation or crisis around the world, and therefore, in the war-torn Afghanistan too. Therefore, India believed Afghan-led and Afghan-owned or controlled peace process. According to Satinder K. Lambah, "The basic tenets of India's aims, policy and approach towards Afghanistan in respect of bilateral and regional cooperation remain unchanged. India has always wanted a democratic, stable and strong Afghanistan able to decide its own future."[6] The problem that pained India has been the 'talks with the Taliban' which was supported by Pakistan, China, and Russia and even the USA. China had always favoured the inclusion of the Taliban in Afghan's peace process, but India has shown its reluctance in this direction as of incessantly increasing terrorist activities by the Taliban. India's logic that was sustained that the terrorist mindsets should not be the part of any peace negotiation unless they relinquish their terrorist activities as prerequisites. India held the Taliban as the biggest threat to Afghanistan and its peace process. During a Heart-of-Asia Conference in India, New Delhi conveyed its support to peace process in Afghanistan, but rejected the Taliban's role in it. However, it has stated that "China has always conveyed to the Taliban that it recognized the Afghan government and has encouraged the Taliban to join the peace process."[7] This became one of the nubs of problems between India and China as an impediment to work in tandem towards the well-being of Afghanistan, besides, unsymmetrical leverages between them. In fact, both have 'status dilemma' in the regional and international levels.[8] Both have incepted their activities aiming to establish stability in Afghanistan, however, with different modus operandi. The significant fact of the matter is that India faced major challenges in accomplishing its national interests in Afghanistan posed by Pakistan, the Taliban and the great power's rivalry. However, for India, "Afghanistan becomes important as it provides a land bridge between the central Asia in north and South Asian in south. Moreover, the central Republics have always been keen to extend their oil, gas and transportation linkages with South Asia to the south, through Afghanistan in order to reduce their dependence on the existing linkages with Russia. This will become possible only after Afghanistan becomes peaceful and stable."[9] India's foreign policy towards Afghanistan had aimed at first, to extend supports to the secular government in Afghanistan providing equal representation to all the ethnic groups; second, to arrange the situation in Afghanistan for its connectivity to the other states especially for trade, however, Afghanistan has extended its support to China's OBOR initiative; third, to provide training to the Afghan security forces so that they to be capable enough to fight against the Taliban and other extremist outfits in the country; fourth, to help Afghanistan in becoming economically sustainable and well off to establish better socio-economic structure; and to engage multilaterally with the other states within and outside the region to find the mechanism for Afghanistan's reconstruction and also importantly to establish peace and stability in the state.[10] By and large, India's Afghan policy focused on the security situation, internal stability, the external dimension to the conflicts and Afghan forces capability to sustain Taliban's attack. Moreover, Paliwal identified "the three drivers of India's Afghanistan policy—striking a balance between Afghanistan and Pakistan, evolving international political environment, and the changing nature of Afghan domestic politics—determined which of the two policy advocacies won the day to influence policy output."[11] However, with the transformation of Afghanistan's powers in the hands of Taliban in August 2021, the domestic politics in Afghanistan also have envisaged paradigm shift. And this shift therefore pulled India's Afghan policy in perplexing situation in terms of its interests in Afghanistan and how to deal with the Taliban which is supported by India's hostile countries such as Pakistan and China and friendly countries Russia and Iran and even the US.

India's Interests in Afghanistan

With the increasing economic and military leverages and having global power ambitions, India has been trying to extend and influence the world. In view of India's influence and its capacity and also as the responsible regional power, India could not and cannot afford to abstain from looking into the dire situation in Afghanistan or "...it cannot afford to see itself as an innocent bystander anymore,"[12] and therefore, India's responsibility remained of moving towards extending proactive plan for the Afghan's peace, stability, and reconstruction. It has argued that "the overarching principle that guided Indian material presence and engagement in Afghanistan was the idea of democracy and how to empower the Afghan state."[13] India's role was seen as "crucial for the long-term stability of Afghanistan and India realizes that a stable, prosperous and democratic Afghanistan is also in its strategic interests."[14] However, India has strategic and economic interests in Afghanistan, and had been seeking a "strategic autonomy" there. To expand economic presence in Afghanistan has been India's honest interest that lied in the stability and security in Afghanistan as of its many projects prevailing there. India has significantly been seeking to facilitate its investment in affluent and rich natural resources of Afghanistan and the Central Asian countries (CAC), and Afghanistan offers India a strategic route to the CAC. India is fascinated by Afghan's unlimited coal and rare earths worth of $1 trillion. Moreover, India's presence in Afghanistan has been seen as to compete with the Chinese presence in Afghan's copper mines and in reviving old oil and gas fields.[15] There are 1400 regions within Afghanistan identified with mineral deposits such as high quality of copper.[16] In fact, Afghanistan offers great opportunity for India, without doubt, to extend its contacts with the Central Asian countries and that will be possible only when Afghanistan becomes internally stable, peaceful, and politically strong.

India's 'Connect Central Asia Policy' moves via Iran and Afghanistan because of Pakistan's blocking of its lands to India's outreach to. During his visit to Central Asian countries in July 2015, Indian Prime Minister Narendra Modi expressed, "India and Central Asia have a special place in our hearts for each other. But, we have not paid as much attention to each other as we should. This will change".[17] India has looked towards Afghanistan by developing the Iranian port Chabahar to connect Central Asian countries. India's Central Asia policy is said to be focused on; soft power which includes Bollywood films and music; education and technology; trade and investment in the wider energy sector and security tie-ups.[18] It has argued that "A friendly and stable Afghanistan is a *sine qua non* for India in order to sustain the traditional relationship between the two countries; ensure that it does not once again become a breeding ground for terrorism or come under the influence of forces inimical to India; and remain available as India's bridge to Central Asia."[19]

In terms of security, "Afghanistan is critical not only for the rest of South Asia but for the other adjoining regions as well."[20] The internal security of Afghanistan is serious matter of concerns for India in terms of its paramount national interests. In other words, "Afghanistan features high on India's national security radar, and has direct and indirect repercussions on India's interests. India dreads an Afghan government not in control of its territory, allowing extremist militias to make up the supply side of the insurgency in Indian-administered Kashmir."[21] Afghanistan is grappled with the strongly consolidated violent activities of the Taliban, and the terrorism by Haqqani group, and even the ISIS looking forward to step in, which posed serious implications for India. However, it has also observed that the Taliban and the ISIS may vehemently indulge in rivalry against each other to dominate the region that would further complicate the security situation in and around Afghanistan. India will have very meager chances of escaping from its probable repercussions. The other possibility also cannot be ruled out that the emergence of the ISIS and its possible intimate contacts with the terrorist factions in the region and their collective terrorist action pose bigger security challenge that further heightening the concerns in the region. Further the presence of militancy in Pakistan's territory close to India has also compelled India to be alert and tightened its security architecture. In fact, India's soft power approach in Afghanistan is criticized stating that "although India's security remains deeply affected by what happens in Afghanistan, India's disadvantage is that it is not involved in Afghanistan's security in any meaningful way."[22] On the other hand, Pakistan sees India's presence in Afghanistan against its interests and a problem of probable security threat. Moreover, India's presence in Afghanistan and its increasing people-friendly gesture provides India an opportunity to put an eye on Pakistan and to observe and defuse its anti-India activities. "India's primary interest in Afghanistan is to prevent Afghanistan from being a proxy of Pakistan...(as)...Pakistan's geopolitical importance allows Pakistan to play significant role in Afghan affairs."[23] But Pakistan is making all its efforts to push India back from the Af-Pak region. Besides, Harsh Pant, by and large, has seen the range of India's interest in Afghanistan such as countering Pakistan, containing Islamic Extremism, a bridge to Central Asia and expanding Regional Influence.[24] However, in pursuing its interests in Afghanistan, according to most analysts, India adopted the "soft power" approach and even this approach has been seen critically by many. For Pant, India's

"...soft power approach has yielded no real strategic gains..."[25] However, despite many assumptions or evaluation of India's soft power approach, India's soft power influence in Afghanistan has been increasingly at its height between 2014 and 2017.[26] And, as a result, India became one of the most friendly nations of Afghanistan. According to "a 2010 ABC/BBC/ARD poll, 74 percent of Afghans viewed India favorably, while only 8 percent expressed similar feelings towards Pakistan."[27]

Diplomatic Engagement

India and Afghanistan have a very long history of relations, as believed, which are traced back to the Indus Valley Civilization. India's relations with Afghanistan are said to be underwritten by social, cultural, economic and security ties. According to Dr. Manmohan Singh, former Prime Minister, "Our cooperation with Afghanistan is an open book. We have civilization links and we are both here to stay."[28] In fact, Pakistan has always been headache for both India and Afghanistan that reduced the distance between them only to enhance bilateral cooperation and healthy friendship between India and Afghanistan. On January 4, 1950, both the Government of India (Prime Minister Jawaharlal Nehru) and the Royal Government of Afghanistan (Nadjibullah Khan, Afghan Ambassador to India) had signed "Treaty of Peace and Friendship" and both agreed to "recognize and respect the independence and rights of each other, to strengthen and develop cultural ties" and "to assist each other's industrial and agricultural progress."[29] Moreover, both the countries agreed to promote the mutual diplomatic exchanges and the strengthening of trade and other links. However, it has stated that by this treaty, India could not influence Afghanistan's foreign policy and also could not continue the supply of arms to the Afghan forces which was planned according to the 1945 bilateral agreement and only training to the Afghan officials was permitted in the Indian soil.[30] However, this treaty had permitted the opening of consulates in each other's country. Since this treaty both states have signed several treatise with the various governments in Afghanistan especially Soviet-supported governments to maintain and promote bilateral cooperation that led to the increasing India's investment in Afghanistan's various areas such as industry, power, irrigation, etc.[31] Moreover, on 4 April 1950, both the countries signed another "Treaty on Trade and Commerce", which subsequently, on 13 January 1952 was ratified, and that opening up of "a new arena of cooperation between the two countries and since then India has signed number of diplomatic, cultural, economic and social exchange programmes with Afghanistan."[32] Further, in 1955 in Asian-African Conference for International Order which was also known as the Bandung Conference, both India and Afghanistan could develop their bilateral engagements.[33] In fact, realizing and understanding India's neutrality gesture in the world politics, the Afghan King Zahir Shah had visited New Delhi in 1958 and followed by the visit of Afghanistan's Prime Minister Mohammad Daud Khan in 1959. Exhibiting its diplomatic and friendly gesture towards Afghanistan, in 1959, India's Prime Minister Jawaharlal Nehru also had visited Kabul. By exchanging their diplomatic visits, both the countries tried to strengthen bilateral relationship. Consequently, this development anguished Pakistan which had always been detrimental in India-Afghan relations and had joined the US-led Western military bloc. And because of Pakistan's negative gesture towards them, both the countries had used the non-alignment forum to criticize Pakistan's joining of the Western forces during the cold war politics. Pakistan had joined the SEATO and the CENTO in 1954 and 1955 respectively. However, despite better diplomatic relations, it has stated that Afghanistan always exhibited hesitancy in supporting India on its conflicts with Pakistan especially in 1947-49, 1965 and 1971. In this context, as quoted by Paliwal, according to former Indian diplomat Chinmaya Gharekhan, "Afghanistan never sided with India in India's disputes with Pakistan. Afghanistan voted against Pakistan's membership in the UN...but on issues like Kashmir, especially Kashmir, we (India) have not had any support from Afghanistan."[34] Afghanistan has also not opposed India either. The logic behind Afghanistan not supporting India or keeping its neutrality during China's India aggression in 1962 and India's war with Pakistan in 1965, could be that India had also not supported Afghanistan over the issue of Pashtunistan against Pakistan and remained neutral by viewing the Pashtun problem as a problem between both Afghanistan and Pakistan.[35] In fact, India had stayed away from this issue keeping in mind its hostility with Pakistan. However, with India and Afghanistan's increasing proximity, Pakistan was perplexed with the perception that both would strategically maneuver plan against Pakistan or "to capture Pakistan in a pincer attack", and both trying to provoking separatist tendencies in Pakistan. However, by 1974, both India and Afghanistan had become increasingly alarmed by Pakistan's propaganda.[36] During this time, Pakistan established its economic and diplomatic relations with the Islamic world and also had tried to impress the Afghans also, but, Afghanistan had not turned positively towards Pakistan. Contrarily, Afghanistan further consolidated its ties with India. In 1976, Indian Prime Minister Indira Gandhi had visited Kabul to strengthen bilateral ties.

Even during the 1980s, especially during the Soviet intervention[37] in Afghanistan, India was the only South Asian country to keep extending support to the existing and succeeding political set ups in Afghanistan and especially by supporting the pro-Soviet government.[38] During the Soviet presence in Afghanistan, India had sheltered over 60,000 Afghan refugees.[39] In fact, India was against any interference in domestic affairs of Afghanistan and had adopted the stand to deal any de facto government. However, in this context it was expressed as quoted by Paliwal that "We (Afghans) are unhappy with the Government of India for not supporting the Afghan people and for supporting the Soviet troops. But that has not lessened our admiration and affection for Indians, who were close to us and who had helped us before the Soviet invasion and occupation."[40] In fact, because of the situation that occurred in the South Asia after the Soviet intervention, the then Foreign Minister of India, Atal Bihari Vajpayee, in the Janata Party government (1977-80) had recognized the threat to India's security. He had held that "the supply of American arms to an 'over armed Pakistan' and Soviet military presence in Afghanistan would endanger peace and stability in South Asia," and further he had asserted that "the Soviet Union must make a prompt declaration that it will withdraw its forces and the US must not use the developments in Afghanistan to induct arms in Pakistan."[41] Moreover, on

India's stand, Amin Saikal noted, "India continued to be the only major democracy that consistently accepted and reiterated the official Soviet version of events that Soviet forces 'invited' into the county by the Afghan Revolutionary Council and were acting to stabilize the country," and "the Soviets would withdraw upon the request of the Afghan government."[42] It has also stated that "India continued to abstain each year that the UN General Assembly voted on the resolution calling on foreign forces to leave Afghanistan."[43]

After the Soviet withdrawal in 1988-89, India had maintained just normal ties with the Afghan government led by Ahmad Shah Massoud till 1996; however, Afghanistan could not provide a strong government due to internal fractions within the government. During the Afghan wars of 1980s and 1990s, in fact, India was on the losing side in Afghanistan as it was seen that India's relations with the Babrak Karmal's government and later Mohammad Najibullah's regime (both unpopular regimes) and its relations with the Soviet were held by the Afghans as "an illegitimate representative of foreign interests."[44] Consequently, the Taliban group grabbed power in Afghanistan, which the international community had not recognized. Even India did not extend its support and closed all its relations with the Taliban-led Afghan government. In this context, argument was made that "India's lack of relations with and open aversion to the Pakistan supported Taliban regime are highlighted as markers of a 'proxy war' or 'competition between New Delhi and Islamabad,' and India's Afghanistan policy in 1990s is often termed as a zero-sum game of influence with Pakistan."[45] During the Taliban regime from 1996 to 2001, India abstained from any involvement in Afghanistan and lost its contact and influence, and also failed in safeguarding its interests. Worsening the situation more, the Taliban had earned defame by hijacking India's IC814 plane in 1999. Moreover, India extended covert support to the non-Pashtun Northern Alliance against the Taliban. As a result, with the deteriorating mutual gesture, it has argued that both Indian government and the Taliban government made no efforts to fill the increasing gap between them and both the sides lost opportunities in establishing bilateral ties for the period.[46] Contrarily, Pakistan gained manifold influence in Afghanistan. India's policy staunchly opposed the Taliban's political and social gesture and believed in containing the Taliban.[47] According to Shyam Saran, former Foreign Secretary of India, "the Taliban was seen as trying to exclude India from Afghanistan and proved to be very hostile to India. That is one of the reasons why India withdrew its diplomatic representation from Afghanistan."[48] However, in 1999, India became one of the supporters (Russia, Iran and the Central Asian counties) of the anti-Taliban Northern Alliance or United Front which was formed in 1996[49] in Afghanistan. India has also activated its aids and arms supplies to the Northern Alliance along with Russia and Iran.[50]

In 2001, after the 9/11 havoc, the US President George W. Bush (jointly with the British special forces) made intervention in Afghanistan throwing the Taliban (the ultra-conservative political and religious faction that ruled Afghanistan from 1996 to 2001 had provided sanctuaries to Al-Qaeda, the perpetrators of the terrorist attack on the US on 11 September 2001) out of the power and later to dismantling of the Al-Qaeda. The US intervention made the congenial situation for India to re-engage proactively with Afghanistan under Hamid Karzai who became acting President in December 2001. "India saw the fall of the Taliban government as a major strategic gain."[51] According to Paliwal, "the massive II-76 carrier of the Indian Air Force descended at Bagram airbase after a 17-hour flight from New Delhi...that included two stopovers—near Dubai and Meshed, Iran...India had dispatched a team of intelligence officers, diplomats, and doctors to restart diplomatic links with Kabul."[52] In the post-Taliban regime, India was the first country to open an embassy in Afghanistan in December 2001. Moreover, India opened four regional consulates in Jalalabad, Kandahar, Mazar-i-Sharif and Herat, besides the full-fledged embassy in Kabul in 2002. In other words, since 2001, India adopted proactive policy towards Afghanistan, as this was a time, as Pant stated "when Indian capabilities—political, economic and military—have increased markedly and India had become increasingly ambitious in defining its foreign policy agenda."[53] It has also argued that "In contrast to its perspective during the Soviet intervention, India welcomed US and NATO military involvement in Afghanistan and has made clear on several occasions that it does not want this role to end prematurely."[54]

In fact, in the late 1990s especially during the Taliban regime and thereafter till 2004, India's Afghan policy had been premised on the Gujral Doctrine of Non-reciprocity and later in the BJP government, Prime Minister A.B. Vajpayee's prioritization of "India's global rather than its regional importance," however "none of these India's approaches helped India achieve its goals vis-à-vis Afghanistan."[55] Subsequently, during Congress-led UPA government under Dr. Manmohan Singh as a Prime Minister (2004-14), "India showed a renewed commitment towards its regional role" and its Afghan policy.[56] Further, by proposing Afghanistan's membership in SAARC in 2005, India consolidated its relations with Afghanistan, and in 2007, Afghanistan became the member of SAARC.[57] Both the countries, in August 2005, when India's Prime Minister Dr. Manmohan Singh visited Kabul, had reiterated their commitment for building a new partnership for the 21st century towards bilateral cooperation in various areas. And this visit was held very significant and "highlighted the edifice of a new democratic beginning in Afghanistan with the foundation-stone lying ceremony of Afghan Parliament building, a symbolic gesture of the world's largest democracy restructuring and rebuilding the youngest democracy."[58] During President Hamid Karzai's visit to India in April 2006, both the sides signed memorandums of understanding (MOUs) for strengthening cooperation in the fields of rural development, education and standardization. Furthermore during his visit to Kabul on 23-24 January 2007, India's then Foreign Minister Pranab Mukherjee had stated, "Indian-Afghan bilateral relations are fast developing into a partnership which is very special to us...we are glad to be able to contribute to the reconstruction and rebuilding of Afghanistan."[59] Moreover, during the 15th SAARC Summit (1-3 August 2008) in Colombo (Sri Lanka), India pledged the bulky amount for the ongoing and the other thereafter projects. In May 2011, Dr Manmohan Singh visited Kabul and further signing of Strategic Partnership Agreement (SPA) in October 2011 strengthened bilateral political ties between two countries, and this visit sent the message that "India will not consider an exit strategy from Afghanistan.[60] After this agreement, Karzai called India as friend and Pakistan as brother.[61] The SPA contains the provisions of assistance to help in rebuilding Afghanistan's "infrastructure and institutions, education and technical assistance to re-build indigenous Afghan capacity in different areas, encouraging investment in Afghanistan's natural resources, providing duty free access to the Indian market for Afghanistan's exports support for an Afghan-led, Afghan-owned, broad-based and inclusive process of peace and reconciliation, and advocating the need for a sustained and long-term commitment to Afghanistan by the international community."[62] In July 2011, the former President of Afghanistan and Chair of the High Peace Council, Burhanuddin Rabbani visited Delhi, and since then India has supported an Afghan-led and Afghan-owned peace process.[63]

In the post-2014 period, India's engagement with Afghanistan was seen increasing. When India's External Affairs Minister Sushma Swaraj visited Afghanistan, the then President Karzai jointly with her inaugurated a monumental Afghan Flag on 10 September 2014, the flag was held as a symbol of Afghan unity and nationhood. India announced US$ 1 million for creation of a national public park around the flag. Indian initiative was widely appreciated by Afghans and the international community. Sushma Swaraj also inaugurated the new chancery complex in Kabul from which the embassy started operating since July 2014. She also had pointed out the clearest statement of 'no exit' policy by India.[64] Furthermore, India extended its assurance and commitment in terms of security and development of Afghanistan by allying with Afghanistan in its undergoing political, security, and economic transitions in 2015. During Heart-of-Asia-2015 in Pakistan, India stressed on increased connectivity, regional trade and openness with Afghanistan....[65] Moreover, while on India visit from 31 January-4 February 2016, Abdullah Abdullah, Chief Executive of the Islamic Republic of Afghanistan, held discussions with Indian Prime Minister Narendra Modi on bilateral, regional and global issues of mutual interest including the security situation and peace and reconciliation in Afghanistan. During this time,

India reiterated its abiding commitment to stand by and support Afghanistan in its all possible ways during its on-going political, security, and economic transitions. Moreover, both leaders also strongly condemned the terrorist attacks in Afghanistan and in Pathankot in India, and both stressed and expressed the need of complete elimination of all forms and manifestations of terrorism as well as support they have been receiving so that to establish peace and stability in the region.[66] In a meeting during the Heart-of-Asia Conference which was held in Amritsar in December 2016, Prime Minister Modi assured the President of Afghanistan Ashraf Ghani of "India's continued support for ensuring peace and stability in Afghanistan." Further, at the time of his visit to India on 10 September 2017, Afghanistan's Foreign Minister Salahuddin Rabbani suggested India for the larger role to play in the regional diplomacy. While appreciating India's assertive role in Afghanistan, he further expressed their (Afghan) expectation from India that to convince the other states like Russia and Iran to work with the Afghan government to support the peace process in Afghanistan. During this time India's Minister for External Affairs Sushma Swaraj called the India-Afghanistan strategic relationship as "Article of Faith",[67] and also said that "we remain united in overcoming the challenges posed by cross-border terrorism and safe havens and sanctuaries to both our countries."[68] In September 2017, during his visit to India, Afghanistan's Chief Executive further expressed Afghan's trust in India's constructive role in reconstructing Afghanistan.

Further on 10 September 2018, India's Foreign Secretary Vijay Gokhale held bilateral discussion with Afghan's Deputy Foreign Minister Hekmat Khalil Karzai convening the joint working group on Political and Security Cooperation. In this regards, India's Ministry of External Affairs in statement stated, "Both sides stressed the need to continue working together towards a stable, peaceful and prosperous region that is free from terrorism and extremism."[69] The Afghan's Ambassador to India, Shaida Abdali in an interview, ahead of Afghan President Ghani's India visit on 19 September 2018, said, "Afghanistan and India are strategic partners. Afghanistan is seeking India's support for its peace process as well as for military hardware," and he further said that "Afghanistan is currently facing a very critical time in all respects, and we certainly need to sit down with all our friends and strategic partners like India to discuss how to deal with terrorism and security issues that ultimately affect all of us."[70]

During Afghan President Ghani's long day visit to India (19 September 2018), both the countries expressed their firm determination to strengthen connectivity by multiple means that also including through the Chabahar Port and the Air Freight Corridor. Besides, during a meeting with Prime Minister Modi, Ghani highly appreciated India-China cooperation in the war-torn Afghanistan. India and China had jointly planned to start a joint training programme for Afghan diplomats or it may also be called as a joint capacity building programme. The Foreign Ministry of India released the statement that "It was agreed to deepen the New Development Partnership in the areas of high impact projects in the field of infrastructure, human resources development and other capacity-building projects in Afghanistan." Both the leaders decided and agreed to strengthen their coordination and consultation on activities at various international forums and also to work together even more closely with their regional and international partners for prosperity, peace, stability and progress. However, President Ghani's this visit to India held as a low-key visit because of "the growing sense of uncertainty that prevails."[71]

Reconstruction and Economic Engagement

As mentioned earlier, after the treaty in 1950, both the countries had economic and cultural exchanges. In fact, "India and Afghanistan have a long standing record of technical and economic cooperation in various field, and prior to 1979, Afghanistan was the largest partner in India's technical and economic cooperation program."[72] India extended trainings to many Afghan officials and students in various academic and technical colleges and institutions.[73] But India's contribution towards the infrastructure development was not adequate before or during the Taliban regime, however, India involved in the post-Taliban Afghanistan proactively. After the ouster of the Taliban from power in 2001, India planned a comprehensive strategy for rebuilding of Afghanistan and also to contribute towards it to bring it out from the dire situation. As a result, along with the international community, India actively played a significant role in Afghan's economic reconstruction and infrastructure development. In the Bonn Conference of 2001, India had participated and announced $100 million construction aid to Afghanistan. Since then India "continued to pursue a policy of high level engagement with Afghanistan through extensive and wide-ranging humanitarian, financial and project assistance as well as participation in international efforts aimed at political reconciliation and economic rebuilding of Afghanistan."[74] India was "the fifth largest bilateral donor country (behind US, Japan, UK and Germany) having pledged US$750 million, committed US$701.67 million and disbursed US$204.26 million," as has been reported in 2007 by Shanthie Mariat D'Souza for various purposes including infrastructure, education, communication, healthcare, etc.[75] The Indian assistance to Afghanistan during the financial year 2005-06 was ₹ 383 crores.[76] Further, India contributed by extending humanitarian assistance worth of $2 billion in 2012 for various purposes that includes power generation, education, transport, health, defense, and diplomatic activities. Moreover, both India and Afghanistan have formed strategic and military partnerships to combat regional militants.[77] However, according to Paliwal, "India had introduced various developmental projects in Afghanistan by the 1970s. These included the Chardeghorband Microhydel Scheme, the Indira Gandhi Hospital in Kabul, and the series of technical assistance schemes in the field of planning, industry, mining, irrigation and power. Agricultural research stations were also established in Bamiyan, Kandahar, and Kabul for rice, wheat and potatoes."[78] Moreover, India had also agreed "to adopt 100 villages in Afghanistan to promote rural development by introducing solar electrification and rain-water harvesting technologies."[79] India's over-all role in Afghanistan from 2002 to 2014 was limited to humanitarian and developmental, strictly abstaining from any military role. During this period, India was described as 'the most friendly country' of Afghanistan which was considered possible because of a special trust that developed by the then

President Hamid Karzai and his fellow political colleagues about "the shared vision of Afghanistan emerging as an independent, sovereign, stable, plural and moderate country, focused on development and determined to turn its back on decades of conflict which had consumed an entire generation."[80] It has also stated that "the well-known Indophile sentiments of President Karzai, who was educated in India...have provided a further boon for India's influence in the country."[81] In fact, during the mid-1970s, India had become the second most important country after the Soviet Russia.[82]

The bilateral trade at $683.02 million for 2013-14 ($474.25 million export and $208.77 million import by India) was at a modest level given the vast potential between two countries.[83] India was also emerged, besides the overall fifth world-wide, as the region's largest donor of Afghanistan. The US also appreciated India's constructive economic investment towards Afghanistan's holistic stability as India made commitment to spend about $3 billion in Afghanistan. According to Satish Chandra, "India's popularity in Afghanistan is currently at a high due to its no-strings-attached economic assistance programme, which is meaningful, effective and geared to local needs."[84] Moreover, India has helped Afghanistan in its political establishments; such as given its political and democratic experience, India extended training to Afghan's officials on electoral processes and even provided electronic voting machines to facilitate the elections there. Besides, in 2008, both the countries signed MoU on "cooperation of local governance to train Afghan government local officials."[85]

India's programme of assistance activities and development partnership with Afghanistan focuses on four key soft power areas: first, humanitarian assistance; second, major infrastructure projects; third, small and community-based development; and fourth, education and capacity building.[86] India's major infrastructural projects in Afghanistan are: building of the 218 km long Zaaranj-Delaram Highway connecting West Afghanistan to Iran's Chabahar Port at a cost of $150 million, which was completed in 2008;[87] the bronze-domed parliament building in Kabul was constructed at the cost of $90 million funded by India (however, $178 million were budgetary committed) and which was inaugurated on 25 December 2015 by Indian Prime Minister Narendra Modi, the Salma Dam (power generating India-Afghan Friendship Dam) on the Harirud river in Herat province with cost of $130 million (completed in 2015 and inaugurated on 4 June 2016 by Modi) and the 220kv power transmission line from Pul-e-Khumri (Uzbekistan) to Kabul with cost of $120 million.[88] The Steel Authority of India (SAIL) secured mining rights at Afghan's largest copper mining deposit site in Hajigak in 2011. Moreover, India started hundreds of the Small Development Projects in South and East Afghanistan (Pashtun-dominated areas) and other parts of the country worth of $130 million, provided food assistance for primary schools and supplied 250,000 tons of wheat and also agreed to train about 1000 Afghan army officers every year among other forms of assistance.[89] It has also reported that India had finalized plan to build a 900 km rail route from the Afghan province of Bamiyan to Chabahar port, upgrading of telephone exchanges in 11 provinces and others.[90] One of India's construction companies has built roads exceeding the length of 700 km in total which cost around US $250 million.[91] Moreover, India assisted in other projects like a 400-km power line, and a hydro-electricity plant.

In the areas of humanitarian assistance and education initiatives in Afghanistan, India's role has been significantly commendable. Afghanistan became the largest recipient of international students scholarship offered by India. India extended studies to 1000 Afghan students every year (initially it was 500 students) in Indian universities on scholarships, and Afghan civil servants were also accessed to Indian training institutions. The Indian government has run a program that provided lunch meals to around two million Afghan school children and built many field clinics and a children's hospital.[92] The Charikar substation project was inaugurated by the Chief Executive of Afghanistan in December 2015; the Doshi substation and the restoration of Star Palace were also expected to be completed in 2016. India has provided high protein biscuits through WFP in schools throughout Afghanistan. India also gave $1 million assistance for flood relief programme in Badakshan in

May 2014. Moreover, in December 2015, India had assured to expedite the supply of more 1,70,000 MT wheat to Afghanistan, which was part of 1.1 Million MT wheat donation committed by India.[93] The prominent Indian companies that were doing their business in Afghanistan are: KEC, Electrical Transmission Lines; Phoenix, Consultancy in Electrical Transmission; AIPL, Establishment of Higher Power Project in Hilmand province; WAPCOS, Salma Dam; ANGELIQUE International, Salma Dam and other power project; APTEC, Computer and management Education; GAMMON INDIA, Power Transmission Line and Power sub-stations; KPTL, Power Transmission Line; ANAAR GROUP (Air India GSA); Spice Jet, etc.[94]

Earlier, in April 2015, Afghan President Ashraf Ghani visited India, and "both the sides discussed about the cooperation and assistance in various sectors including health, education, agriculture, disaster management, power sector and electoral management. During this time, India extended assistance for the annual maintenance of M/s Habibiyar School, Kabul and Indira Gandhi Institute of Child Health; $5 million fund to ARCS to treat Afghan child with Congenital Heart Disease (CHD) in India for five years; extension of ICCR scholarship till 2020 and indicated readiness to sign a bilateral motor vehicle pact to allow vehicles from both sides to travel across each other's countries."[95] During his visit to Afghanistan on 25 December 2015, Modi inaugurated the newly built Afghan Parliament. India, further, announced 500 scholarships for the children of the martyrs of Afghan Security Forces in school and colleges both in Afghanistan and in India.[96] Besides, in September 2017, during Afghan Foreign Minister's visit to India, India's then External Affairs Minister Sushma Swaraj announced 500 new scholarships for children and kin of the Afghan National Defence and Security Forces to honour their sacrifices for the cause of entire humanity and ensuring the safety of the Indian citizens working in Afghanistan.[97] Under the small development projects (SDPs) Phase I and II ($20 million) and Phase III ($100 million) India, along with Ministry of Economy of Afghanistan, had committed more than 200 small projects with less gestation period covering public health, education, and community infrastructure in various provinces of

Afghanistan. Earlier in 2014, under aid to Afghanistan budget, India established Agriculture University ANASTU in Kandahar. In 2016, India approved the III phase of small development projects comprising 92 projects in Afghanistan.[98] Besides, during their visits to Iran in May 2016, Modi, Ghani, and Iranian President Hassan Rouhani signed an agreement for the expansion and development of Chabahar port in Iran. India, while discussing with Iran, made commitment for the expansion of the port through India's development financing. The Chabahar port was aimed at serving as a hub of transit goods route to Afghanistan and Central Asia and also to connect with Western Asia.[99] The operation of the Chabahar port, as potentially measured, intended substantially to increase Afghanistan's exports to trade with India and the rest of the world. In a very recent past, India approved \$85 million for upgrading the capacity of Chabahar Port to facilitate an alternate trade transit route for Afghanistan. On 29 October 2017, India sent wheat from Kandla port in Gujarat to Afghanistan vie Iranian Chabahar port which was said to be the first wheat consignment through the new route.[100] In fact, most of the Indian goods have been sent to Afghanistan vie Iran, and therefore, to make it more viable, India, in 2003, had signed a 'tripartite preferential trade agreement' with both Iran and Afghanistan. In 2003, India had sent goods to Afghanistan vie Iran's Bandar Abbas port. Besides, the Indian Prime Minister announced a fresh \$1 billion worth of aid in 2016. Further, in 2017, India allotted ₹ 350 crores in its budget 2017-18 for Afghanistan. The \$1-billion aid also includes the construction of the \$250-million Shahtoot dam outside Kabul.[101] In September 2017, India further announced 116 new development projects across Afghanistan. By and large, as was observed, India's major role in the reconstruction and rehabilitation of Afghanistan can be seen as

> ...a strong signal of its abiding commitment to peace, stability and prosperity in Afghanistan during the critical period of security and governance transition...India believes that sustainable development of Afghanistan requires long-term investment in Afghanistan that can help it exploit its natural resource wealth. India is, thus, at the

> forefront of the promotion of investment in Afghanistan and a consortium of public and private Indian companies has been selected to make one of the biggest investments in the country's mining sector, in the Hajigak iron ore reserves.[102]

Till the Taliban's regime was re-established in 2021, India-Afghanistan trade was reached to about 900 million dollars that received a boost from special "air corridor" between Kabul, Delhi and Mumbai which was established in 2017.[103] While appreciating India's positive and constructive role in Afghanistan, Javid Faisal, a former government official, stated, "India, as a trustworthy partner in Afghanistan, has contributed and continues to contribute to the reconstruction and development of Afghanistan in a number of different ways."[104] Moreover, Illyas Kamavi, a civil activist from Nangarhar province of Afghanistan, while defending Indian presence in Afghanistan, argued, "Sure, India had its own interests as every country does who support us. But the role India has played here since 9/11 has been construcitve."[105] Moreover, India has already committed to provide lifesaving medicines and one million doses of Covid vaccines to the Afghan people, and has already dispatched the three shipments of humanitarian aids that consist of the medicines including for the Covid.

Defence/Security Cooperation

India has provided "transport, logistical and engineering" equipment to Afghan government and also conducted all the training sessions for Afghan's security forces and personnel in India. In fact, India always remained and nurtured hesitancy in sending and deploying Indian military forces in Afghanistan. However, after a series of attacks on Indian facilities there, India had deployed a small contingent of paramilitary forces in terms of protecting its diplomats and workers on the projects prevailing there, and these forces were not allowed to engage in any combating activities against the terrorist activities or any other military combat mission. According to the SPA of 2011, India had planned to provide military assistance to Afghanistan. The India-Afghanistan SPA mainly had four provisions that are "political and security cooperation; trade and economic cooperation; capacity development and education; and social, cultural, civil society and people-to-people relations". The then Indian Prime Minister Dr. Manmohan Singh, during SPA-2011, had stated, "India will stand by the people of Afghanistan as they prepare to assume responsibility for governance and security after the withdrawal of international forces in 2014."[106] In fact, Afghanistan frequently urged India to provide hard military aid in view of the post-withdrawal of the international security forces from Afghanistan in the end of 2014. But, India always committed for assisting in training, equipping and capacity-building programmes for the Afghan forces. India's Manmohan Singh government, following Nehru's line of thinking, had "stalled Afghan requests for military hardware, fearing they could derail its peace negotiations with Pakistan." Jawaharlal Nehru, the first Prime Minister, had thought that "Afghanistan's military demands could potentially become an irritant in India's quest for peace with Pakistan."[107] India perceived it as risk and limited its assistance to police training unit and small paramilitary contingents involved solely in the protection of Indian facilities in Afghanistan. During his India visit in 2013, Karzai had handed over the list of the military hardware to the Indian government, though it was not the first time. However, India remained hesitant[108] as usual and just had committed to provide defence enhancement to Afghanistan to develop the capabilities of the Afghan National Security forces, in terms of offering training regarding to conduct of counter insurgency and counter-terrorism operations, especially in the built-up areas and rural areas. But India did not respond positively for the supply of weapons to Afghanistan because of the US influence, which was against it as this was later stated by Karzai.[109] Moreover, in 2014, India and Russia had made an agreement and arrangement that the Indian government had to pay Russia that would supply arms and military equipments directly to Afghanistan.[110] However, this proposal also could not be materialized. C. Raja Mohan had narrated the main factors constraining India from providing military arms and equipments to Afghan military according to the SPA 2011 that were

> First, Delhi did not want deeper security cooperation with Afghanistan that could cast a shadow over its ties with Pakistan.... Second, is geography. The lack of physical access has imposed substantial limitations on Delhi's military role in Afghanistan.... Third, the US resistance to a larger India security footprint in Afghanistan.... The US was convinced that any India military role in Afghanistan would grate Pakistan's political sensitivities.[111]

India's assistance to Afghanistan has mostly been civilian and humanitarian especially in power plants, road construction and medical aid and the non-lethal military assistance and always been hesitant in providing robust or hard weapons to Afghanistan considering the geopolitical constraints, as mentioned earlier, because of relations with Pakistan and others. Therefore, because of India's frequently denial for lethal weapons, Afghanistan, as reported, has expressed unhappiness over India's hesitancy of supply of military hardware as it was "grappled with intensified Taliban attacks ahead of the US-led NATO troops drawdown from the war-torn country." In this context, it has stated from the Afghan side that the relationship between India and Afghanistan would be based on 'reciprocity' and India could play a vital role in ensuring peace in the region. But, questioning India's role in Afghanistan, it has stated that India has its strategic interest in the country and if India could believe in the principles of reciprocity.[112] However, China has filled this vacuum in Afghanistan when India did not supply the required weapons. In July 2016, China sent the first consignment of military assistance to Afghanistan. As a result, China's role in Afghanistan appeared larger as compare to India. In fact, India cannot compete with China in any sphere. Afghanistan has significant place in China's foreign policy towards the Central Asian countries and importantly in terms of its BRI initiative. However, in December 2015, India gifted three of four MI 25(Mi-24D) attack helicopters to Afghan Air Force and the fourth was handed over to Afghanistan in December 2016. India, for the first time, has transferred lethal military equipment (these helicopters) to Afghanistan. In fact, these helicopters were not considered as more tactically 'game changer' for the Afghan government to fight its war against the Taliban, but its importance remained as 'more symbolic'.[113] Moreover, India had planned of stepping up its assistance to war-torn Afghanistan by offering to pay for repairs to grounded Afghan Air Force (AAF) helicopters and military transport aircraft. The repairing of 11 grounded Mi-35 helicopters and seven military transport aircraft were estimated at about $50 million.

In August 2016, Afghanistan again gave another list of military requirements to India. During a meeting with Modi in the Heart of Asia Conference in Amritsar in December 2016, the Afghan President Ashraf Ghani had raised the issue of defence cooperation. However, Prime Minister Modi assured India's help for the reconstruction of Afghanistan without any military assurance. In this context, however, it was also expressed that "Keeping in mind the long lasting friendship India shares with Afghanistan, it will be a positive development if India can increase the military assistance to Afghanistan. However, it should be in the realm of increase in training, medical aid, supply of both lethal and non-lethal equipment, creating structures for maintenance of the weapons and equipment and reconstruction."[114] While expressing India's soft power approach towards Afghanistan, Modi argued, "You know that India is here to lay the foundations of future, not light the flame of conflict; to rebuild lives, not destroy a nation."[115] The Indian Ambassador to Afghanistan, Manpreet Vohra, stated, "We have been looking at the scale of the challenge the ANSF (Afghan National Security Forces) faces, particularly in one segment, close air support. We are trying to see how we can help. They have a large number of attack helicopters and transport aircraft grounded for want of spares, for expiry of certification."[116] It was also reported that Ajit Doval, National Security Adviser to Indian government, had met with Afghan National Security Advisor Hanif Atmar in Russia and had asked Afghan government to deliver an official invitation to the Indian Government to dispatch Indian troops, and India had planned to send 15000 troops to Afghanistan under United Nations Peacekeeping mission.[117] However, exhibiting its consistent stand, India failed to send any troops to Afghanistan. In fact, as its prolong policy, India will not send its troops to any country on individual basis. In September 2017, India further agreed to enhance existing assistance to Afghan security forces including the capacity building and training of Afghan soldiers in India, which was gladly appreciated by Afghan's Foreign Minister Rabbani when he was on India visit in September 2017. Moreover, Afghanistan Ambassador to India Shaida Mohammad Abdali, in the same month in 2017, confirmedly said that after training provided to Afghan forces, to expand India and Afghanistan Security Partnership, India had planned to extend training to Afghan police officers by having MoU under the UNDP. In this context, he expressed, "India has always been an excellent partner for all our capacity-building programmes. And we do have similarities in some of the aspects of the conflicts we face, so Indian knowledge and experience is going to be very successful for us, especially in counter-terror, and counter-narcotic (programmes)."[118] After the US's New Afghan Policy, the then Indian Defence Minister Nirmala Sitharaman denied the sending of Indian troops to Afghanistan. In this regards, the Afghanistan's Chief Executive Abdullah Abdullah during his visit to India in last week of September 2017 stated that Afghanistan had made no such request for Indian troops. He further held the New US Policy as an opportunity for India-US-Afghanistan cooperation on security and other development issues and also an opportunity to strengthen the India-Afghanistan security ties. In this direction, it has suggested that "India has to balance both soft power and hard power elements in its approach towards Afghanistan in the near future while aligning with countries which have convergence of interest with India."[119] On India's reluctance to troops to Afghanistan, Happymon Jacob stated, "The deployment of troops by foreign powers in Afghanistan has led to disastrous consequences. It is a historical fact and India understands it very well," and India cannot do militarily positive alone, and "if things go wrong, India stands to lose the goodwill it enjoys among the Afghan public and leadership." In the same line of argument, Rajesh Rajagopalan also stated, "Indian troops won't be able to help Afghanistan in any case. It will only drag the country into an unwinnable and costly intervention and tarnish its positive image."[120] Furthermore, the US Defence Secretary James Mattis stated that India's "no troops to Afghanistan" stand has been because of Pakistan's consideration that such step would develop more new complications in the region especially against Pakistan. However, he applauded India's holistic developmental approach in Afghanistan.[121] Further, during the Afghan President Ghani's India visit in October 2017, Modi has reiterated India's cooperation to supply military equipments on the basis of Afghan forces needs. However, from the beginning, given its long-standing perception, India has always paid no serious attention towards Afghan government's appeal for hard military assistance. In this context, Bose and Panda argued, "the Indian government's reluctance to engage militarily in Afghanistan is not a sustainable strategy; the Indian government will be unable to sustain civilian casualties (in Afghanistan or in India—resulting from terror acts) in pursuit of its soft power-oriented developmental activities, in the long run."[122] It has believed that

> India's only pathway to achieve its security goals has been reliant on its developmental and humanitarian assistance to cultivate goodwill within the masses and the political community. However this goodwill hasn't necessarily translated into leverage or capacity to influence outcomes in the security sphere. This capacity is as much limited by lack of cost-effective direct access to Afghanistan territory as it is by choice. Within the strategic community in India the view that holds traction is that putting boots on the ground is neither possible nor advisable.[123]

India's Concerns and the Future Prospects

India's humanitarian trajectory in Afghanistan has not been silky. With the increasing presence and influence in Afghanistan, India has also been facing multiple impediments in accomplishing its objectives and interests in the war-torn country. India's political and economic influence including significant development efforts and financial investment, though, is largely benefiting the Afghani people, but, this is seen as likely to exacerbating the regional tensions and encouragement to Pakistan's countermeasures in Afghanistan or India.[124] India's presence in Afghanistan also has panic Pakistan making it uncomfortable the way China's presence in Pakistan or India-Pak border makes India uncomfortable. In fact, it has also stated that the Pakistani security establishments are said to be suspicious even of India's developmental assistance to its western neighbour, as a result, Pakistan has consistently adopted the policy of blocking India's overland engagement with Afghanistan and Central Asian republics through which India has been seeking to import energy resources and also the export of Indian goods. However, according to 19 July 2010 'Afghanistan-Pakistan Transit Trade Agreement,' Pakistan allowed Afghani trucks to carry goods to Wagah border to deliver to India, but, the reverse has not been permitted.[125] Moreover, because of Pakistan's recalcitrance and terrorism in the region, the TAPI pipeline facing challenges in materializing.[126] Even for that matter Pakistan also blocked India's humanitarian assistance to Afghanistan and also has been trying to de-influence India in the region. Therefore, Pakistan's obstacles in India's outreach to Central Asian countries through Afghanistan remain the bigger challenge to India's national interests in the region. Pakistan sees India's presence in Afghanistan as a threat to its national and security interests. In this context, it has believed that "Without a wholesale change in thinking within the Pakistani security establishment vis-à-vis India, any security role in Afghanistan by Rawalpindi is likely to jeopardize Indian interests...."[127] However, by learning Pakistan's perception, Afghanistan side balancing its relationships had clarified that "Pakistan is a twin brother, India is a great friend," and the engagement with our friend will not affect our brother... Afghanistan's strategic engagement with India is not aiming against any country including Pakistan. And India-Afghanistan engagement is for Afghanistan's benefits and development from the strength of India. As stated, "Pakistan has created the Taliban and other terrorist groups in the region and continues to nurture these forces as its strategic assets to manipulate the situation in Afghanistan. Pakistan always hoped to seize power and rule the country through its surrogates, and, thus creates the so-called strategic depth."[128] According to the editorial in *The Hindu*, "The suspicion is quite self-serving: it heightens the bogey of 'Indian encirclement' of Pakistan, provides justification to the Pakistan Army's idea of building 'strategic depth' in Afghanistan, and strengthens the military's position within Pakistan. That the India-Afghanistan agreement has come at a time when Afghan-Pakistan relations are at a particularly low point does not help...."[129]

The growing bonhomie between New Delhi and Kabul coupled with the increased presence of India's development projects in Afghanistan could not be abstained from the targets of the Taliban-led insurgency, which included a huge array of insurgent and anti-government forces operating in tandem beyond south and east Afghanistan, with increased symbolic and high-profile attacks around Kabul.[130] The Afghanistan-Pakistan border region has always been burning because of the heavy terrorist activities as it provided safe sanctuaries to the extremist groups that have been posing major security threats to Afghanistan and the region as well, which have optimum potentials to further spill over the terrorist activities across that victimizing India intensively. With targeted attacks towards India in Afghanistan, security of Indian establishments including workers remained a key issue. In this context, Sumit Ganguly argued

> Indian policy makers, quite understandably, are concerned that the end of the US military presence in Afghanistan may well open the floodgates to the expansion of Pakistan's military influence within that country and the possible return of neo-Taliban regime. Such an outcome could well have significant adverse consequences for India's standing in the country and once again make it a haven for various anti-Indian terrorist organizations.[131]

However, the Trump's New Afghan Policy which was declared on 21 August 2017 could have dissolved this possibility for some extent as the US forces would stay in Afghanistan for the undeclared period which might have provided shields to the Indian interests. But the possible intensity of terrorism increasing further cannot be ruled out. India's alliance with the US in Afghanistan would not have been tolerated by the militant groups like the Taliban, as they believed in the US's friends as their enemy. The US would not provide security structure to India outside Afghanistan. However, India's "presence in Afghanistan has been consistently targeted by the Haqqani Network and the Hizb-i-Islami cadre," which are supported by the ISI of Pakistan.[132] Further, China's greater role in Afghanistan poses more challenges to India's interests there. As China, among other anti-India states, has been trying to influence Afghanistan by providing all probable needs. Moreover, Afghanistan-China proximity has been taking strategic shape. Even for that matter, China supports the Taliban also. And, this development would create an optimum leverage to China to bargain/impose its influence over the Afghan government or leadership of the day. The Taliban-led Afghanistan would offer more space to the country which would provide holistic assistance, despite pre-Taliban India-Afghan strong relationship. As India had overtly supported the Afghan government by staying against the Taliban. India and China would possibly display or indulge in 'status rivalry' in Afghanistan. In such a juncture, India would face China's challenge there. Therefore, it has believed that India could not yet "achieve its strategic autonomy vis-à-vis Afghanistan," as Indian foreign policy in Afghanistan "lacks an instinct of power", as argued by Sunil Khilnani, moreover, it has believed that "Pakistani and US strategies on Afghanistan also contribute toward undermining India's quest for strategic autonomy."[133] Bose and Panda narrated that

> India has failed to develop a strategic agenda commensurate with its rising capabilities. This lack of an instinct for power is palpable in the military/security realm where India has failed to master the deployment of its military instruments in support of its national objectives...India needs to develop its economic and military might without being apologetic.[134]

The dilemmatic situation for India, however, for not supplying military equipment to Afghanistan, as stated earlier, has two major constraints: the Taliban and Pakistan. The Taliban had already warned India for its military supply to Afghanistan and Pakistan also had raised objections over India's military equipment supply to Afghanistan on the plea that India may encircle Pakistan from Afghanistan's territory. By and large, India felt possibility of multiple terrorist threats emanating from Pakistan, the Taliban and probably from the ISIS. However, there seemed no objection from the Taliban and Pakistan over China's increasing influence and multiple supplies in Afghanistan as China has developed its substantial engagement with both Afghan government and the Taliban because of China and Pakistan proximity. Therefore, India had the pressure of China, Pakistan, and the Taliban, and unfortunately, at present, Russia (India's all-weather friend), has also begun seating with them since when the India-US proximity increased. As a result, because of inadequate security structure of its own, India was appeared dependent on the US in terms of seeking its security and other interests in Afghanistan. India's relations with Pakistan and China were further deteriorate with India's stand in Afghanistan appeared against Pakistan. In fact, despite Trump's New Policy envisaged pressure on Pakistan, but India was also under major pressure because of more presumed terrorist activities from Pakistan. Pakistan does not hesitate to dare India. The Pakistan-China proximity would obviously further consolidate as against to India's alliance with the US in the region and elsewhere. Therefore, the challenge is how and upto what extent India remains ready to cope with the imminent security threats and other issues after. The Pakistan government had rejected US's New Afghan Policy and also stated that Indian policies have been inimical to peace in the region. As a result, Trump's offering of greater role to India in South Asia could prompt Pakistan to rethink its decades old policy.[135] Moreover, India's strongly increasing ties with Tehran also were seen as provocation to Pakistan to play as a spoiler in Afghanistan. According to Pant, "India's ability to cultivate ties with Iran and Afghanistan leaves Pakistan vulnerable as it finds itself surrounded by states with a distinct anti-Pakistan orientation. Pakistan remains concerned about deepening India-Iran ties and Afghanistan's gravitation towards such as axis."[136] Therefore, to protect its diverse, including dysfunctional, interests in and around Afghanistan from India's ties with Iran and Afghanistan, Pakistan could not be a silent actor in the regional politics, but rather indulged in maneuvering a stormy dysfunctional strategy to destruct their anti-Pakistan motives or policy.

Earlier during the 1970s-1990s, India had better tuning with Russia and Iran in its Afghanistan policy, and the regional tri-alignment (India-Russia-Iran) was considered to be strategically viable. All the three had collectively supported the Northern

Alliance or United Front against the Taliban in Afghanistan. However, at present, the scenario has been appearing to be shifting as Russia and Iran have been appeared supporting Pakistan, and having engaged with the Taliban in terms of looking into the Afghanistan mess despite India's healthy relations with both Russia and Iran. But, therefore, the analysts have observed that Moscow and Tehran had challenged India's advocacy of an Afghan-led, Afghan-owned, and Afghan-controlled reconciliation process. And their aim was to undermine the United States and to reassert their leadership in Afghanistan.[137] Iran is also offering greater space to China. Moreover, China, Iran, Russia, and Pakistan have been indulged in meetings with the Taliban that remained proactive in Afghanistan. This group of the countries carried potentials for collectively de-influencing India's alliance with the US in war-torn Afghanistan. Further, the so-called great power game also seen taking place that further putting strategic impediments in peace and stability of Afghanistan particularly and India's interest generally. Therefore, in such a complex situation, India failed in playing active role alone as it needed the collective security mechanism of almost all the countries involved in and around Afghanistan. In fact, there are many neighbouring states such as Russia, Iran, China, Pakistan, Central Asian countries and even Saudi Arabia, and India and the long distanced US playing either role in Afghanistan and almost all of these states have their defined interests in Afghanistan. And the states like Russia, China, and Iran tried their best efforts to marginalize the US's influence and role in Afghanistan. However, even today with the regime change in Afghanistan, there seems group rivalry between the US and its allies and the other anti-US states, this consequently, making Afghanistan further the battleground of great power rivalry for their respective interests. This situation may be adverse to pose threats to India's interests and even the future possibilities are uncertain given the uncertain posture of Taliban regime 2.0. On India-US partnership and its impact on Pakistan in view of involvement in Afghanistan, Joshua White, the former Director for South Asian Affairs at Barak Obama's National Security Council, "There is value in signaling that the US sees India as a critical partner for Afghanistan. But there is also a risk, because feeding Pakistan's anxiety about Indian influence in Afghanistan is not necessarily helpful to either Washington or New Delhi."[138] C. Raja Mohan also observed that "the strategic rewards (to India) in Afghanistan might be as large as the risks."[139] It had prophesized that "India-US partnership would add further to Pakistan's imaginary fears about India's role in Afghanistan. Pakistan's army is already troubled by Trump's embracing of India and has publicly rejected US demands to shut down terrorist sanctuaries. Pakistan could expand its role as 'the godfather of militancy' by increasing its support to militant groups aimed at Afghanistan and India, and Islamabad can torpedo future peace negotiations with the Taliban."[140] Further, Shyam Saran, the former Foreign Secretary of India, stated, "The actual roll-out of India's policy towards its neighbours has been hampered by slow delivery mechanisms. This is a systemic issue, needing urgent remedy. One problem is the lack of adequate numbers of trained professionals to manage relations with our neighbours across the political and economic spectrum."[141] However, perhaps, India also realized that peace and stability in Afghanistan could not be achieved without the role of Taliban in the peace process. Therefore, India also seemed to be ready to talk with the Taliban for the Afghan's cause to safeguard humanity. In this direction, on 1 October 2018, India expressed "readiness to work towards implementing the Tashkent Declaration of March 2018 that called for direct talks with the Taliban without preconditions."[142]

Furthermore, India may face major challenge after the US forces withdrawal from Afghanistan. Because, no doubt, as the US had been desperate to leave Afghanistan and the Taliban was also highly desperate to control the Afghan power by confronting the Afghan government. The US had been seriously involved in peace talks with the Taliban and also had ready to accept almost all the demands of the Taliban, and, ultimately, it has proved that America has lost the Afghan war, its longest ever in the history of the US's wars in the world around. President Trump's patience was faded completely and even later President Biden eventually finished job of the withdrawal of its forces from Afghanistan vacating space for the Taliban regime. Therefore, it has assumed that India's vested interests in Afghanistan, under the Taliban will face debacle and disdain. In this context, C. Raja Mohan had opined

> Delhi is certainly not alone in being both skeptical about the prospects for these talks and concerned about their success. For, there are not many who vouch for the Taliban's trustworthiness. And American military presence since 2002 has allowed the construction of a modernizing Afghanistan and let India deepen its engagement. This is not a moment, however, for Delhi to stand by and criticize or call for ideal solutions. It is about preparing for significant change in Afghanistan—for good or bad.[143]

However, India needs to be much proactive on multiple fronts to safeguard its interest in Afghanistan without carrying pressure of any sort as the others like China are also moving in Afghanistan to work on almost all the fronts. India also will have to maintain and protect its leverages adroitly by not just sticking to its idealistic approach, but must proactively be realistic. Further, India should also adopt its own method of engaging with Afghanistan rather believing a borrowed or followed one. The fact is that India should deal diplomatically with all the forces present in Afghanistan. In fact, Pakistan has not been stopping its terrorist assaults on India in either situation. Therefore, India should believe in very assertive approach to further its holistic engagement with Afghanistan given its interests. India's hesitance in Afghanistan would marginalize India's leverages as a crucial and major power. Until date India's present policy could not stop the impediments in India's national interest in its borders and in Afghanistan. How long India would persist to its present stand when results are not positive? India needs to change its approach and to dare tough moves in international politics, wherever it demands. India needs to act like a major and responsible power while looking at the interests of both India and Afghanistan.

In fact, during American military presence in Afghanistan, India's some of the interests in terms of security were protected there while playing the role of rebuilding of Afghanistan. Therefore, with the new development in the US's foreign policy, it was believed that India must start preparing for the "inevitable geopolitical turbulence, including the insurgence of the Islamic State and the potential return of the Taliban to power in Kabul, that could follow the American retrenchment in the Middle East and Afghanistan."[144] The slashing of troops from Afghanistan by the US had added multiple concerns for Afghanistan and that also had put impact on the Chabahar route. The US had given temporary waiver to India on its engagement in the Chabahar port project. However, with the setbacks to India on Chabahar port, Pakistan remained the happiest country in the region and continued playing as a spoiler in the Chabahar, where India was the major stakeholder. In fact, the Chabahar port has been seen as a rival warm water port to Pakistan's Gwadar port, in which China is a stakeholder. Therefore, with the increasing shadow of concerns and competition over the Chabahar, India had to adopt a sustain diplomacy to protect its interests and to defend the reality of geopolitical challenges emerging in the region with the changing whimsical minds of the leaders of the various countries peeping in and around the region. However, India in the post-US Afghanistan and the Taliban in power needs to focus on what and how it can contribute further to establish and maintain peace and stability there and for the reconstruction of the Afghan society. Steps to be taken rationally keeping in mind its interests to be protected. Mohammed Ayoob, a scholar of international relations had argued that

> It's rightly being pointed out that India has to be prepared for the potential consequences of the withdrawal of US troops from Afghanistan. While New Delhi is weighing its options it must take into account that for all its antipathy toward the Afghan Taliban, the latter does represent, in a distorted form, a facet of Pashtun nationalism. What has given added potency to the Taliban's appeal is this: its ability to couch in religious terminology traditional Pashtun aspirations for dominance in Afghanistan as well as the aversion of Pashtun tribes to foreign interference in their land.[145]

The Taliban is a group of the largest ethnic group in Afghanistan, and its significance in the Afghan's politics or its influence over the Afghan people cannot be discarded. Moreover, "India's stakes in Afghanistan are not less than those of its other neighbouring countries." Therefore, given the relations of the stakeholders in Afghanistan have established relations with the Taliban regime, India should also need to establish formal relations with the Taliban. Satish Chandra, the former Deputy National Security Advisor of India had opined that "India should not hesitate to reach out to the Taliban, as it is on the cards that some elements from amongst them will be co-opted into the power structure, sooner or later, and once in power their nexus with Pakistan, under the stress of national interests, will inevitably tend to fray."[146] In fact, it has feared that "for the Indian government, however, a bad security situation or the return of the Taliban could lead to significantly larger and more consequential losses...."[147] However, for gaining the confidence of the Afghan people especially the Pashtun's along with the others, Ayoob expressed that "It will take a great deal of creative thinking and imaginative refashioning of New Delhi's policy towards Afghanistan for India to recover lost ground vis-à-vis the Pashtuns. Depending on the US, itself on the verge of cutting its losses in Afghanistan, or on other powers such as Russia and Iran to protect Indian interests in that country will be foolhardy and counter-productive.[148]

However, the new Taliban regime has posed probably new challenges to India in accomplishing its interests. India's influence is fading in Afghanistan which is impacting on India as a strategic loss and may possibly put its investments there at risk. However, India has pledged to continue its humanitarian commitment towards the people of war-torn Afghanistan, and also trying to contact the Taliban through various diplomatic means. For the first time since the Taliban return in power, India has sent humanitarian assistance including the medicines for the Afghan people, which the Taliban government received with Thanks. And even the Taliban government has shown its interest to continue Afghan's political, economic and cultural relations with India. In fact, the Taliban also realized the significance of India's assistance and contribution for the development of Afghanistan.

Notes and References

1. Sourish Ghosh, India's Difficult Transition in Afghanistan: From the Centre to the Periphery, in Harsh V. Pant (ed.), *Afghanistan's*

Regional Dilemma: South Asia and Beyond, Orient Backswan, New Delhi, 2016, pp. 47-48.

2. Vikash Yadav and Conrad Barwa, Relational Control: India's Grand Strategy in Afghanistan and Pakistan, *India Review*, Vol. 10, No. 2, 2011 (pp. 93-125), p. 106.
3. Avinash Paliwal, Afghanistan's India-Pakistan Dilemma: advocacy coalitions in weak states, *Cambridge Review of International Affairs*, Vol. 29, No. 2, 2016 (pp. 465-91), p. 466.
4. Avinash Paliwal and Harsh V. Pant, Afghanistan-India Relations: Normative Sources of Bilateral Ties in Chris Ogden edited *New South Asian Security*, Orient Blackswan, New Delhi, 2016, p. 114.
5. Emilian Kavalski, India's Bifurcated Look to Central Eurasia: The Central Asian Republics and Afghanistan in David M. Malone, C. Raja Mohan and Srinath Raghavan (ed.), *The Oxford Handbook of Indian Foreign Policy*, Oxford University Press, New York, 2015, p. 430.
6. Satinder K. Lambah, Solving the Afghan Riddle, *The Hindu*, 22 September 2017, p. 8.
7. Baisali Mohanty, China-India Rivalry could have Deadly Consequences for Afghanistan, *The Diplomat*, 9 March 2017, http://thediplomat.com/2017/03/china-india-rivalry-could-have-deadly-consequences-for-afghanistan/, accessed on 9 September 2017.
8. *Ibid.*
9. K. Warikoo, Central Asia and South Asia: Opportunities and Challenges, *India Quarterly*, 72 (1), 1-15, 2016, p. 2.
10. Smruti S. Pattanaik, India's Afghan Policy: Beyond Bilateralism, *Strategic Analysis*, 36(4), July-August 2012, pp. 569-83.
11. Avinash Paliwal, My Enemy's Enemy: India in Afghanistan From the Soviet Invasion to The US Withdrawal, HarperColins Publishers India, Noida, 2017, p. 112.
12. S. Bose and A. Panda, Indian and Chinese Foreign Policy Imperatives and Strategies vis-à-vis Afghanistan, Indian Review, Vol. 15, No. 4, 2016 (pp. 379-406), pp. 384-85.
13. Avinash Paliwal and Harsh Pant, 2016, p. 123.
14. Harsh V. Pant, India in Afghanistan: A test case for a rising power, *Contemporary South Asia*, Vol. 18, No. 2, June 2010, pp. 133-53, pp. 133-34.

15. Bharat Karnad, *Why India is not a Great Power (Yet)*, Oxford University Press, New Delhi, 2015, p. 171.
16. Shaji S., Withdrawal of the NATO and the Indo-Afghan Relations in Rajen Harshe and Dhananjay Tripathi (ed.), *Afghanistan Post 2014: Power Configurations and Evolving Trajectories*, Routledge, New York, 2016, p. 173.
17. Aparna Pande, *From Chanakya to Modi: The Evolution of India's Foreign Policy*, HarperCollins Publishers India, Noida, 2017, p. 168.
18. Bharat Karnad, 2015, p. 172.
19. Satish Chandra, India's Options in Afghanistan, *Strategic Analysis*, Vol. 35, No. 1, January 2011, (pp. 125-27), p. 125.
20. Sourish Ghosh, 2016, p. 47.
21. Joy Mitra, India's Policy Thinking About Its Security Objectives in Afghanistan Needs Reimagination, *The Diplomat*, 23 October 2018, https://thediplomat.com/2018/10/indias-policy-thinking-about-its-security-objectives-in-afghanistan-need-reimagination/, accessed on 11 February 2019.
22. S. Bos and A. Panda, 2016, p. 384.
23. Jin Wang, India's Policy Toward Afghanistan: Implications to the Regional Security Governance, *Asian Journal of Middle Eastern and Islamic Studies*, Vol. 11, No. 4, 2017, p. 119.
24. Harsh V. Pant, India in Afghanistan: A Rising Power or A Hesitant Power?, Working Paper, 3P, Centre for International Peace and Security Studies, University of Montreal and McGill, April 2012.
25. Harsh V. Pant, The Afghanistan Conflict: India's Changing Role, *Middle East Quarterly*, Vol. 18, No. 2, 2011, pp. 31-39.
26. Tanvi Pate, Soft Power, Strategic Narratives, and State Identity: Re-assessing India-Afghanistan Relations post-2011, *India Review*, Vol. 17, No. 3, 2018, pp. 320-51.
27. Emilian Kavalski, 2015, p. 432.
28. Quoted by Jin Wang, 2017, p. 112.
29. Sourish Ghosh, p. 49.
30. Avinash Paliwal, 2017, p. 31.
31. Rajen Harshe and Dhananjay Tripathi, *Afghanistan Post-2014: Power Configurations and Evolving Trajectories*, Routledge, New York, 2016.

32. Sourash Ghosh, p. 49.
33. Avinash Paliwal, 2017, p. 31.
34. *Ibid.*, p. 34.
35. Sourish Ghosh, p. 50.
36. Avinash Paliwal, 2017, pp. 32-37.
37. In December 1979, Soviet troops entered into Afghanistan and established pro-Russian regime to be more amicable to Russian desires. This intervention is referred as "Russia's Vietnam," by many as the Soviets poured endless amounts of money, weapons, and manpower into the Afghanistan's civil war. However, in 1988, the USSR President Mikhail Gorbachev finally started the withdrawal of Russian troops nearly after 10 years.
38. Over Soviet intervention, India had the dilemma of whether to support, or not, the action because of two factors: one NAM factor and other was the friendship with Soviet Russia which had supported India in 1971 war and also further supported India with the military equipments. However, the then acting Prime Minister of India Charan Singh had chosen to declare India's stand against the Soviet intervention in Afghanistan, but subsequently and immediately within a fortnight, Indira Gandhi who became Prime Minister of India on 20 January 1980, initially hinted its pro-Soviet stand in Afghanistan, however, later she reverted India's stand of supporting the Soviet invasion. However, latter for damage control she had called the invasion as "inadmissible". For details see Avinash Paliwal, *My Enemy's Enemy*, 2017.
39. Satish Candra, 2011, p. 125.
40. Avinash Paliwal, 2017, p. 47.
41. Sourish Ghosh, p. 52.
42. Vikash Yadav and Conrad Barwa, *India Review*, 2011, p. 106.
43. *Ibid.*, p. 107.
44. *Ibid.*
45. Avinash Palival, India's Taliban Dilemma: To Contain or to Engage?, *The Journal of Strategic Studies*, Vol. 40, Nos. 1-2, 2017 (pp. 35-67), p. 35.
46. *Ibid.*, 2016, p. 473.
47. *Ibid.*, *My Enemy's Enemy*, 2017, p. 106.
48. *Ibid.*, p. 107.

49. Ahmad Shah Masood was a Mujahedeen leader who had played major role in the formation of the anti-Taliban Northern Alliance and also led the struggle to wage against the Soviet intervention, however, he was assassinated on 9 September 2001, for details see, Frank Clements, Conflicts in Afghanistan: *A Historical Encyclopaedia*, ABC-CLIO, California, 2003, p. 165.
50. Harsh V. Pant, India in Afghanistan, June 2010, p. 135.
51. Srinjoy Bose and Ankit Panda, p. 384.
52. Avinash Paliwal, *My Enemy's Enemy*, 2017, pp. 181-82.
53. Harsh Pant, June 2010, p. 135.
54. S. Bose and A. Panda, 2016, p. 384.
55. *Ibid.*
56. *Ibid.*
57. It has stated that the Nepali delegation had obstructed the Afghanistan Membership in SAARC as they wanted China also to be admitted to SAARC. However, China, the US and Japan were accepted as observers. For details see, Shyam Saran, *How India Sees the World: Kautilya to the 21st Century*, Juggernaut, New Delhi, 2017, p. 65.
58. Shanthie Mariet D'Souza, 2007, p. 835.
59. *Ibid.*
60. S. Bose and A. Panda 2016, p. 384.
61. Avinash Paliwal, 2016, p. 483.
62. India-Afghanistan Relations, Embassy of India, Kabul, http://www.eoi.gov.in/kabul/?0354?000, accessed on 25 August 2017.
63. Rakesh Sood, Searching for an Elusive Peace, *The Hindu*, 16 November 2018, p. 8.
64. India-Afghanistan Relations, Embassy of India, Kabul.
65. *Ibid.*
66. *Ibid.*
67. Suhasini Haider, India to Further Aid Afghan Troops, *The Hindu*, 12 September 2017, p. 11.
68. *Ibid.*
69. Suhasini Haider, Gokhale in Kabul for Trilateral, *The Hindu*, 11 September 2018, p. 11.

70. Shaida Abdali, Kabul Seeks Support for Peace, *The Hindu*, 19 September 2018, p. 11.
71. Rakesh Sood, Seeking a Managed Exit, *The Hindu*, 22 September 2018, p. 8.
72. Harsh V. Pant, June 2010, p. 137.
73. Sourish Ghosh, p. 49.
74. Harsh V. Pant, June 2010, p. 136.
75. Shanthie Mariat D'Souza, India's Aid to Afghanistan: Challenges and Prospects, *Strategic Analysis*, Vol. 31, No. 5, September 2007, p. 833.
76. *Ibid.*, p. 835.
77. Shreshta Balachandar, India's Role in Afghanistan: Past Relations and Future Prospects, *Foreign Policy Journal*, 30 November 2012, https://www.foreignpolicyjournal.com/2012/11/30/indias-role-in-afghanistan-past-relations-and-future-prospects/, accessed on 24 August 2017.
78. Avinash Paliwal, 2017, India's Taliban Dilemma, p. 36.
79. Harsh V. Pant, 2010, p. 137.
80. Rakesh Sood, India's Afghan Dilemma, *The Hindu*, 20 January 2015.
81. Kavalski, p. 432.
82. Avinash Paliwal, India's Taliban Dilemma, 2017, p. 37.
83. India-Afghanistan Relations, Embassy of India, Kabul.
84. Satish Candra, p. 125.
85. Jin Wang, 2017, p. 113.
86. Emilian Kavalski, p. 432.
87. This was built by India's Border Road Organisation despite the stiff resistance from the Taliban, and for the security of the workers in this project was provided itself by India by sending 300-strong paramilitary force, Harsh V. Pant, June 2010, p. 137.
88. Avinash Paliwal and Harsh V. Pant, Afghanistan-India Relations, Normative Sources of Bilateral Ties in Chris Ogden edited New South Asian Security, Orient Blackswan, New Delhi, 2016, p. 121, also see V. Mahalingam, CLAWS Journal 2016.
89. *Ibid.*
90. *Ibid.*

91. Thottam, Jyoti, Afghanistan: India's Uncertain Road. TIME Magazine, April 11, 2011, http://www.time.com/time/magazine/article/0,9171,2062364,00.html, accessed on 8 May 2019.
92. *Ibid.*
93. India-Afghanistan Relations, Embassy of India, Kabul.
94. Ministry of External Affairs, Government of India, India-Afghanistan Relations, 25 December 2016, https://www.mea.gov.in/Portal/ForeignRelation/Afghanistan_Dec_2016.pdf
95. India-Afghanistan Relations, Embassy of India, Kabul.
96. *Ibid.*
97. Suhasini Haider, *The Hindu*, 12 September 2017.
98. India-Afghanistan Relations, Embassy of India, Kabul.
99. Rani D. Mullen and Kashyap Arora, Indian Development Cooperation with Afghanistan and The Afghan-India Friendship Dam, Policy Brief, Central for Policy Research, 16 June 2016.
100. However, in fact, it has reported that Chabahar port was used for the first time in 2011 for the transportation of 100,000 metric tons of grains to Afghanistan as a part of humanitarian aids, Bharat Karnad 2015, p. 171, also see Rebecca Byerly, Why India is trying to expand trade wit Iran, *The Christian Science Monitor*, 29 March 2012, https://www.csmonitor.com/World/Asia-South-Central/2012/0329/Why-India-is-trying-to-expand-trade-with-Iran, accessed on 30 October 2017.
101. Devirupa Mitra, While India, Afghanistan Hail Trump's South Asia Strategy, Questions Remain on What It Really Means, *The Wire*, 22 August 2017, https://thewire.in/170067/india-afghanistan-pakistan-donald-trump/, accessed on 7 September 2017.
102. India-Afghanistan Relations, Embassy of India, Kabul.
103. Suhasini Haider, *The Hindu*, 11 September 2018, p. 11.
104. Ruchi Kumar, On Invasions, Wars and Libraries, *The Hindu*, 6 January 2019, p. 6.
105. *Ibid.*
106. Simon Tisdall, India may pay heavily in future for supporting the Karzai regime, *The Guardian*, 5 October, 2012, http://www.guardian.co.uk/world/2011/oct/05/india-regret-supporting-karzai-afghanistan, accessed on 1 September 2017.
107. Avinash Paliwal, 2017, p. 31.

108. "In fact, in 2003, Afghanistan had an open offer from New Delhi to seek lethal light weaponry for the ANSF. Kabul, however, was not keen to seek military assistance from India at that point in time and wanted to coordinate anything in that sector with the US. That India was vacillating on its offer a decade later fed into Kabul's doubts about New Delhi's reliability as a regional security provider." For details see Avinash Paliwal, *My Enemy's Enemy*, 2017, pp. 205-06.
109. Vidya Ram, India Should Not Fall for US Designes, *The Hindu*, 5 October 2017, p. 12.
110. Emilian Kavalski, p. 433.
111. C. Raja Mohan, New Foray into the Great Game, *The Indian Express*, 26 September 2017, p. 9.
112. PTI, Afghanistan Unhappy over delay in supply of arms from India, *The Hindu*, 30 November 2014, http://www.thehindu.com/news/international/south-asia/afghanistan-unhappy-over-delay-in-supply-of-arms-from-india/article6648833.ece, accessed on 25 August 2017.
113. S. Bose and A. Panda, 2016, p. 390.
114. S.L. Narasimhan, Why India's increased military assistance to Afghanistan is a step in the right direction, Feb. 16, 2017, http://www.firstpost.com/india/why-indias-increased-military-assistance-to-afghanistan-is-a-step-in-the-right-direction-3286278.html, accessed on 5 March 2019.
115. Jin Wang, 2017, pp. 118-19.
116. Franz-Stefan Gady, India Considers Stepping up Military Assistance to Afghanistan, *The Diplomat*, 25 March 2017, http://thediplomat.com/2017/03/india-considers-stepping-up-military-assistance-to-afghanistan/, accessed on 26 August 2017.
117. Prakash Katoch, Will India send 15,000 troops to Afghanistan? Time is ripe for concerted action against Pakistan's terror, *FirstPost*, 10 July 2017, http://www.firstpost.com/world/will-india-send-15000-troops-to-afghanistan-time-is-ripe-for-concerted-action-against-pakistans-terror-3514657.html
118. Suhasini Haidar, India Plans to Train Afghan Police Officers, *The Hindu*, 23 September 2017, p. 10.
119. Shaji S., 2016, p. 179.
120. Murali Krishnan, Why is India Reluctant to Send Troops to Afghanistan?, 27 September 2017, DW, http://www.

dw.com/en/why-is-india-reluctant-to-send-troops-to-afghanistan/a-40706506, accessed on 24 October 2017.

121. Latik Jha, No Indian Troops in Afghanistan because of Pak considerations: US, *The Indian Express*, 6 October 2017, p. 12.
122. S. Bose and A. Panda 2016, p. 390.
123. Joy Mitra, *The Diplomat*, 2018.
124. Shanthie Mariet D'souza, Securing India's Interests in Afghanistan, *The Hindu*, 17 December 2017.
125. K. Warikoo, 2016.
126. The TAPI-Turkmenistan, Afghanistan, Pakistan and India, project is 1,814 kilometre long originating in Turkmenistan and passes through Afghanistan and Pakistan finally to reach India. India is aiming of tapping the Turkmenistan's Galkynysh gas fields, which are the fourth largest in the world. The construction of the project started in December 2015.
127. Jabin T. Jacob, India, China and the Coming US Drawdown in Afghanistan, *Economic & Political Weekly*, Vol. 49, No. 14, 5 April 2014.
128. V. Mahalingam, India's Afghanistan Policy, *CLAWS Journal*, Summer 2016, p. 99, The word 'Strategic depth' was the phrase a previous army chief of Pakistan had used to describe Pakistan's pursuit of a friendly regime in Kabul. According to Gen Kayani, the phrase was merely meant the search for a peaceful neighbor where Afghan Pashtuns were adequately accommodated in Afghan politics. For details see, Steve Coll, Directorates, Allen Lane, New Delhi, 2018, p. 351.
129. India in Afghanistan, Editorial, August 2, 2016, *The Hindu*, http://www.thehindu.com/opinion/editorial/india-in-afghanistan/article2523648.ece, accessed on 25 August 2017.
130. Shanthie Mariet D'souza, 17 December 2017.
131. Sumit Ganguly in Malon, Mohan and Raghavan, p. 155.
132. Ambrish Dhaka, Afghanistan Beyond 2014, *Economic & Political Weekly*, Vol. 49, Issue No. 37, 13 September 2014.
133. *Ibid*., pp. 385-86.
134. Bose and Panda 2016, p. 385.
135. Mubashir Zaidi, US-Pakistan alliance at a crossroads, *The Hindu*, 27 August 2017, p. 5.

136. Harsh V. Pant, 2016, p. 10.
137. Avinash Paliwal, New Alignments, Old Battlefield: Revisiting India's Role in Afghanistan, Carnegie India, 15 June 2017, http://carnegieindia.org/2017/06/15/new-alignments-old-battlefield-revisiting-india-s-role-in-afghanistan-pub-71272, accessed on 8 September 2017.
138. Varghese K. George, 12 September 2017.
139. Inflection point in Kabul, *The Indian Express*, 12 September 2017, p. 9.
140. Ahmad and Gopalaswamy, *The Hill*, 1 September 2017.
141. Shyam Saran, 2017, p. 68.
142. Kallol Bhattacharjee, India Backs Direct Talks with Taliban, *The Hindu*, 2 October 2018, p. 11.
143. C. Raja Mohan, An Afghan Trifecta, *The Indian Express*, 29 January 2019, p. 6.
144. As US Retrenches, *The Indian Express*, 22 December 2018, p. 6.
145. "India's refusal to publicly criticise, let alone denounce, the Soviet invasion of 1979, while understandable in that particular geopolitical context and a consequence of India's gratitude for Soviet support during the Bangladesh war, ended up doing India great harm in the eyes of its traditional friends in Afghanistan, the Pashtuns," for details see, Mohammed Ayoob, India's Options and the Pashtun Factor, *The Hindu*, 7 January 2019, p. 8.
146. Satish Chandra, 2011, p. 127.
147. Jubin T. Jacob, April 2014.
148. *Ibid.*

8

Peace Process in Afghanistan

Introduction

Afghanistan has always been a troubled country, and since the emergence of the Taliban and the other extremist groups, peace and stability there have become a mirage that compelling the country to fall in the category failed state. Therefore, given its turmoil situation, the world community and the Afghan government made hard efforts in pulling out Afghanistan from the dire situation of violence and instability. However, they also faced multiple problems because of the obstinate behaviour of the fundamentalist Taliban. Besides, the country like Pakistan played dysfunctional role in deteriorating the violent situation and further striking forward obstacles in the process of bringing peace and stability in Afghanistan. Pakistan wanted the re-emergence of the Taliban regime in Afghanistan. Significantly, the overt/covert engagement of the other countries like Iran and Russia with the Taliban also complicated the situation there as these countries have their own interests in Afghanistan. However, amidst all, the regional and international actors tried their best to bring reconciliation talks between the Afghan government and the Taliban, but even these actors failed in exhibiting the common understanding for the better future of Afghanistan as they themselves indulged in conspiracies against each other using Afghanistan, strategically, as the playground for their interests and are engaged in counting their individual credits, or some want to maintain status quo in Afghanistan. Since long years, the peace process always failed to bring any positive result in Afghanistan due to the mistrust that prevailed amongst the intra-Afghan parties and the stakeholder countries. Moreover, as the women in Afghanistan also have borne the brunt of war, the matter of their inclusion in the peace process was taken on anvil. In this regards, it was argued that "The bottom line is Afghan women want peace and they want to have a say in how it is negotiated." Besides, "Women in urban and rural settings are already engaged in local-level peace-building and conflict resolution, but they must also be included in national-level peace processes for these efforts to reach their maximum potential and facilitate a sustainable peace throughout the country." And it was also believed that "Without women's representation in peace talks, the fragile gains of the past 18 years could be reversed or not fully addressed as part of a political settlement."[1] But, the fundamentalist forces there obfuscated the women's role in peace and development process. During Taliban Regime 1.0 and even now, the women's role as a whole remained absolutely marginalized in any act of governance or any other area.

The Afghan government had always insisted and believed that the Afghan's reconciliation process must be "Afghan-led and Afghan-owned," and also exhibited its flexible posture for the better future. Therefore, for this, Kabul carefully welcomed the international efforts towards a peace process involving the Taliban. In fact, there needs a stable Afghanistan to ensure stable region, and for this, Afghanistan sought "a sustained stability on the basis of genuine state-to-state relations with the region", which included the "diplomatic, economic, political and security cooperation."[2] As a crucial step towards stability and peace, Afghanistan National Independent Peace and Reconciliation Commission was established in May 2005 to lead the reconciliation process with the insurgent groups; the Taliban and Hizb Islami Gulbuddin Hekmatyar. This effort was subsequently followed by The National Consultative Peace Jirga, which was held in June 2010. This was President Karzai's attempt to offer a public forum for Afghans to voice their views regarding reintegration and reconciliation, and to build a wider domestic and international consensus. According to the reintegration plan, those who had relinquished their affiliation with the insurgency, they were offered amnesty and political position to enemy leadership to bring them into the political mainstream. The Karzai's reintegration plan was supported by the US and, its objective was about offering the Taliban "an honourable place in society, if they renounced ties with the Al-Qaeda, abandoned violence, and pursued their political goals in accordance with the Afghan Constitution." Moreover, the plan had offered the Taliban "amnesties and power-sharing" and also the promise was made for the removal of their names from terrorist blacklists. However, the Taliban rejected Karzai's plan, and intensified their insurgency further against the Afghan government. However, Karzai's peace efforts miserably failed due to "...the lack of a cohesive strategy, poor coordination between the Afghan government and international forces, and the absence of transparency in the process. Further compounding the problem are the long-standing, deep ethnic divisions in the country."[3] Further, President Karzai established the High Peace Council on 5 September 2010, and he also had made peace offers to the Taliban. But the Taliban not only refused it but refused to negotiate with the Karzai government also. The High Peace Council was formed aiming to negotiate with the elements of the Taliban, and this council was headed by the former Afghan President Burhanuddin Rabbani who was assassinated in 2011, and after him his son Salahuddin Rabbani was made the chairman of the council till 2015. The membership was also extended to the former members of the Taliban. In fact, Karzai had offered the Taliban a peace deal by conducting, first, a grand peace Jirga in 2010 and then a Loya Jirga in 2011,[4] but they brought no fruitful results. In fact, Karzai believed and expressed that, "We must reach out to all of our countrymen, especially our disenchanted brothers, who are not part of Al-Qaeda, or other terrorist networks, who accept the Afghan constitution."[5] Further, in late 2012, the number of contacts were made with the different "Afghan factions, representatives of the government and international observers in Chantilly, and in later years, in Oslo and several other venues, including the most anticipated semi-direct talks in Murree, Pakistan, in 2015.[6] According to Thistlethwaite;

> Reconciliation processes have proved useful around the world in addressing deeply entrenched national and international conflicts, and breaking the grip of the past on the present and the future. Using a culturally established model, such as the jirga in Afghanistan, is necessary or the whole idea will be rejected as un-Afghan and un-Islamic. Stories of violence, of division, of corruption, and of a lack of good governance exercise a powerful undertow for any nation. Peace and reconciliation processes have been shown they can be useful for nations struggling to resist the drag of history and move forward, but not without real efforts to build trust and to confront these histories head-on. Sadly enough, key elements of what makes national reconciliation processes work seem to be missing in the current Afghan jirga process.[7]

Reconciliation Initiatives by the World Community

After the US intervention in Afghanistan in 2001, there had been the series of dialogues and discussions processes aiming at the reconstruction of Afghanistan. The goals and processes included, but not limited to, "state-building", "counterinsurgency", "winning hearts and minds", "democratization", "counterterrorism", "development" and "regional stabilization".[8] Given these goals and processes, by and large, many bilateral, tri-lateral or multi-lateral dialogues, summits and conferences have been conducted in the direction of beginning the peace process between the Afghan government and the Taliban so that to see peaceful, stable and better life in Afghanistan. The international community has since long been engaged in its commitment for the better future of Afghanistan, and for this, there had been many efforts such as Bonn Agreement-2001, Tokyo Conference of 2002,[9] London Conference of 2006, which revisited the Bonn Agreement to produce the policy document known as the Afghanistan Compact,[10] Paris Declaration-2008 and 2009, and in the London Conference, which was held on 28 January 2010, President Hamid Karzai had proposed its stand on the negotiations with the Taliban that "The Taliban must accept the Afghan Constitution, renounce violence and sever all ties with al-Qaeda and other terrorist organizations." This stand was unanimously endorsed in the conference. Further various conferences were held subsequently for the peace process of Afghanistan.

Istanbul Conference, 2011: The international conference on Afghanistan of the regional countries was held in Istanbul on November 2, 2011. The conference was focused on security, economic development and stability of Afghanistan and the region around it. This was the first in the series of conferences that had planned for the next few months at that time. In this conference, 29 countries including the US and European countries had participated. A joint declaration was adopted and was singed by 12 countries that included Afghanistan and its neighbouring countries, India, China, Turkey, Russia, Iran, Pakistan, Kazakhstan, Kyrgyzstan, Turkmenistan, the United Arab Emirates, and the Kingdom of Saudi Arabia. This conference was aimed to identify and find how the regional countries could cooperate in securing stability and security in Afghanistan. President Karzai, while addressing the conference, had appealed Pakistan to cooperate in Afghan's reconciliation process with Taliban as Pakistan provided space to the Taliban in it its territory. The conference had adopted the principles such as the "non-interference, respect for Afghanistan's sovereignty, unity and territorial integrity" and the support for "an Afghan-led, Afghan-owned and Afghan-driven reconciliation process." However, nothing fruitful was achieved in this conference, because of the lack of consensus amongst the countries and especially due to Pakistan's opposition. However, the main outcome of the conference was "the integrated economic development of Afghanistan" and also the infrastructure development around the main ports of the region to provide Afghanistan an access to the sea. As of being a land bridge in the 'Heart of Asia', Afghanistan was to be connected with South Asia, West Asia, and Central Asia. By and large, the conference had focused on the "need for greater economic cooperation, infrastructure construction, developing health and education sector, and enhancing cultural relations." Moreover, the Joint Declaration was aimed to deal with the important issues such as cooperation in fighting against terrorism, strengthening border controls, returning of refugees, counter-terrorism and counter-narcotics, and disaster management.[11] The common principles and commitments in the Istanbul Conference were:

> Recognition of the central role of the United Nations in international affairs; Equal and indivisible security; Respect for the territorial integrity of States; Non-intervention in the internal affairs of other states; Support for the stability and peace in Afghanistan, as well as respect for Afghanistan's sovereignty, unity and territorial integrity; Continued support for the Government and people of Afghanistan, as they develop their country, re-construct their economy, and further improve their human capital; Resolutely combating and eliminating terrorism in all its forms and manifestations and violent extremism, and preventing safe havens for terrorists and terrorism in the region; Dismantling terrorist sanctuaries and safe havens, disrupting all financial and tactical support for terrorism; Acknowledging that terrorism poses a threat to international peace and security as well as a common challenge to our societies, to the region, and that it can only be addressed through the concerted efforts of all countries; Facilitating the voluntary, dignified, and orderly return of Afghan refugees; Support for an inclusive Afghan national process of reconciliation, in accordance with the Constitution of Afghanistan and in ways which is Afghan-led, Afghan-owned and Afghan-driven; Constructive and supportive relationship between countries of the region; Refraining from the threat or use of force and not to allow one's territory to be used against another; Elimination of illicit drug production, trade and trafficking; Preventing the cultivation and production of narcotics; Preventing the activities of extremist organizations and organized crime networks through enhanced cooperation; Supporting and promoting law enforcement cooperation; Peaceful settlement of disputes in accordance with the United Nations Charter and international law; Fulfillment of obligations under international law.[12]

Bonn Conference, 2011: The Bonn Conference was held on 5 December 2011 focusing the three significant issues such as the civil aspects of the process of transferring responsibility to the Government of Afghanistan by 2014; the long-term engagement of the international community in Afghanistan after 2014 and the political process that was intended to lead to the long-term stabilization of the country. Moreover, an intra-Afghan process with regional support was also focused. This political process was aimed to progress on two levels: the reconciliation of the country's various population groups must be remained a process that takes place inside Afghanistan. This conference also reaffirmed to address the essential issues such as Renunciation of violence, cutting of ties to international terrorism, and respect for the Afghan Constitution including its human rights provisions. Moreover, along with this, the process was aimed to be secured by Afghan's neighbours and the regional powers. The stabilization of Afghanistan was viewed in terms of the political stability of the entire region and to which all the countries of the region had to contribute functionally and honestly. The conference also focused on the shift of emphasis in the international community's Afghanistan policy from the military to the political aspect.[13] The Bonn Conference had promised that the participating countries would continue its support for Afghanistan even after the withdrawal of international forces. The German Foreign Minister, Guido Westerwelle told the conference that "We send a clear message to the people of Afghanistan: We will not leave you on your own. We will not leave you in the lurch."[14] Moreover, Simon Gass, NATO's top civilian representative narrated three reasons why the international community would continuously be generous towards Afghanistan despite the fiscal hurdles:

> The first is that the costs after 2014 will be a fraction of what we are spending now because of the large number of troops. Second, Afghanistan will still be one of the poorest countries on earth and would under any circumstances attract a lot of financial help. Third, if we do not fund Afghanistan, for example by not paying for the Afghan security forces, we will put at risk all we have achieved in the last (Eighteen) years.... This is a matter of self interest,

> not philanthropy. If Afghanistan turned back to chaos, our countries would face flows of drugs and migrants, as well as instability in a sensitive part of the world.[15]

About 1000 delegates from nearly 85 countries and 15 regional and international organizations were believed to be participated in this conference. But, there was an absence of participation from Pakistan and the Afghan Taliban. In context of the Afghan National Security Forces (ANSF), the international community strongly extended its commitment to support their training and equipping, financing and development of capabilities even beyond the end of the given transition period. The President Karzai had told the international community in the conference that "about $10 billion worth of international assistance would be required annually until 2025 in the post-Transition period to sustain the ANSF."[16] By and large, in the Bonn Conference, 2011, the Afghan government and the international community mutually renewed their long-term commitments in various areas of governance, security, peace process, economic and social development, and regional cooperation.

Chicago Summit Declaration, 2012: This declaration was made on 21 May 2012 in Chicago (the US) by all the member countries of the ISAF (International Security Assistance Force) and the Afghan government aiming to renew their firm commitment to a sovereign, secure, and democratic Afghanistan and they unanimously also declared and reaffirmed that their close partnership would be continued even after the withdrawal of the international forces. In the conference, they stated that a political process involving successful reconciliation and reintegration had been of an immense significance for "a peaceful and stable Afghanistan" and for this process, the reconciliation must be truly "Afghan-led and Afghan-owned," and must be inclusive, in which the representative of the legitimate interests of all Afghan people, regardless of gender or status, should have participation. Moreover, it was also believed that the reconciliation was focused to contain the reaffirmation of a sovereign, stable and united Afghanistan, the freedom from violence, the delinking of ties to international terrorism, and importantly the compliance with the Afghan Constitution, including the provisions of human rights, especially the women's rights. Further, it was expected that a peaceful and stable Afghanistan would positively contribute to economic and social development in the entire region, and consequently, the designing of the mechanism to fight against the narcotics trafficking, illegal migration, terrorism and other multiple crimes. In this context, they held "regional cooperation" and "support for stability" in Afghanistan as important factors. Furthermore, the ISAF countries stated that during their long years of partnership with Afghanistan, the lives of Afghan's people including all men, women, and children, have improved significantly in terms of security, education, health care, economic opportunities and an assurance of rights and freedoms. However, despite their long standing presence there, they realized that the expected achievements were not met and more work left to be done further there. Therefore, the ISAF countries expressed that they would continue extending support to Afghanistan on its path towards achieving self-reliance in the areas of security, political, social, and economic development or improved governance so that Afghanistan would be able to prevent its territory from again becoming a safe haven for terrorists that had been threatening life in Afghanistan, the region, and the world as well. On their long-term partnership, the Afghan government confirmed its resolution on its commitment to form a democratic society that to be based on the rule of law and good-governance, no compromise in the fight against corruption, the protection of human rights and fundamental freedoms of its citizens especially the equality of men and women and to provide better opportunities to both in the active participation in Afghan society. It was also declared that they would value the full participation of all Afghan women in the Afghan's reconstruction, political, peace, and reconciliation processes and they also had committed the implementation of UNSC Resolution-1325 on women, peace, and security and the protection of children from the damaging effects of armed conflicts. The commitment of building the NATO-Afghanistan Enduring Partnership and Afghan security even beyond 2014 were also reaffirmed.[17]

Tokyo Conference, 2012: In this conference, the Tokyo Declaration on Partnership for Self-Reliance in Afghanistan from Transition to Transformation was issued on 8 July 2012. The Afghan government and the international community met in Tokyo (Japan) to reaffirm, and further consolidate their partnership from Transition to the Transformation Decade. The Tokyo Conference established a renewed stronger foundation for partnership to support sustainable growth and development of Afghanistan throughout the Transformation Decade (2015-24). The conference was chaired by the Japanese and Afghan governments with the participation of ministers and representatives from 55 countries and 25 international and other organizations from around the world. The participants, on this platform, had reaffirmed the importance of the peace and reconciliation process to end the prevailing conflicts and violence and also to restore peace and security permanently in the country. The "inclusiveness and legitimate interests of all Afghans" was the important feature which the participants collectively had believed for the peace process. The "Afghan-led and Afghan-owned peace process" was the important reaffirmation of this conference also. Besides, the importance of reconciliation principles such as the renunciation of violence, the breaking of ties to international terrorism and respect for the Afghan Constitution including its human rights provisions, notably the rights of women, was also held. The participant countries also "recognized the importance of reintegration as an integral part of the peace process, which would pave the way for community recovery and post-conflict rehabilitation of Afghan society through improving security, community development and local governance." Moreover, the international community reaffirmed "its strong support for the peace efforts of the Afghan government through the High Peace Council and the Afghan Peace and Reintegration Program," and, further, appealed the regional countries, which could contribute their positive efforts "to extend all possible cooperation to ensure the success of the peace process." In the conference, the participants also held the importance of the participation of civil society organizations and women's groups in support of the peace process and the culture of peace and human rights in Afghan society. The participants had reassured their full support to the Afghan government "to realize the aspirations of the Afghan people for a peaceful, stable and self-sustaining Afghanistan," and with the support from the international community, the Afghan government aimed at to its progress on issues such as security, with a focus on terrorism and counter-narcotics, poverty reduction, humanitarian needs, provision of basic social services, food security, protection of human rights in particular the rights of women and children, respect for individual dignity, promotion of education and culture, improvement of governance, reducing corruption, lessening reliance on international assistance, and promotion of private investment, thereby contributing to human security." Besides, the participants in the conference put emphasis on the Governance and Strategy for Economic Self-Reliance, Regional Cooperation, importance of private sector and civil society for the development of Afghanistan.[18] Furthermore, "the sustainable development of Afghanistan" was also important motive of the conference for which the increasing roles of new partners and neighboring and regional countries were collectively recognized. In the conference, the participant countries reaffirmed their respect for the "sovereignty, unity, territorial integrity and independence of Afghanistan" which were said to be important and integral components of the "peace, well-being and prosperity of the region and beyond." They also reaffirmed that peace and security were the foundation on which a stable and prosperous society was possible to be built. In fact, terrorism posed the main threat to Afghan's security and stability, and this threat directly affected the "regional and international peace and security," and therefore, they decided, in the conference, to end the "regional dimensions of terrorism and extremism including terrorist safe havens," and they also emphasized on the stringent need of sincere and result-oriented efforts for regional and international cooperation to end terrorism completely from the region so that to form secure Afghanistan and to provide safeguards to the region and the world from the terrorist threats. Besides the collective determination for the fight against terrorism and extremism, they also renewed and reiterated their conviction not to allow Afghanistan to become a sanctuary for international terrorism again. Moreover, the drug production and trafficking have been another challenge/or threat to Afghanistan and the entire world community, and therefore, the international community, in the conference, had deliberated and aimed and stressed on reducing the drug production and trafficking. In fact, it is not only Afghan's security and economic development that was struggling with this challenge but, this menace has posed major challenge to the entire international peace and stability. As a result, by learning the consequences of the threats, the participant countries believed in the need of collective responsibility especially of the neighbouring and the consuming countries to be dealt with the threats of narcotics to the human life. In this direction, both the Afghan government and the international community had reiterated their determination to counter the menace of illicit narcotic drugs. Therefore, in view of this, they decided to focus the means such as "crop eradication, dismantling of drug production infrastructure and promotion of alternative agriculture and law enforcement, cooperation against illicit drugs and precursor chemicals"; besides, "money laundering and corruption" linked to such trafficking. Furthermore, the international community reaffirmed its intention to support the training, equipping, financing, and capability development of the Afghan National Army (ANA) and Afghan National Police (ANP)" to counter all forms of security and other threats.[19] In 2012, the Afghan's Ambassador to India Shaida Abdali, underscoring the significance of the regional cooperation for peace and stability in Afghanistan, had stated that in the months and years ahead, the opportunity to further secure and develop Afghanistan would be widen for the regional leadership and cooperation, and they looked forward to working with India and their other neighbours to consolidate the collective gains made towards the durable peace in Afghanistan. He further said that the collective success was very much within their reach in Afghanistan, however, it would only be resulted from very sincere cooperation among all of its neighbouring countries.[20]

London Conference, 2014: This conference was held on 4 December 2014 in London, which was co-hosted by the UK and the Afghan government, which was also participated by international community and other partners aiming to reaffirm and consolidate their partnership with the beginning of the

Transformation Decade; 2015-24. The London Conference was held as the first opportunity for the new Afghan government, the international community and the other stakeholders to set out on the world stage their collective commitments to Afghanistan's future after the 2014 drawdown of the ISAF as they jointly proceeded into the Transformation decade. In this conference, the participants confirmed that the Afghan government reform programme entitled "Realizing Self-Reliance: Commitments to Reforms and Renewed Partnership" that providing the credible framework for improving security, political stability, economic and fiscal stabilization, advancing good governance, etc. "The Conference provided a platform for the government of Afghanistan to set out its vision for reform and for the international community to demonstrate enduring solidarity and support for Afghanistan."[21]

Quadrilateral Coordination Group (QCG)

The QCG was set up in January 2016 to find a political solution to the Afghan conflict. It was comprised of Pakistan, Afghanistan, China, and the United States. Before the formation of the QCG, a quadrilateral (2+2) meeting of these countries was held in Islamabad on 10 December 2015, on the sidelines of the Fifth Heart of Asia Ministerial Conference which was held on 9 December 2015, in which a quadrilateral framework was announced for the revival of the Afghan Peace Process. In the QCG meeting, Pakistan Prime Minister Nawaz Sharif, Afghan President Ashraf Ghani, Chinese Foreign Minister Wang Yi and the US Deputy Secretary of State Antony J. Blinken had recorded their participation. This meeting reiterated its support for Afghanistan's unity, sovereignty, and territorial integrity, and also affirmed its full support to the democratically elected National Unity Government of Afghanistan. Besides, the member countries also agreed that the authority of the Afghan State and the legitimacy of Afghan's constitution should be fully respected by the international community. In the meeting, the member countries agreed to work together "to enhance mutual trust and confidence between Afghanistan and Pakistan" to create congenial environment for the peace talks, and also to broaden the political, economic, and security cooperation. Importantly, this meeting also expressed and extended full commitment to "an Afghan-led and Afghan-owned" political process in view of promoting "a dialogue between the Afghan Government and Taliban groups," and it also focused on reduction and renunciation of violence in Afghanistan. They agreed and emphasized on the reconciliation as significant factor "to end violence and promote stability in Afghanistan and the region." Moreover, the member countries also agreed "to work together to create a conducive atmosphere" that to encourage the Taliban groups "to engage in meaningful and sustained negotiations."[22]

The first meeting of the QCG members on Afghan Peace and reconciliation process was held in Islamabad on 11 January 2016. The participants aimed to bring back the Afghan Taliban to the negotiating table to resume the stalled peace talks. The participant countries had decided and considered the mutual efforts to facilitate "an Afghan-led and Afghan-owned" peace and reconciliation process with a view to achieve lasting peace and stability in Afghanistan and the region. Emphasizing on the significance of ending the conflict in Afghanistan, all the four countries expressed their determination to stop senseless violence on the Afghan people and also to breed insecurity throughout the region. For this, they believed and emphasized "the immediate need for direct talks between representatives of the Government of Afghanistan and representatives from Taliban groups in a peace process that aims to preserve Afghanistan's unity, sovereignty and territorial integrity." The participants in their "discussions focused on undertaking a clear and realistic assessment of the opportunities for peace and reconciliation in Afghanistan, and anticipated obstacles and measures that would help create a conducive environment for commencement of peace talks with the shared goal of reducing violence and establishing lasting peace in Afghanistan."[23] The group had tried to ease the path to direct talks between the Afghan government and the Taliban, however, with the little success. Usually, the Taliban continued putting unacceptable conditions for the talks with the Afghan government.

Furthermore, during the second QCG meeting in Kabul on 18 January 2016, the participating countries had invited all the groups of Afghan Taliban for the negotiations with the Afghan government to resolve the mutual differences. However, responding to the invitation for the peace talks, the Taliban had put forward pre-conditions for the peace talks such as "the withdrawal of foreign troops from Afghan soil; to lift the UN sanctions against their leaders; to re-open their political office in Qatar; to release their prisoners and to end propaganda against the group." Subsequently, by learning the preconditions, in this direction, the third QCG meeting was invited on 6 February 2016 in Islamabad, and the member countries extended the continuation of their efforts for the talks between Afghan government and Afghan Taliban. In the fourth QCG meeting on 23 February, 2016 in Kabul, it was announced that Pakistan would host the first round of talks between the representatives of the Afghan government and Afghan Taliban.[24] The fifth QCG meeting for the Afghan peace and reconciliation process was held in Islamabad on 18 May 2016. The participants in the meeting reiterated the political settlement as the only option for the peace negotiations, and they unanimously condemned the violence which serves no purpose. Therefore, they reaffirmed to use their respective leverages and influences. Moreover, they expressed "their continued determination with shared commitment to advance the goal of an Afghan-led, Afghan-owned peace and reconciliation process."[25] Subsequently, on 16 October 2017, the sixth round of meeting of the QCG held in Muscat (Oman) to revive the moribund peace process in Afghanistan. The Foreign Secretary Tehmina Janua had led the Pakistan's delegation and she emphasized the need for a peaceful political solution of the Afghan conflict. The high level officials from the US and China also attended the meeting. This meeting, for the Afghan peace, aimed at the discussions on bringing the Taliban to negotiation table, counterterrorism efforts, and eradication of 'terrorist main bases' on the other side of the border in Pakistan as the main issue as stated by the Afghan delegation. Besides, Pakistan also rejecting the allegations for its providing safe haven for terrorist had stated that "there should be an end to the blame game and all the nations need to make coordinated efforts towards the peace and stability in Afghanistan and beyond."[26]

Kabul Process, 2017

The First Meeting of the Kabul Process for Peace and Security Cooperation was held on 6 June 2017 having objective to work towards peace in Afghanistan with the support of neighbouring countries and the international community. In this meet, delegates from 23 countries, the European Union, the United Nations and the NATO had recorded their participation. While officially opening peace meeting, Afghan President Ghani stated that Afghanistan was on the frontline of terrorism in the world, and while extending peace offer, he stated that if the Taliban joins the peace negotiations, he would allow them to open office in Kabul. However, in front of the gathering, Ghani had accused Pakistan for waging an undeclared war. Besides, he also spoke tough for the Western countries for their attempts to negotiate with the Taliban on their own. He stated, "There are too many players running too many parallel tracks with too little clarity on who they are and what they represent," and "we also ask that you respect the integrity of an Afghan-owned and Afghan-led consolidated process and not set up separate tracks of your own."[27] However, as opposed to this, the Taliban held the Kabul Process as futile by stating that the "talks about peace during the presence of foreign invaders will not yield results and are meaningless."[28] Furthermore, during the second meeting of the Kabul Process, which was held on 28 February 2018, the Afghan government issued a four-page declaration on peace and reconciliation, security cooperation and counter-terrorism. The Taliban again refrained from this meeting also. In this meeting, all the participants reiterated their continued support to the "Afghan-led and Afghan-owned" peace and reconciliation process, and they collectively agreed that the direct talks between the Afghan government and the Taliban, without any preconditions and without the threats of violence, constituted the most viable way to end the ongoing agony of the Afghan people. The Afghan government also reiterated its will and determination through dialogue. All the participants assured the warring parties about their "strong will and commitment to stand behind an intra-Afghan dialogue for sustainable peace and security in Afghanistan."[29]

Ghani's Proposal

In February 2018, Afghan President Ashraf Ghani announced a bold proposal for peace and offered a ceasefire, the removal of sanctions, release of prisoners, the recognition of the Taliban as a political party in return of peace, the conduct of fresh elections, and a review of the constitution. Further in the Tashkent Conference in March 2018, Ghani reiterated the offer. Moreover, in April 2018, he invited the Taliban to participate in the October 2018 parliamentary elections. Further, political dialogues were held in Mecca, Tashkent, Jakarta, and elsewhere and Mr. Ghani's efforts displayed Afghan's "realization of the importance of creating an international consensus on peacemaking in the country and bringing the Taliban into the political fold. However, parallel processes that seek different outcomes for short-term gains can be counterproductive."[30] In fact, it was believed that Afghanistan could achieve and maintain peace only when the Afghan state would be capable enough for governing, accountable to its citizens and if had acted as a responsible member of the international community. Afghanistan cannot be stabilized when the international actors rely on non-state actors to secure their perceived national interests.[31] In fact, the Afghan government had offered to meet the Taliban without any precondition, but the Taliban never turned up for any direct talks. Furthermore, on 28 November 2018, President Ghani announced and formed a 12 member negotiating team for prospective peace talks with the Taliban. This team comprised of both women and men, and led by presidential chief of staff Abdul Salam Rahimi. Moreover, President Ghani also laid out a "road map" for the talks and four important principles to form the backbone of any agreement. The principles included the respect to the Afghan Constitution and a total rejection of interference in domestic affairs by foreign terrorist groups. Ghani said, "we seek a peace agreement in which the Afghan Taliban would be included in a democratic and inclusive society."[32] On 18 December 2018, the Afghan government sent a team for peace talks with the Taliban to Abu Dhabi, a day after, the talks was attended by the US and the Taliban representatives in Abu Dhabi for ending the prolonged war. This team was led by the chief negotiator Abdul Salam Rahimi aiming to begin proximity dialogue with the Taliban delegation and to prepare for a face-to-face meeting between the two sides.

Moscow Format/Process

Since the expulsion of the Taliban regime in 2001, Russia had supported the prevailing system and extended its contributions in multiple ways for Afghan's reconstruction efforts. However, gradually, the Taliban re-emerged strongly in the Afghan territory and began war against the Afghan government and the international forces. Amidst, Afghanistan, Russia, the United States, China and other regional powers such as India, Iran, and Pakistan also tried to seek a political solution, though some of them were hypocritically active. Russia also tried its best for the peace process by reaching out to the Taliban. However, Russia's role in peace-making process in Afghanistan seemingly appeared to be confused and not explicit. In 2016, Russia initiated a series of meetings with the Afghan's neighbouring countries for the political solution to the Afghan crisis, which is known as the Moscow Process/Format. In the first meeting, Afghanistan and the US were not invited and only Russia, China, and Pakistan had attended the meeting. The First Round of the Moscow Format was held in April 2017, which was participated by the representatives from Afghanistan, China, Iran, India, Kazakhstan, Kyrgyzstan, Pakistan, Russia, Tajikistan, Turkmenistan, and Uzbekistan, and importantly, this was for the first time, as believed, the Afghan Taliban were invited to an international forum. The US had declined to attend the discussions. However, subsequently, Afghanistan, India, and some Central Asian countries became the part of the Moscow Process. The United States did not attend any of the meetings and perceived them as an overlapping effort that lacked clarity. The second round, which was to be held on 4 September 2018, was cancelled and postponed as the Afghan government declined to participate. India also refused to participate on the pretext of unwillingness of sharing the table with a Taliban and without the participation of democratically-elected Afghan government. Further, a third multilateral dialogue was planned to organize by inviting the Taliban. But, again the Afghan government declined to participate because of the invitation to the Taliban, and even the Taliban had also refused to engage in direct talks with the Afghan government. The Afghan government believed that such initiative would have undermined legitimacy of its own initiative, the US-backed Kabul Process, as a result, the multilateral dialogue was ultimately postponed.[33] However, Russia in August 2018 had proposed of organizing a multilateral peace talks in Moscow and also had invited 12 countries and the Taliban to attend a meeting in the following month. But, the meeting could not take place and was postponed again due to Ghani's rejection to invitation on the plea that such talks with the Taliban should be led by the Afghan government. The US had also extended its declination to attend the Moscow meeting. In fact, Afghan government was reluctant for Moscow's pressing ahead with the proposal for peace talks. In this direction, it was believed that the Afghan government had requested Russia not to organize the meeting on the plea that "talking to the Taliban at multiple forums will further complicate the peace process backed by the US", however, Russia rejected the request of the Afghan government.[34]

Later, on 9 November 2018, Russia organized a "Moscow Format" meeting on Afghanistan, where the Taliban also participated. According to Moscow, the aim of this meeting was to help narrowing the gaps in the stands taken by the Afghan government and the Taliban to holding a direct intra-Afghan dialogue. However, the Afghan Foreign Ministry had not participated, but the Afghan High Peace Council, a government-appointed body which was given a task to talk to the Taliban on the reconciliation process, participated the Moscow meeting. The regional countries such as Pakistan, China, Iran, and India, the five Central Asian countries (Kyrgyzstan, Tajikistan, Uzbekistan, Kazakhstan, and Turkmenistan) and a five-member Taliban delegation led by Sher Mohammad Abbas Stanakzai, head of the Taliban's political council in Qatar, and even the US had also recorded its participation by sending its Moscow Embassy diplomat to observe the discussions in this meeting. Significantly, this was the first time when all the stakeholders attended the meeting and shared the tables in tandem. For Russia, this conference was an attempt "to make a conducive environment to promote a direct dialogue between the government, the Taliban, and wider representatives of other social and political circles of the country."[35] The Russian Foreign Ministry that stated the main issue on the agenda of the meeting was the "coordination of regional efforts to assist the process of national reconciliation, in the interest of restoring peace in Afghanistan." This format held significant as it provided "Moscow a leadership position in the Afghanistan situation, at a time when the US has been ceding the space."[36] In fact, it has believed that the Afghan government opposed to participate the proposed September 4 meeting under US pressure. In fact, the meeting was cancelled because of the pulling out of the US. However, this time, Afghan government moving ahead carefully tried to prevent the Russia-US clashes and balanced the Russian and US interests by recording its participation through the Afghan High Peace Council's representatives. About the participation in this meeting, Sibghat Ahmadi, spokesperson of the Afghan's Ministry of External Affairs, stated, "Our agreement with the Russians is that this meeting should lead to direct talks between us (Afghan government) and the Taliban, if it does not happen like this, then this will reflect the intention of the Taliban and this means they (Taliban) are not prepared for peace."[37] While making remarks at the second meeting of the Moscow format consultations on Afghanistan on 9 November, 2018, Russia's Foreign Minister Sergey Lavrov stated

> This format is designed to coordinate the development of an inclusive intra-Afghan dialogue towards promoting the process of national reconciliation and the restoration of peace as soon as possible in the long-suffering Afghan state. This process is in the best interests of the people of Afghanistan.... All countries in the region and the international community as a whole sincerely want to see the revival of a peaceful, independent and prosperous

> Afghan state free from terrorism and drug trafficking. Afghanistan's problems can only be settled politically, through the attainment of national accord and with the involvement of all parties to the conflict.[38]

Further, Lavrov stated

> Russia as the organizer of this event sees its role in working together with its regional partners and Afghanistan's friends to help launch a constructive intra-Afghan dialogue.... We hope that responsible politicians will not be guided by personal or group considerations but by the interests of the people of Afghanistan. We deeply empathize with the suffering of the Afghan people, and we are resolved to do everything in our power to help them turn a new page in the history of Afghanistan.... Our countries and the multilateral organisations active in the region must help the people of Afghanistan...root out the terrorist threat. Russia stands for the preservation of a unified and indivisible Afghanistan.... We must not think in terms of geopolitical games, which can only make Afghanistan an area of international rivalry with grave consequences for the people of Afghanistan and their neighbours.[39]

On Russia's posture in organizing this meeting, former Indian Diplomat Rakesh Sood stated, "Aware of the differences, the Russians refrained from attempting a final statement or even a group photograph. Nevertheless, with this meeting, Russia has sent a signal that it is back in the game in Afghanistan."[40] In fact, Russians have their links with the Taliban which were acknowledged by them in 2015 and that they had only communication and information sharing links with the Taliban. However, it has believed that

> Russia's overarching security interests, mainly transnational terrorism and drug trafficking, align with Afghan and American objectives. Moscow's efforts can be useful when they are well defined and are held in unison with efforts by Afghanistan and the United States, as two major parties to the conflict. Engaging with the Taliban for humanitarian causes and the initiating of a peace process is inevitable.

> Nonetheless, contacts that can embolden and disincentive the group to come the negotiating tables goes against the stabilization needs of Afghanistan. Russia's peacemaking efforts must meet Afghanistan's needs, which include initiating negotiations, achieving a political solution, and ultimately peace, and then maintaining that peace. This entails encouraging the Taliban to the negotiating table without undermining the Afghan government.[41]

Furthermore, in February 2019, Moscow facilitated talks between the Taliban leaders and the mainstream Afghan politicians led by former President Hamid Karzai. This talk was held as substantial and significant step towards the peace process, as this was Taliban's first such attempt of public contact with the prominent Afghan's leader. Hamid Karzai declared the talks as, "a big achievement" that would help to push forward the "peace, stability and an Afghanistan free of foreign forces."[42] However, in these talks, the Taliban again exhibited its anti Afghan government posture by not inviting the Afghan government's representative that further putting problem in the outcomes of the peace talks. Therefore, it was suggested to prevail upon the Taliban to talk to the Afghan government. In fact, this process was held as a similar approach with the US-led talks with the Taliban in Qatar.

India's Stand on Moscow Format: India also participated in the second meeting of the Moscow Format at the non-official-level. The former Indian Ambassador to Afghanistan, Amar Sinha, and former Indian High Commissioner to Pakistan, T.C.A. Raghavan, attended this meeting as India's representatives. In fact, this was considered as a significant development. In the last meeting hosted by Russia (Moscow Format), India had not participated in a multilateral meeting involving Taliban, and without participation of the Afghan's democratically elected government led by Ghani on the issue of dealing with the Taliban. In the last meeting hosted by Russia in 2017, India had sent its joint secretary in charge of Pakistan, Afghanistan, and Iran. However, in that meeting, the Taliban did not participate. By maintaining India's support to the "Afghan-led reconciliation process," Raveesh Kumar, official spokesperson of MEA, stated that India extends support to all efforts for "peace and reconciliation in Afghanistan that will preserve unity and plurality, and bring security, stability, and prosperity to the country. India's consistent policy was that such efforts should be Afghan-led, Afghan-owned, and Afghan-controlled, and with the participation of the government of Afghanistan."[43] In fact, this was the first time since the IC-814 hijack in 1999 by the Taliban that India has publicly shared table with the Taliban representatives in the Moscow meeting. During the 'Hijack-1999', India had publicly engaged with the Taliban Regime to free the IC-814. The then Indian officials including Ajit Doval of IB, C.D. Sahay of RAW and A.R. Ghanshyam of the Indian High Commission in Islamabad had talked to the Taliban regime's interlocutors headed by the then Taliban regime's Foreign Minister Wakil Ahmad Muttawakil.[44] Therefore, welcoming India's decision to participate in the talks on 9 November 2018, the Russian Embassy stated, "We highly regard Indian support in the peace process in Afghanistan and welcome Indian readiness and that of other partner countries in the Moscow format."[45] On India's significant shift to participate this meeting with the Taliban, India's former diplomat Rakesh Sood said, "India would have preferred a direct process between the Ghani government and the Taliban, but since that is not possible, a regional process like this one is the next best option. It is to Russia's credit that they have been able to bring everyone to the table for this round of talks."[46] However, in this meeting, the Indian representatives neither have made any official statement nor signed any document there on the half of India. And even for that matter, India made it clear that its participation in this meeting was not because of any compulsion. India, on its participation, stated, "Our participation was decided only after consultations with the main actor in the process, the Afghan government. Since the Afghan Foreign Ministry did not attend and instead sent Afghan High Peace Council representatives, we decided to send people outside the Indian government."[47] This time, India's position on Taliban seemed to be changed. Earlier, when the Taliban had occupied power in Kabul, India had not extended recognition to them. And as stated by the former Foreign Secretary of India, Shyam Saran, "Throughout the 1990s, India gave military and financial assistance to the

Northern Alliance fighting the Pakistan-sponsored Taliban regime in Afghanistan."[48] As reported by Roy, India refused to talk to the Taliban when they re-emerged in 2006-07 to challenge the US forces. Furthermore, India, in the International Conference on Afghanistan in London in 2010, had declared its stand that the elected government of Afghanistan should draw the 'red lines' or the term and conditions for negotiations with the Taliban.[49] However, there were mixed perceptions on India's engagement, though unofficial, with the Taliban. Some argued that it was not the Afghan-led and dominated by Russia and others like the US. It was also clearly appeared that India also wanted to be engaged with the Taliban for the better future of Afghanistan. Over India's participation in talks with the Taliban, in fact, India was also criticized for being the part in the Moscow Format as by this India intended of offering international legitimacy to the Taliban which once opposed. However, as quoted by Roy, according to the former Foreign Secretary of India, Shiv Shankar Menon, "Radical ideologies and religion cannot be defeated on the battlefield, particularly if their military manifestation has state support as is the case with the Taliban and the LeT."[50] However, India, despite a major power in South Asia, has not initiated any peace talks or process on Afghanistan because of its calculated limitations such as its hostile relations with Pakistan and its non-legitimate recognition to the Taliban. By and large, India failed to lead any peace process in Afghanistan.

The US-Taliban Negotiations

By learning that war or military cannot be solution to the Afghan problem, the United States also started believing in the diplomatic and political negotiations as suitable option for the Afghan crisis, and for this, decided to engage at the multiple levels. And importantly, the US believed in the regional cooperation in Afghanistan. Therefore, in this direction, the Trump administration had appointed Ambassador Zalmay Khalilzad as US Special Advisor for Afghan's reconciliation process. Khalilzad started his work by traveling to the region and contacted with the leaders of the regional countries such as Pakistan, Saudi Arabia, the UAE, and Qatar and even Russia.

Even for that matter, the US also started contacting with the Taliban including direct official contacts with the group's political office in Doha. Earlier the US was reluctant to have talks with the Taliban with which it had been fighting its longest war in Afghanistan. However, it has stated that "US engagement with the Taliban has taken place in consultation with, if not with the permission of, the Afghan government."[51] In fact, the US-Russia talks on Afghanistan, initially, could not take place, and the US had avoided the Moscow Process, and had emphasized on the Kabul Process for reconciliation in Afghanistan. However, later, the US sent its representative in Moscow Format which was held in November 2018. Russia, on the other hand, had insisted on the usefulness of its own process. By learning that each stakeholder in Afghanistan especially Afghan's neighbouring countries such as Iran, Russia, China and even Pakistan, which had been maneuvering anti-US strategies or which were proactive against the US's presence in the region, had established contacts and engaged in peace talks with the Taliban, therefore, the Trump administration also understood the significance of engagement with the Taliban to reach to the desired results in Afghanistan.

Earlier, on 23 July 2018, the four member Taliban delegation met with the US senior official Alice Wells to resume the peace negotiation in Doha, Qatar. This was the first face-to-face talks in seven years between the US and the Taliban.[52] In fact, before this, the US was unwilling to have direct talks with the Islamist insurgents and it had said that it would sit on the sidelines of an "Afghan-led, Afghan-owned" peace process. However, the Trump administration by changing its stand extended steps towards the Taliban. On the other hand, the Taliban was unwilling to enter negotiations with the Afghan government without first discussing the removal of foreign troops in the US However, it has believed that the Taliban negotiators exhibited their ready-ness "to compromise on the longstanding demand to evict all foreign troops before any negotiations with the Afghan government", and "the Taliban could even countenance a remaining US force in the country so long as it was involved in the political process that reached such an agreement."[53] On this, Michael Semple, an expert on the region and former deputy to the EU special representative in Afghanistan, viewed that "those predicting an imminent breakthrough in peace negotiations were engaged in "Pollyanna thinking."[54] Further, to boost the long-stalled Afghan Peace Process, the meeting between the American diplomat, Zalmay Khalilzad, and the Taliban was held in October 2018. This was the second meeting that the US representative had talks with the Taliban representatives in Doha (Qatar) since when the Trump administration ordered direct talks in the summer 2018. Since long, it has believed that the Taliban had been demanding that they were interested to meet with the US directly instead of the Afghan government. This was held as "American's direct contact with the Taliban as 'talks before talks' that could then grow into negotiations between the Taliban and the Afghan government." According to Taliban's spokesman Zabihullah Mujahid, six of their representatives met with the US representative Khalilzad. In the meeting, as stated by the Taliban, "they talked about the end of occupation and a peaceful resolution for the Afghan issue.... Both sides agreed to continue their meetings in the future." In fact, "the Taliban have long stipulated that an agreement to withdraw remaining American troops from Afghanistan is essential to negotiating an end to the war."[55] On 14, 15 and 16 November 2018, the Taliban held three days of talks with the US envoy Zalmay Khalilzad in Qatar (Taliban's political office). As it was stated, in a marathon talks, Khairullah Khairkhwah, the former Taliban governor of Herat, and Mohammed Fazl, a former Taliban military chief, were present in the meeting. During the meeting, the Taliban stressed for the postponement of next year's presidential election and the establishment of an interim government under a neutral leadership and to lead the interim government, the name of Abdul Sattar Sirat, an ethnic Tajik and Islamic Scholar, was recommended. However, in this meeting there was no agreement made on the release of the prisoners, opening the Taliban office or lifting Taliban travel ban. Furthermore, on 4 December 2018, the US envoy Khalilzad met with Pakistan's Foreign Secretary and army officials to held discussion on how to bring the Taliban to peace talks. Besides, he also had schedule to visit Afghanistan, Russia, Uzbekistan, Turkmenistan, Belgium, UAE, and Qatar for the same objective.

Abu Dhabi/UAE Talks

On 17 December 2018, the Taliban held another round of talks with the US officials in United States of Emirates (UAE) for the negotiation to end the prolonged Afghan war. The Saudi, Pakistani and Emirati representatives were also involved in the talks. This time also, the Taliban did not provide space to any representative of the Afghan government. But, according to Khalil Manawi director of Afghanistan's Bakhtar news agency, Afghan government's officials also had attended the meeting. This, in fact, created shadow of ambiguity on the government's participation. The Taliban had consistently been refusing to hold direct talks with the Afghan government and they had been insisting that they would only negotiate with the US[56] During these talks in Abu Dhabi, the Taliban officials believed to be said that "the US delegation was pressing for a six month ceasefire as well as an agreement to name Taliban representatives to a future caretaker government."[57] In this context, a senior Taliban official said, "If these three countries—Saudi Arabia, UAE and Pakistan—become guarantors and the US appoints the head of the caretaker government in Afghanistan that we nominate, then we can think about ceasefire."[58] In fact, the Taliban stated that during the talks on 17 December, they held preliminary talks with the US state department's special envoy Zalmay Khalilzad. They also stated that they had held extensive meetings with the officials from all the above mentioned three countries, and repeating their demands for the withdrawal of the international forces from Afghanistan. However, the US had not officially confirmed whether the meeting took place between its envoy and the Taliban officials.[59] In this meeting, the Afghan High Peace Council which attended the Abu Dhabi Peace talks and according to council's deputy spokesperson, Asadullah Zahiri, the meetings were very fruitful and took place in a positive environment and they stated that they met with the several non-political actors and had held informal meetings with the Taliban and other parties. Further, he said, "We got the sense that the Taliban was very serious about negotiating peace and even discussed long term ceasefire."[60] In fact, the Taliban were reluctantly rejected to have talks with the Afghan government calling them as "puppet regime", and the Afghan government always reiterated that the peace process should be "Afghan-owned and Afghan-led". After the Abu Dhabi talks, Afghan National Security Adviser, Hamdullah Mohib said, "As a sovereign country, no other country or individual has the right or the authority to discuss new governance formulas or structures for Afghanistan, including political dispensations, which violates the Afghan Constitution," and further also stated that "There is no substitution for an elected government."[61] On the Abu Dhabi Talks, the UN's Secretary-General's special representative for Afghanistan expressed, "the possibility of a negotiated end to the conflict has never been more real in the past 17 years than it is now."[62] Besides, on the peace process, Zahiri said, "we expect the Taliban to make good use of this opportunity that has arrived for Afghans to find a solution for all these security and political disagreements."[63]

Doha/Qatar Talks

From 21 January to 26 January 2019, the US and the Taliban held a six days long series of discussion in Qatar, that reaching to some seemingly fruitful results, however, leaving many future uncertainties. In fact, this was the longest period of negotiations between them since their bilateral engagement for the peace negotiation. Khalilzad said that those talks were more productive than they had in the past.[64] During these meetings, the Taliban appointed, Mullah Abdul Ghani Baradar, one of its co-founder as the new head of its political office in Doha where these talks were held to strengthen and properly manage these negotiations process and to talk with America. However, he did not participate in these talks, but, it was stated that he would be the part to future business between the US and the Taliban. In fact, this series of talks was described as "unprecedented" by the analysts of the international affairs. During the negotiations, the US tried to make major efforts for a peace deal so that to pave the way for the Taliban's participation in the next government. The discussions were mostly focused on the "troop's withdrawal".[65] However, finally, as reported, that the US and the Taliban were agreed to the "framework" of a peace deal in which the Taliban extended a guarantee to prevent Afghanistan from being used by the terrorists, the complete withdrawal of the foreign troops (within 18-month period after final agreement) in return for the ceasefire, and more importantly, the Taliban's talks with the Afghanistan government to settle the post-conflict political arrangements. In an interview in Kabul, Khalilzad said, "We have draft of the framework that has to be fleshed out before it becomes an agreement.... The Taliban has committed to our satisfaction to do what is necessary that would prevent Afghanistan from ever becoming a platform for international terrorist groups or individuals."[66] The outcome of the framework of peace was briefed by Khalilzad to the Afghan government, thereafter on 27 January 2019 when he returned back to Kabul. However, Afghan President Ghani fearing of further escalation of violence and bloodshed if the peace deal had not been implemented quickly. He said, "We want peace quickly, we want it soon, but we want it with prudence. Prudence is important so we do not repeat past mistakes," that had happened during the withdrawal of the Soviet forces from Afghanistan in 1988. In fact, he expressed that despite the peace deal promises, Afghanistan was broken into civil war and anarchy.[67] On the peace deal between the US and the Taliban, Satinder K. Lambah, the former special envoy of the Prime Minister of India, said, "The Government of Afghanistan should be consulted before critical decisions are taken that could alter the power equation inside Afghanistan. Taliban captives are in custody of the Afghan government so it is fair to hear what the government has to say regarding this first."[68] The Taliban has always demonstrated its disinterest and unwillingness to talk to the Afghan government. Shyam Saran, India's former Foreign Secretary opined that "the endgame has begun in Afghanistan." However, C. Raja Mohan raised some doubts, besides others, that of "the nature of the post conflict-arrangements in Kabul, potential changes to the Afghan Constitution and...the mechanics for peaceful transition to a new political order."[69] Emphatically, Khalilzad stated in his twitter that the US agreement to withdraw from Afghanistan has been contingent on agreement on all issues. "Nothing is agreed until everything is agreed, and 'everything' must include an intra-Afghan dialogue and comprehensive ceasefire."[70] After this development, US Secretary of State Mike Pompeo welcoming the Doha talks expressed that "the US wants to strengthen Afghan sovereignty, independence and prosperity."[71] In fact, to achieve the US objectives in Afghanistan looking at both the Afghan government and the Taliban, according to C. Raja Mohan, Khalilzad identified three big problems that the US had faced. The *first* was that Donald Trump's "patience with America's longest war was wearing thin…for the political weariness with America's longest war had grown steadily as he had apparently asked for plans to cut a significant number of troops from the existed deployment of about 14,000." However, no formal decision had been announced. Therefore, at that time, it was contingent on what the Taliban and Pakistan could do. *Second,* "the Taliban was playing hard ball" as its insurgents were engaged in deadly attacks on Afghan security forces while seating down with Khalilzad and his team in Doha. The Taliban said that it would continue "fight Kabul and talk to Washington at the same time." In fact, "The Taliban's diplomatic assertiveness was rooted in Afghanistan's changed ground reality.... The Taliban made frequent and intense attacks at will across Afghanistan...." *Third* challenge was Pakistan. "Geography makes Pakistan critical for either war or peace in Afghanistan. Trump's predecessors seemed willing to acquiesce in Pakistan's Afghan double game—hunting with America and running with the Taliban."[72]

Furthermore, three days of peace talks were held between them in Doha from 25 February to 27 February 2019, and the US envoy twitted on 28 February that it was decided to put the talks on hold for further two days for the internal deliberations of both sides. This time for the negotiation with Khalilzad, the Taliban was represented by a high-level team led by Mullah Abdul Ghani Baradar.[73] This session of talks was held as exclusive discussions and the main focus of which was on how foreign troops could be withdrawn from Afghanistan and how to guarantee the Afghan territory not to be used again by the terrorists or other forces to attack the other countries. Khalilzad, describing the talks as "solid" and "productive," twitted that "We continue to take slow, steady steps toward understanding and eventually peace."[74] Further, peace talks between them resumed in March 2019. The negotiations between the US and the Taliban were focused on four key interconnected issues to end the Afghan war or that going to compose any future agreement; counterterrorism, troop withdrawal, intra-Afghan dialogue and a ceasefire.[75] Moreover, it has reported that under the peace plan with the Taliban, the US had to withdraw its military from Afghanistan over the next three to five years. In fact, plan of the US withdrawal of its forces raised the fears across the world as "it could lead to the fall of the Western-backed government in Kabul and a return to the extremist rule of the Taliban. The track record for US-supported governments after peace treaties or troop withdrawals" was held "shaky at best." For instance, "US-trained South Vietnamese fell to communist forces two years after the US withdrew from Vietnam in 1973. Large portions of the Iraqi army collapsed in the face of an IS offensive in 2014, just three years after US withdrawal."[76]

Pakistan's Stand on Peace Process

Pakistan has always perceived India's suspicious role in Afghanistan. However, for the first time, Pakistan in December 2018 felt India's cooperation as significant to resolve the Afghan turmoil. In this context, Pakistan's Foreign Minister Shah Mahmood Qureshi, after India, which moved positive steps towards Afghan peace problem, attended a dialogue for peace process with Taliban in Moscow Format and said that India's cooperation would be needed for bringing peace to war-torn Afghanistan. He further stated, "Although Pakistan was committed to facilitate a negotiated end to the 17-year-old Afghan war, it could not do the task alone and that other regional countries, including India, needed to play their part." Qureshi said that Pakistan alone was unable to bring peace in Afghanistan as it has been the shared responsibility of the regional countries including India, Iran, Tajikistan, and China, and since India has been one of the stakeholders present in Afghanistan, its cooperation in this regard was held significantly essential. Moreover, he also expressed Prime Minister Imran Khan's stand stating that the peace establishment in Afghanistan through military power was not possible. Therefore, the US, Pakistan, Afghanistan, and Taliban also wanted a solution through deliberations and dialogues. However, earlier, Pakistan had accused that India was playing the role of spoiler in Afghanistan and therefore, objected the inclusion of India in Trump's September 2017 New Policy on Afghanistan. Moreover, the former Pakistan Foreign Office spokesperson Nafees Zakaria accused that India, in the name of development assistance, had used the Afghan soil to carry out subversive activities against Pakistan. However, India has always denied Pakistan's accusations.[77] On 15 December 2018, the foreign ministers of China and Pakistan attended the second China, Pakistan, and Afghanistan Trilateral foreign ministers dialogue in Kabul, where the three countries signed a Memorandum of Understanding to cooperate on counter terrorism and to coordinate to call on the Taliban to return to the negotiation table and to move forward "the Afghan-led and Afghan-owned reconciliation process." In this context, it was held important for the three involved parties "to enhance counter-terrorism cooperation and to enhance communication to move forward the trilateral cooperation." All the three countries expressed that they would seize an opportunity to move forward the Afghan's reconciliation process with Afghanistan by playing the main role. Moreover, it was also decided in the meeting that both Afghanistan and Pakistan would put positive efforts further to improve their bilateral relations by resolving the mutual trust deficit and they would also engage in more constructive interactions through friendly contacts further by resolving their bilateral tensions. In this context, China assuring its positive role in Afghanistan stated that "China is a friend to both Afghanistan and Pakistan and would like to play a constructive part to help improve their bilateral ties."[78] Pakistan's Prime Minister Imran Khan, on 18 December 2018, said that Pakistan would do everything possible within its power to advance the reconciliation process in Afghanistan as Pakistan has sponsored the talks between the US and the Taliban which were held in the UAE to end the prolonged bloody war. In fact, Prime Minister Khan highlighted the role Pakistan played in conducting the talks. He said, "Pakistan has helped in the dialogue between the Taliban and the US in Abu Dhabi. Let us pray that this leads to peace and ends almost three decades of sufferings of the brave Afghan people."[79] Moreover, while giving an interview to Arab

News, Pakistan Army's spokesman, Major General Asif Ghafoor said, "we are a facilitator. We have done our job of bringing them to the negotiation table. What is discussed and how the process moves forward will depend on progress during every meeting."[80] Furthermore, after the Trump administration decided to slash half of its troops from Afghanistan, to cope up and to plan strategy to resolve the probable new concerns, Pakistan's Foreign Minister Shah Mahmood Qureshi met his Chinese counterpart on 25 December 2018 in Beijing and discussed the situation arising out of it. Both the leaders reiterated with the optimum determination to carry a joint course of action for the regional peace and stability, to promote connectivity and work for Afghan-led and Afghan-owned peace process. However, this development has put its repercussion as the neighbouring countries of Afghanistan felt concerns and fears that there might be the risks of refugee crisis in the region as hundreds of thousands of refugees fleeing across their borders. As a result, the states involved in the peace process were panic due to sudden and abrupt decision of the withdrawal of the US forces. Pakistan's proposal of hosting a meeting between the US and the Taliban in Islamabad was rejected by the Taliban. In fact, the US was seeking help from Pakistan to held talks in Islamabad with the Taliban in the mid-January 2019, and this was highlighted by the Pakistani media that Pakistan was playing this role. But, the Afghan Taliban rejected any such talks with the US's envoy Zalmay Khalilzad in Islamabad. The talks had also offered space to the Afghan government because which, as usual, the Taliban rejected the talks in Islamabad. Moreover, the Taliban accused that Khalilzad was straying from the agreed agenda between them. One of the Taliban leaders said, "we have made it clear again and again that we would never hold any meeting with the Afghan government as we know that they are not capable of addressing our demands."[81]

After the US-Taliban reaching to peace deal as mentioned earlier, looking at Pakistan's role in it, C. Raja Mohan believed, "Pakistan's support is the source of optimism about US engagement with the Taliban."[82] In fact, President Trump had taken stringent stand against Pakistan and had cut off US military assistance and also threatened to put Pakistan under international financial sanctions. Therefore, looking at the US-Taliban engagement, it was stated that "we don't know anything about the price that Rawalpindi has set for its cooperation and what the US is willing to offer," and besides, "If the US effectively uses its considerable residual leverage in Afghanistan, Pakistan does not try and turn Afghanistan into a weak protectorate, and the Taliban does not overreach inside Afghanistan, there is reason for optimism. But if you are a sceptic, you might argue that an Afghan trifecta is near impossible."[83] Though Pakistan played important role in bringing the US and the Taliban on negotiation table up to some extent, but, after the withdrawal of the US forces from Afghanistan, doubtfully the concerns were raised that the militant groups supported by Pakistan would continue their attacks in Afghanistan. According to Dean Coats, Director of the US's National Intelligence, "Pakistan's narrow approach to counterterrorism cooperation using some groups as policy tools and confronting only the militant groups that directly threaten Pakistan—almost certainly will frustrate US counterterrorism efforts against the Taliban," and further he said, "Militant groups supported by Pakistan will continue to take advantage of their safe haven in Pakistan to plan and conduct attacks in India and Afghanistan, including against US interets."[84] However, "Pakistan, long at odds with the United States over the war in Afghanistan, has begun to play a behind-the-scenes but central role in supporting US peace talks with the Afghan Taliban, including by facilitating travel to negotiations."[85] Moreover, Pakistan has also pressurized ("unprecedented pressure") the Taliban leaders who failed to cooperate, even by detaining members of the militant's families, and this time Pakistan had worked more seriously for the talks.[86] In fact, Pakistan's role has been optimum in bringing the Taliban on negotiation table with the US and on this, one of the US officials expressed, "we know it just wouldn't be possible without their support. They have facilitated some movement and travel to the discussions in Doha."[87] Besides, the Taliban held Pakistan's role as "instrumental" and in one of the incidences, "Islamabad sent a message to the militants through religious leaders that they had to talk to the United States or risk a cut-off in ties."[88]

Challenges to Peace Process

The peace process in Afghanistan faced multiple challenges. Importantly, there was a complete lack of cooperation and coordination amongst the stakeholder countries in Afghan peace process, for example, Russia and the US and the others. In fact, the countries like Russia and the US remained engaged in peace process which was initiated by them individually and seemed to be busy counting their credits. However, the most prominent factor in the peace process was the Taliban. The initiation of peace process by any country was incomplete and impossible without the participation of the Taliban, and therefore, by learning this adroitly, the Taliban had always put forward its conditions. There had also been the matter of trust deficit between the Afghan government and the Taliban for the peace process. After the Taliban, the internally emerged insurgency group, the ISIS also posed major security threat to Afghanistan. Moreover, given hardcore hostility between the Taliban and the Islamic State, they were involved in attacking each other wherever they came across face to face in Afghanistan. Russia provided moral and material support to the Taliban as a counterweight to the Islamic State. The Islamic State's main area of domination has been the south of Nangarhar Province, in eastern Afghanistan, besides, they had also another major group in the northern province of Jowzjan, particularly in Darzab district. The increasing fighting between the Taliban and the Islamic State, and the attacks of the IS have posed major challenged to the peace process in Afghanistan. The political and territorial rivalry between the Taliban and the Islamic State Khorasan Province (ISKP), the ISIS affiliated militant group in Afghanistan has been growing since 2014. It has believed that the ISKP has been hostile to the west and its allies, and therefore, they were trying to disrupt the peace process there.[89] It has reported that the Islamic State's offensive appeared to be partly in response to the increasing operations by the US and the Afghan forces to root out its fighters in Deh Bala and other rural districts of eastern Nangarhar province and thereby to disrupt supply lines reaching into Pakistan. Moreover, the IS's lethal escalation of assault has also been seen coincided probably with the "signs of progress in renewed efforts to halt the 17-year-old, US-orchestrated war between the Afghan government and the Taliban."[90] President Trump had urged to eliminate the ISIS which posed threat to the entire world, and therefore, the US operations in Deh Bala were designed to curb the ISKP's ability to attack cities such as Jalalabad, however, he failed in its objective.[91] "Despite the fact it has also been split, into eastern and northern factions, the ISKP was believed to have been strengthened by Taliban defectors, fighters displaced from Iraq and Syria, and militants from Sudan, Chechnya, Uzbekistan and Tajikistan. Its funding supposedly comes from private donors, Arab Gulf states and informal local taxes."[92] Moreover, "The ISKP's mostly foreign origins, its extreme brutality—including beheadings and forcing victims to sit on explosives—and its documented, systematic use of rape and abduction in terrorizing women and girls have done much to alienate the Afghan civilian population. Now, in a strange twist, the US and the Afghan government appear to be relying on their bitter Taliban enemies to help them vanquish this greater evil and simultaneously end the war."[93] In fact, as it appeared crystal clear, the reconciliation process in Afghanistan faced dual threats; one from the Taliban and the other from the ISIS. And most of the actors including the Taliban came closer against the ISIS in and around Afghanistan. Besides, Pakistan's dysfunctional role in Afghanistan has also put forward multiple hindrances in the Afghan peace process, though it showed hypocritically playing positive and constructive role.

By and large, despite multiple efforts since 2001, the peace and stability remained unachieved in Afghanistan due to multiple factors and reasons. And even despite that the efforts of the countries in and around the region have been consistently in progress for the better future of Afghanistan. In fact, it has believed that achieving peace and stability in Afghanistan has been held impossible without an "institutionalization of good governance and rule of law," which was based on Afghan's progressive constitution, and therefore, "to secure the future of its youthful population with 70 percent under the age of 25—is to fight and eliminate endemic corruption. Corruption weakens Afghanistan's nascent state and empowers its enemy. It is the mother of all threats to Afghanistan's stabilization and sustainable development."[94] However, to fight the roots of corruption, the Afghan President Ghani had initiated "a national anti-corruption strategy," and this strategy included the five pillars: "national leadership; security sector reform; improving the quality of civil service recruitment; and increasing our ability to oversee how money is transferred and spent."[95] But all that went in vain. Furthermore, according to Mohammad Shafiq Hamdam, the key reasons for failure of the Afghan's peace talks were:

> A lack of a unifying strategy within the Afghan government. Conflicts of interest and disagreement between government officials and their international partners. Absence of a firm commitment and position of the engaged parties. Overestimating the role and influence of Pakistan, negotiating through the wrong tribune, by wrong moderators, with the wrong actors in the wrong places to fail process. Lastly, a variety of pre-conditions from the many parties prevent the peace process from even really getting off the ground.[96]

Furthermore, according to the former Indian diplomat, Rakesh Sood, "after the fall of the Taliban in 2001, there was an international consensus on rebuilding Afghanistan and ensuring that it should not become a source of regional and global instability. That consensus has eroded over the last 16 years." He further stated that the Afghan citizens who had returned back to their homes in large numbers who had been determined to reclaim their country and rebuild it were left with major frustration because of the continuously declining situation in both security and governance. Besides, the newly created Afghan government's institutions were found unable to adequately address the challenges without adequate international support in both financial and material terms. And, however, because of the major breakdown in the international consensus, Sood said that "it may not be long before the slow fuse reaches ignition point. And 2019 may well become the critical year."[97] In fact, further, extending the message to all the militants in and around Afghanistan including the Taliban that the solution to the peace and stability of Afghanistan has been impossible in the battleground as long as they are continued in fighting against each other, the Afghan government stated that "they can choose to accept Afghan government's offer to negotiate a political settlement for peace. Indeed, peace is not simply what the Afghan people desire but need to thrive toward a secure future in peaceful and prosperous co-existence with all their near and far neighbors,"[98] and "that is why Afghans often emphasize the complete leadership and ownership of the peace process. Its success foremost hinges on the resolution of Afghanistan-Pakistan undeclared hostility, which the Afghan government stands ready to address on a state-to-state basis."[99] Harsh V. Pant believed that "Regional cooperation, time and again, has been declared as the only viable alternative to the festering regional tensions that have plagued the country for decades," and further "various South and Central Asian governments...have underscored that they recognize that Afghanistan's problems of terrorism, narcotics trafficking and corruption affect them all and have to be addressed through cooperative efforts."[100] By and large, the countries in the region believed in the role of regional cooperation for the peace and stability in Afghanistan. However, the problems of lack of regional cooperation and the regional power struggles in the region also have further undermined the success of the peace process in Afghanistan. Pant has rightly observed that "India shares a common interest with the regional states with respect to Afghanistan but is unlikely to find support from them in given the nature of regional power realities. China shares common interests with India in Afghanistan but does not want to realize them at the cost of its friendship with Pakistan."[101] Even more, the relations between/amongst the countries involved in Afghanistan such as India's mounting better relations with the US and Iran, Pakistan's rivalry with India and Iran and the growing relations between Russia and Pakistan have further complicated the matter of regional cooperation and the Afghan conundrum. Moreover, Afghanistan problem has been providing the platform for the rival countries involved in to play their hostile interests on the Afghan land. In the post-2014 troops withdrawal, both Russia and Pakistan tried to reach each other, and, with there increasing proximity, in June 2014, Russia decided to lift an embargo on the supply of weapons and arms hardware to Pakistan. Further, boosting Pakistan's military capabilities, Russia was negotiating the delivery of several Mi-25 helicopter gunships to Pakistan.[102] However, despite that, Ghani had continuously looked at and reached out to its neighbouring countries to contribute positive efforts towards achieving the permanent solution to the Afghan's prolonged problem. In fact, as has observed, regional instability would prevailed as long as Pakistan plays dysfunctional double dealing in context of Afghan's domestic politics especially by favouring the Taliban.

Moreover, the major challenges to all sorts of Afghan's peace processes were mostly emanated from uncertain and unreliable behavior of the Taliban. Though the Taliban leaders exhibited their willingness towards a peace talks, but found unwilling to engage with the legitimately elected Afghan government, which shows Taliban's recalcitrance and obstinacy towards the objective for the better future of Afghanistan. The Taliban has always been appeared rejecting the peace offers moved forward by the Afghan government. In this direction, the Taliban spokesman Mujahid said that the Taliban leaders would not have talks with the Afghan government. However, as has reported that Ghani said that his government would keep trying to form a direct link of diplomatic communication with the Taliban leaders. On the contrary, the Taliban showed its willingness to have dialogues with the US and also engaged with it for the peace negotiation, but, surprisingly, amidst the peace talks between them, the Taliban urged the US on 27 December 2018 to leave Afghanistan, and if not, they warned the US that they would have to face defeat by the Taliban in Afghanistan just like the Soviet Union had faced in late 1980s. Here, the Taliban has used the derogatory words towards the US In fact, this was the reaction of the Taliban after the US's declaration of the slashing of its half of troops from Afghanistan. However, it has reported that with the aim of the Taliban's joining of the peace process in Afghanistan, the Trump administration offered safety network that included job opportunities for the insurgents and the plan of rehabilitation for them in a New Afghanistan.[103] Initially, the Taliban believed and insisted that they would first reach to an agreement with the US, which they saw as the main force in Afghanistan since

2001. But later, on the Taliban, on 6 January 2019, said that they would not attend the planned peace talks with the US in Saudi Arabia and had urged the shifting of venue to Qatar. Unfortunately, later, the Taliban, on 8 January, declared that it had called off the peace talks with the US officials in Qatar that was scheduled in Qatar on the logic of "agenda disagreement," especially over the US stressed on the involvement of the Afghan officials and the other issues of the possible ceasefire prisoner exchange. According to the Taliban sources, "The US official insisted that the Taliban should meet the Afghan authorities in Qatar and both sides were in disagreement over declaring a ceasefire in 2019."[104] In fact, even the other regional countries were also requesting the Taliban to allow the Afghan officials to participate in the peace talks, but, the Taliban always rejected and showed its unwillingness for this. It has believed that the Taliban had demanded the US to release 25,000 prisoners and they would free 3000, but they said that the US officials had not been ready for these exchanges. Therefore, the Taliban officials said, "we would never announce any ceasefire until and unless we achieve major gains on the ground...."[105] In fact, the volatile attitude and the decision of the Taliban over the peace talks had further put the peace talk process on the standstill that led to the failure in achieving the set objectives for the better future of Afghanistan. Afghan's National Security Adviser, Hamdullah Mohib said that the factor of factionalism within the Taliban has slowing down the dialogues for the peace process. He said, "So far, the teams that the Taliban sent for talks in Abu Dhabi, Moscow, or in Qatar have revealed that there are many factions in the group. They sent different people for different dialogues. The Taliban should appoint a single negotiating team first."[106] He also said that the "intra-Afghan" peace dialogue has not taken shape yet. In fact, the US-Taliban negotiations, and the Taliban's engagement with the other stakeholder countries in Afghanistan, somehow, appearing to de-marginalizing the legitimate Afghan government and its importance as all the countries mainly the major powers are focusing on the Taliban and what it wants? Almost all the formats of the peace talks seemed to be Taliban-centric. By engaging with the Taliban, though separately, "the

US and Russia have accepted the idea that peace in Afghanistan is not possible without major concessions to Taliban, including dialogue without insisting on a cessation of violence."[107] Further, "the US and Russia have...agreed to sidestep the Ashraf Ghani regime in Kabul, and accepted the Taliban's condition that it will not negotiate with the elected Afghan government at this stage. And both the Russian and US processes are dependent on cooperation from Pakistan, which remains its influence over the Taliban leadership."[108]

In fact, the declaration of the US withdrawal created the atmosphere of uncertainty and the specter of instability in Afghanistan, South Asia, and Central Asia. Therefore, the security situation in Afghanistan was a sheer possibility of inviting the regional powers to take the responsibility to stabilize Afghanistan. And in this direction, India and China can and should work together at bilateral as well as multilateral level to build a secure Afghanistan after the withdrawal of the US forces.[109] It has suggested that "New Delhi must intensify its dialogue with regional and global stakeholders, and impress upon them that any dialogue with the Taliban must not come at the cost of the hard-fought victories of the Afghan people in the past two decades; on establishing constitutional democracy and the rule of law, and securing the rights of women and minorities."[110] However, the Taliban stubbornly seemed unwilling to form a coalition government with the existing Afghan government or the liberal leaders there, and believed in the sole government of its own or a "sole Taliban Regime", and the Taliban was seen manipulating all the equations in this direction by dealing with the world community especially the US, Russia, and Pakistan among others.

However, despite various peace process and formats initiated by the stakeholders in Afghanistan, the democratically elected government could not be saved, and eventually, the Taliban regime was re-established in Afghanistan in August 2021, and the US forces left the country by 30 August 2021 leaving the Afghan people in further great turmoil of uncertainties. Significantly, the major countries in the region China and India did not initiate any peace process; however, they became the part of various processes. In fact, India had its limitations because of its adverse relations with the Taliban. But China, despite having direct contacts with the Taliban failed to do something substantial.

Notes and References

1. Belquis Ahmadi and Marjan Nahavandi, for the Afghan Peace Process to Work, Women must be Involved, United States Institute of Peace, 29 October 2018, https://www.usip.org/publications/2018/10/afghan-peace-process-work-women-must-be-involved, accessed on 6 November 2018.
2. The Kabul Process, Pajhwok Afghan News, 6 June 2017, https://www.pajhwok.com/en/opinions/kabul-process, accessed on 8 November 2018.
3. Vinay Kaura, Understanding the Complexities of the Afghan Peace Process, ORF Occasional Paper 151, April 2018, pp. 5-6.
4. "A Loya Jirga, or grand council in Pashto, is a mass national gathering that brings together representatives from the various ethnic, religious, and tribal communities in Afghanistan. The Loya Jirga is a centuries-old institution that has been convened at times of national crisis or to settle national issues." For details see, Frud Bezhan, *Loya Jirga—An Afghan Tradition Explained*, 20 November 2013, RadioFreeEurope, RadioLiberty, https://www.rferl.org/a/afghanistan-loya-jirga-explainer/25174483.html, accessed on 5 March 2019.
5. Susan Brooks Thistlethwaite, The Peace Jirga Model, Centre for American Progress, 8 June 2010, https://www.americanprogress.org/issues/security/news/2010/06/08/7891/the-peace-jirga-model/, accessed on 8 November 2018.
6. Said Sabir Ibrahimi, Can Russia Help Bring Peace to Afghanistan?, *The Diplomat*, November 2, 2018, https://thediplomat.com/2018/11/can-russia-help-bring-peace-to-afghanistan/, accessed on 5 November 2018.
7. Susan Thistlethwaite, 8 June 2010.
8. Tim Bird and Alex Marshall, *Afghanistan: How the West Lost its Way*, Orient Balckswan, New Delhi, 2012, p. 4.
9. Aiming the job of security sector reform in Afghanistan; see, Tim Bird and Alex Marshall, *Afghanistan: How the West Lost its Way*, Orient Blackswan, New Delhi, 2012, p. 119.

10. *Ibid.*
11. Smruti S. Pattanaik, Istanbul Conference on Afghanistan: A Feeble Attempt at a Regional Solution, Institute for Defence Studies and Analyses, 4 November 2011, https://idsa.in/idsacomments/IstanbulConferenceonAfghanistanAFeebleAttemptataRegionalSolution_agupta_041111, accessed on 8 November 2018.
12. Istanbul Process on Regional Security and Cooperation for a Secure and Stable Afghanistan, 2 November 2011, Ministry of Foreign Affairs, Republic of Turkey, http://www.mfa.gov.tr/istanbul-process-on-regional-security-and-cooperation-for-a-secure-and-stable-afghanistan.en.mfa, accessed on 8 November 2018.
13. The International Afghanistan Conference Bonn 2011, Permanent Mission of the Islamic Republic of Afghanistan to the United Nations, New York, http://afghanistan-un.org/2011/12/the-international-afghanistan-conference-bonn-2011/, accessed on 9 November 2018.
14. Julian Borger, Afghanistan conference promises support after troop withdrawal, *The Guardian*, 5 December 2011, https://www.theguardian.com/world/2011/dec/05/afghanistan-conference-support-troop-withdrawal, accessed on 9 November 2018.
15. *Ibid.*
16. Vishal Chandra, The Bonn II Conference on Afghanistan: A Step Forward Amidst Uncertainty, Institute for Defence Studies and Analyses, 19 December 2011, https://idsa.in/idsacomments/TheBonnIIConferenceonAfghanistan_vchandra_191211, accessed on 9 November 2018.
17. North Atlantic Treaty Organisation, 21 May 2012, https://www.nato.int/cps/en/natohq/official_texts_87595.htm, accessed on 13 November 2018.
18. Ministry of Foreign Affairs of Japan, 8 July 2012, https://www.mofa.go.jp/region/middle_e/afghanistan/tokyo_conference_2012/tokyo_declaration_en1.html, 13 November 2018.
19. *Ibid.*
20. Harsh V. Pant, 2016, pp. 4-5.
21. Available at https://www.gov.uk/government/topical-events/london-conference-on-afghanistan-2014, accessed on 6 March 2019.

22. Statement of the Quadrilateral Meeting among Afghanistan, Pakistan, China and the United States, US Embassy in Afghanistan, 10 December 2015, https://af.usembassy.gov/statement-quadrilateral-meeting-among-afghanistan-pakistan-china-united-states/, accessed on 13 November 2018.
23. Joint Press Release of the Quadrilateral Coordination Group on Afghan Peace and Reconciliation, US Department of State, 11 January 2016, https://2009-2017.state.gov/r/pa/prs/ps/2016/01/251105.htm, accessed on 13 November 2018.
24. Fahad Nabeel, Resuming the Stalled Afghan Peace Talks, Center for Strategic and Contemporary Research, 15 March 2016, https://cscr.pk/explore/themes/politics-governance/resuming-stalled-afghan-peace-talks/, accessed on 14 November 2018.
25. Pajhwok Afghan News 18 May 2016, https://www.pajhwok.com/en/2016/05/18/fifth-meeting-quadrilateral-coordination-group-qcg-afghanistan-pakistan-united-states-and, accessed on 14 November 2018.
26. QCG Discusses Afghan Peace Efforts, Business Recorder, 17 October 2017, http://fp.brecorder.com/2017/10/20171017226797/, accessed on 14 November 2018.
27. Sune Engel Rasmussen, Afghanistan Holds Peace Conference Amid Violence and Protests, The Guardian, https://www.theguardian.com/world/2017/jun/06/afghanistan-peace-conference-violence-protests-kabul-bombing, accessed on 8 November 2018.
28. *Ibid.*
29. Govt Issues Declaration After Kabul Process Meeting," Tolo News, 28 February, 2018, https://www.tolonews.com/afghanistan/govt-issues-declaration-after-kabul-process-meeting, accessed on 6 November 2018.
30. Said Sabir Ibrahimi, 2 November 2018.
31. *Ibid.*
32. Agence France-Presse, Ghani Forms Team for Talks with Taliban, *The Hindu*, 29 November 2018, p. 12.
33. Said Sabir Ibrahimi, 2 November 2018.
34. Reuters, Russia to host Taliban dialogue, *The Hindu*, 2 November 2018, p. 12.
35. Harsh V. Pant, The Afghanistan Conundrum: Russia's Peace Plays and India's Room for Maneuver, *The Diplomat*,

12 November 2018, https://thediplomat.com/2018/11/the-afghanistan-conundrum-russias-peace-plays-and-indias-room-for-maneuver/, accessed on 21 February 2019.

36. Shubhajit Roy, 9 November 2018.
37. Suhasini Haidar, India to Join Afghan Peace talks Today, *The Hindu*, 9 November 2018, p. 10.
38. Sergey Lavrov, The Ministry of Foreign Affairs of the Russian Federation, 9 November 2018, http://www.mid.ru/en/foreign_policy/news/-/asset_publisher/cKNonkJE02Bw/content/id/3403878
39. *Ibid.*
40. Rakesh Sood, Searching for an Elusive Peace, The Hindu, 16 November 2018, p. 8.
41. Said Sabir Ibrahimi, 2 November 2018.
42. Andrew Higgins and Mujib Mashal, Taliban Peace Talks End with Hope that US Exits, if not too Quickly, *The Indian Express*, 8 February 2019, p. 9.
43. Shubhajit Roy, Taliban at Afghanistan talks table today, Delhi sending 'non-officials', *The Indian Express*, 9 November 2018, pp. 1-2.
44. Shubhajit Roy, The Shift in India Position on Taliban: From Rejection to Unofficial Talks, *The Indian Express*, 15 November 2018, p. 10.
45. Suhasini Haidar, 9 November 2018.
46. *Ibid.*
47. Shubhajit Roy, Taliban at Talks Table, Russia says: No Room for Geopolitics, *The Indian Express*, 10 November 2018, pp. 1-2.
48. Shyam Saran, How India Sees the World? *Juggernaut*, New Delhi, 2017.
49. Shubhajit Roy, 15 November 2018.
50. *Ibid.*, for more details see, Shiv Shankar Menon, *Choices: Inside the Making of Indian Foreign Policy*, Penguin, New Delhi, 2016.
51. Said Sabir Ibrahimi, 2 November 2018.
52. Memphis Barker and Sami Yousafzai, Taliban hails 'helpful' US talks as boost to Afghan peace process, *The Guardian*, 13 August 2018, https://www.theguardian.com/world/2018/

aug/13/taliban-hails-helpful-us-talks-as-boost-to-afghan-peace-process, 22 November 2018.

53. *Ibid.*
54. *Ibid.*
55. Mujib Mashal, US Officials Meet with Taliban again as Trump Pushes Afghan Peace Process, *The New York Times*, 13 October 2018, https://www.nytimes.com/2018/10/13/world/asia/us-talks-taliban-afghanistan.html, accessed on 22 November 2018.
56. Kathy Gannon, Pakistan, Saudis, UAE Join US-Taliban Talks, *The Washington Post*, 17 December 2018, https://www.washingtonpost.com/world/the_americas/taliban-say-another-meeting-in-middle-east-with-us/2018/12/16/91aaafe2-01ae-11e9-958c-0a601226ff6b_story.html?noredirect=on&utm_term=.2bee92d00092, accessed on 18 December 2018.
57. Reuters, Focus on Afghan Ceasefire as US, Taliban Talks Peace, *The Indian Express*, 19 December 2018, p. 9.
58. *Ibid.*
59. Reuters, Afghan Government sends Team for Peace Talks with Taliban, *The Hindu*, 19 December 2018, p. 12.
60. Ruchi Kumar, Changing Peace in the Middle of War, *The Hindu*, 23 December 2018, p. 6.
61. *Ibid.*
62. *Ibid.*
63. *Ibid.*
64. Rod Nordland and Mujib Mashal, Afghanistan Peace Talks: US, Taliban Edge Towards Deal to End America's Longest War, *The Indian Express*, 28 January 2019, p. 9.
65. Agence France-Presse, Talks with the US have entered 4th Day: Taliban, *The Hindu*, 25 January 2019, p. 12.
66. Mujib Mashal, US Declares it has Agreed upon Peace Framework with Taliban, *The Hindu*, 29 January 2019, p. 12.
67. *Ibid.*
68. Kallol Bhattacherjee, Experts Flog Impact of Latest US-Taliban Talks, *The Hindu*, 28 January 2019, p. 11.
69. C. Raja Mohan, An Afghan Trifecta, *The Indian Express*, 29 January 2019, p. 6.
70. *Ibid.*

71. *Ibid.*
72. *Ibid.*
73. Mullah Baradar was one of the four top commanders who had formed the Taliban in 1994, and was freed by Pakistan government from jail in 2018, and he is believed to be the highest ranking Afghan Taliban prisoner released so far; Lalit K. Jha, 7 March 2019, p. 11. It has believed that he comes from the ruling Durrani tribe represented by the founder king of Afghanistan, Ahmad Shah Durrani. "When Baradar was captured in 2010 by a join Pak-US effort, the ISI took him in custody, promising the CIA that he would be handed over to them next day. To the amazement of the ISI personnel, Baradar disclosed to them that his capture was arranged for him to negotiate a deal with the CIA unbeknownst to Omer and to the ISI." For details see, Khaled Ahmed, The Mullah Baradar Mystery, *The Indian Express*, 23 March 2019, p. 6.
74. US, Taliban Pause Peace Talks in Doha for Two Days, Gandhara, 28 February 2019, https://gandhara.rferl.org/a/u-s-taliban-pause-peace-talks-in-doha-for-two-days/29796051.html, accessed on 7 March 2019.
75. Lalit K. Jha, Talks with Taliban Focus on Four Key Issues to End Afghan War, *The Indian Express*, 7 March 2019, p. 11.
76. Thomas Gibbons-Neff and Julian E. Barnes, Under Peace Plan, US Military Would Exit Afghanistan within Five Years, *The Indian Express*, 2 March 2019, p. 11.
77. Shubhajit Roy, India's cooperation needed for Afghan peace: Pakistan foreign minister, *The Indian Express*, 12 December 2018, p. 5.
78. Press Trust of India, Afghanistan, China, Pak sign MoU on Counter Terrorism, *The Indian Express*, 18 December 2018, p. 8.
79. Sajjad Hussain, The Indian Express, 19 December 2018, p. 9.
80. Nirupama Subramaniam, US-Taliban Talks: What's on Table, Why it is being Greeted with Action, The Indian Express, 30 January 2019, p. 6.
81. Jibran Ahmad, Afghan Taliban Rejects Talks with US in Islamabad, The Indian Express, 20 January 2019, p. 18.
82. C. Raja Mohan, 29 January 2019, p. 6.

83. *Ibid.*
84. Lalit K. Jha, Pak-backed Groups will Continue Attacks in India, Afghanistan, says US Intel Chief, *The Indian Express*, 31 January 2019, p. 10.
85. Phil Stewart, Idrees Ali and Jibran Ahmad, Pakistan Starts Backdoor Aid to US-Taliban Talks, *The Indian Express*, 9 February 2019, p. 8.
86. *Ibid.*
87. *Ibid.*
88. *Ibid.*
89. Simon Tisdall, Islamic State attacks show group is intent on killing Afghan peace hopes, *The Guardian*, 1 August 2018, https://www.theguardian.com/world/2018/aug/01/afghanistan-us-look-taliban-for-help-isis-attacks-rise, accessed on 27 November 2018.
90. *Ibid.*
91. *Ibid.*
92. *Ibid.*
93. *Ibid.*
94. M. Ashraf Haidari, Afghanistan in 2017: Achievements and Challenges, *The Diplomat*, December 28, 2017, https://thediplomat.com/2017/12/afghanistan-in-2017-achievements-and-challenges/, accessed on 13 November 2018.
95. *Ibid.*
96. Mohammad Shafiq Hamdam, Pieces of Afghan Peace, Huffpost, 6 October 2015, https://www.huffingtonpost.com/mohammad-shafiq-hamdam/pieces-of-afghan-peace_b_7548794.html, accessed on 8 November 2018
97. Rakesh Sood, Afghanistan, On a slow Fuse, *The Hindu*, 25 Janaury 2018, p. 8.
98. M. Ashraf Haidari, December 28, 2017.
99. *Ibid.*
100. Harsh V. Pant, 2016, p. 4.
101. *Ibid.*, p. 5.
102. *Ibid.*, p. 9.
103. Amid Talks, Taliban Urge US to Exit Afghanistan or Face Defeat, *The Indian Express*, 28 December 2018, p. 9.

104. Jibran Ahmad, Taliban Call off Peace Talks with US, *The Indian Express*, 9 January 2019, p. 9.
105. *Ibid.*
106. Kallol Bhattacherjee, Internal Peace Process Yet to Take off in Afghanistan, *The Hindu*, 7 January 2019, p. 11.
107. Editorial, Tough-Talking, *The Hindu*, 7 February 2019, p. 8.
108. *Ibid.*
109. Anita Inder Singh, The Great Game is not a Zero-Sum Deal, *The Hindu*, 10 January 2019, p. 8.
110. Editorial, Tough-Talking, *The Hindu*, 7 February 2019, p. 8.

Index

J

K